Russian Jews on Three Continents

Russian Jews on Three Continents

Identity, Integration, and Conflict

Larissa Remennick

Transaction Publishers
New Brunswick (U.S.A.) and London (U.K.)

Library of Congress Catalog Number: 2006052605
ISBN: 978-0-7658-0340-5
Printed in the United States of America

Library of Congress Cataloging-in-Publication Data

Remennick, Larissa I.
    Russian Jews on three continents identity, integration, and conflict / Larissa Remennick.
        p. em.
    Includes bibliographical references.
    ISBN 0-7658-0340-2 (alk. paper)
    1. Jews, Russian—Israel—Social conditions. 2. Jews, Russian—North America—Social conditions. 3. Jews, Russian—Germany—Social conditions. 4. Jews—Identity. 5. Social integration. 6.Immigrants—Israel—Social conditions. 7. Immigrants—North America—Social conditions. 8. Immigrants—Germany—Social conditions. 9. JewsCultural assimilation—Israel. 10. Jews—Cultural assimilation—North America. 11. Jews—Cultural assimilation—Germany. I. Title.

Ds113.8.R87R46 2006
305.892'4047—dc22   2006052605

I dedicate this book to my informants, fellow immigrants of former Soviet origin, who are spread today across the globe. I am grateful for your time, trust, and frankness of your narratives. I wish you all the best in your new lives – in Israel, America, or Germany.

Contents

Acknowledgements

I am grateful to my Israeli and American colleagues Larisa Fialkova, Vera Kishinevsky, Dimitri Liakhovitski, and Olga Gershenson for their thoughtful comments on the earlier drafts of this book.

Introduction

"Russian Jews on Three Continents": Ten Years Down the Road

Over the last two decades, perhaps a dozen or so books have been written about the dramatic story of Soviet Jews, their lives in the shadow of state-sponsored anti-Semitism, and their two recent waves of emigration. Why did I decide to add yet another volume to this already respectable collection? Because I believe that this book stands out in the existing literature on Russian and Soviet Jewry in three main respects: its time and place frame, analytical concept, and authorial identity. This book offers a follow-up on what happened to the Jewish émigrés from the former Soviet Union (FSU) some fifteen to seventeen years from the inception of their last exodus and in all major countries of their resettlement. This last point means that my analytical frame is broadly comparative, juxtaposing the challenges of social integration experienced by Russian Jews in the different national settings of Israel, the U.S., Canada, and Germany. Finally, this tale of immigration and adaptation of Russian Jews is narrated by a participant observer of this process—a Russian-Jewish immigrant woman who happened to be a professional sociologist. Most previous accounts of Russian Jewish experiences, before and after emigration, have been written by outside observers of Russian Jewish culture—social scientists and journalists raised in North America and Israel. The best-known chroniclers of Russian Jewry—such as Zvi Gitelman, Robert Brym, Rita Simon, Steven Gold, Fran Markowitz, Theodore Friedgut, Tamar Horowitz, Eli Leshem, and Yaakov Ro'i—have all been onlookers rather than participants, however expert and sympathetic. The insider perspective significantly alters the researcher's standpoint, access to informants, and data sources in the native language, and can also redress the interpretation of the findings. Although this book centers on the immigrants who left the FSU on the "Jewish ticket," my general sociological goal is to understand the modes of economic, social, and cultural adjustment to life in the West among the people molded by state socialism, the infamous *Homo Sovieticus*. The saga of their meeting with the economic marketplaces, lifestyles, and everyday cultures of their new homelands unfolds in this book, based on many years of my comparative research among former Soviet immigrants.

The migration movement of Soviet Jews to Israel has been part of the late twentieth—century global flows of the so-called *ethnically privileged* or *return migrations*, ideologically framed as the in-gathering of diasporas, or homecoming by co-ethnics historically detached from their homelands by wars, demise of multinational empires, and change of borders (Brubaker, 1998; Capo Zmegac, 2005). The returning migrants may have lived outside their historic homelands for several generations (like East-European Germans, Brazilian Japanese, or ethnic Russians in former Soviet republics), for hundreds of years (like Pontiac Greeks and Germans who had settled in Russia in the late eighteenth century), or since time immemorial, like Jews spread across Europe, the Middle East, and later the Americas, since the destruction of the Second Temple. The ingathering of the Jewish Diasporas to the State of Israel after 1948 was the largest global project in return migration, although the *return* in this case has been purely symbolic, given thousands of years of life in the Diaspora. During the last few decades of tightly regulated immigration regimes in the West, the gateway for Soviet Jews' entry to America, and later on to Germany, was also legitimated by ethno-religious affinity, and Soviet refugees were expected to join these countries' Jewish communities. However, in most societies gathering back their ethnic diasporas, the processes of economic and social integration have been fraught with conflicts between the established and migrant populations. The remote ethnic kinship could not offset multiple cultural gaps and conflicting intentions: nationalist-ideological of the hosts and pragmatic-economic of the migrants (Capo-Zmegac, 2005). The case study unfolding in this book—former Soviet Jews joining their co-ethnics in Israel and in the West—adds more evidence to this general assertion.

Throughout the second half of the twentieth century, the condition of Jews under Soviet rule has been that of a special ethnic (rather than religious) minority, which was both persecuted and privileged, but always mistrusted (Pincus, 1988; Zaslavsky and Brym, 1983; Remennick, 1998). After an upsurge of emancipation and upward social mobility during the first three decades of Bolshevism, since the end of World War II Soviet Jews were subjected to covert institutional policies of exclusion from higher education and prestigious careers and lived in the shadow of anti-Jewish and anti-Israeli media campaigns, augmented by everyday social anti-Semitism. Yet, by way of paradox, having faced routine institutional discrimination from school age and across their working lives, Jewish parents aspired to excellence in education and cultivated the value of hard intellectual effort in their children, which eventually earned them a respectable place in most professions such as medicine, science, education, law, culture, and the arts. It can be argued that Soviet Jews excelled both despite and due to their discrimination. This twisted need-hate relationship between Russian Jews and Soviet power made Jewish professionals an indispensable part of the Soviet technological and cultural elite ever since the early 1920s, and, despite ups and downs in the waves of state anti-Semitism, they retained this special status up until the end of the twentieth century (Branover et al., 1998). Some of them were devoted loyalists of the regime, others cynical collaborators, still others—convinced dissidents, overt or covert; yet all carried for life a stigma of their "ethnic disability" vis-à-vis the surrounding Slavic majority. Careers of many talented Jewish professionals were stifled due to the built-in anti-Semitic filters of the omnipotent System. Many Jews hated and despised the communist regime and, after the short-lived Thaw, lost any hope for political and economic reforms. Wishing for a better future for themselves and their children outside of the Iron Curtain, where their efforts would get higher returns, many Jews quietly considered the subversive option of emigration.

This wild dream became true in the early 1970s, when Brezhnev's regime had to make some concessions to Western pressure, and Jewish emigration became its chief bargaining chip in trade negotiations with the U.S. Although small trickles of other ethnic migrants were allowed to leave around the same time (mainly Germans and Armenians [Heitman, 1989]), Soviet Jews became effectively the only ethnic group granted the exceptional privilege of mass emigration from the Soviet empire under the pretext of return to their historic homeland of Israel. Between 1971 and 1981, around 250,000 Jews left the USSR, forming the Third Wave of Russian Jewish immigration in Israel and in North America (the two previous waves arriving at the turn of the twentieth century and after World War II [Gitelman, 1997]). During the following decade (1980–1989) the deteriorating Soviet regime reversed its emigration quotas to the pre–1970 level, so that only a few thousand Jews could leave under exceptional clauses (Brym and Ryvkina, 1994; Tolts, 1997).

The demise of state socialism in Eastern Europe in the late 1980s marked the onset of the great New Exodus of now former-Soviet Jews, along with a few other ethnic minorities who could claim the right of return to their historic homelands or family reunification. Since 1988, well over 1.6 million Jews from Russia, Ukraine, and other Soviet successor states have emigrated to Israel, the U.S., Canada, Germany, Australia,[1] and a few other Western countries. Some others left the FSU with job visas as research scholars and high-tech specialists, winners of the Diversity Lottery or via marriage. The process of social incorporation of these newcomers has been rather different from the experiences of their predecessors during the 1970s, reflecting multiple changes in the global economy and geopolitical context of the late twentieth century, as well as the unprecedented scope of this exodus. Those leaving the FSU in the early to mid–1990s were survivors of the wild "market capitalism" and unpredictable, "drunk" Yeltsin's democracy; many also had a chance to travel abroad, had relatives and friends in Israel and in the West, and knew much more than their predecessors about their potential immigrant destinations. While Russian-Jewish émigrés of the 1970s have been rather well depicted in both American and Israeli scholarly literature of the 1980s and 1990s by Gitelman, Markowits, Brym, Simon, Horowitz, and other social scientists, the sociological analysis of the latest immigration wave is ongoing, and its collective portrait still waits to be drawn. This mass resettlement of Russian-speaking Jews (and their non-Jewish kin) in the end of the twentieth century has emerged as a fascinating social experiment, whereby large communities of former Soviets sharing a common past and socio-cultural background found themselves in the diverse national contexts of the host countries that share the common grounds of market capitalism, democratic government, and fairly generous (albeit shrinking) welfare systems.

Although former Soviets continue to leave the FSU to this day, many changes have occurred since the beginning of the exodus in the late 1980s, affecting the distribution between destination countries and many aspects of their social composition. There were several distinct periods (or sub-waves) in the course of the post-communist migrations of the late twentieth century. The first one began around 1987–1988 as a pivotal point of perestroika, whereby those left behind by the closed gates of the 1970s (*refusniks*) were allowed to leave, both for Israel and for the West, although the latter destination was never openly stated. The majority of those who left the USSR with Israeli visas between 1987 and 1990 (around 85 percent) arrived in the USA under Jewish refugee status (their total number is estimated at about 127,000 [Dominitz, 1997]). Then at the end of 1989, the U.S. government changed its refugee policy towards Soviet Jews and drastically reduced the quotas and the terms of entry, limiting them mainly to family reunification. At the same time, Israel opened direct flight routes from the major Soviet cities to Tel Aviv, closing the transition camps in Vienna and a few other European cities where earlier waves of Soviet émigrés had been waiting for their visas to the West (departure to Israel had always been expedient). Since the early 1990s, these simultaneous changes effectively redirected the bulk of Jewish emigrants leaving the USSR to Israel, reducing the so-called dropout rates (*neshira*) to 20–25 percent (Dominitz, 1997). The swings in the numbers and directions of the migrant flows reflected multiple political tensions and compromises between the Israeli government and Diaspora (mainly American) Jewry (Gitelman, 1997; Lazin, 2005), but for Israel their net results entailed adding over 950,000 newcomers to its Jewish population, significant fortification of the secular Ashkenazi majority, the economic boom of the 1990s, and the emergence of a new thriving subculture on the Israeli ethnic map. In America and Canada, about 370,000 post–1988 Soviet immigrants, although a relatively small immigrant population (vis-à-vis Hispanics or Chinese), became the main source of demographic growth of North American Jewry. Germany has also experienced a gradual increase in the numbers of applicants for its "special refugee" program tailored for former Soviet Jews, and by the early 2000s has received about 200,000 Jewish newcomers and their family members.

Sociologists, anthropologists, and social historians manifested their interest in the last migration wave of former Soviet Jews soon after its inception. In the summer of 1993, the first international conference

Russian Jews on Three Continents, looking into the mechanisms of mass emigration and the interim results of the resettlement, convened at Tel Aviv University, and its proceedings have later been published by Frank Cass as an edited volume under the same title (Lewin-Epstein et al.1997). The conference and the book examined the condition of Soviet Jews during the last years of the deteriorating Soviet empire, documented their mass exodus as well as the challenges of resettlement and initial contact with the host societies. The present book can be seen as a follow-up and reappraisal of the social incorporation of this large immigrant community in Israel and in the major host countries of the West some fifteen years later. My goals here are both broader and more sharply focused. They are broader due to the comparative lens I draw upon: while the volume mentioned above juxtaposed the experiences of former Soviet Jews in their homelands (mainly Russia and Ukraine) with the challenges of resettlement in Israel and in the U.S., my analysis covers two additional locations of post-communist Jewish migrations—Canada and Germany. On the other hand, this book has a more specific focus as all "country-bound" chapters address a similar set of research questions centering on the socio-economic adjustment and cultural encounter with the receiving society. Vis-à-vis many earlier writings on post-Soviet Jewish émigrés, I am also paying considerably more attention to the heterogeneity of their adaptation experiences along the lines of gender, age, ethnicity, and pre-migration social background.

The book opens with a chapter providing a backdrop to the social forces that shaped Soviet-Jewish identity and lifestyle during the last decades of state socialism and after its fall. Although much has been written about this topic, I believe that my take on Russian-Jewish identity is different as I base my reflections mainly on the so-called soft data—ethnography rather than surveys and statistics—trying to understand the "thin fabric" of Russian Jewish culture and the social boundaries between Jews and other former Soviet citizens. I also focus my analysis on the features of this culture that played a role in the subsequent social adaptation (or its lack) among Jewish immigrants in their new homelands. The following chapters elaborate on the difficult processes of social integration of the newcomers as well as the evolution of their cultural identity, community life, interactions with the established Jewish communities, and perceived social inclusion and exclusion. Within this broad framework, I highlight some of the recently emerging phenomena in immigrant life on the "Russian street" that were not yet evident to observers during the early 1990s: the gender differentials in the adjustment process, the social locations of the so-called 1.5 generation, the emerging transnational lifestyle, and more.

As the majority of the last-wave immigrants have moved to Israel, reinforcing its role as demographic and social center of the expanding Russian-Jewish diaspora,[2] the case of Russian Jewry in Israel of the 1990s and early 2000s occupies a significant portion of this volume. This emphasis also reflects my own standpoint as an Israeli scholar of Russian background and the agenda of my recent research among Israelis with a Russian accent. A central place of the Israeli scene of *Aliyah ve-Klita* (Hebrew for immigration and absorption) is also explained by the intensity and versatility of the integration experiences of Russian Jews in the Holy Land. They were not only influenced by the hegemonic Hebrew majority, but have also made a significant impact on the country's economy, cultural, political life, and the very boundaries of its Jewish identity. Indeed, in most other receiving countries, Russian-speaking Jews comprise a tiny minority, while in Israel they make fully 20 percent of its Jewish population, and in some towns and cities—a "critical mass" of between 30 percent and 40 percent. Another unique feature of the Israeli scene is a highly institutionalized and policy-driven approach to the social project of *Alyah ve-Klita* seen as a principal source of growth and security in Israel, while in all other destination countries Russian Jews are just another immigrant group left to accommodate for themselves. Reflecting this high social investment in the newcomers (*olim*), their encounter with veteran Israelis has been ideologically loaded, rife with mutual expectations (mostly unmet!), debates over public assistance and its economic returns, the tenuous Jewishness and Zionism of the new arrivals, and their continuous loyalty to the Russian language and culture. Although the expectations and "strings attached" in the reception of Russian Jews in the U.S., Canada, and Germany were not as apparent and intense, the tacit conflict between the established Jewish communities and the newcomers has been unfolding there also. The chapters discussing the lives of Russian-speaking Jews in major North American cities refer to a different, and in a way "pure," case of encounter of former Soviets with Western economies and lifestyles, where they dived into unfamiliar waters with relatively little public support and had to swim on their own. The German case is unique in the extent and duration of welfare aid to the Jewish refugees, which partly discouraged them from labor market participation. While aliyah to Israel is ideologically constructed as homecoming (repatriation), and many olim internalize this view of their resettlement, with the ensuing expectations of support and social inclusion, immigration to the West is perceived by both parties as a pragmatic decision taken by the émigrés at their own risk. A comparative study allows exploration of the role of ideological framing of migration, local policies towards immigrants, and their expectations from the host society as factors shaping the experiences of integration.

Another salient aspect of the Russian-Jewish experiences in the post-communist diaspora (largely overlooked by earlier writers) embraces complex relations between Jews and non-Jews in the emerging Russian speaking migrant communities. Due do the decades of assimilation and mixed marriage (exceeding 60 percent in the recent demographic cohorts), the Jewish and non-Jewish circles of former Soviets are closely intertwined, both in the homelands and after emigration. Younger generations of Russian-Jewish immigrants are predominantly of mixed ethnicity (Toltz, 2003). In Israel, the public discourse around Russian immigrants of the 1990s includes the controversy around the growing share of non-Jews in their ranks as a potential "fifth column" unwilling to identify with the national agenda. In a twisted way, the attitudes towards non-Jews in Israel resemble the precarious status of Jews in Russia as mistrusted "others." Entitled to aliyah by the Law of Return but deprived of some basic civil rights as non-Jews by religious law (*Halacha*), tens of thousands of Russian-speaking immigrants became second-class citizens in the "ethnic democracy" of Israel (Kimmerling, 2001). In Germany, members of the Jewish "special refugee contingent" of the 1990s cross paths with a 2.5 million immigrant community of *Aussiedler*—ethnic Germans from the vast territories of the FSU, and despite their shared Soviet background these communities maintain separate social networks. The American and Canadian landscapes of Russian-speaking minorities include several groups that had arrived via different channels: Jewish refugees of the late 1980s and 1990s mingle with former Soviets of any ethnic background who came to work on job visas in science and high-tech, on one hand, and as domestic and nursing workers, on the other. In Toronto, Vancouver, and other Canadian cities, independent Russian-speaking immigrants who arrived directly from the FSU meet those who re-migrated from Israel, unable to achieve economic success and/ or integrate there socially. To complement the picture, there are winners of the Green Card (Diversity) Lottery, members of persecuted religious minorities (Pentecostals and Baptists), Armenian refugees, and former Soviet spouses and parents of American and Canadian citizens—to name just the main groups comprising the "Russian mosaic." Where are the social and cultural boundaries of these groups and in which realms do they intersect? What, if any, role is played by lingering anti-Semitism in shaping relations between Jews and non-Jews as immigrants in foreign lands? Some initial insights into these issues will draw on my ethnographic observations collected in the early 2000s, when the main lines of coexistence and conflict came to the fore.

Finally, a novel stance taken by this book is the analytical framework of transnationalism applied to the emerging global Russian-Jewish diaspora. The great exodus from the FSU over the last fifteen to eighteen years has split families and social networks of colleagues and friends: some stayed put while others resettled in Israel and in the West. After getting an initial foothold in the host countries, these dispersed individuals started to reassemble their old social networks, strongly enabled by the new technologies of communication and travel. Former Soviet Jews have been molded by the Russian-Soviet culture, which they cherish and wish to preserve and transfer to the next generation. Some may feel isolated from the mainstream in their new homelands and seek kindred souls in the familiar Russian social spaces, both local and global, for example in the Russian Internet forums and dating websites. Many others wish to stay plugged in their old social networks despite being well integrated in the new country. Thus, Russian-speakers scattered across different locales are gradually forming an increasingly dense social space held together by physical and economic ties (mutual visits, joint business ventures, and scientific projects) as well as spiritual and virtual means (cultural exchange, educational projects), fortified by the advent of the Internet and the global Russian-language media. Some of the key expressions of the emerging transnational lifestyle of Russian Jewish global citizens will be highlighted in the following pages.

At this point, I owe an academic reader a few words on my research paradigm and method. My personal credo as a scholar draws on a broad view of sociology as a synthetic and multifaceted discipline and includes constant shifting of the focus between the macro and micro levels of social inquiry. I deem myself a holistic social observer, merging the elements of sociology, social anthropology, and cultural analysis (in any case, the boundaries between these disciplines mainly reflect institutional conventions and are constantly crossed in the research praxis). In order to compile a genuine picture of social reality it is essential to combine different research tools and perspectives, both structured (surveys, statistics) and interpretative-qualitative such as personal narratives of the immigrants, observations of their interactions with host societies, and analysis of the cultural artifacts produced by the Russian-speaking diaspora (mass media, Websites, fiction, folklore, etc). I also find great epistemological value in the unobtrusive methods of social observation that zoom in on spontaneous human environments and interactions, inevitably altered by structured tools and formalized settings of the orthodox social research.[3] Finally, I believe in the intrinsic value of "thick description" (Geertz, 1973) as a salient insight into social reality, especially when statistical patterns are rapidly changing or hard to establish. Through the diversity and flexibility of my methodological tools I hope to construct a fuller and more realistic picture of the processes of immigrant integration and cultural conflict with host societies.

At the same time, no first-hand account of immigration (or any other social experience) can be "objective" and free of the reporter's personal biases, so this work can be seen as my humble effort at an interpretation of the complex reality of the Russian-Jewish exodus. Throughout this book, I tried to downplay my own opinions and political sympathies but sometimes they do "hang out," and most readers will probably decrypt them. Whenever possible, I preferred intellectual honesty to political correctness, often resulting in an unflattering portrayal of my subjects (especially when I quote their uncensored speech). Last but not least, I am also well aware of the challenge entailed by my complex analytical template, which draws not only on four different countries but also on multiple intersections of gender, age, and human capital factors that simultaneously shape the experiences of the newcomers. As this is the first comparative study of this kind and scope, it inevitably suffers from limitations and blanks in the data, substituted where possible by educated guesswork. I hope that this book will spark interest in the Russian Jewish community even in

countries where it comprises a small minority and inspire future research on the Jews and other diasporic immigrants of former Soviet
origin (e.g., Germans, Greeks, Armenians, and Finns).

The genre of this book can be defined as analytical overview en-
compassing my own research of the last decade and multiple other
sources from Israeli, American, German, and Canadian social science
literature. Throughout the book, my own reflexive voice as participant
observer will be intermingled with more formally reported research
findings. As the readers of this book may have diverse interests and
not necessarily peruse it from beginning to end, I framed individual
chapters as fairly self-standing articles; each of them can be read
independently of the others, with some necessary cross-references.[4]
The empirical base for this analysis includes a major Israeli survey
that I developed and conducted in 2001, as well as rich qualitative and
ethnographic data (over 500 hours of interviews and group discussions) that my assistants and I collected among Russian-speaking immigrants in Israel, the U.S., Canada, and Germany between 1994 and
2005. In view of the diversity of research questions, participants, and
tools of different studies comprising together my empirical database, it
would hardly make sense to provide one general chapter on methodology. Instead, whenever citing my earlier work, I briefly describe research participants and methods and refer the reader to the relevant
publications for the details. By doing so, I am trying to keep at the
necessary minimum methodological and technical details so that this
book could appeal to a broader readership. I believe that this unorthodox approach to explaining methodology is a reasonable compromise
between scientific rigor and readable writing style that suits the unusual character of this project. Transcending disciplinary boundaries,
this book addresses a diverse potential readership: sociologists, anthropologists, and political scientists studying immigration and integration, ethnicity and ethnic identity, global diasporas and transnationalism,
as well as scholars and wide public interested in the former Soviet
Union, Jewish affairs generally, and Soviet Jewry specifically.

Notes

1. The available estimates show that between 10 and 15,000 former Soviet Jews
   have left for Australia after 1989, now forming over 10 percent of Australian
   Jewry (www.naa.gov.au). Exact numbers are hard to establish as their entry to

this country was framed under Point System (i.e., evaluating their age and human capital) as economic migrants, regardless of the ethno-religious criteria. As virtually nothing has been published on the integration experiences of this small group of former Soviet Jews (and for budgetary reasons I could not travel there to collect my own data), I did not include Australia in this book.

2. I am using the term *diaspora* in its primary meaning of *dispersion*, referring to ethnic groups living outside their historic homelands (see Saffran, 1999). For the former Soviet émigrés of any ethnicity, Russia, Ukraine and other parts of the former USSR had been, until recently, their historic homelands. This was the home they left after the fall of communism, and this allows me to speak of the *post-communist diaspora*. As Russian Jews count many generations on Russian soil and their cultural makeup is largely Russian, FSU serves as a much more tangible historic homeland for the current wave of immigrants than Israel, the virtual and symbolic one. These unorthodox twists on the notions of *home* and *diaspora* certainly debunk Zionist mythology, but they are much more in line with the lived human experience of late twentieth-century Jewish migrations.

3. Former Soviet immigrants (especially their older part) pose a challenge for the social researcher: formal interviews and structured questionnaires almost never reflect their true lives and opinions due to the lingering fears of misuse of personal information by "the authorities" (whoever they are, real or imagined). Social desirability, that is, the wish to please the interviewer and/or meet the perceived social norms in one's answers, is also common in this group (Remennick, 2004a-c; Kishinevsky, 2004). In-depth research conducted by insiders understanding these cultural codes (as opposed to mainstream sociologists and observers) has greater chances to glean frank answers.

4. Although this had not been my initial intent, the size of the chapters is congruent with the size of the Russian-Jewish communities in the individual host countries, with the Israeli chapter being the largest and the American one the second largest, followed by the German, and the shortest one, Canadian. I let the reader decide if this observation has any analytical value.

1

Soviet Jewry and the Dilemma of Emigration

"—How do Jews even know they are Jews? They are not so different from the rest . . .
—Oh, they won't mind forgetting all about it, but they are constantly reminded . . . "
                                                    —from a short story by Fazil Iskander, 1978

It is common wisdom now that there is no single and monolithic Jewish identity that would be valid across historic periods and cultures; Jewish identities in different countries of the Diaspora have been as diverse as were the conditions of their lives. For most of Diasporic Jewish history, and especially since the inception of assimilation in the nineteenth century, Jewish identities and cultures have been split between their national or local halves (Russian, German, Moroccan, etc.) and their Jewish halves. Across written history, Jews have been the single most multilingual and multicultural ethno-religious group. Jewish communities have been able to survive in hostile environments and adjust to whatever life had to offer in a specific time and place, trying to make the best of it. Another trait typical of most Jews is their being dynamic, mobile, fast learners, and often brokers of social change in their countries of residence. Historical studies reflecting on the Jewish people's role in modern civilization generally and in Russian history specifically, exemplified by *The Jewish Century* by Yuri Slezkine (2004), attest to impressive Jewish adaptive potential and social mobility, which Slezkine reckons to be the Jewish people's most basic common feature across times and places. Multiple monographs over the last decade have addressed more specific and local-ized dilemmas of Jewish life in different contemporary societies (*Jewish Survival*, by Krausz and Tulea [1998]; *Mapping Jewish Identities* by Silberstein [2000]; *Forging Modern Jewish Identities* by Berkowitz et al. [2003]; *American Judaism* by Sarna [2004], to cite only a few notable volumes); their very number points to complexities and con-troversies involved in understanding what it means to be Jewish today. What is the special place of former Soviet Jewry [1] on the global map of modern Jewish experience and how did life under the Soviet system shape its collective identity and the eventual drive toward emigration? Without going too far back into the history of Russian Jewry (for which I refer the reader to the concise and cogent account in chapters 3 and 4 of the Slezkine book, as well as chapter 2 in Brym and Ryvkina's 1994 book), I will focus on the last three decades of state socialism that preceded the inception of the last Jewish exodus from the USSR.

Demographic Profile of Soviet and Post-Soviet Jewry

I will begin with a brief demographic sketch of Soviet Jewry that has direct bearing on its social characteristics; for more detailed statis-tical data on Russian-Jewish demographics the interested reader can consult publications by Mark Tolts (1997, 2003, 2004). Accounting for the assimilative processes, demographers usually distinguish be-tween what they call *core Jews* and the *Jewish periphery*, or *enlarged Jewish population*. The former term refers to those who have two Jewish parents and self-identify in censuses and surveys as Jews; the latter—to persons with one Jewish parent or grandparent, as well as non-Jewish spouses of Jews. Although socially these two groups are closely intertwined, the percentage of their Jewish blood, so to speak, often made a real difference both in the face of Soviet-type institu-tional anti-Semitism and in contexts where religious Judaic authorities set the tone and policies regarding their rights as Jews, in Israel and in some other Orthodox communities in the Diaspora. As a result of mixed marriage between Jews and non-Jews, the share of partial Jews has been growing from one generation to the next, while the share of core Jews has been shrinking. The ratio between the enlarged Jewish population and its core in the Russian Federation increased from 1.5 in the late 1970s to 1.8 in 1994, and probably approached 2.0 by the time of the last Russian census of 2002 (Tolts, 2003).

Respectively, the estimates of the size of the Jewish population of Russia and the FSU may broadly vary depending on the chosen definition of the Jews and political agenda of those using these statistics. Religious Jewish organizations in the FSU, and their foreign sponsors, are usually interested in the "genuine Jews," that is, those born of two Jewish parents or at least of Jewish mothers. Their numbers in the USSR and successor states have consistently dropped from one census to the next, from 2,279,000 in 1959, to 1,480,000 in 1989, 544,000 in 1999, and an estimated 400,000 in 2002 (the last censuses in Russia and the FSU had multiple organizational and performance flaws, so the numbers are estimates at best). By 2002, the majority of the remaining Jews (233,600) lived in Russia (vs. 551,000 in 1989), less than 90,000 remained in Ukraine, and all the other former republics counted together about 55,000 of core Jews (Tolts, 2003, 2004). At the same time, The Jewish Agency (Sochnut) that brokers and manages immigration to Israel, bases its count on the entitlement for aliyah and Israeli citizenship that embraces also half and quarter Jews, with their immediate families. Counted in this way, the enlarged Jewish population of Russia may exceed half a million (and according to some estimates, stands closer to one million), and for the whole FSU— 800,000 (1.2 million, by the upper-end estimates). The World Jewish Congress, United Jewish Appeal, and other international Jewish organizations also prefer to cite the upper-limit figures to facilitate their fundraising for Jewish causes in the FSU. The broad range of the existing estimates is impressive and leaves a lot of room for ideological and pragmatic speculation.

The demographic decline of Soviet and post-Soviet Jewry is explained by four major factors: mixed marriage, low fertility, advanced-age composition, and accelerated emigration. Mark Tolts estimated that between 1989 and 2002, the core Jewish population of Russia has dropped by 55 percent; about 42 percent of this decrease reflected negative vital balance (i.e., excess of deaths over births) and 58 percent was due to emigration. In 1994, 63 percent of Jewish men and 44 percent of Jewish women in Russia were married to non-Jews, compared to 51 percent and 33 percent, respectively, in 1979. Among Ukrainian Jewry, the shares of out-married men and women in 1996 were 82 percent and 74 percent, respectively; the same was true about Jews in Latvia (86 percent and 83 percent). No data on out-marriage are available for the early 2000s, but these numbers have definitely climbed further up. The greater tendency to out-marriage among Jewish men reflects, to some extent, the lack of Jewish brides in the major Russian cities where young Jewish men had migrated earlier in great numbers. Culturally, it can also reflect lower attractiveness of Jewish women vis-à-vis Jewish men as potential marital partners for non-Jews, reflecting popular stereotypes of Jewish men as hard-working, sober, and devoted to the family and of Jewish women as demanding and haughty ("Jewish princesses") or, alternatively, as meddling and petty (Gershenson, 2006). As a result, among Soviet/Russian half-Jews, the share of those with Jewish fathers (who are not recognized as Jews in Orthodox Judaism) significantly exceeds those with Jewish mothers. Between 1988 and 1995, the percentage of children born to Jewish mothers and non-Jewish fathers, out of all children born to Jewish mothers, rose from 58 to 69 percent, and by the early 2000s has probably exceeded 80 percent. As a result of these trends, in the younger generations (sixteen to twenty-four year olds) the share of youths having two Jewish parents, among those having any Jewish relation at all, stands at 25–28 percent (Tolts, 2003, 2004).

In contrast to their forefathers in the Pale of Settlement and their counterparts in Israel and some Diaspora countries, Soviet Jews have typically had fewer children than the surrounding majority. During the post-communist years, their fertility rates dropped even lower: from 1.5 children in the late 1980s to 0.8 in 1994, compared to 1.9 and 1.25, respectively, in the general population of Russia. Besides low fertility norms in Russia and the modest living standards of most citizens, Jews limited their offspring to one or two children due to a strong emphasis on the quality of their upbringing and great parental investment in each child. Reflecting many decades of low fertility combined with high life expectancy among the Jews, their age pyramid was inverted, pointing to the rapid aging process. By the mid–1990s, death rates among Russian Jews surpassed birth rates by 27 units, leading to a steady decline of their numbers. Similar trends have occurred in other successor states. The Jewish population of the FSU is the oldest one among all Diasporic Jewish communities: the mean age of a Russian Jew today approaches sixty.

While during the turmoil of the post-communist 1990s the life expectancy of Russians plummeted to the unprecedented levels of 57.9 among men and 71.3 among women, the longevity of the Jews showed only a slight downward turn and remained relatively high: 69.6 and

73.2 for men and women, respectively. For comparison, the figures for one of the last years of socialism, 1988, were 69.9 and 65.4 for Jewish and Russian men, and 73.3 and 74.2 for the Jewish and Russian women. Thus Jews had always had an advantage in longevity vs. non-Jews, but in 1993–94 a Jewish man in Russia lived on the average almost twelve years longer than his fellow Russian, and a Jewish woman lived two years longer than a Russian one (Tolts, 2003). I will elaborate more on the reasons for the Jewish survival advantage (especially on the male side), but one apparent conclusion from these statistics is that Jews as a group have adjusted much better than Russians to the drastic changes in the economic and social environment of the post-communist years.

Former Soviet Jewry of European (Ashkenazi) origin has been the most urbanized ethnic group in the FSU: over 95 percent of them lived in the cities, mostly in the capitals and other large urban centers (in the Russian Federation, 54 percent of the Jews lived in Moscow and St. Petersburg*). Ever since the 1920s, Jews have also been the most educated ethnic minority, over half of them receiving postsecondary education. In certain birth cohorts of Jews, the percentage or carriers of university degrees was as high as 75 percent and about 90 percent worked in white-collar occupations. Jews who grew up in Moscow, Leningrad, Kiev, Minsk, Odessa, Tashkent, Novosibirsk, and a few other mega-cities had a lot more opportunity to study in good schools, read diverse literature, and develop their talents in various cultural venues vis-à-vis their provincial counterparts. Some of the ambitious small-town Jewish students and professionals could, of course, relocate to the capital, but this was a small minority as, besides anti-Semitic barriers in education and careers, Moscow and Leningrad had tight administrative regulations of residence, and one could get a living permit in these cities only via marriage or job contract (not unlike the U.S. Green Card). Thus, due to their disproportionate concentration of cultural and educational resources, Moscow and Leningrad became hothouses for a multifaceted Jewish professional and intellectual elite, represented in a whole range of scientific, medical, educational, artistic, legal, and technical occupations. According to the last Soviet census of 1989, the percentage of Jewish adults with a university education or equivalent in Moscow and St. Petersburg was 60.4

---

* In 1991 Leningrad had its pre-revolutionary name St. Petersburg restored. This is the second largest Soviet/Russian city, often called "the Northern Capital."

percent and 55.2 percent, versus only 45 percent among provincial Russian Jews. The Jews of the smaller cities and towns of Russia, and the majority of Ukrainian and Belorussian Jewry, typically belonged to skilled industrial and technical occupations rather than humanistic or free professions (Tolts, 1997).

By contrast to the educated, secular, and urban Ashkenazi Jews, the minority of Jews living in Central Asia (Bukharan Jews) and the Caucasus (Georgian, Mountain Jews, and Krymchaks) comprised together a minority of 8–10 percent among Soviet Jewry and had a very different social profile. These communities, living in remote and less urbanized areas, where the hold of Soviet power was weaker than in the big cities, managed to keep many of their ethnic and religious traditions and did not try to assimilate into the mainstream. These Jewish communities spoke Jewish languages of their own, various dialects of Farsi, Azeri, and Georgian (and often Russian as a second language), had organized Jewish life, married each other in arranged marriages, raised relatively many children, and confined most of the women to the homemaking roles. The levels of formal education among Asian and Caucasian Jews have been much lower than among European Jews (roughly similar to the Soviet average of 20–25 percent holding postsecondary degrees) and their occupational structure was dominated by tradesmen, artisans, and since the 1990s—small business owners. Virtually all of these Jewish communities left the FSU—some back in the 1970s and the majority after 1989—and resettled in Israel, and (in smaller numbers) in Europe and the U.S.

As mentioned above, emigration significantly depleted the ranks of Soviet and post-Soviet Jewry from the early 1970s on. At this point, I will only cite the available statistics and will develop my argument on the social mechanisms of emigration in the following pages. The first emigration wave that left the USSR over the decade of the 1970s counted about 250,000; among them about 130,000 moved to Israel and 120,000 continued to the West, mostly to the U.S. When the gates of the deteriorating Soviet empire reopened in the late 1980s, Jews were the first ones to take their leave; ethnic Germans, Armenians, Greeks, and Finns soon followed in their steps. The majority of those who left the USSR with Israeli visas between 1987 and 1990 (around 85 percent) arrived in the U.S. under Jewish refugee status (their total number is estimated at about 235,000 [Dominitz, 1997]). Then at the end of 1989 the American government changed its refugee policy towards Soviet Jews and drastically reduced the quotas and the terms of entry. At the same time, Israel opened direct flight routes from the major Soviet cities to Tel Aviv and closed the transition camp in Vienna where bifurcation of the migrant stream took place in the past.

Since the early 1990s, these simultaneous changes effectively redirected the bulk of Jewish emigrants leaving the USSR to Israel, reducing the so-called dropout rates (*neshira*) to 20–25 percent (Dominitz, 1997). Between 1989 and 2002, over 1.6 million former Soviets emigrated from the FSU on the "Jewish ticket," that is, as ethnically privileged migrants. About 60 percent of them belong to the Jewish core and 40 percent are partly Jewish or married to Jews. The four major receiving countries after 1989 have been Israel, the U.S., Germany, and Canada; smaller groups resettled in Australia, New Zealand, and a few European countries. Demographers estimate that roughly one-half of the 1.6 million *core Jews* born in the USSR/FSU reside in Israel, about one-quarter remain in the FSU, and the rest are spread between North America and Germany, with a few percent living in other countries (Tolts, 2004). In the wake of this exodus, the Jewish population of Russia shrank to 45 percent of its size in 1989, and for the FSU as a whole to some 30 percent. By the early 2000s, the out-migration flow of Russian-speaking Jews turned into a trickle of several thousand per year. The remaining Jews are either too old to migrate or fully assimilated into the Russian mainstream; many of them have achieved economic success under the new market economy and lead comfortable lives (Gitelman et al., 2003). In any event, it seems clear that the major potential of emigration of former Soviet Jewry has already been exhausted.

The Imposed Jewish Identity vs. the Perceived One: Passport Jews and Others

While demographers are interested in numbers and statistical trends, sociologists try to explain and interpret them. Let us now look at the social context behind the facts of Soviet Jewish demography and the forces that shaped Russian-Jewish identity, with its built-in emigration streak, during the last decades of the twentieth century. As the epigraph to this chapter reminds us, being Jewish had never been a matter of choice for Soviet Jews. Since the mid–1930s, internal passports of all Soviet citizens included a *nationality* entry, meaning ethnic origin, the infamous fifth paragraph (*piatyi punkt*) that became synonymous with Jewish "social disability" among other "normal" citizens. At the age of sixteen everyone was ascribed the ethnicity of one's parents; those born of mixed marriage could choose either ethnic designation. Thus a person born of two Jewish parents entered society officially defined as a Jew. Among the youths, who could choose between their Jewish and non-Jewish affiliation, about 90 percent registered as Russians, Ukrainians, etc., in order to avoid a negative label that could hinder their future education and career prospects. By the mid–1990s, only 6 percent of these youths chose to register as Jews (Tolts, 2003), suggesting that the popularity of Jewishness did not increase much in the post-Soviet era. Besides the overt statement of their *nationality* in the passport and most other documents (including medical records and library cards!), Jews were easily recognizable by their non-Slavic last names and typical patronymics such as Izrailevich or Abramovich, as well as their physiognomic features and some aspects of their speech and demeanor. So Jews were visible in the midst of the Slavic majority regardless of what their documents said. As the punchline of a sad Jewish joke goes, *They* [anti-Semites] *hit you on your face, not on your passport.*[2]

During the first two post-revolutionary decades, Jews became a privileged minority group as the young republic of peasants and workers needed their relatively high professional and administrative skills, as well as their political loyalty. As Slezkine shows in his book (2004), Russian Jews had a long-standing affair with communism as ideology and political regime, which ultimately entailed rather destructive results both for them and the country. By the late 1930s, the regime had recruited and trained enough cadres from the ranks of Russians and other Slavs so that the ubiquitous presence of Jews in high-ranking posts in the party apparatus, government, and secret services was rapidly reduced via relentless cleansing campaigns (Martin, 1998; Zeltser, 2004). Ever since, the rising and falling tides of anti-Semitic plots and campaigns, masterminded by the Kremlin and conducted by the NKVD-KGB in team with the central party press, served as a mechanism for controlling Jewish social mobility and ethnic representation. Admittedly, the Russian chauvinism of the Soviet authorities, inherited from the tsarist regime and peasant mentality, targeted other non-Slavic minorities too (e.g., ethnics of the Asian and Caucasian republics). Yet, the position of Jews on the scale of ethnic intolerance has always been outstanding, both due to age-old anti-Jewish sentiment and the lingering possibility of emigration, automatically rendering Jews untrustworthy, a black sheep in the flock of Soviet nations, a suspect neighbor in the infamous communal apartment (Slezkine, 1994). Having no designated land of their own in the USSR (besides the failed project of Birobidjan) but having a historic homeland of Israel and a thriving diaspora abroad, Jews (along with a few other minorities, most notably Germans, Greeks, and Armenians) had a kind of extraterritorial status on the Soviet geopolitical map and did not fit into the scheme of the party's "nationality policy" (Friedgut, 2003). Given their propensity for higher education, they also competed with Russians and other "titular nations" (e.g., Ukrainians in the Ukraine) for positions in the public service and various professions, and often won the competition whenever merit rather than a "nomenclature principle" was at work. By the late 1960s, Soviet powerholders could no longer tolerate disproportionate representation of Jews in prominent positions in the sciences, education, technology, and culture; Jewish ambition and mobility had to be contained (Altshuler, 1987).

The price Jews had to pay for their unprecedented social mobility under state socialism was the virtual destruction of Jewish culture (Altshuler, 1987, 1998). By the early 1950s, the system of Jewish schools and cultural institutions has been almost completely destroyed, as were synagogues and yeshivas. The majority of Jewish educated professionals and civil servants who grew up in the large Soviet cities did not speak any Yiddish and knew little about Jewish traditions. Some reserves of the Ashkenazi Jewish lifestyle still remained in the provincial towns of the former Pale of Settlement (parts of the Ukraine, Belorussia, Moldavia, and the Baltic states) but they were also fading away as their carriers grew older and died. Reflecting forced secularization over seventy years of Soviet power, Jews became an ethnic minority rather than a religious denomination. Jewish affiliation became defined by purely bureaucratic means—parental ethnicity and registration in civil papers—and lost any direct connection with Judaic faith or religious practice. At the same time, Jews were the most Russified of all ethnic minorities: in the last Soviet census of 1989, about 90 percent of the Jews named Russian as their native language, compared to 30–60 percent among other ethnic groups (Remennick, 1998).

Given the wide prevalence of mixed marriages between Jews and non-Jews, growing from one generation to the next, the ranks of half-Jews and quarter-Jews expanded as well over the decades of the Soviet regime. In contrast with the religious Judaic principle defining Jewish ancestry on the maternal side, in Soviet mixed families the father's ethnic origin always mattered more for the identity of the offspring. Hence half-Jews on the paternal side were often more prone to identify as Jews, both psychologically and officially; some of them even chose to register as Jews in the passport. Yet, the majority of half-Jews grew up as Russians, or else as "internationalists," with only a small fraction of them discovering their Jewish side in later life (Nosenko, 2004). In terms of the dominant culture and lifestyle of the mixed households, Russian wives of Jews more often adopted Jewish features of everyday living and child rearing than vice versa (i.e., Jewish women who married Russians and other non-Jews tended to adapt to their lifestyles). In other words, in most mixed marriages between Jews and non-Jews the woman was usually the party to adjust and make changes, reflecting the dominant patriarchal gender culture. Many of these women willingly followed their husbands to Israel where, by an irony of fate, they assumed a minority status and had to undergo religious conversion (*giyur*) in order to become "normal" (I will say more about these women in the pages to follow). Whether a family kept any signs of Jewish traditional lifestyle was also defined by the size of the city they lived in, the presence of the Jewish elders in the household, education and occupation of the middle generation, and other circumstances. Usually educated urban professionals were more distant from the Jewish traditions than their small-town and less-educated counterparts (Altshuler, 1987).

Some recent research suggests that young people of mixed ethnicity became aware of their Jewishness later in life and under different influences than their peers with two Jewish parents. A survey in a representative sample among the Jews living in the major cities of Russia and Ukraine conducted twice (in 1992/3 and 1997/8) by the Jewish Research Center via face-to-face interviews (Cherviakov et al., 2003) compared the responses of pure or "passport" Jews with those of half-Jews. As all but a few of the mixed ethnics registered in their passports as non-Jews and had Russian last names, their exposure to institutional anti-Semitism was much weaker and many of them were not aware of their Jewish affiliation until early adulthood, typically their student years. Their self-awareness as Jews was developed mainly by cognitive practices (e.g., reading literature on Jewish history or the current Jewish press) rather than direct personal experiences. Most of the pure Jews recounted that they became aware of their "ethnic disability" early, usually in elementary school, and mainly through direct encounters with anti-Jewish remarks or actions of their peers, teachers, neighbors, and others. When asked about the people who shaped their Jewish self-awareness, pure Jews more often named one or both parents, while half-Jews mainly named their friends and colleagues (suggesting that their parents did not discuss Jewish matters with them). Finally, pure Jews were more inclined to observe some of the Jewish traditions at home (30 percent vs. 18 percent in the Russian sample) and to attendance in Jewish organizations. Pure Jews were also twice as likely to perform any of the religious rituals, although the percentage of positive answers here was low in both groups (between 3 percent and 10 percent). A recent narrative-based study by Elena Nosenko (2004), including eighty-three oral histories of half-Jews living in the major Russian cities, largely confirmed these trends, showing that the Jewish component of their self-identity was diffuse and situational, with anti-Semitic attacks serving as its main trigger. Some respondents "recovered their Jewish roots" via participation in the Jewish educational and community projects (usually sponsored from abroad), which most attended for social and pragmatic reasons. Nosenko failed to trace any major role either of the Holocaust, or of Zionism and Israel as salient axes of their Jewish self-perception; most informants did not consider emigration and saw Russia as their homeland.

Ethnic groups are defined by their common cultural signifiers (language, art, cuisine, etc.) and boundaries vis-à-vis other groups. Given that Soviet Jews lost their religion and traditional culture and immersed themselves in the midst of the general urban populace, what was the remaining ground for their self-identification as Jews? Was it mainly due to the ambient anti-Semitism or were there also some other specific qualities they ascribed to themselves and their ilk? Zvi Gitelman in his article "Thinking about Being Jewish in Russia and Ukraine" (2003) reflects on the signs and expressions of what he calls a "thin" Russian-Jewish culture that remained in the wake of their destroyed "thick" culture, based on common religious practice, language, and organized community life. What special cultural fabric, however thin, made Jews different from other ex-Soviets? No academic work was done on this topic during Soviet times, but quite a few social scholars explored the issues of perceived Jewish identity during the post-Soviet era (Brym and Ryvkina, 1994; Gitelman et al., 2003; Ryvkina, 2005). Important reflections about Russian Jewish intelligentsia are found in the writings by the Russian Jewish historian and activist Mikhail Chlenov (1997), physicist and ardent Zionist Alexander Voronel (1997), and psychologist who joined political reforms of the early 1990s Leonid Gozman (1997). The construction of Russian-Jewish identity in contemporary fiction by Jewish authors is discussed by Mikhail Krutikov (2003) and Olga Gershenson (2006) explores the images of Russian Jews on screen. Multiple insights on the lifestyle and mindset of Russian Jews can be gleaned retrospectively, by analyzing the narratives of the Jewish immigrants in the U.S. and Israel, quite a few of which have been collected and published over the last decade (see for example Siegel, 1998; Orleck, 1999; Yelenevskaya and Fialkova, 2005).

When researchers coming from the Anglo-Jewish world and raised in the "cultural Judaism" of the contemporary Diaspora first tackle the issue of Russian-Jewish identity, they are shocked by the apparent absence of the recognized pillars of the Jewish identity—knowledge of the Jewish history and holidays, keeping some household and cooking traditions, the imperative to marry other Jews, religious rites of passage and Jewish education for the children, knowledge of the Jewish languages, and identification with Israel. These components of the international Jewish cannon were obscure or foreign for most Soviet Jews, and are even less relevant for those who remain in the FSU today (Ryvkina, 2005). In the previously mentioned survey among Russian and Ukrainian Jews (Chervakov et al., 2003), only 0.5 percent to 5 percent of the respondents named the features listed above as essential for being a "genuine Jew." By contrast, in both countries and at both times the majority (between 20 percent and 33 percent) chose the answers "*to be proud of your nationality,*" "*defend Jewish honor and dignity,*" "*not to hide one's Jewishness*" and "*remember the Holocaust*" as chief expressions of their Jewish identity. It seems that the Holocaust memories form the only common denominator between the Soviet and other Diaspora Jews. In the survey among 1,000 Jews of Moscow, Kiev, and Minsk conducted by Brym and Ryvkina (1994), the most salient factors of respondents' perceived Jewish identity (in the decreasing order in a regression model) were exposure to Jewish culture while growing up, plans to emigrate, mother's and spouse's "passport nationality," experience of anti-Semitism, father's nationality, fear of anti-Semitism, and city size. Among those self-identifying in this latter survey as pure Jews, only 12 percent celebrated high Jewish holidays or tried to pass some Jewish traditions on to their children; 8 percent participated in Jewish organizations, and 4 percent regularly read the Jewish press. Only 14 percent expressed interest in religion, among them more leaned towards Russian Orthodoxy than Judaism. In Brym and Ryvkina's view, the Russian Jewish identity manifests as both elastic and pragmatic, that is, coming to the fore only when it serves a purpose (mainly related to emigration) and subdued for the rest of the time. Most of the building blocks of Soviet-Jewish identity were imposed by state policies or came in reaction to discrimination and humiliation (so-called reactive ethnicity, described in the American context by Alba [1990], amongst others).

The concept of identity is so complex and dynamic that in order to capture it one must to go beyond statistics and structured survey items and employ ethnographic tools such as in-depth interviews and group discussions letting people speak in their own voices. I will offer the reader some of my reflections about the *positive core* of Russian-Jewish identity drawing on multiple discussions with friends and on what is wryly called by anthropologists "home ethnography," that is, a researcher's first hand experiences in her own social circle. Multiple reinforcements for these observations come from the fieldwork of folklorists Larisa Fialkova and Maria Yelenevskaya (see, for example, their 2004 articles and 2005 book), anthropologists Fran Markowitz and Natalie Zilberg, media and culture scholars Olga Gershenson and Nelly Elias. Novels and stories written by contemporary Russian-Jewish authors, both in Russia (e.g., by Ludmila Ulitskaya) and abroad (e.g., fiction by Dina Rubina and Svetlana Schenbrunn in Israel, Svetlana Boym, Gary Shteyngart, Ludmila Stern, and Lara Vapnyar in the U.S., David Bezmozgis in Canada, Fridrikh Gorenshtein and Vladimir Kaminer in Germany) also helped me compile a fuller retrospective picture of Jewish lives and self-perceptions under socialism. My reflections pertain of course to this "thin culture" that evades strict definition and adequate measurement, but is nevertheless very real for its carriers.

Perhaps the pinnacle of the perceived Russian-Jewish identity was (and still is) the ambition for excellence and achievement, in any given sphere of activity, with the corollary high valuation of education, hard effort, and intellectualism. Another related trait is the respect for professionalism and its central place in an individual's self-identity and self-esteem. The value of professional achievement and self-actualization for many Soviet Jews exceeded the value of material wealth coming with higher occupational status, although they were not blind to the link between the two. This cult of education and professional mobility, juxtaposed with the discriminatory reality of the Soviet schooling system and most white-collar workplaces, resulted in the built-in fighter spirit and the drive to overcome the barriers erected by institutional anti-Semitism. *You can make it, just be ten times as good as any Russian, and they will have to give in,* was the wisdom that many Jewish youths digested with maternal milk. Hard effort often yielded Jewish students places in elite high schools and colleges, despite carefully designed attempts to fail them during entry exams. Jewish children and youths more often than their Russian peers had busy after-school schedules attending chess and music classes, studying foreign languages, drama, and pursuing numerous other activities that developed their abilities and ambitions. Jewish teenagers seldom participated in street gangs or hung out aimlessly in public gardens smoking and drinking alcohol. Like their parents, they knew too well that education and hard work would eventually earn them a place in the middle class, with its better access to both the material and cultural resources that Soviet urban life had to offer. The alternative would be the gloomy, drunk, and violent existence of the Russian working class, in whose ranks they would experience a full measure of hatred and humiliation as Jews. While among ethnic Russians heavy drinking and alcoholism have always been a national plague, Jews were usually moderate drinkers and also had low rates of criminal behavior and imprisonment (Shkolnikov et al., 2004). These features gave Jews a solid advantage in collective competition vis-à-vis their Slavic neighbors.

Another identity-shaping feature of Jewish life (in Russia and elsewhere) is the central place of the family in a person's life as a safe haven and primary support network, especially in the face of hostile outer society. The connections between husbands and wives, parents and children, siblings, and other relatives were usually those of duty and mutual care, regardless of intimate affections involved. Jewish parents are known for intense investment of time, effort, and emotion in their children's upbringing and education (the flipside of which is sometimes excessive protection, control, and mutual dependence in parent-child relations). Jewish families stay connected over the life course, grandparents helping the middle generation with childcare and being cared for, in turn, after becoming old and frail. The co-residence of multi-generational families under one roof, sometimes voluntary but mostly caused by the shortage of housing throughout Soviet era, also facilitated provision of mutual hands-on help and intense emotional ties in the Jewish families. When the older generation could arrange for separate living quarters for their adult children, both parties preferred living in the same neighborhood or at least in the same city. The incidence of child or spousal abuse in Soviet Jewish families was much lower than among the hegemonic majority, as were the rates of abortion and sexually transmitted diseases, other common Russian plagues (Remennick et al., 1995). By and large, Soviet Jews led healthier lives compared to the non-Jewish majority, marked by balanced nutrition, engagement in outdoor sports and hiking, moderation in drinking, lack of violence, social support, and optimal use of available health services and medication for their ailments. As was already mentioned, this modus vivendi found its ultimate expression in a significantly longer life expectancy of Soviet Jews, which even during the worst post-soviet years of general decline exceeded longevity of non-Jews by five to ten years (Tolts, 2003).

Ever since the short-lived Thaw of the 1960s, Jews were among the most consistent opponents of the Soviet regime, reflecting both their own predicament and general intellectual contempt towards the stagnating System, inefficient, immoral, and ridiculous at every level (Chlenov, 1997; Voronel, 1997). Although only a few brave ones would come out of the closet as open dissidents, most others cultivated subversive ideas, read dog-eared *samizdat* (outlawed writings that no Soviet publisher would print) and *tamizdat* (banned Western publications), and ridiculed the Soviet system in late-night kitchen discussions. Political and ethnic anecdotes (jokes with deeper meaning reflecting social and political irony embedded in Soviet reality and virtually untranslatable) thrived as the chief genre of Soviet folklore.[2] The culture of subversion and scorn, more rarely—explicit resistance, common in most Russian-Jewish homes, was the principal yeast on which young Jewish men and women of the 1960s, 1970s, and 1980s had been raised. Of course, such an atmosphere was not limited to the Jewish social milieu but was also typical of certain sectors of the Russian, Ukrainian, Armenian, Georgian, and other intelligentsias (let alone constant intersections of these social circles in mixed families as well as between colleagues, friends, and neighbors), but among the Jews "anti-Soviet attitudes," as they were called in official parlance, were paramount. At the same time, some Jewish professionals and bureaucrats excelled in the Soviet-style doublethink and doublespeak, were members of the Communist Party, and kept two separate ethical codes: one for external and the other for personal use.[3] This was also part of their successful adaptation strategy.

Featuring last but not least on the map of Soviet Jewish identity was the sense of common destiny and in-group solidarity in the face of harsh reality. Russian Jews could not help but divide the social world into *us* and *them*, easily identified each other in the crowd, and stuck together in informal social circles. Given their common problems in the face of institutional anti-Semitism (of which their Russian peers were often naively oblivious), the lingering dilemma of emigration, a peculiar sense of humor, and references to the common past experiences, their conversations were often strange and impenetrable for the outsiders. There were so many matters that they simply could not share with non-Jews without risking misunderstanding, tension, and even greater dislike of Jews. Such landmarks of Soviet-Jewish history as *Delo Vrachei* (see *The Doctors' Plot* by Rapoport, 1991), and persecution of "rootless cosmopolitans" (a pure euphemism used for vilification of Jews as foes of Russia) were often unfamiliar to fellow Russians, or were differently interpreted by them. Many non-Jews were oblivious of the terrible losses most Jewish families had suffered during Nazi occupation and mass executions of Jews in the Ukraine, Baltic states, and other western parts of the USSR. In brief, Soviet Jews shared a common history and common language to talk about it.

As a result, informal Jewish networks were often rather self-enclosed and exclusive of others: over 80 percent of Soviet Jews stated in the surveys that all or most of their best friends were Jewish (Brym and Ryvkina, 1994). In most social institutions Jews who had achieved positions of influence would support and promote other Jews (e.g., senior professionals would help younger ones, put a word for them, etc.), albeit usually rather tacitly, in order to avoid allegations of "ethnic protectionism." Throughout Soviet times, Jews were connected by the special grapevine, a chain of mutual informal aid, helping their friends (and even remote acquaintances) to find a good doctor, a tutor for the children before college exams, a babysitter or a caregiver for the parent. When emigration became reality, Jews helped and advised each other about how to by-pass Soviet bureaucrats, gave free Hebrew and English classes, disseminated letters from those already living abroad, exchanged names and telephones of their acquaintances who could help out during the first months in New York or Tel Aviv. This mutual support network comprised the most precious social capital that Soviet Jews had accumulated; some of these networks survived or replicated themselves in immigration, while others were irreversibly lost.

It is hard to say if their dense presence in many professional guilds brought Soviet Jews much excessive material wealth. Throughout the postwar period Jews where ushered by the state educational policy towards technology, engineering, and science and were effectively discouraged from entering the prestigious faculties of humanities, social sciences, culture, and journalism as they were seen as a gateway to the ideological front where Jews were mistrusted. Despite harsh competition to enter medical schools, many Jews became physicians and other health professionals. Let me remind the reader that throughout the Soviet period educated professionals such as engineers, teachers, and physicians were universally low paid, often less than skilled industrial workers. They had no professional autonomy and were defined as civil servants trained and allocated to their jobs by the state (Jones, 1991). So the majority of Jewish rank-and-file doctors and engineers lived as modestly as their non-Jewish peers, dwelling in small urban apartments and riding buses and the subway rather than private cars (which had been a luxury). A more successful minority who had climbed to the top of Soviet organizations gained access to additional sources of wealth such as cars, summer cottages, larger apartments in prestigious housing complexes—all granted to them by the authorities rather than acquired on the non-existing free market. However, most educated Soviet Jews had greater than average access to invaluable non-monetary resources such as better schooling for their children, better health care, cultural events, and entertainment—though informal networking with each other and better ability at navigating the Soviet system. As an old Russian proverb says, *Ne imei sto rublei, a imei sto druzei* (What matters is having a hundred friends, not a hundred rubles). In the unpredictable Soviet economy plagued by permanent shortages of basic goods, the exchange of favors was a universal form of barter, so the most important factor of individual well-being was to get to know the right people and have something to offer them in exchange for their aid (Ledeneva, 1998; Pesmen, 2000). Most former Soviets had to make moral compromises and partake in informal economic practices (barter, black market deals, bribery, and other connive-to-survive schemes) in order to get what they wanted. Jews were usually rather good at the art of networking with the right people and were themselves part of this vital exchange network.

Across the Soviet empire but especially in its east and south, Jews (along with Armenians, Chechens, and other Caucasus ethnics) were also active participants in the socialist shadow economy that existed in parallel to the inefficient and corrupt "command economy," providing the citizens with the merchandise and services unattainable via official channels. It included such branches as smuggling/import of foreign goods, underground manufacturing of consumer products, for instance false brand-name clothing items (e.g., Levi jeans), sidetracking and resale of goods from special warehouses catering to the Soviet nomenclature. An opportunistic entrepreneurial spirit and informal mode of operation were necessary to bypass the omnipotent system in achieving one's goals, and over time this behavior was molded into the social norm for most business-minded *Homo Sovieticus*. Ewa Morawska, one of the foremost cultural historians of Eastern Europe, describes three basic principles of Soviet-style entrepreneurship: (1) deeply ingrained "beat the system, bend the rules" modus operandi (instead of legal-institutional approach) in pursuit of business goals; (2) reliance on personal patronage and informal networks instead of legal-civic arrangements, including the lack of formal written contracts and reliance on the "word of honor" of one's business partners (the sanctions for the breach of trust being in-group ostracism and loss of income at best, violence at worst); (3) consumption-oriented capital accumulation instead of long-term investment and production development; immediate rewards take priority over deferred gratification. Businessmen Russian-style are prone to flashy public show of their wealth, for example by driving expensive cars, wearing furs and diamonds, and staffing their homes with middle-class status symbol objects (e.g., art, antiques, home electronics, kitchen appliances, etc.). These traits, molded in the clandestine Soviet business life, soared during the years of post-communist economic transition, when the established systems of regulation were demolished and new legal rules changed almost daily, asking to be bypassed. Moreover, this "cultural toolbox" of the former Soviet people with a business streak (many

Jews among them) came in extremely handy in the gray sector of liberal market economies where they found themselves as immigrants during the 1990s (Morawska, 1999).

In sum, Jews occupied a special place in the economic, social, and cultural landscape of Soviet society, providing a unique example of so-to-speak "discriminated elite." By this I mean that, despite constant policies of their control and containment at the entry to attractive career tracks and in all social institutions, Jews have achieved prominence in most important domains of professional activity and often accumulated significant influence and wealth due to their hard work, talents, entrepreneurial and social skills. In response to the policies of exclusion and vilification, Soviet Jews fortified some features of their traditional culture that helped them adapt and achieve upward mobility: cultivation of intellectualism, respect for hard effort and know-how in one's line of work, strength of family networks, in-group solidarity, moderation in their lifestyle, quiet negation or sheer manipulation of the Soviet system, in which they had to partake in order to achieve any success in their profession or business. All these features formed the basis of the unique Russian-Soviet Jewish identity and defined ethnic and cultural boundaries between the Jews and other Soviet people. The typical lamentation about the Jews often voiced by Slavs was that they "can always get by and make it" (a-hard-to-translate Russian adage *evrei umeyut ustraivat'sia*), hinting at the Jewish smarts, malleability, and self-interest vis-à-vis Slavic selflessness and naiveté.

Despite all the barriers, not a few Jews made it to the top of the Soviet hierarchy in various domains of public life, aside from the party, politics, and administration. Soviet high and popular culture featured many Jewish high-flyers: composers Isaak Dunaevsky and Matvei Blanter authored most popular songs of early socialism, stand-up comedians and satiric writers Arkady Raikin, Mikhail Zhvanetski, Genadi Khazanov, and Gregory Gorin molded ironic self-reflection among *Homo Soveticus*, writers and poets Boris Pasternak, Osip Mandelstam, Mikhail Svetlov, David Samoilov, Boris Slutsky, and Josef Brodsky became household names of the Russian intelligentsia; in many homes one could find the tapes and records of amateur (bard) singers Alexander Galich and Alexander Gorodnitsky; most Soviets learned at school about the great Russian chemist Dmitry Mendeleev (who compiled the Periodic Table of the Elements), Soviet-era physicists Nobel Prize winners Abram Joffe and Lev Landau, and so on and so forth. By the virtue of their affiliation with this prominent group, ordinary Jewish people were often proud of their Jewish origins and somewhat arrogant towards their Slavic neighbors. Affinity with the great Jews in Russia and all over the world gave them moral compensation for living under the shadow of anti-Semitism and formed an important source of a positive Jewish identity, partly offsetting the negative identity based on common problems and discrimination. (A popular Russian-Jewish hobby was taking a painstaking inventory of Jewish figures of fame in history and in modern life, carefully peeling away various disguises such as Christian and literary names). This sense of belonging to the cultural elite, regardless of their personal achievements, often made a disservice to Russian Jews after emigration, when they suddenly found themselves at the bottom of the new social pyramid.

Russian Jews, Russian Culture, and Russian Orthodoxy

As was mentioned earlier, Jews were the most Russified of the Soviet ethnic minorities and counted Russian as their mother tongue. Having moved far away from the traditional Yiddish-based culture of their forefathers, Russian-speaking Jews across the USSR became ardent adepts of the Great Russian Culture, or in Yuri Slezkine's ironic definition, "eagerly professed the cult of Pushkin." The attitude of urban middle-class Jews towards their vanished shtetl culture and its language varied between nostalgic and pejorative; Yiddish was mainly used by the elders to keep secrets from the children. Reflecting their propensity for higher education and broad cultural interests, Jewish professionals of any kind were usually well read and often knew Russian history and fine literature better than many ethnic Russians. Naturally, few Russians enjoyed revelations of their ignorance by these outsiders, only enhancing the mutual antagonism. As was already mentioned, many Jews were among the prominent creators of the twentieth-century Russian culture. Many Jews occupied a highly visible place in the Soviet cultural pantheon as theater and cinema actors and directors, stand-up comedians, composers of popular music, chess champions, writers, and poets. They were also highly active on the backstage of Russian Soviet cultural production as editors of newspapers, magazines, television and radio shows, often working under Russian-sounding literary names in order not to "stick out" as Jews.

The biographies of renowned figures in the Soviet culture, science, and society comprise over half of the two thick volumes of *The Encyclopedia of Russian Jewry* (1998). One specific example of a highly influential, and explicitly Jewish, figure on the cultural scene of the 1980s was a satiric writer and stand-up artist Mihkail Zhvanetskii, whose bitter witticisms about every aspect of life under decaying socialism became an indispensable part of late Soviet folklore and in many ways spearheaded the advent of glasnost and perestroika (Nakhimovsky, 2003). This means that throughout the twentieth century Russian Jews have been at the core of the social category known as Russian intelligentsia. The intersections and complex relations that linked Russian and Jewish intellectuals over the twentieth century, and the Jewish contributions to the so-called "Russian national vision," caused heated debates during the post-communist years, after the taboo on the overt discussion of the Jewish matters had been lifted (Krakhmalnikova, 1994). Jews were also ardent consumers of high culture of all available shades and sorts, attended concert halls and theaters, collected impressive home libraries, and vehemently discussed recent publications in the influential literary magazines such as *Novyi Mir* (New World) and *Inostrannaya Literatura* (Foreign Literature). Thus, despite their lingering label as rootless cosmopolitans, Russian Jews surely had deep roots in the Russian cultural soil. Although they were generally more rational and pragmatic than their fellow Russians, the famous keyword trio symbolizing Great Russian culture—*sud'ba*/destiny; *dusha*/soul, and *toska*/melancholy—formed a salient semantic frame through which they often construed themselves and their lives (Wierzbicka, 1996).

For a part of Russian-Jewish intellectuals, the Russian Orthodox version of Christianity became an important spiritual anchor, helping them to fill in the void left by the Soviet atheist ideology in their inner lives. For many Russians of any ethnic background, joining the Church was a form of protest against the system, an escape or "internal emigration" in the times when actual emigration was impossible. Discovering religion in the atheist milieu was for many a salient part of what Russians call *dukhovnost'* (spirituality in a broad sense as a spiritual drive rather than material pursuits). Christianity was also an easier spiritual outlet for many Jews, as it has few regulations of everyday lifestyle, as opposed to the tenets of Judaism. Its emphasis is on faith and moral living, not strict observance of daily rules of conduct. Although most religious confessions were under pressure and control under state socialism, the Orthodox Church as the most traditional and deeply rooted religious institution in Russia was still better preserved and represented than either the Judaic or Muslim faiths. For those interested in religion, there have always been many more churches than synagogues, and many more devoted Orthodox fathers than ordained rabbis. Up until the late 1980s, in Moscow, with its tens thousands of Jews, there was only one functioning synagogue closely supervised by the KGB, while dozens of churches welcomed all those seeking faith and were relatively free of surveillance.

The high Russian culture of the nineteenth and twentieth centuries, on which most Russian Jews had been raised, was rife with Christian symbols, arguments, and references: Dostoevski, Tolstoy, Bunin, Berdiayev, Soloviev, and many other important writers (whose books were banned or silenced during the Soviet era) have all positioned themselves vis-à-vis Orthodox philosophy and theology. At the same time, the writings by Gogol, Dostoevsky, and other twentieth century Russian classics often featured anti-Jewish sentiments typical of their time. So in many ways the closeted Christian faith was an attractive spiritual respite for many Russian intellectuals, including Jewish ones. As most of the urban Jewry knew virtually nothing about Judaism and had been raised as atheists, they did not perceive their turn to the Orthodox faith as betrayal of their original faith (as they had none) but as a discovery of a new spiritual world. When asked about their religious identity, they would answer that they are ethnically Jewish but Russian Orthodox by faith, seeing no conflict between the two. In her in-depth study among baptized Russian Jews, Judith Deutsch Kornblatt (2003) discovered that some converts even felt more Jewish after their baptism and more in touch with their Jewish roots and ancient history because Jesus himself was a Jew. Thus, during the 1980s a few passionate and articulate Orthodox priests have developed a sizeable following among younger Jewish men and women seeking meaning and purpose in the stifling confines of the Soviet society. The best known of them was definitely Father Alexander Men (himself a converted Jew) whose small parish in the vicinity of Moscow attracted multiple believers and fresh converts, Russian and Jewish alike. Father Men was also an original Christian philosopher and ethicist; his books, tapes, and public lectures carried a strong educational and humanist message going far beyond Orthodox dogma and offering an attractive moral alternative to late Soviet cynicism. His brutal murder in 1990 (unsolved until today but probably ordered by the KBG) was a harsh blow for many decent people, believers, agnostics, and atheists alike.

After the fall of communism Russia experienced a true religious renaissance, allowing different confessions to bloom and proselytize. Jewish religious organizations, Chabad the most visible and active among them, rushed into the open competition for the hearts and minds of the remaining Russian Jews. While both Russian Orthodoxy and several Judaic denominations welcomed those leaning towards organized religion, many chose the predominant and well-familiar Christian faith. Those interested in Orthodox Judaism went to religious schools and joined the synagogues for a short while only to realize that true Jewish life is hardly possible in Russia; eventually most of them left for Israel or U.S. Liberal Judaic confessions (Reform and Conservative) have weak representation in the Soviet successor states, and Orthodox Judaism is too dogmatic and obsolete for most former Soviets. Political power games between various rabbinical officials (e.g., the chronic conflict between the two chief rabbis of Russia— Adolf Shaevich representing the old Soviet/Russian version of religious Judaism and Berl Lazar appointed as a leader of "New Russian Jewry" from Chabad's global headquarters in New York), aggressive proselytism of Hasidic organizations, their cozy relationship with the Kremlin and flashy demonstrations of alleged philo-Semitism by the current power holders (e.g., Chanukah celebration in the Kremlin Palace) further repelled many decent people from joining any Jewish activities. Secular (or cultural) Jewish schools in large Russian cities can only survive with external funding, and only if their curriculum is not "too Jewish," that is, compatible with the national standards allowing their graduates to bid for higher education. There is not enough indigenous grass-roots initiative and drive to let Jewish causes thrive in Russia; many articles in the 2003 volume *Jewish Life after the USSR* edited by Gitelman et al., as well as my own recent visits to Moscow and conversations with few remaining Jewish relatives and friends—all attest to this sad conclusion. David Shneer's upbeat depiction of the "Jewish revival" in Moscow (Schneer and Aviv, 2005) reflects the author's outsider's stance, highly selective sources, (interviews with Jewish activists) and certain naiveté in his interpretations. The remaining Jews are largely of mixed origin and/or well assimilated and consider Russian cultural traditions, with their built-in Orthodox streak, their own. Having no long-term cultural and demographic basis in Russia and other Slavic countries, the Judaic boom is superficial and will probably prove short-lived. It will dissolve along with its corollary social and financial aid programs sponsored from the West that, indeed, helped many Jews survive the hard times of the post-communist transition. Those ethnic Jews who chose Russia not only as their cultural anchor but as their homeland will hardly ever coalesce into a Jewish community or profess Jewish faith. In the end of his *Jewish Century* Yuri Slezkine cogently noted that in the Brave New Capitalist Russia the social and cultural distance between Jews and Russians is rapidly closing from both ends: not only are Jews becoming more Russian, but Russians are becoming more "Jewish" in terms of entrepreneurial spirit and dynamic lifestyle, adopting the business, trade, and mediation skills traditionally exemplified by the Jews. It seems unavoidable to conclude, along with Slezkine (p. 360), that the Jewish part of Russian history is (almost) over.

"Suitcase Moods": The First Wave and the Great Exodus

Proneness to migration has been an important feature in the Jewish collective portrait ever since the destruction of the Second Temple. It reflected both their attempts to flee persecution and mass violence and their eternal search for better economic opportunities and more tolerant host societies. The driving forces and the push-pull factors involved in the two recent migration waves of Russian Jewry are not so different from this age-old pattern (Slezkine, 2004). Stalin was not so wrong when he coined the term "rootless cosmopolitans" as a collective second name for Soviet Jews; many of them have harbored dreams of leaving the Socialist Paradise ever since their affair with Soviet power began to dwindle, and especially after the end of the Great War and the shock of the Holocaust. For many years, these dreams were a dangerous diversion and could hardly be voiced, even between friends and relatives. Jews who had close relatives in Israel, the U.S., and capitalist Europe (and many did) had to conceal their existence, let alone correspond with them or exchange phone calls; having relatives abroad was a serious liability. All this started to change in the early 1970s. There is little doubt that the very possibility of emigration, even playing with this idea, became one of the main axes of Soviet-Jewish identity throughout the last three decades of socialism.

Three historic events were involved in the upsurge of emigration motivation among Russian Jews: Israel's impressive victory in the Six Day War of 1967, with the ensuing re-emergence of Zionist sentiments among parts of Soviet Jewry; anti-Zionist ideological backlash and the rising tide of state-sponsored anti-Semitism in the wake of these events; and finally the ruthless destruction by the Soviets of the Prague Spring in 1968. The last hopes for political reform and economic liberalization, still lingering after the short-lived Thaw, were gone now and many of the more active and self-conscious Jews realized that they, and especially their children, had no future in this country. Another potent push factor came in the form of severe restrictions for Jews in higher education. The tacit quotas for Jewish applicants to the universities and colleges were reintroduced by the Soviet administration (emulating the tsarist practice of the late nineteenth—early twentieth century) soon after Israel's victory in the Six Day War and the ensuing anti-Zionist backlash in Soviet propaganda. Since the early 1970s, when Jews started to emigrate in significant numbers, most prestigious schools virtually closed their doors to Jewish candidates as all of them were seen as potential émigrés. The state did not want to grant free education and exposure to military and scientific secrets to this "nation of traitors." State universities (following the initiative of the Moscow State University, the most prestigious national school) and the best science and technical colleges in the major cities stopped admitting Jewish students, with few exceptions. This campaign, signaling a red light in social mobility for the next Jewish generation, greatly boosted the moral readiness for emigration among parents and children alike (Altshuler, 1987; Orleck, 1999).

The first real chance to leave presented itself with the beginning of détente and concomitant warming of East-West relations in the early 1970s. The analysis of the political forces that set in motion the emigration movement of Russian Jews in the 1970s can be found in multiple works of historians and political scientists, to which I refer the reader.[4] I will simply note that Jewish emigration had for decades been a political bargaining chip in the Soviet politics, making ordinary Jewish citizens hostages of the give-and-take deals between the Kremlin and the White House, and later on—in the contested interests of American Jewry and Israeli government (Lazin, 2005). At the same time, Jews were the only ethnic group granted the privilege of exit relatively early (only for Israel and only on the grounds of family reunification as a sole legitimate rationale for emigration by Soviet law); other diasporic minorities joined the movement only in the early 1990s. For my purposes now, it is important to understand the social profile of those who dared to start the emigration process during the 1970s vs. those who stayed put until the moment in the late 1980s when the gates opened again.

Declaring one's wish to leave was a brave and risky step to take in the 1970s as it was defined by the authorities, and perceived by the broad public, as the act of treason and meant severing one's links with other "good citizens," becoming an outcast. In order to apply for the exist visa to the Ministry of the Interior's Visa Department (the infamous OVIR) every employee had to collect multiple papers authorized by his or her administration, certifying that s/he had no access to state secrets (those in occupations with access to classified data could not even apply). Thus early in the process one had to come out of the closet in front of one's bosses and colleagues and reveal one's "real face" as anti-Soviet scum (in addition, one also had to collect different papers in one's residential administration, local medical center, and a few other offices, so soon enough everybody around knew that X or Y were applying for emigration). Several rituals of punishment had to be performed over every defecting Jew, excluding him or her from the ranks of the Party or Komsomol (if they had been members) and expressing public disgust over their deed. After revealing their plans to emigrate, most Jews had to quit their jobs in order not to cast a shadow over their collectives or were simply laid off, losing the sources of livelihood. Many were also subjected to the KGB surveillance and if they showed signs of political activism for Zionist or other dissident causes, they could be further prosecuted by means of the Soviet law prohibiting "parasitism," that is, having no formal employment. An additional sanction came in the form of the so-called diploma fee (ironically called the brain drain tax) introduced in 1972, that is, the requirement to pay back to the state the costs of higher education that Jewish émigrés had received for free and were now taking out with them for the benefit of other countries. The fee was very high vis-à-vis the average Soviet income, especially given that most Jews had lost their jobs after application to exit. After intervention from the American pro-Jewish lobby, this tax was lifted in 1974. But another ridiculous tax—that for "declining Soviet citizenship" against their will—was collected from Jews before departure, meaning they could not carry a Soviet foreign passport. They left their step-motherland without any personal documents but a small green piece of paper with their name and photo—an exit visa.

As waiting for the exit visa was rather protracted and the response could always be negative, the "applicants" had to live from hand to mouth, often relying on the support of their parents and friends. Between 1971 and 1977 most applicants finally got their exit permits and Israeli visas and left the USSR; after 1977 the process slowed down and came to a halt in 1979–1980, the year of the Soviet invasion of Afghanistan and the ensuing international boycott of the Moscow Olympics. Those who applied for emigration in the 1970s and early 1980s and were refused exit visas (because of their alleged exposure to state secrets or without any clear reason), became so-called *refusniks* (*otkazniki* in Russian), and were stuck without jobs and income for an indefinite time as social pariahs. Their survival hinged on the mutual support, and thus dense social networks were formed by refusniks over the 1980s that included running free Hebrew and English classes, helping each other to find manual jobs, lending money, updating each other on any changes in emigration politics, distributing Western aid packages that reached them every now and then, spreading tamizdat publications, etc. The social groups formed by refusniks were chief fertile ground for the clandestine Soviet Zionist movement of the 1980s[5]; they were also intertwined with other streams of political dissidence and their leaders experienced harsh KGB persecution and imprisonment. Yet, at the same time, hunger strikes, sit-ins, and street demonstrations organized by desperate refusniks gave international visibility to the "plight of Soviet Jewry" and increased the political pressure on the Soviet government from the West (Gitelman, 1999). By early 1980, over 22,000 Soviet Jews found themselves living in an economic, legal, and political limbo for years at a time. The growing stream of letters, literature, and other alternative information sources from abroad (with mostly good news about life in emigration), the support from the Western Jewry, and the hope for the inevitable reopening of the emigration gates in the near future were forces that helped Soviet Jews to live through the final trying years of the Soviet regime, marked by material privations and new anti-Semitic campaigns inspired by the 1982 Lebanon war (Friedgut, 1989).

The social composition of the Jews who were leaving the USSR during the 1970s was rather mixed. The first category included Jewry from the Soviet periphery—the Baltic republics and the western parts of Ukraine, Belorussia, and Moldavia that had been included in the USSR only before the war, in 1939–40, and had experienced relatively less Sovietization and secularization than the central areas and cities. Jews living in the western parts of the USSR, especially in smaller towns, were much more Jewish in the traditional sense, had strong Zionist orientations, and even some active Zionist cells. Similar processes occurred among the Georgian Jewry and in smaller groups of Tats and Mountain Jews from the Caucasus. When the green light from the Kremlin was first given to the local authorities to let the Jews out, the bureaucratic process was expedient and by the mid–1970s the majority of these pioneers found themselves in Israel (a small number made a home in Vienna, West Berlin, and a few other European cities). The majority of these immigrants had average Soviet educational attainments and belonged to the varied ranks of clerical and technical workers, teachers, white-collar service, and trade occupations. After the Jackson-Vanik amendment of 1974 that conditioned U.S.-Soviet trade relations on the right to emigrate (reserved only for the Jews), the emigration movement received a new impetus, involving also the Jews of Moscow, Leningrad, Kiev, and other major cities (Gitelman, 1999). Those who ventured out at this time were mainly educated professionals and intellectuals seeking freedom and economic prosperity rather than wishing to join the ongoing Israeli battleground. Some of them were Zionists (and went to Israel), but the majority were merely disillusioned refugees from state socialism. Additional discouragement from making aliyah had to do with the shock and losses of the Yom Kippur War of 1973 and the bitter realization that Israel was destined to fight for its existence for many years ahead.

Thus an Israeli invitation and visa became mere procedural elements on the exit routes of Soviet Jews, as fake as everything else in their relations with the state that refused them an alternative excuse for leaving the country. Since the mid–1970s, the increasing numbers of those who arrived to the transit camps in Vienna opted to continue westward, mainly to the U.S., and proceeded to Rome where they waited for U.S. visas. By 1979, over 85 percent of the potential repatriates to Israel "dropped out," in Israeli terms, and "defected" to the West. This "violation of the initial intent" (i.e., exiting on Israeli visas but not actually going there) was one of the pretexts used by the Soviet authorities to explain the virtual stoppage of the emigration by the early 1980s (Zaslavsky and Brym, 1983; Friedgut, 1989; Lazin, 2005). The Israeli government was very angry at the U.S. Jewish organizations (HIAS and JDC) that allegedly lured Russian Jews to America by offering them generous financial aid. Responding to Israeli pressure, HIAS agreed in 1982 to accept in Vienna only those émigrés who already had first-degree relatives in the U.S. Therefore the few Jews who managed to leave in 1982–84 were compelled to go to Israel regardless of their wishes. The same scenario in the U.S.-Israeli trade for Russian Jewish souls was reproduced later, after the inception of the mass Jewish exodus in 1989 (Dominitz, 1997).

After the dead-zone period of the early 1980s, the first winds of change blew after Gorbachev declared his perestroika and glasnost plans in 1985–86, with the following renewal of the emigration movement in 1987–88. The refusniks and other Jews who had been morally prepared ("ripe," as a euphemism of the time went) to leave were the first ones to apply for the exit visas. Then in the early 1990s, Russia and most other successor states enacted a new "Law of Exit and Entry," according to which any citizen could receive a foreign passport and travel abroad for any private purposes, not having to justify it before the authorities and ask for an exit visa (but contingent on getting an entry visa for their destination country). The only difference between those leaving for good and those traveling abroad for a limited time was that the former had a stamp in their foreign passports saying *Exit for a Permanent Residence Abroad*. The émigrés also had to revoke their housing registration (*propiska*), return their apartments to the state, and hand in their internal Soviet passports. Following mid–1991, those leaving the country for good remained Soviet/Russian citizens and could register as such in the Russian or Ukrainian consulates in their new countries. This practically meant that anyone, regardless of ethnic belonging, could leave Russia and the FSU for any amount of time and for any destination, the limitations emerging on the receiving end. This was a real revolution in the Soviet legal regulation of the citizens' movement across borders: the Iron Curtain fell down and, sure enough, tens of thousands of former Soviet citizens soon lined up at the embassies of Western countries seeking better fortunes abroad.

Russia, Israel, or the West? Deliberations of the 1990s

What happened with now former-Soviet Jews and their deliberations on the eternal Jewish question: to stay or to move on? Is it
preferable to live in the New Russia as a Jew, given the signs of the
diminishing state anti-Semitism, a green light for every kind of social
and economic activity, and the ability to travel and see the world as a
tourist? Or is it still safer to leave Russia and make a fresh start
elsewhere, where democracy is established and the economy stable?
The country was rapidly changing, new opportunities appeared for
industrious and talented people, along with new risks and stresses. The
liberal reforms of the first half of the 1990s engendered severe economic polarization of the population whereby the majority sank into
poverty or barely survived by juggling multiple jobs, while a minority
gained access to the country's incredible natural resources and industrial might in the chaotic campaign of privatization. Many Jews rapidly learned how to swim in the rising waters of the market economy
and readily entered the entrepreneurial world; their material wealth
and lifestyles significantly improved. Several highly visible Jewish
figures moved in the newly emerging economic elite (the so-called
oligarchs) also intimately involved in Kremlin politics; their thriving
did not go unnoticed by the anti-Semitic propagandists (Goldman,
2003). At the same time, many other Jews, especially older people or
those with a less developed business streak, led subsistence lifestyles
on small academic, medical, or scientific salaries, especially bitter in
the face of the booming consumer choice of goods and leisure venues.
Mass unemployment and impoverishment, an influx of ethnic Russians and other migrants from the successor states to most large cities,
rising nationalism and ethnic conflicts, the unending war in Chechnya,
and growing signs of corruption and nepotism under "drunken Yeltsin's
democracy" gradually exhausted any remaining trust in democratic
government, with the ensuing nostalgia for "good old communist times"
with their predictability, modest but stable, and allegedly equal, living
standards.

As always in the times of change and turmoil, anti-Semitism, rising
this time from the bottom rather than sponsored by the government,
was a corollary of pluralism and democratic freedoms. The anti-Jewish sentiments found their pivotal expression in the activities of the
first and rather ominous NGO of "free Russia"—the so-called Society

for History and Culture Pamyat (Memory) whose main activity was publishing and distribution of anti-Semitic materials, both old (*The Protocols of the Elders of Zion*) and new, blaming the Jews for all historic grievances suffered by Russians and other Slavs before and after the Revolution. Many Jews found anti-Semitic flyers in their mailboxes almost daily and some were preparing to fortify their doors in anticipation of pogroms. Although pogroms have never materialized, the anti-Semitic streak has always remained part of Russian nationalist discourse, and the emergence of the Jewish nouveau riche has only added oil to its flame. Once again, Jews were reminded that they have always been a foreign element in this country and would be better off leaving it for good (Friedgut, 1989).

Thus, throughout the 1990s the decision to leave was shaped by a constellation of multiple factors: the accommodation to the new realities of "jungle capitalism" in the FSU, employment and career prospects in Russia vs. abroad, fear of anti-Semitism, age, state of health, and the wish to join family members already living abroad. The social costs of emigration became much lower: the formal procedures of exit after 1991 became easier and rituals of exclusion and punishment at work vanished with the rest of communist ideology. In addition, many urban residents had privatized their apartments by 1992, 1993 and could sell them for real market prices, making some initial resources for resettlement abroad. In any event, the emigration decisions of Russian Jews in the 1990s were driven by pragmatic rather than ideological considerations, that is, the careful weighing of the push and pull factors (or gains vs. losses) in the FSU vis-à-vis possible destinations abroad.

Then the second crucial decision was: where to go? Israel and the U.S. had been the chief options during the 1970 and late 1980s; in 1989 alone 38,395 Soviet Jews have entered U.S. as refugees and another 30,000 or more had applications pending. The veto on the special status of Soviet Jews in the U.S. refugee program was introduced by late President Reagan before stepping down and confirmed by the newly elected President George Bush (the Senior); from the early 1990 on the influx of Soviet Jewish refugees sharply decreased, as new visas were now granted mainly to those already having close relatives in the U.S. In Western Europe, only Germany became an increasingly possible destination after 1992–93, but many Jews had strong anti-German attitudes and could not imagine living in the country that organized the extermination of European Jewry only one generation ago. For many others, though, the possibility of living in the heart of "civilized Europe" and the generous welfare policy of the German state towards "special refugee contingent" of Soviet Jews had been very enticing and outweighed anti-German sentiments. Many émigrés with partial Jewish ancestry and mixed families opted for Germany as no deep inquiries into their Jewish "purity" had been enforced by German embassies up until the late 1990s. A few other Western countries (mainly Australia and Canada) screened the candidates not by their Jewishness, but by education, occupation, age, and language skills; their immigration programs were generally small-scale and hardly known outside the capital cities. Throughout the 1990s and early 2000s, Israel was the only country receiving all Jewish émigrés without any conditions or screening. The checks into Jewish "purity" were relaxed over time as the demographic potential for aliyah was fast running out, but the Israeli political establishment and Sochnut wanted it to continue no matter what.[6] Yet, Israel was not an attractive destination for many pragmatically disposed Russian Jews: a small country in the Middle East with few job opportunities, a hot climate, a difficult language, and an ongoing military conflict with its neighbors. For many parents who went out of their way to save their sons from the draft to the Soviet Army and possible participation in the Chechen war, mandatory military service in Israel was another strong deterrent. This is not to say that Zionist sentiments were completely missing among Soviet Jews planning emigration, but they were certainly less common than in the early 1970s wave.

Several surveys of the early 1990s (Brym and Ryvkna, 1994; Gitelman, 1997; Levinson, 1997) explored the emigration deliberations of Russian Jewry, trying to understand how the destination countries had been chosen. Their conclusion was that, if a free choice of destination had been available, over two-thirds would opt for the West (mainly the U.S., Canada, and Germany) and about one-third for Israel. Respondents preferring to move to Israel were usually those with stronger Jewish identity as measured by such indicators as some traditional observance and perceived exposure to or fear of anti-Semitism. Often these respondents were older people, residents of smaller cities (not Moscow and St. Petersburg), as well as those with lower education and less developed professional identity. Another pull factor for migration to Israel was the wish to join family members and friends who had moved there earlier. On the other hand, America was perceived by many former Soviets as a country with unlimited opportunities, the *goldene medina* of their forefathers, where everyone can find their place and fortune. But the final destination was, of course, determined by the combination of their wishes and available opportunities.

While Russian Jews were contemplating emigration, covert but intense political struggle about their fate and destination was going on between the two chief interest lobbies: the Israeli government and its Zionist arm Sochnut versus American Jewish organizations involved in immigrant aid—HIAS, JDC, and UJA—and their lobbyists in the White House. As a result of their efforts to reverse the restrictions introduced in 1989, the refugee quotas for ex-Soviet Jews were once again increased after 1992, and almost 157,000 of them were resettled in the U.S. by the HIAS till the end of 1996 (HIAS, 1997). The Israeli government observed the continuing influx of Russian and Ukrainian Jews to the U.S. with the growing frustration. In the words of a high-ranking Israeli official, Yehuda Dominitz (1997:121), "The start of the Soviet Jewish exodus to Israel was considered an historic opportunity to increase the Jewish population of Israel, build the nation and strengthen Israel's social fabric and cultural foundations. *To forfeit such an opportunity by letting tens of thousands of Jews opt for other countries of migration would be unforgivable*" (my emphasis). Thus, Russian Jews were treated once again as a tool for reaching macro-level political and ideological goals of state powerholders rather than individuals seeking better lives and making independent decisions. American Jewry was rather split on this issue: the Zionist circles believed that artificial direction of the wave of migrant Jews to Israel was necessary and morally justified, while a liberal lobby insisted on individual agency and freedom of movement for those leaving the FSU. Both sides realized that the U.S. would be the destination of choice for the majority of the new migrants. The Israelis remembered too well the dropout of Russian Jews in Vienna during the late 1970s, and made sure that this transit camp was closed in 1990. Soon after the reopening of the Israeli embassy in Moscow, Israel established direct flights to Tel Aviv from several major cities; those who wished to travel via Europe had to stop for a short while in Budapest, Bucharest, and a few other cities where they were carefully isolated from any contact with American representatives. Both applications and issuance of the visas to the U.S. (on case-by-case rather than automatic grounds) moved directly to the American Embassy in Moscow, eliminating the need to use Israeli visas for the transit. Ever since then the process of emigration to Israel was fast-tracked (one could complete all the necessary paperwork and get free tickets to Israel within a few months), while emigration to the Western countries for ex-Soviets became as protracted and impeded as for other international applicants.

As a result of this restructuring in the policies of the main hosting countries, Israeli authorities could proudly report that from 1989 to 1993, almost twice as many Soviet Jews made aliyah to Israel than moved to the West (close to half a million and 250,000, respectively[7]). 1990 and 1991 were record years in the aliyah movement: over 183,000 and 147,000 new immigrants, respectively, arrived in Israel in just two years (33 percent of the total size of the last wave). In historical terms, the mass exodus of 1990–91 came in the wake of the deep economic and political crisis surrounding the demise of the Soviet Union, with a concomitant rise in Russian nationalism and populist anti-Jewish propaganda. But in their personal narratives of immigration many Jews recollected that their decision to leave everything behind and rush into the unknown was party irrational, boosted by the social panic, by seeing that most of their Jewish friends, colleagues, neighbors, and everyone else were on the move, with the ensuing "fear to remain the last Jew in Russia, alone and trembling," in the words of one of my informants. Many Jews shared the apocalyptic feeling that the fall of the USSR would practically mean the end of Russian history and will bury everyone under its debris; "leave now or never" was a popular motto of the time. The eternal Jewish "fight or flight" instinct propelled to move even those who considered themselves deeply rooted, well-to-do and never wanted to emigrate before; the need to erase one number after the other in one's phone book acted as a strong incentive to change your mind.

After 1993–94 the emigration drive of Jews diminished in line with the improving economy and living standards in Russia and the relaxation of anti-Jewish sentiments, now redirected to the new hate object—the growing ranks of Chechen refugees and other migrants from the Caucasus in the big cities. The pull to Israel was further diminished by the discouraging news from friends and relatives about the hardships of adjustment there: the lack of jobs for professionals, the challenge of learning Hebrew, housing shortages, and a broad cultural gap with Israeli Jews. Together, these changes curtailed the stream of migrants to Israel by 300 percent, so during the mid–1990s between 68 and 50 thousand were registered annually as Russian olim (Hebrew for new immigrants [8]), and a similar number left for various Western destinations, mainly U.S. and Germany. A brief upsurge in immigration to Israel occurred in 1999—over 67,000, vs. 46.000 in the previous year—in response to the financial crisis (default of the ruble) in 08.1998 in Russia, after which many citizens lost their savings and small businesses. Mark Tolts (2000, 2005) observed that throughout the post-Soviet period there had been a high and consistent negative correlation between the socio-economic situation in the successor states and the size of their Jewish population embarking on aliyah. After each local crisis there is an upsurge in the numbers of applicants for Israeli visa as the most accessible and expedient venue of exit. There has also been a clear inverse association between living standards in different parts of the FSU and aliyah harvest collected by the Sochnut in these places. Thus in Russia itself, Birobidjan (with the World Bank's index of socio-economic well-being comparable to this of Jordan or Peru) has lost the highest share of its Jews to aliyah, and Moscow (rated roughly on par or higher than other East European capitals) —the lowest share, proportionate to their base Jewish populations in 1989. This is a strong indication of the push factor's dominance in the aliyah movement of former Soviet Jews, and the perceived image of Israel as a shelter country. In the new millennium, the flow of new immigrants to Israel narrowed down to some 34,000 in 2001, and then to slightly over 10,000 in 2004. Since 2002, more ex-Soviet Jews immigrated annually to Germany than made aliyah to Israel; the numbers of those coming to the U.S. as refugees dropped to less than 5,000 per year.

The social composition of the immigrants to Israel has significantly evolved over the seventeen years since the inception of the Great Aliyah, as it is called in Israel. The first to move this time was the top professional echelon from the capitals and other big cities, many of whom missed the train to the U.S. after 1989 but felt compelled to leave Russia fearing chaos and violence. In 1989–90, 34 percent of the olim came from Moscow alone and by 1993 their share dropped to 17 percent; the respective figures for the Jews of St. Petersburg were 28 percent and 12 percent. The share of immigrants from smaller provincial cities and towns grew respectively from 54 percent in 1989 to 71 percent in 1993, and reached 95 percent in 2001. Over time, fewer olim came from Russia and more from the Ukraine, Belorussia, Central Asia, and the Caucasus. As mentioned above, the size and location of the city of origin strongly correlates with the "human capital" of Soviet Jews, the professional elite usually coming from Moscow, St. Petersburg and a few other major industrial and academic centers such as Kiev, Kharkov, Odessa, and Novosibirsk. The share of university educated olim with academic and scientific occupations diminished in line with their being more provincial and often less Jewish (the share of core Jews dropped to one-third after 1999). The percentage of olim with higher education in 2002 was 35 percent, vs. 72 percent in 1990. This of course reflected the features of the increasingly assimilated Jewish population still remaining in the FSU, when and if they embarked on aliyah.

As a result of these temporal changes, the current composition of the Israeli Russian-speaking community is a virtual blueprint of the enlarged Jewish population of the FSU, with some 15–20 percent of educated and well-adjusted professionals at the top and the majority coming from all possible regions, occupations, and walks of life typical of the late Soviet society. Although I have no direct statistical data to vouch for this, but a similar pyramid structure probably typifies Soviet Jewish immigrants who settled in North America and in Germany. However, the upper and middle tiers of these (Western) pyramids, that is, the proportions of educated middle-class Jews, are probably wider vis-à-vis Israel reflecting both their self-selection for the West, better information and access to Western embassies in the major cities, and some filters at the entry (such as Canadian point system). Due to the unselective character of its immigration policy aside from ethnic identity (and even this being broadly defined), Israel has received the older, less healthy, and less professionally fit part of the Soviet Jewish migration pool.

In conclusion, let me point out the major features in the collective portrait of the Soviet Jewry that affected their migration movement and the processes of social integration in the receiving countries. The identity of this group was shaped along three main axes—Russian, Soviet, and Jewish, with dramatic individual differences in the manifestation of each component of this ideological mix. Over seventy years of socialism and mandatory atheism, the overwhelming majority of Soviet Jews drifted far away from their religion and Yiddish-based cultural practices. If they had any deities at all, these were Pushkin and Chekhov, Pasternak and Bulgakov (as the icons of the Russian high culture), on one hand, and social mobility (expressed in the cult of education and professionalism), on the other. Getting one's children a higher education was a must for the majority of Jewish parents, although the number of professional domains open to Jews had been gradually shrinking, and they were steered mainly towards engineering, science and technology occupations. As a result, engineer became the most common occupational title for a Russian Jew, both before and after immigration. Familial ties have been of paramount importance for the Jews, hence their propensity to migrate as extended families, together or in a chain, and choose destination countries by the location of their next of kin and close friends. The internal differentials within Soviet Jewry were largely a reflection of their geographic and social location with the ensuing access to economic and cultural resources, which in Soviet society were concentrated in the capitals and a few other major cities. Former residents of Moscow and St. Petersburg typically formed the elite of Soviet Jewry vis-à-vis those who had lived in smaller provincial towns.

Although atomized and not having any organized community life, most Jews were nevertheless involved in the far-reaching informal social webs (in Fran Markowitz's definition, "a community in spite of itself") that were in fact their main survival and advancement resource in the face of the hostile outside world. Their collective identity was mainly based on the common past, which left a painful historic dent in almost every Jewish family, and on a difficult present in the face of systemic institutional discrimination or, in other words, on the sense of common destiny. They also shared their peculiar mental and social duality as "discriminated elite" of Russia and other FSU countries. Ambivalence may be the key trait of Russian-Jewish identity, shifting between the feelings of inferiority and superiority, self-loathing (as internalized anti-Semitism) and self-idealization (Gershenson, 2006). The constant need for adjustment and social mimicry (e.g., modifying Jewish names into Russian-sounding ones) has shaped their ethnic identity as highly elastic and pragmatic one, subdued or underscored depending on the circumstances.

Molded by the Soviet system and at the same time excelling in the art of manipulating it to their own benefit, Soviet Jews emerged as a perfect sample of the social type known as *Homo Sovieticus*, although most of them would adamantly reject this label. Their mindset and conduct paradoxically combined social dependency on the womb-to-tomb welfare state with mistrust of the establishment and great diligence in manipulation of different bureaucracies, bending the rules, and "oiling the wheels" to achieve their goals. The feelings of the shared fate, and the revival of the closeted Jewishness, were further reinforced by the advent of emigration possibilities, and for some, an ensuing predicament of life in the social limbo as refusniks. Like most members of the Soviet intelligentsia after the Thaw, Jews had a strong distaste for any kind of imposed state ideology, be it Marxism-Leninism or Zionism. Some of them embraced the tenets of Zionism when it was outlawed and dangerous, but it was usually a form of dissidence and resistance rather than a strong ideological commitment. An even smaller minority converted to Orthodox Judaism and rejected altogether the Russian/Soviet components of their cultural identity.

In stark contrast to their forefathers who had been in the front lines of every revolutionary movement in Russia, Jews who came of age during stagnation of state socialism shunned any form of political participation and concentrated on their private and professional lives. They seldom joined the Party and other Soviet organizations, and even after the fall of communism had low participation in organized parties and groups, including the Jewish ones. As any self-organizing initiatives growing from below have been sanctioned by the Soviet state, and most forms of activism sponsored from above were distasteful and/or forced, most Soviet Jews were suspicious of any social activism as such. The very concept of voluntary or self-help organizations lying at the core of civil society was unfamiliar to most of them (some informal groups of refusniks were an exception to this rule, but only a small minority was involved in them). Despite their strong ties with the Russian language and culture, many Soviet Jews never felt at home in the country, and when opportunity presented itself, ventured on a long and difficult journey of emigration. Although this wave of migrants was endowed with impressive human capital in terms of their formal education and professional background, many of them turned out to be poorly equipped for economic and social readjustment in the West. More often than not, Soviet-type qualifications and skills proved to be as unconvertible a currency as were Soviet rubles. Some of the Russian-Jewish adjustment strategies proved to be useful in immigration, while others turned into disadvantages. At the same time, Soviet Jews carried their real treasure of social networks with each other (or social capital, in current sociological parlance) that was traveling with them due to the mass character of this resettlement. The next chapter will explore how this constellation of assets and flaws has played out in the process of social adjustment of Russian olim of the 1990s in Israel.

Notes

1. Throughout this book, I am using the terms Russian, Soviet, and former Soviet Jews (after 1991) as virtual synonyms. The most inclusive term is perhaps Russian-speaking Jews, pointing to the lingua franca of the Soviet Empire as the main common ground for otherwise diverse groups of Soviet Jewry. In the last Soviet census of 1989, about 90 percent of the Jews named Russian as their first language.

2. For an excellent collection of Soviet Jewish anecdotes in Russian see *Evrei Shutiat* (*The Jews are Joking*) by Leonid Stolovich, 2001. Some English translations (rather awkward but still informative) are cited on the Russian-American website http://russia-in-us.com/humor. Russian and Soviet history in anecdotes is represented in the new book by Bruce Adams Friend (Taylor and Francis, 2005).

3. A vivid example of this double life is chief protagonist of Yuri Druzhnikov's 1989 novel *Angels on the Head of a Pin*, editor of a central Party newspaper Yakov Rapoport, a cynical chef in the kitchen of Soviet ideology. He is fully aware of the fact that his paper feeds its readership pure garbage but would never try to challenge his bosses, after having spent a few years in Stalin's Gulag.

4. See for example a book by Victor Zaslavsky and Robert Brym *Soviet Jewish Emigration and Soviet Nationality Policy* (Macmillan, 1983), edited volume by Murray Friedman and Albert Chernin. *A Second Exodus: The American Movement to Free Soviet Jews* (Brandeis University Press, 1999), and multiple books and articles by Zvi Gitelman. The most detailed account of this matter is found in the recent book by Fred Lazin *The Struggle of Soviet Jewry in American Politics: Israel Versus American Jewish Establishment* (New York: Lexington Books, 2005).

5. Although political activists, and especially the "Prisoners of Zion," were of course the most famous members of the refusniks, broadly covered in the Western media and literature, they were certainly a small minority among all Soviet Jews who were living in the limbo of refusal and did not dare to further jeopardize their condition by open dissent.

6. Russian-Israeli author Dina Rubina who served as Cultural Director for Sochnut office in Moscow in the early 2000s, describes in her sharp recent satire The Syndicate (Moscow: EXMO, 2004) the frantic attempts of Sochnut officers to "dig out of the ground" the few remaining Jews entitled to aliyah by all kinds of dubious tactics, including luring, misinformation, etc.—in order to fill in the expected quotas and justify their own existence and shrinking budgets (see part 1 of the novel at her website www.dinarubina.com).

7. Here and below I am referring to the numbers of new immigrants published by Israeli Ministry of Immigrant Absorption and Central Bureau of Statistics (see www.cbs.gov.il), and in relation to the U.S. entrants, also Dominits, 1997; Gitelman, 1997; and HIAS statistics published on their website.

8. Both Hebrew terms applied to new immigrants are ideological labels ensuing from the Zionist tenet of homecoming. Aliyah means ascent or pilgrimage, derived from the ascent to Jerusalem as a holy site located in the hills of Judea. Olim literally means the rising ones, or the pilgrims. These terms are in common use in contemporary Hebrew, despite multiple challenges to the Zionist master narrative and growing realization that aliyah is no different from any other immigration experience, entailing losses, adjustments, and cultural gaps to the hegemonic majority.

2

Newcomers in the Promised Land: Integration or Separatism?

"I was shocked to see the loud and flamboyant crowd in the streets of Jerusalem: the people of every skin color, dress and style—are they all Jews? I found it hard to believe. Jews were my Kiev friends—engineers, teachers, musicians—cultured and decently dressed people. . . . I was at a loss. Did I have a place in this crowd?"
—from an interview with an architect from Kiev, 1993

"I was Jewish in Russia, now I am Russian in Israel. Is it our fate to always be 'others' and second-rate citizens?"
—from an interview with immigrant security guard, former engineer, 1994

"Russian Jews have changed the face of Israeli society, boosting its economy and culture. They are also destined to take over future political leadership and show the way out of the current deadlock in the conflict with Palestinians."
—from an interview with a Knesset member of Russian origin, 2000

Russian Jews in Israel of the 1990s: Setting the Stage

Ideology, Expectations, and Reality

Just as immigration to Israel is ideologically framed as homecoming, or ingathering of the dispersed diasporas, the Hebrew words aliyah (ascent to Jerusalem) and olim (the ascending returnees) are used in

53

the Israeli vernacular instead of the neutral international terms "immigration" and "immigrant."[1] Referring to repatriation as a voluntary and enthusiastic endeavor, the Zionist narrative implies warm welcome and expedient accommodation (absorption in Israeli terms) of the newcomers via magic chemical transformations they allegedly undergo in the famous Israeli melting pot. This myth carefully ignores the historic fact that most waves of mass migration to Israel had been driven by adversity and persecution of the Jews in their origin countries rather than by their Zionist persuasion, making Israel a true shelter country (Levy and Weiss, 2002). In reality, emigration of Jews from their former homelands and resettlement in Israel is as fraught with losses, challenges, and cultural gaps with Israeli mainstream as any other international migration, including that of ethnic return (Capo Zmegac, 2005). Until recently, the Israeli establishment adhered to the rhetoric of "natural" and relatively rapid absorption of olim from all over the world, allegedly united by their Jewish religion and/or ethnic bonds and tried to ignore a de facto existing multicultural social structure (Shuval, 1998; Kimmerling, 2001). The increasing presence of Russian-speaking Jews, especially resistant to the melting pot expectations, gradually debunked this favorite Israeli myth (Horowitz, 1999; Lomsky-Feder and Rappoport, 2001). On the other hand, the message of homecoming and expected warm welcome by the Israeli Jews spread by Sochnut and other Israeli agencies—brokers of aliyah in the FSU—set too high the expectations of the émigrés, who considered themselves invited to Israel, entitled to a smooth resettlement experience, and in a way doing the Jewish State a favor by moving there. These unrealistic expectations made the actual encounter with Israeli society a harsh exercise in disillusionment for many newcomers.

By the beginning of the last great aliyah in the second half of 1989, Israel had a small (about 120,000) but well-established community of former Soviet Jews[2] who had arrived during the 1970s. Most of these people espoused Zionism and had moved to Israel because they wanted to live in the Jewish State and not because no other country would receive them (for the details of their emigration story see chapter 1). They had spent their first year in the state-sponsored Absorption Centers, where all they had to do was study Hebrew and get to know their new country. The integration experience of the 1970s wave had been rather smooth and expedient; the professional skills of the émigrés had been in high demand on the Israeli market still lacking locally trained doctors, engineers, and scientists, so most immigrants had been successfully employed in their old Soviet professions. Private housing had been inexpensive in the 1970s and 1980s, and many olim of these years also got access to the subsidized public housing. Having little if any sentimental tie to anything Russian and Soviet, most of them had switched to Hebrew as their primary language (or remained bilingual) and did not even try to speak Russian with their children. Many of them changed their Russian names to Hebrew ones, symbolically shedding their old identity. In brief, they rapidly joined the Israeli middle class and blended very well into the secular Ashkenazi[3] mainstream of the time.

By the early 1990s, the social and economic context of the resettlement of tens of thousands of former Soviet newcomers has changed dramatically. Israel became a post-industrial society, with a typical proliferation of service industry, information technologies, and consumerism in its various forms; the traditional industrial and agricultural sectors were shrinking, leaving thousands of unemployed in their wake. As a result of the ongoing "Americanization," the dominant ideology gradually shifted from collectivism and social solidarity (at least within one's own ethnic group) to individualism, competitiveness, and achievement-oriented behavior (Weissbrod, 2002). By the early 1990s, the skilled labor market of Israel had enough locally trained professionals in virtually every field, and in some professions even a surplus (e.g., the number of physicians per 1,000 of the population in Israel was the highest in the world after Russia). The political scene of that period featured the Likud-based government headed by Yitzhak Shamir, the first Palestinian Intifada raging in the occupied Palestinian territories, and the nearby Gulf War of 1990–91 with Iraqi missiles targeting Israeli towns and keeping citizens in shelters. The country's internal agenda was certainly full and its resources stretched as thin as ever; adding to the strain, the Russian immigrants kept arriving by the thousands. The Great Russian Aliyah, for which Israeli politicians fought so hard in the international arena (Lazin, 2005) and whose strategic importance for the country's future was recognized by most Israelis, turned out to be as a harsh challenge for the receiving society (Horowitz, 1999). While after several difficult years this aliyah spearheaded the Israeli economic boom of the 1990s, in the beginning it looked very much like a human disaster. Overwhelmed by the challenge, the Israeli government had to apply for financial support from the U.S.

On the eve of the Great Aliyah, Israel's Jewish population was about 4 million; in the following decade it added over 870,000 Russian immigrants, who together with the arrivals of the 1970s, came to comprise one million Russian-speakers, or 20 percent of the Jewish population. Almost half of the last influx took place in just three years—1990–1992; on some days a thousand or more Russian-speaking olim landed in Ben-Gurion Airport. To further complicate the picture, about 18,000 Ethiopian immigrants have been resettled to Israel over the same short period, constantly crossing paths with the Russian Jews (Statistical Bureau of Israel, 1997). The small country was flooded by the newcomers, looking for house rentals and jobs, lining the corridors of the Sochnut, Ministry of Immigrant Absorption, and Social Security to apply for various subsidies and services. The institutional approach to immigrants' initial accommodation used in the 1970s had to be abandoned, as the existing housing and other public facilities could not cater to all the newcomers. The new policy of so-called direct absorption (*klita yeshira*) meant that most new arrivals received direct financial aid for six months (the so-called absorption basket) that was ostensibly sufficient for them to rent an apartment on the free market, buy basic home appliances, and devote most of their time to studying Hebrew in full-time free classes (*Ulpanim*). For the next six months, those who did not find jobs could get an interest-free bank loan that had to be repaid after three years (Geva-May, 2000).

In practice, this financial aid was barely sufficient to cover housing rentals as the costs were skyrocketing in line with the demand, and most olim had to find manual jobs soon upon arrival in order to supplement their rapidly depleting absorption basket. Housing costs were especially high in Tel Aviv and central Israel, the areas to which many olim were driven due to their more developed job market. The two consequences of high housing costs (unanticipated by the policymakers) were the olim's early dropping out of the Ulpanim, with resulting slow improvement in the Hebrew skills, and co-residence of multi-generational families under one roof to lump together limited resources. The established Israeli homeowners gained handsome revenues from the rise of the rental prices, but other Israelis of modest means (e.g., young families) suffered along with the "Russians" from the soaring housing costs and shortage of apartments. In response to the housing crisis, the Israeli government embarked on a large-scale program of construction of cheap housing complexes, mainly in the sparsely populated periphery of the country, hoping to redirect the main flow of the newcomers into the so-called development towns. In the meantime, the new arrivals who could not find accessible housing in the urban centers (Russians and Ethiopians alike), were moved to the caravan campsites equipped with only the most basic commodities where their "temporary residence" often lasted as long as seven to eight years. These caravan towns soon became sites of poverty, petty crime among school dropouts, and ethno-racial tension between the Russians and Ethiopians.[4] Black Jewish tribes were as far from Russian Jews in terms of their culture and everyday habits as one can get; this objective cultural gap was augmented by a common xenophobia of former Soviets who had never lived in proximity to people of other races. To cite one of my female informants in her early fifties, "If I had known that I'd find myself living in a suffocating plastic box in the middle of nowhere, next door to a savage black tribe that never heard about the WC and electricity—well, I'd hardly ever leave my small but comfortable apartment in Kiev."

The situation with the occupational adjustment of the newcomers was also very difficult (more on this below). As public financial aid to the newcomers is both modest and short term (compared to the package received by Jewish refugees in the U.S. and especially in Germany), all able-bodied olim had to earn a living wage soon upon arrival, which was not easy. In the early 1990s, the unemployment level among Russian immigrants reached 40 percent, slowly going down afterwards and reaching the national average of 10–11 percent by the late 1990s. Yet, throughout this period, just over a quarter of the olim holding academic degrees from the USSR worked in their original professions. The small and saturated white-collar labor market of Israel could only absorb a small fraction of the skilled immigrants, while the rest had to turn to retraining or downgrade into manual occupations. The extent of occupational downgrading was especially dramatic for women and older professionals of either gender, who had often been senior specialists before emigration (Raijman and Semyonov, 1998; Remennick, 2003b; Stier and Levanon, 2003). Governmental programs of retraining and aid in the first employment was of help mainly to the younger and more dynamic immigrants. Although policymakers had anticipated occupational downgrading of Russian olim (due to skill incompatibility, language barrier, etc.), it was highly traumatic for educated immigrants, who overnight found themselves in the bottom tier of the workforce. The feelings of social displacement were augmented by an overarching sense of insecurity—financial (due to unstable income and mounting debs), physical (reflecting ongoing military conflict and acts of terror), and psychological (reflecting poor command of Hebrew, misunderstanding of local norms, and loss of support networks).

Thus, the early years of resettlement of the post-Soviet immigrants in Israel were wryly described by one of my informants as "moving from one madhouse to another," referring to a simultaneous challenge of economic survival, linguistic and cultural adjustment, facing constant security threats, military draft of most youths, and, on top of everything else, adjusting to the swings of Israeli climate, sweating during long and hot summer and freezing in unheated apartments in the winter. By the mid–1990s, the country could somewhat relax its muscle as the influx of Russian immigrants diminished to a "normal level" of fifty to seventy thousand a year. The acute housing shortage had been mitigated, albeit with many strategic mistakes, as few newcomers wished to settle in remote development towns with no jobs where most of the new houses had been built. The superb survival skills of formed Soviets stood them in good stead: most found ways to make a living, drawing on both the formal and thriving informal (immigrant-dominant) economic sectors. Yet, every subsequent group of olim professionals faced deeper downgrading as most available skilled positions had already been taken. On the other hand, immigrants who left the FSU in the mid—and late 1990s often had acquired some initial capital and entrepreneurial experience, and found new economic footholds by opening small businesses in Israel.

The political turmoil stirred by the Oslo peace accords of September 1993, their inconsistent implementation, and the ensuing Yitzhak Rabin assassination in November 1995, pushed many Russian immigrants out of their usual social apathy and boosted their political engagement on both sides of the barricades (but mainly on the right). By and large, the old survival skills of former Soviet Jews, their readiness to face adversity and negative attitudes of the surrounding majority, to manipulate the laws and regulations to their own advantage, and rapidly learn the new rules of the game were of great service to this wave of newcomers in their old-new homeland. The social composition of former Soviet immigrants has evolved over fifteen years of immigration, starting from educated Jewish professionals from the major cities of Russia and Ukraine during the early 1990s and including, over time, more and more families from smaller provincial towns of the FSU, coming to Israel as de facto refugees from the by poverty-stricken areas, unemployment, and ethnic conflict (e.g., the Caucasus, Moldova, and Central Asia). In parallel, the share of educated immigrants with white-collar professions has dropped from over 70 percent in 1990–92 to less than 40 percent in 1999–2002, and the share of core Jews plummeted to about 30 percent. Due to the lower cultural capital of these latecomers, as well as full saturation of the labor market by the late 1990, they typically found themselves in the lower tiers of economy and on the margins of Jewish society. After 2000, the flow of immigrants almost stopped, and those few still arriving from the remote and troubled areas of the FSU are ready to take any manual jobs available. Some of them are, in fact, temporary labor migrants who came to Israel to save money, send remittances to their families in the FSU, and eventually return there. After this brief overview, let me turn to the specific facets of the encounter between new Israelis with Russian accents and mainstream Israeli society.

Russian Jews and Israeli Judaism: Jewish Goyim and Simply Goyim

Immigration to Israel is regulated by the Law of Return enacted in 1950 and revised in 1970, which allows entry and immediate citizenship to Jews, their children, and grandchildren on both sides (maternal and paternal). At the same time, the Orthodox religious establishment and Rabbinical Courts draw on the Halacha (Jewish Common Law) that defines Jews only as children of Jewish mothers. The discrepancy between the civic and religious definitions of Jewish affiliation means that non-Halachic Jews (e.g., those with Jewish fathers and non-Jewish mothers) can live in Israel as citizens but cannot enjoy some basic civil rights. Since the State of Israel is an unusual polity founded on the ethno-religious principle and the ensuing default expectation of the privileged status of its Jewish majority (Kimmerling 2001, Levy and Weiss, 2002), there is no legal separation between the state and religion in many important aspects of its legislature and government.[5] Orthodox Judaism dominates all official religious institutions, whereas Reform, Conservative, and other liberal Judaic denominations have small congregations but no influence on national politics. Although a minority (12–14 percent) among Israeli Jews profess the strictest version of Ultra-Orthodox Judaism, and another 22 percent belong to a more moderate Modern Orthodoxy (also called the National Religious or *leumi dati*), a large segment of the population (about 40 percent) describe themselves as traditional, that is, observing some key rules of Judaism, and only the remaining 20–25 percent are completely secular in their beliefs and lifestyle (data from an early 1990s cited by Sharot, 1998; no large-scale studies on religiosity of Jewish Israelis have been conducted since then). Thus, the newcomers from the FSU could either join one of the existing "camps," or invent a new category for themselves.

A special role in safeguarding of the Jewish majority in the population is played by the Ministry of Interior, which issues both internal ID cards (*teudat zehut*) and foreign passports of Israeli citizens and permanent residents. Since the inception of the Russian aliyah, this Ministry has been controlled by religious and conservative politicians who tightly guarded secured the gateway to Israeli citizenship by crosschecking the "ethnic purity" of the arriving Jews and side-tracking all the "suspects." Besides other demographic details, the blue Israeli ID card has an entry for Nationality (*leom*), which can be Jewish, Arab, other minority (e.g., Druze), or Unstated. The latter category was mostly used for the non-Jewish olim, unless they asked to write Russian, Ukrainian, or other specific ethnic designations. Since the early 2000s, the notification of *leom* became optional, but most citizens still carry their old ID cards with this entry stated in black and white. (One cannot help noticing clear similarities in the ways Israel and the USSR framed the issues of citizens' official ethnic affiliation). Although in most important domains, such as labor market, health care, and political participation, non-Jewish olim did not face tangible discrimination; their "non-kosher" origins were known to every official and could cause various adverse reactions, at least on the level of gossip and attitude. The matters of marriage, divorce, registration of newborns, and burials are all controlled by the religious authorities, which exclude non-Jews from their proceedings; so far, few civil alternatives have been available in the matters of personal status. This means that non-Jewish olim cannot get married in Israel, although their foreign marital certificates are recognized by the state for all official purposes. They also have more trouble getting divorced, registering their non-Jewish children as citizens, and inviting their non-Jewish parents or siblings to visit or join them in Israel.

Marriage to non-Jews had been common among Soviet Jews, and growing from one generation to the next, reaching 70 percent in the recent cohorts (Tolts, 2003). The high tide of aliyah has swept entire families to the Israeli shores—two or three generations, many of them including non-Jews—who migrated together or in succession. The share of the immigrants who had been granted entry but not recognized by the Orthodox establishment as Jews, has been constantly growing since the early 1990, reaching roughly two-thirds of the new arrivals after 1999. The estimated number of non-Jews among the last-wave Soviet immigrants currently living in Israel is around 350,000, that is, over one third of the total, as indicated on the Interior Ministry's website. Their actual number is probably even higher (some authors estimate it to be one half of the total) as some émigrés had probably invented their Jewish ancestry with the help of diligent document forgers who had always been in business in the FSU, selling real birth certificates or fabricating false ones. The allegations of forgery of Jewish identity among Soviet immigrants, quite vocal in the Hebrew press and popular discourse since the mid–1990s, [6] are difficult to prove or refute, so the scope of this phenomenon will hardly ever be known. Moreover, I do not believe it to be strongly relevant for the issue of identity and integration. While half-Jews on paternal side often self-identify as Jews and are interested in Jewish life, those with one real Jewish grandparent (i.e., still legitimate olim by the Law of Return) are hardly much closer to Jewish traditions than their purely non-Jewish peers (Cherviakov et al., 2003). What is more important though is that in many domains of life, especially private ones (marriage, divorce, and family reunification[7]), these newcomers were in fact reduced to the status of second-class citizens. Although the arrival of thousands of non-Jews could be anticipated on the basis of Soviet Jewish demography, the Israeli institutions were largely unprepared to find acceptable legislative and practical solutions to the presence of multiple "non-kosher" citizens in a whole range of issues, staring from issuing guest visas for their Russian relatives and all the way to their burial in non-Jewish cemeteries[8].

Russian and other non-Jewish wives of Jewish men found themselves in an especially precarious position, as they not only felt like unwanted outsiders themselves but also inadvertently complicated the lives of their children who inherited their Russianness. Non-Jewish men were at least spared the trouble of proving or changing their personal status, as the responsibility for Jewish lineage lay solely on the woman's side. The only way to help the children of mixed marriages to enter Israeli mainstream was their mothers' conversion (*giyur*) in its most severe Orthodox version, as the religious establishment does not recognize modernized and flexible Reform or Conservative conversions, nor does it accept any giyur certificates from the FSU. During the early and mid–1990s, thousands of Russian, Ukrainian, and other women studied in the giyur classes, but only about half of them could pass the final examinations (checking into their true observance and home lifestyle) to become "kosher" Jewish women. A weird twist of this situation was that these non-Jewish women had to comply even with the most ancient and peculiar demands of the female hygiene, for example, immersing themselves in the *mikve* (Jewish ritual bath) after the end of their period for symbolic purification before resuming intimate relations with their husbands; their Jewish-born peers were spared these weird practices as they were not tested or under the scrutiny of the rabbis. "I was born Jewish and I will never need even to get near mikve, while my unfortunate (as it turns out!) Russian friend Tanya has to undergo all these obscure rituals in order to lead a normal life in Israel—isn't that absurd?", my Jewish informant was telling me in 1994. One couldn't help admitting that it was, at least from the secular point of view.

As a result of their new indoctrination, some of the converted women have adopted certain features of the Jewish lifestyle (most often the tradition of family gatherings on Friday night with candle lighting and *kabalat shabat*—Sabbath reception), while others could simply shed the label of *goya* (a non-Jewish woman) and get the new set of ID cards for themselves and their children. In any case, by the late 1990s most giyur classes have been closed as the fraction of non-Jewish women (and a few men too) who converted via official Orthodox procedure was small (about 3 percent), reflecting the stringent and unrealistic demands of compliance with the Orthodox rules. It became clear that Orthodox conversions will not solve "the problem" of the growing share of the non-Jewish population; some legal and procedural changes regarding these residents and their rights had to be introduced. Yet the progress in the legislation hinged on the delicate relations between the State and the Orthodox establishment, touching upon the politically charged issue of preserving the Jewish character of Israel. Left in the limbo, some of the Russian wives, who could not "normalize" themselves via giyur or become equal via new legislation, later propelled their husbands to embark on the second emigration to Canada or the U.S., or else to return to the FSU.

Yet, the religious establishment of Israel also held multiple grudges against the "pure ethnic Jews" of Soviet background who know nothing about Judaism as religion and lifestyle. Even Jewish holidays and symbolic rites of passage (bar mitzvah) were novelties for most newcomers, let alone such demanding aspects of Jewish observance as male circumcision, dietary rules, and sexual conduct within marriage. Many Russian Jews had trouble getting used to the Jewish calendar and starting their work week from Sunday, as well as to the closing of all shopping and entertainment places and the absence of public transportation on the Sabbath. As opposed to the 1970s olim, very few of them were ready to trade their Russian names for Hebrew ones, letting Israeli officials struggle and stammer pronouncing names like Svetlana, Vladimir, and Gennady. They were also not willing to change their lifestyles in any drastic way. Kosher eating habits? Forget it! Multiple Russian delis and grocery stores mushroomed in Israel since the early 1990s, selling pork and ham along with caviar, rye bread, and other familiar food items produced locally or imported from the FSU. Despite the outrage of local rabbinical councils, the laws of the free market took over and most of the non-kosher Russian groceries survived, although they often had to move out from the central streets. While many Russian immigrants showed interest in learning about Jewish history and culture (whenever such classes were available in colleges, community centers, etc.), their interest in religion and Orthodox observance was very low. A small minority of the young immigrants (5 to 8 percent in my estimates) opted for Orthodox Jewish education and became later *baalei tshuva* (converts from secular to religious life); some of them joined the core of the radical settlers in the occupied territories.

The majority, though, have learned over time to respect the sensibilities of the veteran Israelis and not to break the main traditions in public (e.g., not to eat outdoors on Yom Kippur), but in their homes and in-group social gatherings most olim kept their old Russian/Soviet traditions of cooking, drinking, leisure, and everything else. Some of them selectively adopted a few Jewish rituals, mainly circumcision of the newborn boys and bar/bat-mitzvah for the children, but many avoided even these mild forms of observance. Yet others became fervent opponents of the "religious obscurantism" of the country and joined political groups fighting for the separation of religion and state. The failure of the Israeli Judaic establishment to attract and convert Russian immigrants reflects not only the latter's very secular upbringing in the FSU but also the single-handed rule of the Orthodox version of Judaism unacceptable for most reasonable people in the twenty-first century, and the virtual lack of alternative forms of Judaic practice more compatible with modern times. In the dichotomous split between Orthodox Judaism and secular Israeli identity, most former Soviets had little hesitation in choosing the latter.

One of the pivots in the conflict between religious Israelis and the newcomers from the FSU revolved around the end-of-year holidays—Chanukah, Christmas, and the non-religious New Year. Since the Communist regime had cancelled Christmas, during Soviet era, New Year replaced it as the people's favorite holiday, one of the few without ideological underpinning. It was celebrated on the night of December 31 and bore little association with the birth of Christ. The only common symbol linking the two holidays was a decorated Christmas tree (called in Russian New Year fir tree), which symbolized the winter and was often kept in the homes for most of January. Soviet families started preparations for the New Year's Eve night dinner long before the holiday, stocking scarce groceries and listing potential guests. The tradition was to eat and drink a lot, sing, tell jokes, flirt, and stay awake until dawn, with the sacred rite to welcome the New Year at midnight with a glass of champagne. Russian Jews loved their New Year celebrations no less than fellow Russians, never associated them with religion, and were determined to continue this tradition also in Israel, despite the lack of snow or any other signs of real winter. Of course, a misunderstanding followed: Israelis interpreted Russian New Year as a version of Christmas, an outlawed Christian holiday, a sign of treason. These Russians, and their pork chops, and their Christmas trees, a familiar angry adage went around Israel. It took some time and patient explanations for Israelis to give up and take no offence at these strange Russian habits, especially because everyone happily celebrated Chanukah as well. By the early 2000s, small Christmas/New Year's Trees are openly sold in the street markets and many young Israelis added the night of December 31 to their calendar of holiday outings. In this case, common sense has won.

Not so in many other cases. The independent behavior of the newcomers, who showed no interest in becoming more Jewish, caused severe backlash on the part of institutional Judaism and Orthodox politicians, who often demanded change in the criteria of immigrants' entry or stop Russian aliyah altogether "to preserve the purity of the national genetic pool and way of life from contamination by the false Jews" (I wrote down this citation from a radio talk show). Major Hebrew newspapers featured heated debates on the problematic consequences of the mass influx of secular Russian Jews, and whether this huge aliyah has generally been a mistake. However, Russian Jews fought back, fortified politically and psychologically by their "critical mass" in the population, with the ensuing electoral weight. The political parties formed by the Russian immigrants were first elected to the Knesset in the mid–1990s, where they lobbied for civil marriage and divorce, burial of non-Halachic Jews in Jewish cemeteries, and other amendments diminishing the exclusive role of the rabbis. They found their political allies first among the Israeli secular Left, and in the late 1990s also in the centrist Shinui (Change) Party that proclaimed the containment of the Orthodox establishment as its chief political goal. However, despite some procedural concessions that had to be made to meet the needs of tens of thousands of non-Jewish residents, no major breakthroughs have been achieved in the contest between the combined secular forces and the Orthodox religious establishment. The sources of its political power have deep roots in the Israeli version of representative democracy, and are constantly augmented by its expanding demographic and electoral basis due to the high natural increase in the Orthodox sector (Kimmerling, 2001). In any event, the cleavage between the secular and religious ideology and lifestyle will probably remain one of the principal battlegrounds in the Israeli society, and Russian immigrants have a special role to play in this debate.

Russian Jews in the Israeli Ethnic Mosaic

Israel is perhaps the purest case of an immigrant society, with an ensuing extreme diversity of its Jewish population originating from more than 100 countries; almost half of all Jewish Israelis were born abroad. Jews form 80 percent of Israel's population, while indigenous population (Israeli Arabs) is the main religious minority of about 20 percent. As Jewishness (whatever that means!) is the only common denominator for this young nation, the main basis for internal stratification is one's country of origin and length of time spent in Israel (Israeli born Jews—sabras—form a separate category). This means that in Israel Polish Jews became the Poles, Moroccan Jews Moroccans, and Russian Jews simply Russians. Jews of European and American origin (Ashkenazim) comprise the historical "White" elite of the country, while dark-skinned Jews who migrated from the Arab countries (mostly Morocco) during the 1950s and 1960s disproportionately belong to the proletariat and underclass, typified by the lingering educational and income gaps (Cohen and Haberfeld, 1998; Kimmerling, 2001; DellaPergola, 2004). The latest addition to the diverse ethnic map of Israel was black Ethiopian Jews saved through aliyah from famine and civil war in their native country. The Israeli ethnic "salad" is spiced by exotic minority groups such as Indian Jews, Cherkese, Druze, and Bedouins, Black American converts to Judaism, and members of different religious congregations (e.g., Messianic Jews) living around Jerusalem. The resulting human mix filling public spaces of Israel is perhaps one of the most diverse and colorful in the world (Rebhun and Waxman, 2004). As the filters of political correctness in Israeli culture are still rather weak (vs. American ones), ethnic references are common in the everyday Israeli vernacular, including the jokes, TV shows, films, and other cultural genres. (Shifman and Katz, 2005).

Most former Soviets came from White society with little racial or social diversity, where most citizens looked, dressed, and sounded almost the same. Although Russia and Ukraine were home to dozens of ethnic minorities alongside with predominant Slavic nations, these minorities were white, secular and culturally Russified, hence not apparently different. Until the early 1990s, the system of residence and work permits prevented people from the ethnic periphery of the USSR from moving to Moscow, Leningrad, Kiev, and other major cities, keeping their population profile intact for decades. Mass migrations and ethnic mixing became possible only after the fall of communism, driven by both ethnic conflicts and the search of economic opportunities. On the level of everyday culture, the allegedly egalitarian Soviet society was split by many invisible lines of social prestige shaped by differential access to resources for different ethnic and social groups. One's location in this pyramid of prestige was defined by the place of residence (Russia vs. other republics; capitals vs. other large cities vs. smaller towns. vs. rural areas); ethnicity (with ethnic Russians on top, Tartars, people of the Caucasus and other Moslems, as well as minorities of the Far North, at the bottom); and occupational status (administrative personnel vs. rank-and-file workers and civil servants). When professionals and workers from the European cities were sent by the state to work in the Caucasus or Central Asia, they tried to keep residential and social distance from the indigenous people and often looked down on them as culturally inferior. The emissaries of Russia seldom learned ethnic languages, expecting that the locals should learn and speak Russian (which they did as most schools were Russian anyway). These imperial attitudes towards ethnic minorities (even in their own lands!) were reflected in the language including many pejorative names for non-Slavs (*chuchmek, churka, natsmen,* etc.). Being educated large-city folks (although not Slavs themselves!), Soviet Jews also partook in this tradition of prejudice and arrogance towards non-white, non-European ethnic groups. Most of them never traveled abroad before coming to Israel, and hence had no chance to see the racially diverse crowd in any major American or European city. Israel was their first "abroad," and they were shocked to see that Jews came in every possible color, size, and appearance. Used to establish social hierarchies, former Soviets had to define their own place on the ladder of prestige vis-à-vis sabras, Moroccans, Romanians, Ethiopians, and other Israelis whom they met in different walks of life.

The issue of ethnic prejudice is ideologically loaded, making it difficult to elicit frank responses in surveys; even so, about 30 percent of Russian immigrant respondents consistently admitted to having prejudice against Moroccan and other Mizrahi Jews; 40 percent expressed negative opinions about Ethiopians and over 80 percent strongly disliked the Arabs (Feldman, 2003). In the ethnographic studies of immigrant folklore by Yelenevskaya and Fialkova (2005), the pejorative attitudes towards Mizrahi Jews often came to the fore in the anecdotes and personal narratives of adjustment in Israel. As recent immigrants, Russian Jews found themselves on the lower tiers of the Israeli social structure where they typically met Moroccans, Yemenites, Ethiopians, and the less-educated part among Ashkenazi Jews as their neighbors, co-workers, landlords, real estate and sales agents. They also competed with these disadvantaged groups for scarce jobs and public housing, which increased mutual antagonism and negative stereotypes. The features typically ascribed by "Russians" to dark Mizrahi Jews are ignorance, boldness, and chutzpah; inability to keep their personal environs clean; sloppiness in appearance and dress (e.g., men's falling low-cut pants and shorts; women's bleached hair, harsh voices, and chain smoking); negligence of children growing wild and ignorant like their parents. In brief, dark-skinned Jews are "rough and primitive Asians," vis-à-vis Russian and Ukrainian Jews, constructed as "cultured and well-behaved Europeans." Russian immigrants often draw on the Orientalist explanatory frame to interpret the demeanor and lifestyle of their Mizrahi neighbors, and Israel's popular culture generally, viewing the cultural gap between West and East as inherent and unbridgeable (Lomsky-Feder et al., 2005). Moroccan and other Middle Eastern Jews are often likened to Arabs as belonging to the same cultural tradition and are ridiculed in the anecdotes, ditties, and other forms of Russian-Israeli folklore (see Yelenevskaya and Fialkova, 2005, for many witty examples that, unfortunately, lose their flavor in translation). After a short acquaintance with Mizrahi Jews, Russian olim did not expect from them any consideration or merit, but fellow Ashkenazi Jews were often a disappointment too. For example, they never lived up to the implicit expectations of Jewish solidarity and equality, cheating naïve newcomers in various deals, renting them run-down apartments at excessive costs[9], and paying minimal wages for their hard work. In brief, taking full advantage of the immigrants, showing former Soviets the "ugly face of Israeli capitalism" (Bernstein, 2005).

Becoming Israelis: The Pathways to Social Inclusion

From the above introduction the reader can easily see that the social encounter between Russian Jews and the Israeli mainstream was far from smooth: reality shattered their mutual expectations and preconceptions about each other. Israel had expected to receive the "historic gift" of one million Zionist Jews and received one million of Soviet atheists, including single-parent families, non-Jewish spouses, and not a few criminal elements. The immigrants expected to arrive to a "civilized Western country, a southern version of Europe" but found themselves "half-way between Medieval Jewish ghetto and noisy Oriental Bazaar" (from an interview with a former Moscow resident). Yet, the marital vows between the Great Russian Aliyah and the State of Israel have already been taken and their bond was fairly irreversible, so both parties had to cope and adjust to each other. Before turning to the detailed discussion of the Russian immigrants' experiences in the different domains of Israeli society, let me introduce the existing theoretical approaches to the study of immigrant incorporation and my own heuristic model of integration that will guide the reader throughout this chapter.

Theoretical Perspectives on Immigrant Incorporation

The terms integration and acculturation are commonly used in the immigration literature, but their meaning and relation to other terms remain rather obscure. Few migration scholars have tried to define them and delineate clear boundaries between various scenarios of host-migrant relations (Faist, 2000; Vertovec, 2004). In the American tradition of migration research, integration refers to the process of the gradual inclusion of newcomers into a host society and is often seen as an initial stage of assimilation. Sometimes assimilation, integration, and acculturation are used in the American migration literature as practical synonyms (Rumbaut, 1996, 1997; Alba and Nee, 1997; Portes and Rumbaut, 2001). It is important to note that the bulk of current research on assimilation/acculturation/integration has been conducted in Western countries hosting third world migrants, typified by low human capital and broad cultural gap with the receiving societies. Theoretical insights generated in this context may be inapplicable to the host-immigrant encounter in the course of "ethnic return" migration (or repatriation) from one group of developed countries to another, where both immigrants' social profile and issues at stake are quite different. Finally, mass repatriation waves are rather recent both in Europe and in Israel, meaning that not enough time has elapsed to draw meaningful conclusions. Therefore, my theoretical reflections are of preliminary nature and serve mainly as a heuristic tool for the interpretation of some recent research findings.

One often-cited typology of the immigrant "acculturation strategies" was proposed by Canadian social psychologist John W. Berry (1990; 2001). Berry regards assimilation, integration, marginalization, and separatism as a continuum stretching from complete inclusion to total exclusion of minority groups by the host society. In his view, separatism is the opposite of assimilation, that is, an individual and community-level tendency to ethno-cultural retention and minimization of contact with the host society. Marginalization is described by Berry and his followers (e.g., Nauck, 2001) as a limbo condition of individual immigrants or a whole minority group, whereby they have already parted with their home culture but did not join the host cultural order. Both latter scenarios usually reflect segregative practices and/or exclusive attitudes on the part of the hegemonic majority. At the individual level, all the four strategies may be found simultaneously, but collectively one of them usually predominates in the immigrant-host relations (Berry, 1990).

Let me turn now to the concept of integration, which will inform my further analysis of the empirical data. In my view, integration differs from assimilation both in dosage and in content. Berry (1990, 2001) and some other migration theorists (Grillo, 1998; Faist, 2000; Nauck, 2001) describe assimilation as total and irreversible dissolution of the minority group in the majority (the Israeli term absorption, originating in chemistry, is used in the same sense). Conversely, integration suggests that the minority group preserves its cultural core, while developing additional adaptive facets of identity, skills, networks, etc. In other words, assimilation is a complete transition from an old culture to a new one, while integration usually emerges in a form of biculturalism, based on bilingualism. Tamar Horowitz (2001) writes about the "hybridism script" of integration in a similar sense. Integrative strategy implies a double cultural competence, flexibility and an effective situational switch between the two cultures (Berry, 1990; Nauck, 2001). Bilingualism and double cultural competence may also be seen as signs of acculturation (this is where the two concepts overlap). Similar understanding of integration and acculturation is offered in the analysis of immigrant youth experiences in the U.S. by Portes and Rumbaut (2001) in their book chapter titled "A Third Way: Selective Acculturation and Bilingualism." Effective integration requires diverse personal resources—languages, education, social skills, and the ability to adapt to different roles. In that sense, assimilation may be an easier option since it implies full adoption of the host culture and hence makes bicultural maneuvering unnecessary (Nauck, 2001).

The feedback provided by the host country's majority, or its hegemonic social groups, is universally important for the integration process in any national context. Negative attitudes and conduct of the hosts towards large immigrant communities—including their negative stereotyping in the media, discrimination on the job market, residential and school segregation—may cause various expressions of separatism and so-called reactive ethnicity among the newcomers, catalyzing their ethnic mobilization (Grillo, 1998; Portes and Rumbaut, 2001; Al Haj, 2002, 2004). When immigrants form a sizeable portion of the host country's population, integration may also be seen as a bilateral process, whereby the majority and minority influence each other in multiple ways and cultural hybrids result from these interactions (Werbner and Modood, 1997; Faist, 2000; Anthias, 2001).

Most immigration scholars agree that complete assimilation, if it occurs at all, is a matter of several generations, while integration is more typical of the first and 1.5 generations (i.e., those who migrated as children or adolescents). Hence, from now on, I will set aside the term assimilation as largely inapplicable to the first generation of Russian-Jewish immigrants. Instead, I will focus on integration as referring to the structural aspects of immigrant inclusion (employment, functional social networks, participation in host social institutions) and acculturation in relation to the cultural aspects of this process, including language shift, informal social networks, and cultural consumption. Biculturalism may be seen as a simultaneous expression of integration and acculturation

Immigrants' choice of a specific integration/acculturation strategy in the host society is certainly not random. Developing Berry's typology, German sociologist Bernhard Nauck (2001) describes several key factors shaping this strategy, based on a comparative studies of various minorities in Germany (Turkish guest workers, Italian and Greek migrants, and Aussiedler, that is, ethnic Germans from Eastern Europe and the FSU), as well as Russian Jews in Israel. These factors pertain both to minority's own social profile and contextual variables: inclusive/exclusive tendency of the host society and cultural distance between the minority and the mainstream. Drawing on a broad view of capital as a set of personal assets, resources and skills available for reaching individual's social goals, minority's social and cultural capital emerged as the major predictor of its acculturation path. (Financial capital is important too, but it is relatively uncommon in mass immigrant waves, and hence omitted from the discussion). In line with other European scholars, (Grillo, 1998, Faist, 2000; Vertovec, 2004), Nauck understands by cultural capital (also known as human capital) education, professional experience, and host language command, while social capital is defined as contacts and personal networks with members of the host society used for meeting various instrumental and expressive needs. Nauck (2001) and Steinbach (2001) argue that both cultural and social capital are essential prerequisites for effective integration strategy, giving first-generation immigrants access to both majority and minority cultures.

Let me focus now on the integration/acculturation processes under conditions of mass migration, when immigrants form a sizeable minority in the receiving society (like Russian Jews in Israel, Aussiedler in parts of Germany, or Latinos in California). Below I outline a number of measurable social indicators for the study of integration based on current research in repatriate communities of Israel (Leshem and Lissak, 1999; Epstein and Kheimets, 2000a; Remennick, 2002a, 2003a) and Germany (Tress, 1997; Nauck, 2001; Jasper, 2005). I suggest four interrelated social indicators that allow operative measurement of the extent of integration/acculturation among first-generation immigrants. Firstly, it is the employment in the mainstream economy (in case of educated migrants—skilled or professional employment), rather than in the ethnic sector that rapidly develops in periods of mass immigration. Successful employment results not only in economic well-being, but also in the development of new interests and loyalties, as well as in contacts with non-immigrant coworkers, which facilitates the learning of the host language and cultural ways. Secondly, it is diversification of communication circles, whereby immigrants' informal networks come to include both co-ethnics and locals. Thirdly, it is gradual re-orientation of the cultural and media consumption from endogenous (i.e., co-ethnic, based on the language and culture of origin) to exogenous (mainstream cultural and media products in the host country's language). Apparently, this indicator of cultural transition is more salient for educated migrants, carriers of significant cultural capital from their home country, but it plays some role for all first generation migrants (who read papers, watch television, attend cultural events, etc.). The fourth factor shaping the pace and scope of integration is the dominant attitude of the hegemonic majority towards the specific immigrant groups. A more open and inclusive attitude on the part of the hosts is conducive to mutual tolerance, biculturalism and greater participation of the newcomers in the host social institutions. At the individual level, age at migration and language skills strongly influence all of the above processes. Younger age usually means faster social learning and greater adaptability, while better language command improves the chances for successful studies and employment, informal networking with the locals, and an easier shift to the mainstream cultural products.

The research framework discussed below drew on this heuristic model, exploring the principal dimensions of the integration process among ex-Soviet immigrants in Israel. My main empirical database was a national survey in a representative sample of over 800 post–1989 immigrants living in various parts of Israel, interviewed face-to-face by trained Russian-speaking interviewers. The survey was conducted in the spring of 2001, by the time that a majority of the respondents have spent several years in Israel (the average tenure in the country was 7.2 years); the mean age of respondents was 46.[10] I will also draw on the synthesis of my other studies, mainly of qualitative nature, that have been conducted in the course of the late 1990s and early 2000s and that looked at the processes of occupational adjustment among Russian immigrant professionals, political participation, patterns of language use and cultural consumption, transnational lifestyles, and immigrants' relations with the old-time Israeli citizens. Finally, this chapter will cast more light on the diversity of the immigrants' experiences, shaped by their gender, age, and ethnicity.

Occupational Integration: Career Continuity or Economic Survival?

For most adult immigrants, the workplace is their main social gateway into a new society. At work they meet their local peers, strike up new friendships, and improve their language skills; as a result they develop cultural competence in the new society and expand the limits of their personal identity. Needless to say, well-paying jobs form the basis of material wealth of immigrant families, improving their housing, lifestyle, and child education, with the ensuing social drift towards the mainstream (Stier and Levanon, 2003). All of the above play a central role in the immigrants' mental well-being and self-esteem, and, on balance, often serve as the main criterion for viewing the whole migration endeavor as success or failure. Apparently, immigrants having a strong professional identity often aspire to career continuity in the new country, while people with lower qualifications and achievements would have modest ambitions and are satisfied with gainful employment in any available job. Many others who may have never liked their former occupations, regard immigration as a fresh start and often venture into entirely new businesses and careers. All of these observations from international research on skilled migrants (Faist, 2000; Friedberg, 2000; Reitz, 2001; Vertovec, 2004) are fully applicable to the Russian Jews in Israel, yet the circumstances of their occupational re-adjustment were rather unique.

Before describing the adjustment and success of specific occupational groups, let me offer some general thoughts on the factors that contribute to immigrants' ability to relaunch their careers upon re-settlement. Of primary importance is the very nature of the profession in terms of its cultural dependency, that is, the embeddedness of professional practice in the language, mentality, and cultural codes. Carriers of culture-dependent professions such as educators, journalists, and entertainers have the hardest time applying their talents on a different cultural soil. Professions drawing on the "objective" internationally comparable qualifications such as physicians, nurses, social workers, and other "helping professions" take an intermediate position on this scale, and their success is contingent on the adjustment to the new professional culture. Engineering, technical and scientific occupations are presumably the most convertible between various national contexts, being "culturally neutral" and based on the verifiable set of skills and credentials.

The second issue is how far apart are the standards of professional education, accreditation, and practice in the home and host countries. The rules of licensure and registration with local professional associations are set in order to preserve proper standards at the face of mass entry of immigrant professionals into practice (Iredale, 1997). For example, in Israel physicians who went to medical school in the U.S., Canada, or U.K. are exempt from the standard licensing procedure required from all the other foreign-trained physicians, since the standards of medical training and practice in the Anglophone countries are very similar to the Israeli ones (Shuval and Bernstein, 1997). For the same reasons, the credentials of Soviet-trained engineers and "hard" scientists are accepted automatically, while economists and social scientists often cannot reconfirm their diplomas, since the gap in social disciplines between Western and eastern bloc countries had been very wide (Lerner and Menachem, 2003). The intellectual and social skills needed for successful professional practice (self-marketing, computing, languages) are also part of the standards that may widely differ between national contexts. Thus, former Soviet professionals often have poor skills of job searching and self-promotion that are needed in competitive occupations since in the FSU professional jobs were stable and relocation, when needed, was organized by employers (Jones, 1991).

The final set of factors shaping occupational prospects of educated migrants has to do with the structural conditions on the host economic marketplace. This includes the demand for a specific occupational group (i.e., for software designers in the years of the high-tech boom), the supply of native specialists, and their reaction to competition with the immigrants in the form of stricter licensing regulation, barriers to senior posts, etc. The personal factors of gender, age, and language proficiency permeate all other aspects of the integration process, with a greater difficulty for women and older specialists due to ageism and male preference of employers in competitive professions in most countries (Raijman and Semyonov, 1998; Menachem and Geijst, 2000; Stier and Levanon, 2003).

The impressive human capital of former Soviet Jews has already been mentioned: about 60 percent of the immigrants, men and women alike, had post-secondary education and, before emigration, most had worked in white-collar and professional jobs (CBS, 2000). This influx of skilled migrants was a mixed blessing for the small and saturated labor market of Israel, as in many professions the numbers of immigrant specialists exceeded the numbers of locally trained ones. Among the arrivals of the 1990s, there were some 38,000 teachers; 30,000 physicians, dentists and nurses; 18,000 musicians and music teachers; 12,000 scientists. Yet specialists in different kinds of engineering and technology were the largest professional group, numbering over 82,000 members (IMIA, 1998). The incorporation of all these newcomers in the skilled workforce was clearly beyond the physical capacity of the small Israeli economy. Besides their sheer excess, the incorporation of Russian professionals was compromised by skill incompatibility between Soviet and Western standards, the need for licensing for many occupations in human services, poor command of both Hebrew and English languages, and low market demand on many common Soviet professions (e.g., mining and metallurgic engineers). Older professionals, who had reached high occupational status in the FSU, usually had slim chances for regaining it in Israel. During most of the 1990s, 25–27 percent of Russian-speaking professionals were working in their original specialty. Others had to opt for retraining for more demanded occupations (e.g., computing, banking, insurance, social work) or to be satisfied with unskilled or "pink-collar" jobs in the industry, sales and services (Naveh et al., 1995; Raijman and Semyonov, 1998; Sicron, 1998).

In most countries receiving immigrants, the state only provides the legal basis for their employment (i.e., issues visas, social security cards, and other formalities granting legitimacy in the host economy), not involving itself in actual licensing, training, and job placement of skilled immigrants. Professional associations typically license immigrants on common grounds with their local colleagues, applying the same state-of-the-art standards. In this ostensibly fair game, immigrants are invariably disadvantaged vis-à-vis. their native colleagues due to the lack of social and financial resources and limited language command (Iredale, 1997; Reitz, 2001). Israeli policy towards skilled immigrants is unique in that the state agencies are actively involved in their occupational adjustment. The best possible utilization of the immigrants' human capital is an important macro-policy consideration. Yet, incorporation of thousands of skilled immigrants is a challenging task, shaped by two opposing sets of values and constraints. On the one hand, there is ideological and moral commitment to aid recent immigrants in their occupational (and, hence, social) adjustment. This is reflected in the institutional support policies, including free classes of advanced Hebrew, refresher or licensing courses tailored for specific professional groups, as well as stipends for scientists and other specialists to endorse their employment in both public and private sectors. On the other hand, there is constant competition for scarce jobs and career tracks between native and immigrant professionals in the small and saturated Israeli market (Shuval, 1995; Stier and Levanon, 2003). The interplay of these forces—market-driven, institutional, and personal or skill-related—has shaped the processes of occupational adjustment of different professional groups in Israel. Let me now take a closer look at the specific cases of career continuity among three largest occupational categories, which were most common among the skilled Russian immigrants of the last wave: engineers, physicians, and teachers.

Immigrant Engineers: Elite Specialists and Technical Proletariat

Besides their sheer numbers, the employment prospects of Russian-speaking engineers in Israel were aggravated by several structural features of engineering education and work in the FSU. To begin with, technology and engineering was one of the few professional tracks relatively open for Soviet Jews. The demand for technical specialists had always been high within huge Soviet industry, technical research, and construction. An engineering diploma promised a stable job and little involvement with the ruling ideology, which made Jewish parents propel their children towards engineering colleges. Engineering education was considered appropriate for both genders, and women comprised about 40 percent of the engineering cadre of the FSU. Although elite engineering colleges (such as the famous PhysTech in Moscow) had very low quotas for Jewish students, Jews often managed to get good engineering education in less prestigious or industry-affiliated schools (such as the Institutes of Chemical Technology, Railway Engineers, Radio-Electronics, and some others). The upscale Soviet engineering education is typified by a broad knowledge base, including good command of math and physics, with the ensuing skill versatility. The specialization of engineers reflected the structure and needs of the Soviet economy, dominated by heavy industry (mining, energy production, metallurgy, machine building, chemical and petroleum production), civil engineering, and construction. The majority of older Soviet engineers had been trained and worked in these areas; fewer specialists worked in modern branches of engineering related to computing and high technology. In the younger cohorts, these proportions started to change in line with the developments in the post-Soviet economy. The elite of Soviet engineers had been employed by the military-industrial complex and aerospace industry; many of them had high security clearance and could not even dream about emigration up until the mid–1990s. Thus, the ex-Soviet engineering corps has been highly stratified including relatively few elite specialists, the middle-class of solid but limited professionals, and the masses of low-grade technical proletariat.

Like other professionals in the FSU, engineers were state employees, had no professional autonomy, and were isolated from any contact with their colleagues abroad (Jones, 1991). As a result, most Russian-trained engineers have only basic (if any) command of English insufficient for professional work in the West. Computer literacy among older engineers was also low: under 20 percent of engineers aged forty-five or older had used computers in their work in the FSU (King and Naveh, 1999). Finally, formal engineering education did not necessarily entail actual engineering experience, as many graduates of technical colleges had been engaged in administrative or other office work. Reacting to the structural changes in the late Soviet industry, many engineers shifted to another area vs. the one they had been trained in, which further complicated an assessment of their credentials. In sum, many immigrant engineers discovered that their experience was non-applicable outside of the Soviet economy and had to find alternative occupational tracks.

Several Israeli studies examined the occupational adjustment of former Soviet engineers (Sicron, 1998). A cross-sectional survey by King and Naveh (1999) was based on a national sample of immigrant engineers (58 percent men, 42 percent women) who arrived in 1989–1994 and were between the ages of 25 and 54 at arrival. Before emigration, 87 percent of the sample worked in different posts related to engineering and technology, with an average experience of thirteen years. This survey has shown that under one-quarter of all immigrants with engineering diplomas, who had registered with the Ministry of Labor (75 percent of the total), worked in their area of training by 1995, and another 8–10 percent worked in related areas. Three immigrant engineers out of four experienced various degrees of occupational downgrading: 44 percent worked as skilled laborers and 25 percent as unskilled ones. Women's chances for professional employment were slimmer than men's: 30 percent of men and 18 percent of women worked in their main specialty. Over half of all respondents had studied in various professional courses sponsored by the state, but this had only a minor effect on their subsequent employment. The categories of engineers that most often regained and/or upgraded their old occupational status were electronics and computing-related specialists, software designers, aviation, civil and construction engineers. The least successful were engineers of the traditional Soviet branches almost inexistent on the small Israeli market—mining, metallurgy, and automotive (all cars in Israel are imported).

On the positive side, the mass influx of qualified engineers in Israel coincided with, and greatly contributed to, the rapid expansion of high-tech industries during the 1990s. By the year 2000, over 40 percent of the employees of Israeli high-tech companies in Israel were Russian immigrants, making a significant intellectual contribution to the global success of Israeli IT and computing industries. Although they usually lacked financial capital and business experience to start new ventures, Soviet-trained engineers and designers often formed the intellectual backbone of many start-up companies due to their broad knowledge base, high work ethics, and developed team spirit. Many engineers with postgraduate degrees and Soviet experience in R&D found employment in the government-sponsored "hothouses"—start-up companies for the development and initial marketing of new technical projects and patents. A handful of elite specialists were grabbed by the Israeli military and aviation industry. Yet, the majority of low-rank engineers were compelled to retrain into other specialties or to work at manual jobs.

My own longitudinal study including a three-wave survey and focus group discussions with immigrant engineers (Remennick, 2003b) has shown that only around 35 percent of all immigrant engineers have found engineering posts in Israel, either in their old specialty or in a new one after retraining. The major challenge faced by the immigrant professionals with no financial means, was entering a career track while simultaneously making a living. These two tasks are often mutually exclusive, since most specialists cannot find relevant jobs soon upon arrival and need to invest in the host language learning and professional orientation first. The latter activities are time consuming and often require formal study in different courses. Small allowances paid by the state to specialists who took retraining courses were not nearly enough to pay for housing, food, transportation, child education, etc. Hence, most specialists had to strike an uneasy balance between manual work for today's survival and studies or job searching for future success. This conflict was usually solved by living on the verge of their physical capacity, for example, taking night classes after toiling for six to eight hours at a factory or in a nursing home. Many gave up and abandoned professional ambitions altogether. In two-career families, the common strategy was taking turns, that is, letting one spouse to study or engage in job search while the other took over as a breadwinner, with the expected role reversal upon his/her occupational success. Not surprisingly, it was often women who decided to provide for the family while their husbands were struggling with professional Hebrew or initial volunteer work (a common entry route to many professions in the early 1990s). Regardless of their own education and experience, most women believed that a career is far more important for men, and that men cope much worse with the loss of their former professional status.

The initial years in the new country proved to be crucial for career prospects: immigrants, who had arrived in the early 1990s and not managed to find engineering jobs by 1997, did not improve their work status by 2001. Hence, those engineers who postponed a professional job search due to the immediate livelihood pressures often lost the momentum and got stuck in the manual labor force. This scenario was more typical for women, who often became the main breadwinners for their families, as well as older engineers and those with less desirable specialties. The delay of career-related activities till "better times" may often be fatal in the sense that the routine of daily unskilled work and detachment from the professional milieu gradually diminish both motivation and ability to return to the professional track. Our focus groups have also pointed to the salience of informal social networks for occupational adjustment of the newcomers and their basic disadvantage in that respect vis-à-vis their Israeli-trained peers. Similar findings have been reported by Vinokurov et al. (2000) who studied occupational adjustment among Soviet immigrant professionals in the U.S. Policy-wise, this means that various resettlement agencies should maximize their efforts to help immigrant specialists return to the professional track soon upon arrival via language training, subsidized professional courses, help in job search, preparation for interviews, etc. Time is of essence and it works against those skilled migrants who wish to regain their career but also must struggle to make ends meet.

Physicians: From Patient-Centered to Managed Care

Doctoring has been another traditional occupation for the Jews, including Soviet ones; over 15,000 Russian-speaking physicians and dentists, as well as over 25,000 nurses made aliyah to Israel since 1990 (IMIA, 2000). The hosting medical establishment was deeply concerned about professional accommodation of these newcomers on the saturated medical market, as the numbers of MDs and dentists in Israel have more than doubled by 1995. According to the calculus made by the Israeli Ministry of Health (MOH) in the early 1990s, the addition to the local practitioners necessary to serve the newly arrived immigrants at the present doctor-to-patients ratios was about 3,000 at the most. What would the rest of the 15,000 physicians do? These institutional concerns reflected the socialized and centrally managed nature of the Israeli health care system, whereby the numbers of medical posts and residencies, as well as medical facilities and beds are regulated by the MOH and delivered by means of four Sick Funds (Kupot Holim), similar to managed care providers (HMOs) in the U.S. Suffering from the chronic budgetary deficits, the Israeli health care could not afford to build new hospitals and staff new clinics in a short time, in order to employ the multitudes of immigrant doctors and meet the needs of the new patients. At the same time, local practitioners and Israeli Medical Association (IMA) representing their interests felt threatened by the lowering of wages and quality of care due to oversupply of physicians and questionable standards of medical education and practice in the FSU (Shuval, 1995).

The systemic response to this crisis emerged in the form of multiple barriers and filters (both overt and tacit) in the way of the newly arrived Russian doctors to clinical practice. In the late 1980s, on the eve of the Great Aliyah, the MOH and IMA established new accreditation rules for foreign medical graduates, which were revised again in the early 1990s in light of the "Russian invasion." The new rules required that all MDs with Soviet diplomas (and all other foreign diplomas except those received in the U.S., Canada, and U.K.) undergo comprehensive medical exams if their professional experience was below fourteen years. Those with fourteen or more years of practice in the FSU were required to have six months of supervised practice in a recognized medical facility, followed by a clinical examination. Upon passing theoretical exams or supervised practice period, immigrant physicians could be granted a general medical license similar to those received after five years of local medical school, regardless of their pre-migration medical specialty (e.g., gynecology or cardiology). In order to regain it, immigrant doctors had to proceed to a four to six year residency side by side with beginning Israeli doctors. Only a small number of senior medical specialists with academic degrees or international reputations were granted the right to specialist practice by the IMA (about ten percent of the total). However, upon setting these stringent demands, the Israeli medical and absorption establishment could not spare the newcomers any help in meeting them. Reflecting the dominant institutional approach to immigrant adjustment, the government offered free classes in medical Hebrew and English, preparation courses for the licensure exams, as well as allowing examination in the immigrant's language of choice (Hebrew, English, or Russian). Thus, the access to the senior medical posts for the newcomers was fully controlled by senior Israeli practitioners, representing the medical establishment, while access to low-rank general practice was made available, pending some reasonable quality control filters. Yet, all things considered, this policy was rather lenient in comparison to stringent American and, especially Canadian, rules of licensure and practice for foreign MDs (Shuval and Bernstein, 1997).

What happened with the thousands of Russian doctors in Israel is often described as a medical marvel. Operating within this harsh system of sticks and carrots, over 70 percent of those who had applied for the Israeli license at the outset (and about 25 percent had not, foreseeing all the trouble involved) managed to complete the accreditation and get a general medical license. Among those licensees, about three-quarters found work as doctors, including some 20 percent who started a new residency to become specialists. As a result of their mass entry into Israeli medicine, doctors with a Russian accent comprise today fully half of all Israeli practitioners under the age of forty-five and one-quarter among those aged forty-five to sixty-five (MOH, 2004). Among immigrant nurses, over 95 percent are working in nursing, usually after some additional training and/or exams; this reflects the ever-high demand for nurses in Israeli health care, not fully met to this day. As a result, former Soviets form a large portion of the medical staff in most Israeli hospitals and outpatient clinics, especially at the lower levels of medical practice (ER, ambulance, night shifts, geriatric and internal wards, etc.). Fewer Russian immigrant doctors are found so far among senior specialists, but this is changing over time as more young and middle-aged Russian doctors complete their residency and start practicing. Thus, it can be argued that Russian immigrant doctors in Israel succeeded against all odds on the small and saturated professional market. Admittedly, they have filled the less prestigious niches of the medical practice unwanted by Israeli doctors, and most of them will never regain their former status as medical specialists. Yet, the majority managed to get back to medicine as their main source of livelihood and intellectual stimulation—an achievement that cannot be taken for granted for immigrant MDs in many other countries (Shuval and Bernstein, 1997). Those who failed at medical licensure procedures, or had not tried to get the license in the first place, often converted to paramedical occupations such as diagnostic imaging or physiotherapy (Remennick and Shakhar, 2003).

Aside from organizational barriers, former Soviet doctors faced significant cultural challenges in the local medical institutions, trying to adjust to the new principles and norms of Americanized Israeli health care (Remennick and Shtarkshall, 1997). Doctoring Israeli-style is very different from the medical care in impoverished hospitals and clinics of Russia or Ukraine, where doctors had to treat patients almost with bare hands, under a permanent shortage of basic equipment and medications. In this context, Soviet doctors had to rely on their classic clinical and diagnostic skills, intuition, sympathy, and hands-on bedside care, which they had often performed because of missing or unskilled nurses. They also approached patients in a more holistic way (e.g., tried to fortify their natural immunity by administering vitamins and food supplements—the functions often left for alternative/complementary practitioners in the West), and if needed performed as counselors and social workers, non-existent in Soviet hospitals. Many good Russian doctors believed in the helping ethos as the core of their profession; they could afford spending time with their patients during long hospital stays, especially when little could be done medically. The romantic image of the doctor as a humane, caring and helping professional is very common in Soviet films and books. On the other hand, Soviet medicine was overflowing with "informal relations" (under-the-table payments, exchange of personal favors, privileges to friends and family, etc.) as a flipside of its lack of enforceable standards (Ledeneva, 1998).

Socialized in this patient-centered but often corrupt and inefficient system, immigrant doctors had to make rapid adjustments to Israeli medicine based on high-technology in diagnosis and treatment, fixed time budgets of doctors and nurses, short hospital stays, standard treatment protocols, and tight financial control of medical expenses—in brief, the managed care environment. Russian-trained doctors had to come to terms with the fact that "there is no time and no need to talk with patients beyond the immediate issues of medication and procedures to be ordered . . . nobody here collects detailed anamnesis or reads the notes written by other doctors. Machinery has replaced everything; doctors don't even touch patients to get first-hand feeling of their symptoms and reactions, they only look at the printouts of tests and CAT scans. Western medicine is a symbiosis between technology and economics; the only trouble is the patient has been left out of the system." Despite being critical of Soviet medicine, in hindsight informants found many positive aspects in their prior medical practice.

Thus, an internist in her mid—forties working in a large Israeli hospital mused:

> Medical treatment here became so specialized that no one is responsible for the patient as a whole, his well-being, his prospects. In our poorly equipped hospitals in Russia, the patients at least knew their leading doctor whom they could always address with questions. Here there is no such a thing as professional responsibility for your patients. Patients just sign so-called informed consent forms, which they do not understand, and everybody's ass is covered. . . . In Russia, post-operative care was very primitive due to lacking equipment, but at least patients were not discharged in five days after heart surgery . . .

Along with adapting to these new rules of professional practice, immigrant doctors also had to cope with the negative stereotyping by both their colleagues and patients as incompetent, unfamiliar with modern technology, and intrinsically corrupt. A former cardiologist recalled with bitter irony the days of his observed practice on a general ward of a large Israeli hospital:

> It took a few months before my supervisor (who was a young resident himself) entrusted me with operating the most basic equipment, thinking that I just went down the tree and never saw these screens, lights, and buttons before. When I tried to administer simple procedures to patients, he paled and snatched the instruments from my hands. The guy knew that I had worked for many years as cardio-surgeon, but where? In Russia, where bears walk on the streets and people stand in lines to buy bread. How cold he ever trust me?

Under similar circumstances, many had to downplay their clinical knowledge, working in junior supervised positions and not daring to state an independent opinion, or, God forbid, to contradict an Israeli doctor on whom they depended for their job and final reference. However, closer encounters between former Soviet and Israeli practitioners working side-by-side eventually mitigated mutual negative attitudes and helped both sides appreciate the merits of the other. It seems that by now most immigrant physicians have found a middle path between their old and new professional ethos, and probably enriched Israeli medical practice with some of their better facets (e.g., a more holistic approach to patients). As about two-thirds of Russian immigrant physicians are women, their entry into practice has also feminized Israeli medical care, adding diversity along both cultural and gender lines (Remennick and Starkshall, 1997).

Teachers: Survival of the Fittest

Another occupational venue available to Soviet Jews was teaching. During the last decades of socialism, educational policy was aimed at the cultivation of academic talents, and so-called specialized schools, majoring in foreign languages, math and physics, life sciences, or athletics were established in most large cities. The teaching and administrative elite of these schools often included Jews; as the schooling system started deteriorating with the end of socialism and teachers' salaries plummeted below the poverty line, many Jewish teachers embarked on emigration. Of course, not all Jewish teachers had been stars, most were rank-and—file classroom workers, including those who had chosen teaching due to the lack of other career options and had never liked it. Over the 1990s, about 40,000 schoolteachers arrived in Israel (85 percent of them women), facing the severe challenge of making it in the Israeli school system. To allow these teachers to get back in practice, the Israeli Ministry of Education provided a series of university-based certification courses, aiming to adapt the skills of former Soviet teachers to the local curriculum and its demands. In the early 1990s, there were enough vacancies in those disciplines less dependent on language proficiency (especially math, the sciences, physical education, art, and music), which were soon filled by immigrant teachers, despite their imperfect Hebrew. The teachers of humanities and languages faced greater challenges—nobody was ready to employ English or French teachers with a Russian accent (given the abundance of native-speakers), let alone teachers of the Russian language and literature which were not taught in most schools.

Like medicine (or perhaps more) teaching is a culturally embedded occupation: the principles and practices of education and teacher-student relations in Israel are very different from those in the Russian/ Soviet schools. Israeli children and youths are raised as free, independent individuals with few limits set by parents and teachers; as a result they are bold and forthcoming in their demands and dissent, and feel little social distance from adults, including educators. Classroom culture is very informal: students can interrupt and challenge the teacher, speak and use mobile phones in class, get out without asking permission, and call the teacher by her first name. Most Israeli teachers take it for granted and respond to students in a similar informal fashion, trying to maintain discipline in class and solving conflicts by joking, placating, or cajoling, but seldom by criticizing, shaming, or punishing. Teachers have to handle large classes (often over forty students in the middle school), and they can hardly enforce even minimal academic standards for everyone. The message to the students is that consistent work and educational achievement are optional rather than a universal expectation, as there is no regular control and feedback (e.g., by checking homework). Up until high school, the students can get good grades without much effort; they largely come to school to socialize and have a good time. In high school, though, they pay a high price for their relaxed previous years, as the workload, the pressure of tests, and competition for the grades with the approaching final matriculation exams all skyrocket between the tenth and the twelfth grades.

The schooling principles in the FSU were exactly the opposite: children were trained to take their studies seriously from grade one, and even the weakest pupils had to be pulled up to meet the minimal demands of literacy and knowledge. It was shameful to fall behind in class, and weaker pupils were often assigned mentors from the ranks of better students. The increment of effort and workload was gradual, and most students were prepared for the final intense years of high school. Finally, the teacher ruled the classroom and it was uncommon to openly challenge her, regardless of the amount of like or dislike (although mean tricks could be played behind her back). From this brief description, it is clear that former Soviet teachers had a very hard time adjusting to work in Israeli schools. Having little respect for teachers generally, Israeli students openly made fun of immigrant teachers, tainted by their lingering Russian accent and short temper in the face of the students' chutzpah.

Disappointed by the local educational standards and their outcomes, Russian immigrant parents and teachers teamed up to develop a complementary or even alternative school framework that would rescue the education of the young generation of Russian Jews (Epstein and Kheimets, 2000b). The Mofet (Excellence) network of complementary classes in math, physics, and Russian language and literature, run by ex-Soviet teachers mainly for the immigrant students, spread across Israel during the early 1990s, despite the persistent opposition of the

Ministry of Education. (All Israeli schools are public and closely supervised by the Ministry, with the exception of independent ultra-Orthodox schools). The cultivation of these isles of excellence was denounced as segregation and elitism, and speaking Russian in class allegedly hampered the prescribed linguistic conversion to Hebrew. Yet, by the late 1990s, persuaded by the tangible educational success of this parallel system (expressed in higher matriculation grades and the rising place of Israel in international student math competitions), the Ministry allowed reframing of a large regional high school in Tel Aviv (Shevah) in line with the Russian educational ideas. Started as an elitist framework for highly motivated immigrant students (but conducted mostly in Hebrew), the Shevah-Mofet project gradually attracted more Israeli-born students, and by now the classed are rather mixed. Soon Mofet's approach to teaching math and sciences has been introduced in many other schools. As a result, the level of teaching of the basic scientific disciplines has improved for all students, a fact grudgingly recognized by the educational authorities.

In the early 2000s, I interviewed nineteen immigrant teachers who continued teaching in Israel and sixteen teachers who left this occupation for different reasons (see Remennick, 2002b for the study details). All of the above-mentioned contrasts between the Russian and Israeli school cultures surfaced in the teachers' narratives as highly bothersome. Many informants referred to natural selection or "survival of the fittest" as a key metaphor of their ability to work in an Israeli school or drop out. Age, gender, and teaching experience emerged as important determinants of success: teachers in their thirties with five to fifteen years of experience (men and women alike) had the best chances for job continuity and satisfaction. In older age groups, school principals often preferred to hire male teachers as potentially more able to keep the class in check. Administrators did everything to avoid hiring older female immigrant teachers, even if they had been allocated these jobs by the Ministry of Education.

Hebrew proficiency was another factor shaping job retention. One teacher recounted: "When I finally was able to tell jokes in Hebrew, class experience has changed for me profoundly. I saw how even the most bold and hostile students melted down and paid more attention to what I said. Language is almost everything in class." Another female science teacher in her early forties reflected:

It wasn't that hard to learn physical terms in Hebrew. The problem was to master all these routine sayings in class—to call students to discipline, to confront their wisecrack remarks — you know how Israeli students are with teachers. When you have to scold, to punish, etc.—acting on the negative side—you get nervous and all the right words you knew suddenly evaporate from your head . . . and you end up sounding pathetic in front of the class. That's the worst.

Disciplinary problems in class and the "guts" needed to control them repeatedly surfaced in the interviews. Many teachers complained that a lot of time had to be wasted disciplining the students, which compromised the teaching process and hampered academic results. Here are some typical quotes: "You have to deal with the infamous Israeli chutzpah all the time, and if you do not develop effective tools for curbing it in class—you are finished as a teacher. The students put you to test all the time, just because you are new and Russian, unlike the teachers they are used to." "When I banned food and drink in class, the students organized the whole boycott of my lessons. The involvement of the principle was needed in order to get them back to class."

Many immigrant teachers also found it difficult to relate to Israeli parents, who often pulled their superior rank as natives vis-à-vis ostensibly naïve immigrants who misconstrued Israeli culture. As opposed to the Russian tradition, in conflict situations Israeli parents tended to side with their children and prove the teacher wrong. "If I raise the voice on him, or dare to expel him from the class, or give him an extra homework—tomorrow his angry mother will attack me and I would surely be found at fault, not her son. I would be shown as insensitive or incompetent—but the boy is always right. Since school administration tries to avoid clashes with parents, I'd rather be safe than sorry . . . "

Special bonds linked Russian immigrant teachers and immigrant students in their classes. Based on common cultural grounds, these relationships often served as safety net for both parties. The following account from an older math teacher was typical:

I know exactly how these Russian kids feel in the Israeli classroom, and I do everything in my power to make it easier for them. I am ready to sit with them after classes to explain new material once again, listen to their complaints, give them a hand in social matters or speak on their behalf with other teachers. . . . These kids have been thrown in the unfriendly waters of Israeli school with very little aid and language training, and not all of them can swim on their own.

Relations with Israeli colleagues were described as rather diverse, as was the amount of support during the accommodation period. Better schools created a friendlier atmosphere for the immigrants (both teachers and students), made more attempts at inclusion and compromise rather than separation and conflict. In better schools with a more educated and secure teaching staff, the newcomers were provided initial assistance and soon given equal footing with others. The welcome was typically cooler in problem-ridden schools in poorer or remote areas, where many local teachers were less educated and perceived Russian newcomers as a threat to their jobs or promotion. In such schools Russian teachers felt more isolated and disliked, and were compelled to seek each other's company and help. The lack of instrumental aid was often aggravated by popular stereotypes about Russian teachers as inflexible and authoritative, ostensibly due to their experience in the autocratic Soviet educational system. Many teachers felt angry about this unfair labeling:

> They think Russian school was a version of the Red Army or a department of the KGB– discipline, drills, and total surveillance. Their ideas about everything Russian date back to the Stalin era, as if we are still living in the 1930s . . . . For some, it's an easy way to discredit any bearer of a Russian accent, not to let us advance on equal terms with Israeli teachers, despite our better education and good teaching record.

Interviews with former teachers who quit this occupation revealed some additional facets. Most "dropouts" said that they never regretted their decision typically explaining it by their inability to adjust to this "messy" school system. "I was overwhelmed by the piling problems— to master new math program in Hebrew and to teach it in this zoo of untamed Israeli kids. . . . My backbone wasn't strong enough for this, and I was lucky to realize it very quickly. If I continued teaching for another year, I could end up in the asylum with a nervous breakdown." Not every ex-teacher used such strong language, but most were sure that they were better off outside of the Israeli school. Some (usually younger ones) successfully retrained into computing, banking, or accountancy; others worked in sales or personal services. Two older male teachers worked in a security service during the daytime and had a thriving tutoring practice in the evening. "I'd rather sweep the streets than enter an Israeli classroom. If I want to keep in touch with my profession, I prefer giving private lessons—the demand on the "Russian street" is rather high."

The bottom line probably was that former Russian teachers were self-selected into these two alternative occupational tracks, depending on the extent of their professional commitment to teaching and the available alternatives. Those who stayed in teaching often paid a high personal cost for their persistence, but enjoyed a strong sense of accomplishment. Personal traits, especially self-confidence and resilience, played a major role in the immigrant's ability to win and keep their place in the local school "jungle." Sensing the vulnerability of immigrant teachers, students may try to take advantage of them, bargaining for higher grades or informal privileges. Israeli parents are often on their children's side in conflict situations about grades and discipline. On the positive side, general work satisfaction among those, who persisted in their teaching career, was rather high. When Russian teachers managed to earn real authority and love of the students they felt fully rewarded for the stressful experiences along the way.

To conclude, the latter two case studies shed more light on the challenges of occupational integration for educated immigrants whose professions are culturally and linguistically sensitive. Our findings show that, even in a society generally committed to the cause of immigrant occupational integration (i.e., providing institutional aid in licensure and job search), there are high cultural barriers to successful professional performance. For Russian teachers, making it in the Israeli school means not only mastering Hebrew and a new curriculum, but also adjustment to the new school culture and relationships between teachers, students, and parents. In many cases, immigrant teachers also have to resist negative stereotyping as professionals by Israeli colleagues. This experience is shared by many immigrant professionals working in education, health, and human services. In this respect, my findings among Russian teachers (Remennick, 2002b), doctors (Remennick and Shtarkshall, 1997), and medical laboratory workers (Remennick, 2004b) fall into the same pattern, showing that, beyond instrumental skills, immigrant professionals have to comprehend and adopt local styles of doctoring, teaching, and socializing with co-workers and clients. Both medicine and teaching are "social" occupations, deeply embedded in local culture, history, and social networks. In the process of professional readjustment, social support provided by local peers of the immigrants and broader mainstream public (including the media that can either dispel or reinforce their negative stereotypes) can make a real difference.

Small Business as an Alternative to a Professional Career

The above case studies show that only a fraction of all educated immigrants could regain their original occupation in Israel. What alternatives were available to those who could not or did not want to get back to their Soviet occupations? Many immigrants had chosen their occupational track in the FSU not because they liked it or had special talents for engineering or teaching, but from pragmatic considerations and limited options. For many others, parents had made this decision for them, relying on their informal personal networks and providing· whatever help they could during the children's studies and job search. Thousands of former doctors, educators, and musicians could not get licensed or find work on the saturated market. In any event, for many young and middle-aged men and women immigration was a good excuse for a fresh start, and not a few of them tested the enticing option of opening their own small business (Light and Isralowitz, 1997). When asked about their motives and incentives, most immigrant entrepreneurs mentioned the wish for independence, autonomy in decision-making and daily management, and the lack of bosses to report to (Lerner and Hendeles, 1996). However, the lack of initial investment capital, business experience, and poor familiarity with Israeli rules and practices of running small businesses made this endeavor rather problematic. As in many other tracks of occupational adjustment, potential business-men and women received institutional support from the Israeli Small and Medium Business Authority, an agency affiliated with the Ministry of Industry and Trade. This Authority organized several intensive courses in business management for Russian speakers, provided ongoing advice for beginning entrepreneurs, and helped them self-organize into the Association of Immigrant Businesses (Lerner and Hendeles, 1996).

Soon enough, most beginning entrepreneurs discovered that they could hardly compete with established Israeli companies and service providers in the mainstream Hebrew-speaking market. In order to survive, small immigrant businesses had to find their own market niche that would allow them to utilize their relative advantage. As in all other pluralist immigrant societies, ethnic entrepreneurs turned to their own co-ethnics as clients (Light and Gold, 2000). Another possibility, which many business-minded olim explored time and again was a joint venture with Russian or Ukrainian partners, usually revolving around export-import of various raw materials (e.g., wood and paper) or ready-made products in demand on the Russian immigrant market (food, books, videos, CDs), or else secondary imports from the FSU of the technology products that are cheaper to buy there than from other suppliers (e.g., home electronics, computers, and related parts). Some immigrants opened business ventures related to their former line of work (e.g., engineers specializing in energetic equipment imported turbine parts from the Ukraine to several Middle Eastern countries, including Israel). Running these joint enterprises, Soviet Jewish immigrants could rely on their old professional and personal networks, good knowledge of the Russian language and post-communist business culture in the FSU. Many of these joint businesses had been started during the early 1990s (when prices in Russia were hard to beat) but few of them survived all the political and economic turmoil in the FSU, compromising supplies, payments, and contract discipline. Many of the remaining joint businesses collapsed after the infamous ruble default in August 1998.

A less ambitious but more realistic option was to run small service-oriented businesses catering to the "Russian street" in Israel. The most popular of those have been grocery stores, restaurants, book/video/music stores importing the latest Russian hits; real estate and home repairs/remodeling services; computer service; translations/notary/legal/ insurance services for Russian speakers; cleaning and personal services such as eldercare, child minding; hair/nail care and cosmetology. A special place on the map of Israeli-Russian business activities belongs to the agencies organizing internal (within Israel) and foreign tourism, which cater to both Russian Israelis and their multiple guests and contacts from the FSU, U.S., Germany, and other countries of the post-communist emigration. Some immigrants combine their day jobs as employees with additional business activities, selling their skills (e.g., computer maintenance, math/chess/music lessons, or statistical advice) to their co-ethnics or to the broad Israeli public. Some entrepreneurs offering intellectual services claim self-employed status as it enables them to deduct many additional expenses from the annual taxes, while others prefer to work in the shadows. Many Russian entrepreneurs have imported their business "toolbox" based on bending the rules, informal networking and exchange of favors, which fitted rather well into the Israeli business culture that often entails "flexible interpretation of the rules," protectionism, and various semi-legal *combinot* (Hebrew for smart moves and deals). A lot of small-time business activities on the "Russian street" go unregistered and un-taxed, comprising a part of Israel's thriving cash economy (Lerner and Hendeles, 1996).

For these reasons, it is hard to estimate the actual prevalence and scope of entrepreneurial activities among last-wave Soviet immigrants. Official statistical sources (CBS, 2002) list about six to seven percent of post–1989 arrivals as solely self-employed (vs. 13 percent among Israeli Jews generally), but then many businesses exist in addition to the main occupation, or are registered in a relative's name (e.g., a retired mother in law), or are not reflected in any papers at all. At the same time, many olim business owners create additional workplaces for their co-ethnics, some of whom are registered as their employees (with the ensuing taxes, health, and social security payments), while others work for cash. Some businesses in construction, plumbing, and home repairs employ foreign workers from the Ukraine, Moldova, and other FSU countries, both legal and undocumented. Multitudes of middle-aged and older women who collect their welfare checks are paid in cash for baby-sitting, eldercare, and household services to their neighbors and others. Thus, quite a few of immigrants in Israel are involved formally or informally, permanently or temporarily in business ventures that form together the web of a Russian ethnic economic sector. The ready availability of work in this sector, although usually for poor pay and with few social benefits, provides economic security for many immigrants (especially most recent arrivals) with few marketable skills and poor Hebrew who could not otherwise make a living in the mainstream Israeli economy. Although the official earned income of Russian immigrant households has been, on the average, about 40 percent lower than that of non-immigrant Jewish households (CBS, 2002), the additional trickles of cash not captured by statistics have probably improved the actual living standards of many newcomers.

From Muteness to Self-Expression:
Hebrew, Russian, and HebRush

The crucial role of Hebrew proficiency has already surfaced in the earlier discussion of occupational and economic mobility of Russian immigrants. As opposed to Jews making aliyah from North America, Argentina, or France, most of whom had attended Jewish schools and had some basic knowledge of Hebrew, most former Soviet Jews were unfamiliar with the Jewish languages. Some older people remembered basic Yiddish from their youth, but Hebrew, both ancient and modern, was totally alien to them. Some immigrants from the large Soviet cities had had a chance to attend Hebrew classes run by the Jewish Agency (Sochnut), where they had learned a survival set of two-hundred to three-hundred words, but the majority did not know even that. Learning a new and difficult language from scratch was a major challenge for the middle-aged and older olim. To make things worse, Hebrew was totally unlike any other foreign language they ever learned: its ancient script, right-to-left direction, lack of capitals, prepositions sticking to the main words, and complex verbal structures scared away many beginners, who decided they would never master it. Knowledge of English, which could help immigrants get around during the initial accommodation period, was also poor; some had learned French, German, or Spanish but few (about 15 percent altogether) had a good working command of any foreign language. Thus, in the multilingual mosaic of Israel, where most people are immigrants or children of immigrants and speak several European languages in addition to Hebrew and/or Yiddish (Spolsky and Shohami, 1999), Soviet Jews emerged mostly as pure Russian monolinguals (Olshtain and Kotic, 2000).

Although most immigrants have studied for at least several months in the state-sponsored Hebrew language classes (Ulpanim), for many this learning experience was ineffective as most teachers did not speak Russian and could not explain the intricacies of Hebrew grammar. The widely used "Hebrew-in-Hebrew immersion" method was good for some (younger and more linguistically able) but useless for many others, especially older students. Making things worse, many students had to miss day classes because they needed to work or dozed off in night classes after days of hard toil. As a result, most olim have mastered the survival or functional Hebrew (from life more than from class) necessary for keeping their jobs and getting by on daily errands, but Hebrew has not become their primary language. The younger and professionally advanced immigrants usually become bilingual, but prefer to speak Russian with their co-ethnics. Several earlier socio-linguistic studies focused on the determinants of language acquisition and use among Russian immigrants (Ben-Raphael et al., 1998; Olshtain and Kotic, 2000; Kheimets and Epstein, 2001; Naiditch, 2004); they have largely shown that younger age, female gender, higher education, employment in the skilled sector, and living in mixed neighborhoods (vs. immigrant enclaves) are all conducive to faster and better acquisition of Hebrew. The survey I conducted in 2001 in a large national sample tried to shed more light on the associations between language patterns and other principal aspects of social integration—occupational mobility, identity, social networks, cultural consumption, attitudes towards and involvement with the mainstream society (Remennick, 2003d; 2004c). As this survey embraced multiple other issues, the data on language proficiency is based on self-ratings rather than objective testing. Here are some highlights from the survey findings.

Hebrew Proficiency and Usage

Respondents were asked to rate their command of Hebrew on a five-point scale (1 for the poorest and 5 for the best). The mean scores for oral fluency and literacy were 3.14 and 2.76, respectively. The score distribution was as follows:

Score	Oral skills	Read & write
1–2	29 percent	42 percent
3	31 percent	30 percent
4–5	40 percent	28 percent

Apparently, respondents reported better oral than reading/writing skills. This is understandable, given a wide gap between spoken and written Hebrew, as well as the difficulties of Hebrew grammar and writing principles for speakers of European languages. Conversely, contemporary spoken Hebrew resembles Russian in some respects (e.g., free word order in sentences, many similar idioms) as Russian migrants to Palestine took an active part in its revival in the early twentieth century. Most respondents perceived their limited Hebrew as a problem and made attempts to improve it. About 31 percent were engaged in active study (in class or with private tutors) and 49 percent tried to increase their natural exposure to Hebrew (via radio/TV, conversations with the natives). The remaining 20 percent reported no such attempts; among them 13 percent said they managed well enough without Hebrew, and 7 percent believed that their level was sufficient for their needs.

As for other languages, English was mentioned as global lingua franca, essential for occupational advancement. Forty-two percent of respondents said they had some knowledge of English, usually rather minimal (the mean score on a five-point scale was 3.17). Many Soviet-trained professionals admit that their poor command of English is the major barrier to high-quality jobs and promotion, in Israel and in the West (Kheimets and Epstein, 2001). In this sample, the principal correlates of a better command of English were younger age, higher education completed in the late 1980s (i.e., in the period of Russia's growing openness to the West), and coming from a large city with greater exposure to international media and better language schools.

As for the language preferences and usage, my findings were in line with earlier research (Lissak and Leshem, 1995; Ben-Rafael et al., 1998). The positive evaluation of Hebrew was related to two aspects: occupational/social mobility in Israeli society and connection with the Jewish heritage. Russian was perceived as the main vessel of culture and personal expression, associated with the European cultural tradition most immigrants identified with. The usage of Hebrew was dominant in the occupational and public realms, whereas Russian remained the language of personal communication with family, friends, and other co-ethnics. Yet, these domains were not isolated from each other. Hebrew gradually invaded the private circles of communication: only 66 percent of respondents spoke pure Russian at home, while 23 percent mixed some Hebrew into Russian, and 11 percent spoke the so-called HebRush (a 50:50 mix of the two languages). Another booster of Hebrew use at home was having school-age children; over half of such households were typified by the constant mixing of Russian and Hebrew.

Hebrew and English as Tools of Socio-Economic Mobility

Our analysis shows that language proficiency is both a prerequisite to and a result of occupational success, but causality between them is hard to establish. In regression analysis, working in a skilled occupation (especially in one's original specialty) was a consistent predictor of better Hebrew and English skills. And vice versa: language proficiency as an independent variable predicted higher levels of employment and job continuity. Among the respondents who had worked in their original profession for three years or more (the most successful category), over 70 percent defined their Hebrew as good or excellent, versus 53 percent among those who had a skilled job after retraining, 30 percent among those working in menial jobs, and 22 percent among the unemployed or retired.

Language, Ethnic Identity, and Attitudes towards Integration

It was not unexpected to find a significant link between Hebrew proficiency and self-identification. I believe that immigrant identity is always a hybrid of old and new elements that may surface in different contexts. Terms such as hyphenated identity, situational identity, and salami-style identity are used to reflect this complexity (Gold, 1997; Faist, 2000). Therefore, I framed the identity item (usually included in immigrant studies) as a scale with three main categories: Regular Israeli (11 percent of all answers), Russian Israeli (69 percent), Russian living in Israel (17 percent), and Other (3 percent). As opposed to the earlier surveys (Ben-Rafael et al., 1998; Lissitsa and Peres, 2000), I deliberately excluded general Jewish or Russian-Jewish categories, framing identity in relation to the host society rather than ethnicity. Indeed, all but few respondents could define their location along the scale of Israeliness and only 3 percent wrote open answers such as Russian/ Ukrainian/ Moldavian Jew. Among respondents with the poorest Hebrew, only 8 percent defined themselves as Regular Israelis compared to 25 percent among those with excellent Hebrew. Among those who identified as Russians living in Israel, only 16 percent reported good or excellent Hebrew, while about 50 percent said their Hebrew was basic or poor. Pearson's r between Hebrew level and identity title (from mainly Israeli to mainly Russian) was inverse and rather high (–0.34). Hence, better Hebrew proficiency is intertwined with a more positive attitude towards mainstream Israeli culture, a greater sense of belonging to Israeli society, and self-perception as a regular Israeli or Russian-Israeli.

The subsequent in-depth ethnographic study (Remennick, 2004a) explored the socio-linguistic patterns in seventeen multigenerational immigrant families in the context of the emerging Russian-Hebrew bilingualism. The fieldwork conducted with these families included over fifty personal interviews and many hours of participant observation during everyday family settings, parties, and other social occasions. The profile of these families was typical of the Russian-Jewish intelligentsia, comprising, in terms of education, about 60 percent of the last immigrant wave. The study embraced the differential experiences of three generations and two time waves of Russian Jewish immigrants to Israel (the arrivals of the 1970s and 1990s), trying to understand how language practice evolves with age and duration of life in the host country. The key theoretical perspective guiding this research was *core values* of minority cultures, developed by Polish-Australian sociologist Jerzy Smolicz and referring to the "fundamental components of the group's culture, symbolic of the group and its membership. From the perspective of the outsider, it is through core values that social groups can be identified as distinctive cultural communities . . . The nature of core values can be most clearly discerned when the group concerned is under threat and needs to defend its culture against external pressures" (Smolicz et al., 2001: 166–7). Some immigrant groups are known for their strong family values and in-group support (Greeks, Italians, and Armenians), others for their religiosity and commitment to ethnic causes (Arabs), still others for the praise of individual effort and achievement (Protestant minorities). For most ethnic minorities, their native language belongs to the core values, whether they use it on a daily basis or not (Smolicz et al., 2001; Bakalian, 1992). As for Russian Jews, their attachment to the Russian language and culture regardless of the country of residence reflects the core values of education, upward social mobility, and achievement through hard intellectual work (Gold, 1997; Kopeliovich, 1999; Kheimets and Epstein, 2001). The transmission of the linguistic and cultural inheritance to their children living outside Russia is an important endeavor for most Russian Jews. Below I highlight the main findings of this qualitative research (see Remennick, 2004a for details).

From Russian to Hebrew via HebRush: The Emerging Immigrant Lingo

In the families that moved to Israel during the 1990s, a clear inverse relationship was evident between age/generation and Hebrew command. School-age children were most fluent in Hebrew and many revealed signs of Russian language attrition, using word order and idioms suggesting inverse translation from Hebrew. In the family gatherings they spoke Hebrew with each other and sometimes with the adults too. Most members of the middle generation had a rather good oral command of Hebrew (their self-estimates on the five-point scale ranged from 3.7 to 4.8), but preferred to speak Russian in the family circle. The grandparents usually had the poorest Hebrew limited to the basic set of words and phrases.

Despite the fact that the bulk of verbal exchanges during family events were in Russian, the speech was generously spiced with Hebrew elements pertaining to the Israeli-based subjects and realities (food and clothing items, forms of leisure, politics, etc.). Sometimes a phrase would be started in Russian and finished in Hebrew, or they would be mixed (e.g., from a tableside exchange: "*Oy, ty posadil mne ketem na khultsy, kakoi tembel!*"—Oy, you stained my blouse, what a fool! The sentence template is Russian and Hebrew words are Russified). The relative shares of Russian and Hebrew in the speech depended mainly on the speakers' age and social placement: students and those in skilled occupations, immersed in the Hebrew-speaking milieu during their workdays, used more Hebrew elements than the unemployed or those having unskilled jobs. Older family members were often excluded from the general discussion conducted partly in Hebrew (unless someone was willing to translate) and struck conversations of their own. Only two families out of ten that my assistants and I visited stuck to pure Russian with almost no Hebrew inclusions throughout many hours of a family gathering.

In the subsequent interviews, most informants admitted that mixing Hebrew and Russian could be a problem for family communication (especially for the elders) and in terms of Russian's preservation by the children. The switch between the two languages often occurred inadvertently, almost automatically, especially when it came to the local realities such as work relations, weather, security problems, etc. Several participants had tried to avoid mixing the languages and to speak only in Russian, but soon gave up since it seemed unnatural to translate from Hebrew such common local terms as *miluim* (reserve army duty), *mazgan* (air conditioner), *hamsin* (dry heat wave), and so forth. Many informants pointed out that Hebrew phrasing was much more concise than the Russian one; it often takes a whole Russian sentence to translate a Hebrew idiom. Alex, a forty-two-year-old engineer, expressed a common view:

I am wondering how some of my friends continue to speak pure Russian with their families and friends. Marx was right saying "Being shapes the mindset": you can't separate yourself from the society you live in. I work mostly among Hebrew speakers and Hebrew is ingrained in my mind;

some Hebrew words come to mind easier than their Russian analogues. . . . I guess the basis of my talk will remain Russian for my lifetime, but mixing Hebrew in is inevitable too.

Marina, a thirty-seven-year-old social worker, expressed the opposite view:

I made it a rule to speak pure Russian at home, and everybody sticks to it. The family is the only place where my twelve-year-old son can preserve his mother tongue, since in every other context he speaks Hebrew, including his pals of Russian origin. If we start mixing the two languages—he will quickly lose good standards of Russian, the way it happened to most of his friends. Every language is an asset, and your native language is a must.

Socio-linguistic studies among recent immigrants (Stevens, 1992; Smolicz et al., 2001; Sposlky and Shohami, 1999; Dounitsa-Schmidt, 1999; Yelenevskay and Fialkova, 2003) often pointed to a clear boundary between public and private realms in language use, whereby the host language is used for instrumental purposes in dealing with social institutions, while the native language serves for private communication with the family and other co-ethnics. Our observations suggest that this partition, although generally still in place, is becoming murky: Russian often penetrates the public realm and Hebrew becomes part of private conversations. The former tendency reflects the large size of the Russian-speaking community in Israel with the ensuing presence of Russian-speakers in every workplace and social setting. Yefim, thirty-five, a civil engineer working in a private construction firm, commented on this:

I learned Hebrew rather soon since I had to speak it at work: in the early 1990s I was the only immigrant in my company. But now it has changed dramatically: I guess half of my coworkers are Russian-speakers. At first it felt wrong to speak Russian at work when Israeli colleagues could hear us, we almost whispered or went out to smoke in order to have a natural conversation. But gradually Israelis got used to this "Russian invasion" and now we can speak Russian openly between ourselves, it doesn't bother anyone. Some Israelis even learned a word or two in Russian and use it jokingly with us.

Older informants and those who worked in manual jobs often admitted that their Hebrew was very poor, but were eager to stress that they did not need it in their daily lives. Maya (fifty-nine), a former accountant, said, "Do I need good Hebrew to sweep the floors in the offices and apartments? I can express my basic needs, like negotiate my wage raise or workload, but who needs more than that? All my friends are Russian like me, I go to the Russian library, watch Russian TV, shop in Russian stores. . . . In Israel today many Russian Jews can live without learning Hebrew beyond the basics . . . unless they have a chance to find real skilled work, of course." This remark underscores the link between host language acquisition and social placement of the immigrants, occupational mobility often being the main motive for the improvement.

Language Choices of Bilinguals

An interesting issue arising from our fieldwork was the language preferences of bilingual immigrants: when and with whom do they speak Russian or Hebrew while both options are available? As was shown in the often-cited study by Joshua Fishman (2000), linguistic choices of bilinguals are shaped by the interplay between the thematic domain in question, social statuses, and fluency of the speakers. Apparently, Hebrew was always used with non-immigrant Israelis, but it was also a common part of exchange between Russian-speakers themselves. Michael, forty-one, a bilingual free-lance journalist, commented:

> I have noticed that in official situations I would speak Hebrew even when I believe that the other party (a doctor, a school principal of my kids, etc.) can speak Russian—you can always guess by the accent and general demeanor. Yet, with the officials who are veteran Russian immigrants you don't feel the legitimacy to speak Russian, it's a matter of social distance I guess. Russian is a language of familiarity, privacy, friendliness—and you cannot impose it on someone you don't know in person, especially when you don't want to provoke their animosity.

It seems that social distance is an important determinant of language choice in potentially bilingual interactions: many informants stated, like Michael, that they only switch into Russian when they are sure of the positive disposition of the other party, feeling that s/he is "one of us." For instance, several bilinguals noted that they never tried to speak Russian with their bosses at work, whom they knew to be old-time Soviet immigrants. Most informants were aware of their Rus-

sian accent as a universal signifier of the group affiliation; some perceived it as a problem, making them self-conscious and uneasy, while
others saw it as an inevitable aspect of their immigrant state and took
it for granted. Lena, forty-five, a receptionist in the municipal social
service center, recounted:

> When we came here in 1991, being Russian was almost a dirty word,
> meaning miserable, unfit—which was in a way true, given what conditions
> we had started from: lousy jobs, run-down apartments, financial need. . . .
> My Russian accent was like a stigma, signaling that I was an alien. Over
> time, things improved, and I felt more secure; my Hebrew grew richer,
> now I can handle any topic. My accent became milder but it is still there:
> when I open my mouth every visitor at work, every sales girl or a bank
> clerk knows I am Russian. . . . Only I don't care anymore, I have no prob-
> lem being Russian in Israel. This society has to accept us on our own
> terms.

Lena's last remark points at the firmer social footing and growing
self-esteem among bearers of a Russian accent in Israel, reflecting the
consolidation of the Russian community along economic, political,
and social lines. The increasing ethnic power of Russian speakers in
this multi-ethnic immigrant society has had another unexpected rami-
fication: the comeback of Russian into the lives of more veteran Russian immigrants.

The Reversal of the Language Shift in the Old-Timers

Seven extended families of Soviet immigrants of the 1970s included in this study maintained dense intergenerational contact by
means of mutual visits, frequent phone conversations, joint trips during weekends and holidays. Most grandparents in these families came
to Israel in their thirties and early forties and are now in their sixties
and early seventies. The informants belonging to the middle generation were usually born in the USSR, moved to Israel as children, and
spent most of their formative years among Hebrew speakers. Most
grandparents, who had embarked on aliyah back in the 1970s, shared
Zionist ideals, had illicitly studied Hebrew, and were highly motivated
to shun Russian and integrate into the mainstream. In Rina's (67)
words, "We had come to Israel to become Israelis and contribute to
the nation building in this land. Those who wished to speak Russian

and read Russian books could stay back in Russia, why bother with all the losses and pains of immigration?"

In most old-timer homes, Hebrew had prevailed fairly soon upon arrival. While spouses could speak Russian, or "HebRush," with each other, they usually made a point of speaking Hebrew to their young children. Three out of seven members of this generation recounted that in the 1970s and 1980s transmission of Russian to the children was not on their agenda; becoming full-fledged Israelis had seemed more important. Three other informants told us that they had felt connected to their Russian linguistic and cultural heritage, did not see it as a threat to Hebrew, and attempted to teach their children to speak and/or read Russian. These families had kept a bilingual lifestyle throughout the 1970s and 1980s and their children (today's mid-generation) had significantly better Russian fluency than the children of the former (Zionist) category. One couple made aliyah in 1978 in their mid-forties and ever since was in and out of employment, remaining mainly Russian speaking; their grown children had the best Russian oral fluency in the sample. Thus, it seems that language attitudes and practice of the parents had a strong bearing on the native language continuity in the children.

Except for the latter couple (that never switched to Hebrew in the first place), all old-timer informants described how during the last decade Russian made a comeback in their lives. Sima, seventy-one, a convinced old-time Zionist, recounted:

> When Russian Jews reappeared in the early 1990s after a long break and soon filled every walk of life, I was shocked and even embarrassed. Why would these people assume that everyone should understand them in Israel? They would approach you in the street and start asking questions in Russian as if they never left their native Minsk or Odessa . . . . At first I feigned not speaking any Russian and responded in simple Hebrew . . . frankly by then my own Russian had gotten a little rusty. But over time Russian became a common language in Israel—and it became more natural for me to answer in Russian, although I still believe that wherever you came from, in Israel you should speak Hebrew.

However, most other informants were happy to return to Russian, feeling the growing acceptance of their native language in Israel. Dina, sixty-four, said:

Most veteran Israelis were threatened by the rapid influx of educated Russian Jews, who often showed their cultural superiority and little interest in the Hebrew culture. In the early 1990s, my co-workers often told me how angry they were hearing several new Russian employees loudly chat in Russian during lunch break or in the smoking corner. "How dare they? Did we wait for this big Russian aliyah for ten years only to get this crowd of aliens?" I tried to explain that adult people cannot switch to a new language right away, and even if they must, they still feel more comfortable speaking Russian among themselves. Don't Israelis speak Hebrew when they live for years in America? Anyway, it's different now, when Russians have their own community life, their press, theatres, Knesset members, and all that. Israelis got used to the sound of Russian in the streets, on TV and radio; it is perceived as yet another language of Israel. And I am very glad that this has happened—now I can speak Russian everywhere without hushing myself.

Semyon, forty-six, who moved to Israel in 1977 at the age of twenty-one, reflected:

Now that you ask about it, I realize that Russian came back to my life during these five to seven years, and I took it for granted. Before the big Russian immigrant wave, we spoke Russian only at home, mainly as a secret language to exclude children from our arguments—the way our own parents (or grandparents) had used Yiddish. And look at us today! Even our kids who grew up in Israel, watch Russian TV sometimes, and use Russian as a secret language to gossip about their friends. . . . And you know what? My seventeen-year-old son told me the other day that his Israeli pals asked him to teach them a few lines in Russian to pick up Russian girls . . . . Of course, his Russian is funny, with a heavy Hebrew accent, but five years ago he would never utter a Russian word at all. That's a big change!

These remarks indicate that the language shift, which had occurred among veteran immigrants some decades ago, proved to be reversible against the backdrop of the mass influx of Russian speakers during the 1990s and the improved social status of this minority language over time. Despite some ideological reservations, most old-timers were quite happy to regain their native tongue and see their children pick up some of it in the new atmosphere of the reemerging Israeli multilingualism.

The Role of Cultural Values in the Transmission of Russian to Children

Even in our small sample, the link between cultural values and language patterns was apparent, regardless of the time spent in Israel. Informants who had strong emotional and intellectual ties to Russian culture were more determined to preserve it and transmit it to their children and grandchildren. These ties were especially salient for those whose pre-migration occupations were deeply embedded in the Russian language and culture—teachers, journalists, and artists. It was not accidental that in Israel these people were often underemployed or changed occupation to make a living. In comparison with those who worked in industry, technology, health care, and other "hard-core" sectors, their Hebrew command was generally worse. These parents were typically less involved with Israeli society and drew on the Russian subculture for their social networks, consumption, and entertainment. This category of parents showed more determination in transmitting their own culture to the children, for instance by placing them in the Mofet school system.

Most Russian homes had rich libraries, including Russian classical literature and modern writers, translations of Western authors, and art books. The majority of these books had been taken to Israel from the FSU, and most participants continued buying new Russian books via multiple Israeli-Russian outlets (stores, mail catalogs). However, in most cases, the consumption of these cultural resources was limited to the older generations who grew up in Russia. The children seldom showed interest in Russian literature; if they read at all, it was in Hebrew or in English. Many older informants expressed bitterness about the "waste of cultural potential" they brought to a new country as their most significant asset. As Olga, a fifty-year-old teacher of Russian literature, put it,

> Look at these shelves filled with Chekhov and Bulgakov! We had naïvely believed that our kids would love these books the way we did! Alas—this is not part of their mental world today. Even if they study some Russian authors at school, they read them in Hebrew! When I look at these books, I often feel guilty that I wasn't persistent enough in my efforts to keep Russian for my children, who could pass it on to their kids. Now it is too late.

In most cases, the maximum the adults could expect from their children was keeping some oral fluency in Russian, but not reading and writing skills. Even when a persistent grandma or grandpa had managed to teach the basics of Russian grammar and reading to their grandchild, these skills deteriorated fairly soon due to non-use. The only exceptions in our sample were three adolescents who attended the Shevah-Mofet school, where most students and teachers are of Russian origin and Russian is taught as a second language. All the other children studied in the regular schools where Russian was not offered at all or was treated as a temporary option for recent arrivals. Many adults were upset by the absence of Russian in the school curriculum, but most children did not see it as an important issue. "We have enough trouble with English and French or Arabic; who wants more workload with Russian?" said one twelve-year old.

Other parents were less concerned about the loss of interest in Russian culture among their children. Dmitri, forty-six, a successful engineer working for a hi-tech firm, said,

> I think this change in interests is inevitable. Our kids grew up in a different time and in a different part of the world. It is much more important for them to be fit in today's competitive world, to get useful skills, than to chase dreams in books, the way our parents and we did. They read books because this was their only source of information and pleasure. Today's kids have many other options—Internet, travel, and all. Frankly, I myself almost stopped buying books unrelated to my work: I have no time and no interest in Russian authors. We live in this country and Russia is far away. So the loss of Russian is part of our migration story, and for the kids it is not even an issue—Hebrew comes naturally to them. It is much more important to learn English in order to succeed in this life.

Beyond language, many parents of the 1990s wave were upset by the way their children spend free time, perched for hours in front of the television screen or playing computer games. What bothered them was not that all the television and cyber-world information was consumed in Hebrew or English, but the very idea of succumbing to mass culture and mindless pastime. The cultivation of excellence, intellectual work, high standards of education—all the core values that the mid-generation of Russian Jews grew up with—turned to be a lost cause with their kids immersed in Westernized Israeli culture. In the words of one informant, "It seems that along with Russian literacy these kids lost access to the whole different world where culture is not about killing time and entertainment but about mental effort, self-improvement, and growth." Similar feelings were expressed by several parents who grew up in the FSU, but not by those whose who had spent their own formative years in Israel, that is, the arrivals of the 1970s. The latter often took for granted their children's lifestyle and did not expect them to be different from other Israeli youths. This was a vivid expression of the gap in cultural values of the two historic waves of Russian-Jewish immigrants. However important parental attitudes were towards Russian language and culture, many additional factors shaped children's knowledge and use of Russian. The external social milieu—school curriculum, peer group, attitudes of their friends towards Russianness, and the child's own preferences were at least of the same influence.

In sum, these studies have shown that bilingualism is an important instrument of social mobility and integration for first-generation immigrants, allowing them to embrace different social roles and switch between alternative cultural codes. The improving command of the host language, with the ensuing feeling of social inclusion, entails multiple psychological benefits: higher self-esteem, sense of achievement, and validation of the whole emigration venture (Yelenevskaya and Fialkova, 2003). The changes in language and culture of Russian immigrants occur in line with the hybridism model: adopting various features of everyday Israeli culture, Russian Jews have also incorporated multiple elements of Hebrew in their speech. The language shift from Russian to Hebrew entails broad use of the emerging amalgam lingo jokingly called "HebRush"—a vivid example of linguistic interference reflecting on-going adjustment to the new realities of life in Israel (Naiditch, 2004). Our findings confirm some earlier observations on the Hebrew-Russian bilingualism, pointing to the additive rather than replacive mode of its formation (Donitsa-Schmidt, 1999; Olshtain and Kotic, 2000; Kheimets and Epstein, 2001). At the same time, due to the gradual attrition of Russian and imperfect command of Hebrew, a large part of the alleged bilinguals are in fact semilinguals, whose articulation is functional but rather limited and exists mainly in the oral domain with poor literacy in both home and host language. A traditional split between public and private language in immigrant lives is becoming more fluid, that is, both languages (albeit in different shares) are used in every social context. There is an apparent crossover in the language patterns between the recent arrivals (the 1990s wave) and the old-timers (the 1970s wave): while the former increasingly shift to Hebrew, the latter return to Russian after many years of oblivion, asserting once again that the reversal of the language shift among ethnic minorities is possible under certain social conditions (Fishman, 1991).

These findings on the individual and family level reflect the rising social status of Russian speakers in Israel throughout the 1990s (Leshem and Lissak, 1999; Epstein and Kheimets, 2000a; Remennick, 2003d; Naiditch, 2004). The increasing legitimacy of this prevalent minority language manifests in many ways: the pivotal presence of Israeli-Russian politicians on the public arena (especially during election times); the growing visibility of Russian artists in Israeli culture and media and audibility of their accented Hebrew; the acceptance of the independent Russian media by the Hebrew-speaking majority, and more. The underlying trend is of course the rising economic potential of the Russian community, defined by its large size (i.e., market share) among Israeli consumers, making it profitable to sponsor a Russian TV channel, show commercials in Russian, hire Russian-speaking operators for marketing goods and services to their co-ethnics, and so on. Suddenly bilinguals are demanded by many employers and get better jobs. These commercial and labor market forces have elevated the Russian language, which used to bear only sentimental and cultural value in the early 1990s, up to a new status with an added economic value. The growing political weight of Russia on the international arena and its mediation in the Israeli-Palestinian conflict may also play a role. All this inevitably adds to the appeal of the Russian language for pragmatic Israeli youngsters, especially those who in any case had Russian as part of their family heritage.

As was shown for other ethnic minorities living far away from their cultural metropolis (Bakalian, 1992; Smolicz et al., 2001), Russian language maintenance and cultural continuity belong to the core values of the Russian-Jewish intelligentsia living in Israel. The pursuit of intellectualism, high educational standards, and upward social mobility cause Russian parents to oppose the influence of mass culture transmitted to the youth via Israeli media. Our interviews confirmed the earlier findings by Kopeliovich (1999) that educated immigrant parents perceive Russian as an important vehicle for transmission of their core cultural beliefs to children via reading, conversations, and other traditional channels. The "Hebrew vs. Russian" dilemma has yet another interface with the core values concept. In the Israeli context, languages have ideological baggage that stretches far beyond their instrumental role as tools of communication and social adjustment. In a society built almost entirely of immigrants from all over the world, the universal use of Hebrew signifies Israeli statehood and is an important icon of national consciousness (Spolsky and Shohami, 1999). Although Hebrew has been firmly established as the national language of Israel since the late 1950s, new immigrants who are unwilling to switch to Hebrew continue to be seen as outsiders, if not as a fifth column. The persistence of the 1990s immigrants in the everyday use of Russian and the expansion of its institutional basis is a continuous cause of cultural conflict between them and veteran Israelis. Thus, the rising socio-economic status of the Russian language goes largely against the traditional melting pot aspirations and the ideology of Hebrew monolingualism. The significant human capital of Russian speakers and their sense of cultural superiority combine with omnipotent market forces to sustain Russian's legitimacy, at least for the time being. The final outcome of this rivalry will be manifested of course, in the language preferences of the second generation.

"Integration without Acculturation" Revisited: Social and Cultural Autonomy of Russian Israelis

In her influential 1989 article on the earlier wave of Soviet immigrants to Israel, Tamar Horowitz wrote about "integration without acculturation," referring to their successful incorporation into all Israeli institutions without actually adopting Israeli culture. During the 1990s, the tendency to socio-cultural autonomy typical of the former Soviets was compounded by their poorer instrumental integration at the workplace and other mainstream institutions. Along with Russian immigrants of the 1970s, the weight of Russian-speaking Jews from the FSU has now reached 20 percent of the country's Jewish population. This critical mass of immigrants has inevitably led to the formation of a self-sufficient ethnic community. Cherishing their cultural and linguistic heritage, adult Russian speakers from the outset resisted the attempts at their rapid Israelization.

Superiority Complex as a Flipside of Social Marginality

Coming from a linguistic and cultural metropolis that for decades dominated all smaller nations of the Soviet empire, most Russian Jews (like their fellow Russians) believe that their European cultural heritage is superior to that of the Levantine and provincial Israel (Lissak and Leshem, 1995; Epstein and Kheimets, 2000; Zilberg, 2000). In many interview quotes cited above, the reader can trace the motives of cultural superiority felt by Europeans living in the midst of a "primitive," "undeveloped," "crude," etc. Middle Eastern, or "Asian" country. Similar images of Israeli society and culture as Eastern (i.e., backward) vis-à-vis Russia and Ukraine as parts of Europe (i.e., advanced, enlightened, Western) often surfaced in oral histories of Russian immigrants collected by Fialkova and Yelenevskaya (2004b). Olga Gershenson (2005) reflects on the place of Gesher—Russian Theater company regarded by many critics as the best Israeli theatre—as an agent of "cultural colonization" of "immature" culture of the "natives in a banana republic" by refined theatrical elite, setting the high standards of European performing arts in the "backward" Middle East. At the same time, the condescending "colonizers" must permanently overcome their de facto inferior status of linguistic and cultural minority, having to switch almost entirely to Hebrew-language performances in order to attract the mainstream audience. Indeed, an interesting dynamic emerging between the migrant "cultural missionaries" and "colonized" natives, the latter often unaware of the patronizing nature of this relationship.

The sweeping critics judged Israeli culture mainly by its everyday "street" expressions, admittedly, not always pretty: the infamous chutzpah of the youth (e.g., loud and bold behavior on buses and trains, talking back to adults who intervene, etc.); blatant advances some men make at women; noise and litter in public places—all these facets of Israeli everyday modus vivendi are in dire contrast to the reserved, polite, and disciplined demeanor the former Soviet intelligentsia is used to. Reflecting the existing social stratification and cultural gaps in Israeli society, these jovial, pushy, and otherwise "uncultured" behaviors are mostly typical of Mizrahi Jews (see note 1), with whom Russian immigrants often cross paths in public transport, poorer neighborhoods, and unskilled workplaces they inhabit. This may partly explain the observation that the ideas of cultural superiority over Israelis are most often voiced by the least integrated immigrants, whose poor Hebrew precluded them from understanding the mainstream media and literature (e.g., few of them could name prominent Israeli writers, media figures, or musicians), who did not have any Israeli friends, and never worked in a white-collar Israeli organization—in brief had few encounters with middle-class Israeli culture. More often than not, these Russian "cultural supremacists" were none too refined themselves, nor were they plugged into the contemporary Russian culture itself, usually referring to the classic icons dating back to their school years (professing "the cult of Pushkin," in Yuri Slezkine [2004] words). Conversely, the immigrants who had socially and economically joined their native middle-class peers, were usually more curious and enthusiastic about Israeli arts, literature, and mass media, adding these new items to their existing cultural interests. It seems that the cultural superiority complex, which some Soviet immigrants proudly wear on their sleeve, is compensatory and defensive vis-à-vis their marginal status and transitory identity in the new society; Israeli psychological research generally supports this assertion (Mirsky, 1998; Horenczyk, 2000). American-Russian psychologist Vera Kishinevsky made similar observations on the sweeping negation of American culture they hardly knew among the less integrated Russians immigrants in the U.S. (personal communication). Socio-linguist Gasan Guseinov living in Germany also wryly noted that lamentations about the low cultural standards, sweeping materialism, and the lack of spiritual pursuits are typical motives found in educated Russian immigrants' discourse on the native German majority (Guseinov, 2005).

Mechanisms of Cultural Continuity

Two main channels help recent immigrants sustain their ties with Russian culture: transnational links with the FSU and other countries of the Russian-Jewish diaspora (Remennick, 2002a) and the creation of the versatile Russian cultural and media market in Israel. During the last decade, over 300 Russian book/video/ music stores have opened across Israel; about twenty newspapers and magazines in Russian are published, including several thick literary almanacs, exceeding the number of similar periodicals in Hebrew, English, and other languages. Although the Russian-language media increasingly focus on Israeli society and current events, the writing style, in-group humor, lingering cultural references, and other features reflect the Russian-Soviet journalistic tradition (Zilberg and Leshem, 1996; Elias, 2003). All pivotal political and cultural events in the FSU are imported to Israel by multiple Russian TV channels (received via cable or satellite in all

Russian-speaking homes); dozens of popular Russian musicians, theater companies, and stand-up comedians tour every year in large and small Israeli towns with Russian presence.

The recently established Israeli-Russian TV Channel (Israel Plus) not only depicts the life of the Israeli-Russian community but also serves as a cultural bridge to the mainstream society, politics, and culture. With the boost of the TV medium, the "Russian street" is now featuring its own celebrities and cultural elite from the ranks of politicians, performers, journalists, writers, etc. Some of these TV personalities wear several hats at a time: for example, the host of a popular weekend show *Sem' Sorok* on Israel Plus channel Jan Levenzon is also a leader of the national KVN team (see below), and owns a Russian restaurant bearing his name. Although some prominent Russian Jews such as Levenzon are quickly becoming a brand name, their aura exists mainly within the boundaries of the Russian community; few Hebrew speakers have ever heard of these names. Several radio channels in Russian cater to the different audiences: the official station REKA affiliated with *Kol' Israel* is popular with the older immigrant listeners, while younger Russians tune to the private stations featuring Russian and international popular music and interactive talk shows. Israeli-Russian theater companies, amateur and professional (the above-mentioned Gesher being the most popular one, playing in both Russian and Hebrew), artistic/literary societies, and Russian libraries serve as vessels of cultural continuity, also for the younger immigrant generation (Zilberg, 2000).

The Israeli literary scene features quite a few prominent authors who continue to write and publish in Russian, targeting both the one million Russian olim and broader audiences in the FSU. Israeli Russian writers and poets have a union of their own, which offers small grants to beginners for publishing their first book. Some authors made aliyah back in the 1970s (e.g., novelist Nina Voronel, satiric poet Igor Guberman, and literary critic Maya Kaganskaya), while others arrived with the last wave. Of the latter, perhaps the most prominent writers are Dina Rubina, Anatoly Alexin, and Gregory Kanovich. All the three had been well-known authors in the USSR; Alexin had even been a functionary of the Union of Soviet Writers, and one of most published authors writing about children and youth. While Kanovich's books had always depicted the lives of Lithuanian Jews, also when this topic was outlawed in Soviet literature, Rubina and Alexin had never touched upon Jewish subjects in their pre-migration books. In Israel, they rediscovered their Jewish side, and now all their writings revolve around Jewish and Israeli subjects: Alexin writes Isaac Bashevis Singer-style historic novels about Jewish families (e.g., *Pevzners' Saga*); Rubina published several hilarious novels and short story collections depicting the lives of Russian olim and their cultural gap with the Israeli society (Rubina, 1999). Her most recent book *Syndicate* is a sharp satire describing her experiences as a cultural liaison officer for the Sochnut office in Moscow, putting in a dubious light Jewish Agency's global bureaucracy and their activities as brokers of aliyah in the country where few interested Jews remain.

In brief, every Russian speaker in Israel can consume as much Russian culture as he or she can possibly digest and pay for. Indeed, my 2001 survey (Remennick, 2003a) showed that about 75 percent of Russian immigrants keep reading fiction in Russian, 97 percent watch Russian TV channels, and 63 percent listen to Russian radio stations. Over half attend Russian cultural events and tours of the Russian artists, often or sometimes (here high ticket costs are a barrier to attendance, but with lapsing time and raising income more immigrants can afford it). However, even among adult immigrants, Russian cultural interests are gradually expanding to incorporate Hebrew and international channels, books and shows (in translation or in original). Younger immigrants, the so-called 1.5 generation, make this shift faster, although many of them continue to read Russian books and listen to popular Russian music after many years of life in Israel (more on this below).

Transplantation of Unique Cultural Genres

Over the last fifteen years of their presence in Israel, Russian immigrants have transferred multiple templates of their cultural life in the FSU to Israeli soil. One vivid example is the establishment—back in the early years of aliyah—of the national Israeli KVN team, as well as many local teams based in cities or universities. KVN—Klub Veselyh i Nahodchivyh (The Witty and Savvy Club, in my free translation from Russian) has been an all-Soviet cultural hobby since the mid–1970s: musical-satiric shows by amateur (usually student) performers revolving around current events and framed as contests between two teams. The jury featuring famous stand-up comedians, musicians, and television personalities rated the jokes and musical scenes and voted for the winning team, which gradually rose from local to regional to national tournaments, all this competition making a prime-time show on the national television. This uniquely Russian/ Soviet cultural genre became a favorite pastime for many students and youth, sharpening their artistic talents and sense of humor, reinforcing team spirit, and always gleaning laughter from enthusiastic audiences. Over the 1990s, KVN teams mushroomed in all countries of post-communist migrations—U.S., Canada, Germany, and even Australia; these immigrant teams stage contests between themselves and with the teams from the cultural metropolis—the FSU. The topics featured in Israeli-Russian KVN programs mirrored the encounter with the hosting society, and its misunderstanding, conflicts, and mutual stereotypes (e.g., a joke from a 1993 show: "Question: Why do Israeli men wear sandals all year round? Answer: Because it helps them count to twenty"). At the same time, these festivals of humor attested to the growing Israelization of young Russian immigrants, including over time multiple Hebrew cultural icons and idioms (see more on Israeli KVN contests in Falkova, 2005).

Another remarkable example of continuity of the old cultural genres in the Russian diasporic life is the tradition of KSP (Russian acronym for Club of Amateur Song), where self-made composers and poets perform their songs with guitar accompaniment, usually in the frame of popular open-air festivals going on for days and continuing on nights near bonfires. This old Soviet dissident tradition dates back to the post-Thaw period when it emerged as a form of the intelligentsia's protest against the relentless regime, with its officially approved sterile popular music. The genre soon caught up with the broad public (disseminated by the newly available tape recorders) and amateur songs with their uncensored lyrics became an indispensable part of social gatherings and wild-nature tourism, the main form of spending vacations for the Soviet intelligentsia. The political content of the songs was complemented over time with lyrical, satiric, and romantic motifs, featuring such late classics as Alexander Galich, Vladimir Vysotsky, and Bulat Okudjava, and current stars such as Yuli Kim, Mikhail Sherbakov, Ivasi Duet, Timur Shaov, Michael Volkov, and others. Some of these authors and singers live in Israel (e.g., Volkov and Kim), others come to tour from Russia; many other young talents, yet unknown, are inspired by this old intellectual and musical "bard" tradition lingering from the Soviet past but constantly evolving. As with

KVN tournaments, KSP festivals spread across the global Russian-speaking community, featuring new styles and authors, gradually incorporating local topics, languages, and cultural symbols of the host societies.

Another example of typically Russian cultural hobbies transferred to Israel (and other countries) are intellectual contests where individual players or competing teams tackle difficult questions, demonstrating their erudition in history, science, literature, politics, and the arts. The blueprint of this genre was TV show *Chto-Gde-Kogda*? (What? Where? When?), that first appeared on Soviet TV in the late 1970s and had probably been molded as "our answer" to American quiz shows but with a higher intellectual content. Many immigrants, adults and youths alike, are still carefully watching Russian intellectual games on TV, and some participate in on-line and live contests blueprinted on *Chto-Gde-Kogda?*, held in local schools, colleges, and community centers. About 670 teams of this brain-ring game have been registered in 2002 by the international Russian-language site www.amik.ru in the FSU countries and in the Russian-speaking immigrant communities (Yelenevskaya, 2005). The tough questions included in these games also evolve, embracing more elements of the local Israeli agenda (and respective local agendas in other host countries).

The Role of ru.net

Last but not least on the Israeli-Russian cultural and media menu is the global kingdom of Russian Internet, spanning both the metropolis and all the diasporic countries (see Fialkova, 2005 for a detailed study). Younger generations of computer-literate Russian immigrants in Israel and in the West rely on a host of websites found on ru.net, operating in the FSU itself (e.g., www.lenta.ru) and on the locally maintained diasporic sites, whose address often follows a similar template (e.g. www.russianlondon, www.russianboston, etc.) for information, dating, social support, and entertainment. The largest Israeli-Russian web-portal is www.souz.co.il, featuring links to multiple other web-pages in Russian, Hebrew, and English. Russian web space, maintained in the FSU but geared to the global Russian-speaking public, includes governmental sites, media portals, on-line newspapers, literary magazines, film libraries, and more. For example, one can download most classic and many contemporary Russian movies from on-line movie sites and enjoy a trip to one's past from one's current home in Tel Aviv, Chicago, or Melbourne. In most countries of Russian immigration, the Internet portals are quickly becoming bilingual (Russian-Hebrew, Russian-English, Russian-German) as for many young surfers reading and writing in Russian only is becoming tedious. Due to its efficiency in real-time communications, the Russian cyber-community came to form a backbone of the incipient post-Soviet diaspora (I am using the term in the most inclusive sense, referring to dispersed minority groups who can trace their mutual origins to a country or area other than that in which they reside—Safran, 1999). In the virtual world of Russian Internet (whether its domain name ends with .ru, .il, .com, .gov, .de, .ca, etc.) immigrants' primary identity is that of Russian-speakers and bearers of Russian culture, regardless of specific ethnic background that allowed them to become "return migrants" in Israel, Germany, Greece, and Finland or refugees in North America. The linguistic and cultural affinity allows the residents of the virtual diasporic space to find common ground despite the diversity of their current experiences in different host countries.

To conclude, despite the apparent tendency of Russian Israelis for linguistic and cultural autonomy, after fifteen years of life in Israel the cultural artifacts produced on the so-called Russian street manifest clear signs of influence if not hybridization with the mainstream Hebrew culture. Reflecting its hegemonic status, the Hebrew media and cultural world is much less aware and receptive of the elements of Russian culture carried by the immigrants, which it stubbornly refuses to see as superior. If anything, Israeli popular culture is mainly shaped by Americanization and global unification of musical styles, TV journalism, entertainment, and fashion. Russian performers and theater companies exist on the cultural margins and gain recognition with the mainstream public only when they switch into Hebrew (the Gesher Theater and opera singer Evgeny Shapovalov are prominent examples of success upon conversion). Russian Israelis enjoy rich choices on their cultural menu embracing Israeli, Russian, and global items. Would they prefer Habima (Israel's oldest national theater) to Gesher; *Yediot Aharonot* to *Vesti* (the largest quality Russian newspaper) or would they reject both for the sake of CNN, BBC or MTV? Would they watch Russian, American, Mexican, or Israeli sitcoms and serials? These choices multiply with younger age, better facility with the languages, and availability of spare time and expendable income. The studies that looked into the patterns of cultural consumption (Remennick, 2003a; Feldman, 2003) suggest that exclusive orientation toward both imported and locally produced Russian culture typifies older immigrants, especially those living in Russian residential enclaves and/or working in the ethnic economy. Younger immigrants, as well as more integrated and economically successful ones regardless of age, are more selective in their choice of Russian cultural products and clearly drift towards Israeli and global-oriented cultural consumption.

Diversification of Social Networks: Who are Your Friends?

While immigrants meet members of the host society in the public domain (workplace, studies, social institutions), their informal personal networks usually remain co-ethnic. The clear divide between formal and informal networks seems to be a universal facet of immigrant experience. Many researchers also agree that the gradual inclusion of natives in immigrants' personal social networks is an important indicator of an ongoing integration process (Epstein and Kheimets, 2000a; Nauck, 2001; Portes and Rumbaut, 2001). A similar divide between formal and informal networks was found in my survey among Russian Israelis (Remennick, 2003a). About 82 percent of the survey respondents said they preferred to spend leisure with their Russian friends and acquaintances, while 16 percent had a mixed circle of friends, and only 2 percent spent time outside work mainly with Israeli friends. Immigrants' personal networks also included family members and friends who stayed in the former Soviet Union or migrated to Western countries. About 70 percent of respondents said that they kept in touch with their relatives and friends abroad, regularly or sometimes, by means of phone calls, letters, e-mail, and mutual visits. These transnational connections within the Russian-Jewish diaspora significantly contributed to the maintenance of Russian cultural and linguistic continuity (Remennick, 2002a, 2004c).

Women and men were similar in their informal socializing patterns, with women reporting somewhat more Hebrew-speaking contacts, probably reflecting (and further reinforcing) their more fluent Hebrew. The in-depth study of gender differences in social adjustment among 150 immigrant couples (Remennick, 2005b) has pointed to women's greater proneness to embark on new friendships, both with co-ethnic and other Israeli women, as well as greater variability in the forms of leisure spent together with these friends. Women more often spent time out of home, visiting various cultural events, shopping, chatting in cafes, and enjoying the beach with their female friends, while men more often preferred to stay at home, tend to their car or work on the computer, watch television, and sometimes host a male friend with a beer in the living room. Women had acquired on the average more new friends in Israel than did their male partners, and they were usually those who initiated friendship between couples, including joint hiking and outings. Reflecting greater versatility and intensity of women's contact with other women, including their Israeli peers, they were more prone to social learning and faster change in their lifestyle, tastes, and ways of dressing, vis-à-vis their male partners.

As for the age differences, younger immigrants tended to include local peers in their informal networks (about 40 percent said they spent their free time with both Russian and Israeli friends, and 10 percent—mainly with Israeli friends). With advancing age, the share of non-immigrant contacts and friends went down, to the minimum of 2–3 percent among the oldest immigrants (aged 65+), in line with decreasing Hebrew proficiency. Respondents, who had white-collar occupations and met Israelis through work, reported more local contacts also in the informal realm (25 percent had a mixed circle of friends and 9 percent preferred Israelis to Russians—vs. 16 percent and 2 percent in the general sample). Besides Hebrew skills, the presence of school-age children in the respondents' households was a positive predictor of having more contact with the natives, probably via children's classmates and other local friends, their parents, and teachers. Among parents of schoolchildren, 27 percent reported spending time with Israeli friends and acquaintance, vs. 16 percent in the general sample (Remennick, 2003a; 2004c).

Another indicator of the social insertion of Russian-speakers into the mainstream are romantic relationships with local partners, both actual and possible. Only 12 percent (15 percent of the women and 9 percent of the men) reported having ever been involved in such a relationship and 22 percent thought it was possible for them in the future, while 25 percent were not sure and 54 percent responded negatively. Most respondents who have had relationships with non-immigrant Israelis noted that they were short-lived, and only 2 percent (all women) had a permanent Hebrew-speaking partner or husband. Understandably, most reported relationships with Hebrew-speakers clustered in the age bracket of less than forty-five, peaking at 30–34 percent in the age group twenty-five to thirty-four. Older immigrants had low chances for meeting a local partner and developing a relationship, reflecting both their poor Hebrew and social isolation from the mainstream. A similar distribution of answers by age and gender was found in response to the question about the potential romantic liaisons with members of the host society.

Trying to glean a better understanding of this finding, I conducted a subsequent focus-group research among Russian- and Hebrew-speaking students on four Israeli campuses (Remennick, 2005a). It has shown that among younger Israelis too cross-cultural relationships between Russian immigrants and Israeli-born youths were uncommon, with most such couples featuring a Russian-speaking woman and an Israeli man. Trying to discern the reasons for higher popularity of Russian women vis-à-vis Russian men as dates and potential spouses, I realized that complex interplay between gender role stereotypes and social status of immigrants was at work. Russian immigrant women are perceived by Israeli men as attractive partners due to their greater compliance with the feminine gender role (passive, easy to please, prioritizing family and motherhood over independence and career), while Russian men are unpopular among young Israeli women (and unwilling to pursue them in turn) precisely for the same reason, that is, these men's attempt to adhere to the traditional, active and assertive, male role in courtship. Since the masculine role in dating is by definition more demanding in terms of personal and financial resources, these immigrant men feel inferior, unable to meet the expectations they ascribe to established Israeli women due to their built-in disadvantage in the new social context: faulty Hebrew, poor familiarity with Israeli youth culture, low income, and no residence of their own. As a result, Russian men prefer to "play it safe," seeking almost exclusively in-group dating partners, while Russian women's choices include both immigrant and native men. Apparently, traditional femininity still "sells well" on both in-group and out-group "romantic marketplace." Some Israeli men feeling challenged by their "assertive, tough, and demanding" Israeli female peers may prefer immigrant women, appearing more easy-going and compliant (time will show if this image is true).

Last but not least, some comment is due on the social relations between Jews and non-Jews of Soviet origin living side by side on the Israeli "Russian street." In general terms, the Russian-speaking community manifests an ironic reverse twist on the relations between Jews and Slavs in the USSR, whereby non-Jews in Israel became somewhat suspect if not second-class citizens denied some basic civil rights (Yelenevskaya and Fialkova, 2005). The non-Jewish Russian camp is very diverse, but only the insiders grasp its internal boundaries; native Israelis usually perceive all Russian speakers as a single category. In demographic terms, the non-Jewish group is constantly growing on account of the recent olim (who can have just one Jewish grandparent, or forged Jewish identity, and bring along their spouses and children), as well as labor migrants from the FSU. The dilution of the "Jewish element" also entails the change of the social profile towards the less educated and poorly adjusted former Soviets. One group includes non-Jews (most commonly Russians, Ukrainians, and Armenians) who came as spouses and children of Jews, as well as part-Jews and their families entitled for aliyah and citizenship. They are largely an integral part of Russian Jewry; many Russian wives of Jews underwent a difficult Orthodox conversion, and some became more observant than their Jewish-born counterparts. On the whole, non-Jewish wives of Jews seem to be economically and socially well integrated, with the non-Jewish husbands falling somewhat behind (reflecting the afore-mentioned gender gap in language and social skills).

Another group includes former Soviets with dated tourist visas working in menial service jobs (work for "tourists" is advertised by every Russian newspaper) and guest workers from Ukraine and Moldova working in construction sites, agriculture, cleaning, and other unskilled jobs. The latter two groups largely arrived after 1995 and are typified by low educational attainment, poor knowledge of Hebrew, and life on the social and economic margins, working in the cash economy and forming a new Russian-speaking underclass. The relations between Jews and non-Jews are largely shaped by their differential social status; for example, working middle-class Jewish women often hire Russian-speaking "tourists" as cleaners or gardeners. Those of the non-Jewish olim who succeeded in their careers and entered Israeli-Russian middle-class, usually blend well with the rest and no longer change their Russian last names; thus, many TV personalities on the Israel Plus channel are Slavic in name and appearance—the most tangible sign of their social inclusion. Religion was not an issue before 1995, when most olim, Jews and non-Jews alike, were atheists. Reflecting the religious revival in the FSU in the second half of the 1990s, a large number of non-Jews entering Israel identified themselves as Christian and now frequents Orthodox, Baptist, and Ukrainian Catholic churches mushrooming across the country. The increasing presence of underclass Slavic immigrants or temporary workers is reflected in the higher rates of heavy drinking, the appearance of street gangs and inter-group violence, and shocking elements of anti-Semitic organization and propaganda. The underground group by the name of Slavic Union is deemed responsible for anti-Jewish graffiti and crosses painted on public buildings, as well reported assaults on elderly Jews in several towns (retrieved from Web portal www.souz.co.il).

Thus, Soviet immigrants manifest the trend toward in-group preference in personal relationships, both friendly and romantic, found among most immigrant groups that face economic and cultural gap to the hegemonic majority (Portes and Rumbaut, 2001; Smolitz et al., 2001). Yet, women, especially younger women, are more willing to embark on new relationships and explore new social opportunities than fellow male immigrants, with resulting broader circle of native contacts and more expedient acculturation. It seems that their greater social skills and propensity for exploration of the new milieu make resettlement a more positive psychosocial experience for women than for men, despite the fact that women often face greater occupational downgrading and role overburden (Remennick, 2005b). The relations between Jews and non-Jews among the immigrants are largely shaped by their social-class affiliation and the extent of social incorporation; yet there are some new signs of the emerging religious antagonism between Jews and Slavs living in Israel.

Political Participation, Citizenship, and Military Service

Soviet Jews, Zionism, and Political Location on the Israeli Map

The historic affair between Russian Jewry and the classic Labor Zionist doctrine peaked in the early twentieth century, when many prominent Russian Jews came to Palestine to build the Jewish national home; all but a few of the founding fathers of the state had been born in the Russian Empire and spoke Russian, Polish, and Yiddish as their main languages. Their children and grandchildren formed the first generations of sabras—brave and assertive, direct and confident, farmers and soldiers, businessmen and politicians of the new kind, who shed the humiliations of *galut* (diasporic life) and the ashes of Auschwitz to start a new nation from scratch (Kimmerlng, 2001; Weissbrod, 2002). They no longer spoke galut languages but only Hebrew; the volumes of Pushkin and Chekhov were discarded from their bookshelves. By the late 1960s, only the melodies of the kibbutz generation songs borrowed from the Soviet musical repertoire (with the lyrics adapted and translated into Hebrew) remained the Russian cultural legacy of the country. The wave of Soviet immigrants, who escaped the Soviet Union during the 1970s and chose Israel as their destination (when they could go anywhere) was also of Zionist persuasion, willingly learned Hebrew and rapidly joined the Jewish mainstream. By the mid–1980s, the link between Soviet Jews and Israel had been almost fully severed by the information vacuum and venomous anti-Zionist propaganda. Only a few enthusiasts among the refusniks still wanted to learn Hebrew and make aliyah. The masses of Jews who embarked on emigration after 1989, when the USSR opened its gates and all Western countries hastily locked theirs, found themselves in Israel not because of their Zionist aspirations, but because Israel was the only country providing them with unconditional shelter and support.

Let me remind the reader that the Israeli polity had been founded as a social democracy, and socialist Labor party (first Mapai, then Avoda) remained in power until the late 1970s. In 1977, Menachem Begin's Likud first challenged its ideological and economic hegemony, as well as Ashkenazi dominance itself, by awakening masses of Mizrahi Jews to political activism. Yet, despite changes of government, the remnants of socialist ideology of the founding fathers lingered much longer in the form of a large public sector and centralized management of the economy, omnipotent trade unions, socialized medicine, and a developed welfare state. With the increasing role of the Likud and other right-wing parties in Israeli politics, the socialist foundations of the state and economy gradually deteriorated, coinciding with the demise of traditional industries (textile, garment, plastic, etc.), and growing unemployment (Goldscheider, 1996). During the late 1990s and early 2000s the series of neo-liberal reforms initiated by Benjamin Netanyahu have led to the growing socio-economic gaps and shrinking welfare support of recent immigrants and disadvantaged groups. On the political scene, the failure of the 1993 Oslo initiative and the aggravation of Israeli-Palestinian relations, with the increasing pace of Arab terror attacks and Israeli retaliations, caused a major disappointment in the peace process and a drift of Israeli public to the hawkish right, perceived as the only force able to provide basic security. Since Yitzhak Rabin's assassination in November 1995, most Israelis have consistently voted for the right-wing coalitions and prime ministers (with a brief exception of Ehud Barak's unsuccessful term in 1999–2000).

This overview of the general political landscape of Israel sets the stage for understanding the political affiliations of Russian immigrants. It had been shaped by a unique syndrome ensuing from their Soviet past and including such traits as dislike of socialism in any form, mistrust of the state and its institutions, pragmatism in political choices, and oftentimes espousal of a hard-line republican doctrine as a strange twist of totalitarian consciousness (the latter is more typical of the older generations). The general rejection of any macro-ideology and ideological indoctrination, political and civil apathy, and retreat into private life are augmented by the negation of the socialized forms of government. These "allergies" are understandable psychosocial reactions to the decades of life under state socialism with its forced unification of citizens in poverty and mediocrity, interference in private life, ineffective economy, and omnipresent hypocrisy and corruption (Khanin, 2000; Mondak and Gearing, 2003). Placed in this perspective, the consistent right-wing and anti-Labor orientation of most former Soviet immigrants in Israel becomes easier to explain. Many external expressions of the socialist politics in Israel of the late 1980s and early 1990s—protectionist policies by Histadrut (General Trade Union) de facto barring of new immigrants from secure jobs in the public sector and large governmental companies; endless strikes by every possible occupational group from doctors and nurses to bus drivers and junk collectors making everyday life difficult; long waiting lists and crowded clinics in the Histadrut-owned General Sick Fund, the major provider of health care; and finally the familiar socialist rhetoric and symbolic arsenal (complete with red banners and singing of "The International" at meetings) still used by the Israeli Labor in the early 1990s—formed together a strong deterrent from joining the left-wing camp. In the words of one informant, as architect from Leningrad in his mid-fifties, "In Israel, we soon realized what happened: we traded one type of Socialism for the other, with a Zionist streak and protection of long-standing Ashkenazi privileges. Can't we just be spared any ideology and live our lives as private persons?"

However, in Israel it is hardly possible to stay away from any ideological and political engagement whatsoever—the flow of current evens is intense and dynamic, and has an immediate impact on everyone's life. Given their immediate access to citizenship, the newcomers also had to decide how to vote in the elections, the first of which came as early as 1992, when Russian olim still had little understanding of the Israeli political landscape. At first, their voting behavior was shaped by pragmatic interests rather than ideological convictions: politicians who promised them greater benefits and support would get their votes (this explains the vote for Rabin in 1992). Ever since this early election campaign, the Israeli politicians realized the huge electoral potential of Russian aliyah, not only due to its demographic size but also high turnout in elections. Olim have also got the taste of their tangible political power in a small country and saw that their votes can make a difference, vis-à-vis their Soviet past when the chief mantra was *"I am a drop in the sea, nothing depends on me."* In every subsequent election campaign, Russian-speaking voters have been showered by politicians' speeches and custom-made media messages geared to glean their votes. Yet, it took them several years of turmoil and indecision to finally occupy their stable position on the center-to-right end of the Israeli political spectrum. Ever since the 1996 elections in the wake of Rabin's murder, Russian immigrants voted either for Likud or ethnic lobby parties of their own, all but one of them right wing (Khanin, 2000; Shumsky, 2002; Feldman, 2003; Al-Haj, 2004). Supporting neo-liberal politicians, they inadvertently spearheaded the attack on the welfare state, from which many of them benefited during times of unemployment, as single parents, the disabled, and the elderly. Like their co-ethnics in the U.S. voting Republican, Russian Jews in Israel often do not grasp the basic discrepancy between their political outlook and pragmatic interests as clients of the welfare state.

Besides their general anti-socialist outlook, two additional vectors have defined political choices of Russian immigrants: strong anti-Arab attitudes and a hawkish view of the conflict, and opposition to the religious influence in politics and society. Reflecting age-old tradition of imperial Russian chauvinism, former Soviet citizens generally manifest high levels of ethnic intolerance towards any minorities often labeled as inferior, hostile, and fraudulent. Although Jews themselves had been a traditional target of ethnic prejudice, they are not free of negative attitudes towards any racial, ethnic, or cultural "Others." In

Israel this ultimate "Other" are Muslim Arabs, who within pre–1967 Israeli borders are a minority of the same size as Russian Jews (20 percent), and form an absolute majority in the occupied Palestinian territories and in the surrounding Arab countries. The attitudes towards Arabs openly expressed by Soviet immigrants resemble those of the White Russians who had settled in the national republics during Soviet times towards the dark-skinned indigenous peoples of Asia and the Caucasus. Added to this cultural superiority complex is fear and hatred of the Arabs as the fifth column and potential collaborators with external Palestinians in the acts of terror and destruction in Israel (Yelenevskaya and Fialkova, 2004). I have already mentioned that anti-Arab motifs surface all the time in different genres of immigrant folklore (Yelenevskaya and Fialkova, 2005); they are clearly manifested in all attempts at ethnic mobilization and political activity of Russian immigrants: all prominent political parties they ever organized or took active part in (Israel be-Aliyah, Israel Beiteinu, Ehud Leumi) were against any territorial compromises, advocated unlimited use of force against Intifada rioters, and preserving the status of Israeli Arabs as second-class citizens (Al-Haj, 2002; Al-Haj, 2004). Although most would deny that in official surveys, in private conversations many Russian olim support the radical right's idea of the transfer, i.e., forced resettlement of the Arabs from Israel and Palestine to the neighboring Arab countries. The typical adage goes, "There are twenty-two Arab countries in the world, and just one tiny Israel for the Jews. There is no place for Arabs here." In recent surveys conducted by Israeli-Russian sociologists David Aptekman and Eliezer Feldman, between 15 to 22 percent of respondents said that in Israel they became Jewish nationalists (Feldman, 2003). Coming from a huge country with abundant natural resources, many former Soviets are acutely aware of the small size and high population density of Israel and are scared by any further shrinking of the country's borders and rapid natural increase of the Arab population.

Anti-religious attitudes are another dominant theme in the way Russian Jews relate to Israeli politics and social life. Reflecting their secular and often atheist background, the majority of Soviet Jews oppose close involvement of religious authorities in most aspects of everyday life and their gate-keeping role in the matters of civil status (marriage, divorce, registration of the newborn, burial). They also detest the monopoly of the Orthodox establishment in deciding who is Jewish and who is not on the grounds of the ancient Jewish legal code Halachah. To cite one middle-aged male informant, "Israeli Orthodoxy asserts that Jewishness and Judaism are one and the same thing, but they are not; there is much more to being a Jew than praying three times a day and keeping kosher. Although I never go to a synagogue, I am as Jewish as they are, if not more." Russian immigrants object to the proliferation of yeshivas and synagogues in the times when schools, hospitals, and other salient public services are declining; they dislike the routing of taxpayers money to support of large Orthodox families averaging eight children, which further encourages unlimited fertility and poverty in this sector. They find it unfair that young Orthodox men spend their time studying Torah while their own sons serve long years in the military, defending the country and risking their lives. There is a small minority of Russian Jews (6–8 percent, in my estimate) who converted to Orthodox Judaism (*baalei tshuva*) or at least chose a religious way of life, among them some prominent academics and journalists

In brief, in the matters of separation between religion and the state Russian olim largely join forces with the secular-liberal camp; the party most closely reflecting their political views was Shinui (Change). Headed by a senior Israeli journalist Tommy Lapid, Shinui combined the center-to-right wing stance in the Arab-Israeli conflict with strong anti-Orthodox message. The electoral success of Shinui in the 2002 elections (fourteen Knesset seats) reflected, among other factors, a massive Russian vote on its behalf (Feldman, 2003). Yet, loud anti-clerical rhetoric of Shinui's leaders did not translate into a tangible legislative breakthrough: civil marriage is still non-existent and religious parties are as strong as ever. In the last Knesset elections of 2006, Shinui split into two weak factions due to internal conflicts and got few votes. A minority of Russian Jews (around 12–15 percent in my estimate) espouse universal liberal values and side with the Israeli Left in the Arab-Israeli conflict, recognizing Palestinians' human and civil rights, including their right to statehood, and supporting full equality of Jews and Arabs within the borders of Israel. An anti-Orthodox stance is an important part of this paradigm: liberal olim espouse Jewish pluralism, reduction of the public funding of Orthodox institutions, and ultimately the separation between the State and Religion. These olim usually vote for Meretz party as chief representative of the above-said aspirations, since the mainstream Israeli Labor (Avoda) has an all too strong association with orthodox socialist and trade-unionist values, especially after Amir Peretz had been elected as its leader. (Democratic Choice headed by Roman Bronfman has merged with Meretz after 2002 electoral failure and did not participate in the last elections). Yet, both minorities—baalei tshuva on one end and the radical left on the other—do not make a significant impact on the political moods of the "Russian street." The political outlook of most Russian Israelis can be summed up as three antis: anti-socialist, anti-Arab/Moslem, and anti-religious. Most of them agree on these three negative tenets, while their positive political beliefs may broadly vary, including a large portion of those with no clear political outlook at all.

From Apathy to Activism: Participation in Political Movements and Civil Organizations

In her 1993 book with the ominous title *A Community in Spite of Itself*, anthropologist Fran Markowitz described the lifestyle of Soviet Jews in Brooklyn, typified by the lack of formal organizations but proliferation of informal social networks immigrants heavily relied on both in business and in private matters. Indeed, the Soviet legacy of forced collectivism created lingering dislike of any formal associations and self-proclaimed activists, always presumed to have a hidden self-interest (Gold, 1997). The mistrust of formal organizations and social apathy are common among all citizens of the former Socialist bloc, which significantly hinders developing of the civil society in the successor states (Mondak and Gearing, 2003). However, the pressing needs of resettlement and conflicts with Israeli bureaucracy over their economic and civil rights soon compelled Soviet Jews to organize into self-help groups and political movements to lobby together for their interests. Signs of community formation among Russian Israelis first appeared in the mid–1990s, when the initial adaptation stress and cultural gap with the mainstream have subsided. By this time, former Soviets have also realized the ethnic-sectarian nature of Israeli politics: immigrant groups can only bargain for a greater chunk of public resources when they mobilize their ethnic power (Al-Haj, 2002, Al-Haj, 2004; Shumsky, 2002). In 1994 a well-known Soviet Jewish dissident and refusnik Natan Sharansky united small local movements of Russian olim into the first Israeli-Russian party Israel be-Aliyah, which engaged several prominent immigrant intellectuals as its leaders and set the goal of winning seats in the Knesset. Backed up by some 300,000 immigrant votes in the 1996 elections, Sharansky and his team indeed won six seats in the 120-member national parliament. Israel be-Aliyah represented a secular centrist orientation and avoided more radical nationalist messages; soon it was complemented by the new party of a radical anti-Arab orientation headed by Avigdor Liberman (Nash Dom Israel in Russian– Our Home Israel). Representing the liberal-left alternative, another immigrant politician Roman Bronfman left Sharansky's party to form the one of his own (Democraticheskii Vybor—Democratic Choice).

Thus, the Russian political spectrum came to reflect the macro-level one, but with the clear bias to the right. The activities of immigrant politicians, and their visibility in the Russian and mainstream Israeli media, peaked in the mid to late 1990s, but started to lose momentum by the early 2000s. The immigrant voters were disappointed by the lack of tangible achievements of their politicians in the contest with religious establishment (e.g., the civil marriage is still nonexistent in Israel, and mixed couples have to travel abroad to get married), and few economic improvements in their living standards (e.g., public or subsidized housing is still in great shortage). The olim voters realized that their alleged representatives strive mainly for keeping their Knesset seats and personal benefits, like most other Israeli politicians (general disrepute of politicians, Knesset, and representative democracy is typical of the Israeli public these days). Thus, the outburst of Russian ethnic politics came to an end by the 2002 elections, when the majority of Russian immigrants voted for the mainstream Israeli parties (mainly Likud, Shinui, and Ehud Leumi) while Sheranky's party won only two seats. Soon after that three immigrant parties merged with the mainstream parties of the relevant orientation as immigrant factions. I am writing these lines soon after the March 2006 Knesset Elections. Most Russian immigrants with moderate-centrist views voted for Kadima (Ehud Olmert) and the right-wing ones opted for Nash Dom Israel (Avigdor Liberman), with a growing number of olim voters (around 25 percent) shunning away from the elections altogether. Both Kadima and Likud have recruited candidates of Russian origin in their lists, hoping to attract olim voters, while the Left did not invest in such an effort. As a result the 17th Knesset is going to have around eight members representing Russian immigrants (out of 120 seats), mainly belonging to the right-center wing of the Coalition.

Apart from political parties, the community life of the "Russian street" featured several voluntary associations that started from local activist groups and gradually achieved national scope. The most prominent of them is the Union of the Veterans of the Great Patriotic War (i.e., World War II on the USSR territory, 1941–1945) a national umbrella organization that embraces dozens of local veteran societies and clubs. The Union organized various social and cultural activities for its members, and its most prominent achievement has been the inclusion of May 9 (the official Victory Day in the USSR) in Israel's national holiday calendar. Due to the veteran's persistent public outreach efforts, more native Israelis are aware today of the Soviet Union's decisive role in the victory over the Nazis, and specifically of the salient contribution of the Jewish soldiers and officers in the war's outcome. The message is, Jews had been warriors, not just Holocaust victims. Every year on May 9 the former Soviet veterans organize a march in the central cities, a mini-version of the Victory Parade staged in the Red Square, featuring gray-haired men and women in their military uniforms with the military medals shining in the sun. Other Russian immigrant organizations that gained national recognition include SOS Chernobyl, representing the interests of some 140,000 olim who came from the regions in the Ukraine, Belorussia, and Russia affected by the radioactive fallout in the wake of 1986 Chernobyl nuclear disaster, among them about 1,200 who worked as cleaners (liquidators) at the explosion site and got exposed to extreme levels of radiation (Remennick, 2002c). These immigrants considered themselves entitled in Israel to special benefits they had received as victims of radioactivity in their home countries, including tax reductions, special medical follow-up, free medications, vacations in state-sponsored resorts, etc. Many of Chernobyl-affected immigrants suffered from stress rather than physical diseases, while their true individual exposure to radiation was impossible to prove and measure; after long bureaucratic struggle with Israeli authorities (Ministries of Health and Immigrant Absorption) their case was lost. Some of them managed (with SOS Chernobyl's aid) to win compensation from the Ukraine, while others had to give up and simply get on with their new lives. By the late 1990s this association quietly dissolved, but several new groups advocating the issues of health care and support of the immigrant patients (e.g., cancer victims) have emerged in its place.

Several successful organizational initiatives belonged to immigrant women, who got together to lobby for their interests as single mothers (The Israeli Single Parents Union) or as non-Jewish spouses of Jews (The Union of Mixed Families). After their initial attempts to lobby for economic benefits or civil rights on the political level have largely failed, these organizations redirected their activities to mutual support (e.g., free babysitting service for single mothers), legal aid (e.g., advice in the matters of divorce, child custody, and citizenship/residence rights for non-Jewish spouses, mostly women), and social activities (outings, child summer camps, etc.). Several major occupational groups of immigrants (e.g., engineers, doctors, teachers, and entrepreneurs) established loosely shaped unions that provide support in job search, legal advice, and mutual referrals of clients. Additional examples of olim associations include different *landsmanschaft* groups, bringing together migrants from specific areas and cities of the FSU.

A more militant group of Russian immigrants has coalesced in the early 2000s under the name of Battalion Aliyah—a voluntary militia consisting of the olim veterans of the Afghan and Chechen campaigns who were not drafted for the IDS service due to older age but wished to contribute their combat experience to Israel's defense. Although the Israel's Defense Ministry did not welcome this initiative, after some lobbying efforts by Russian politicians these militia units were allowed to serve as armed patrols around the Green Line and in the settlements of Gaza (now evacuated) and the West Bank. As a recent interview-based study by Zaika (2006) shows, Battalion Aliyah's members (mostly ethnic Russians, Ukrainians and other non-Jews) espouse an extreme right wing and anti-Arab views and see their voluntary service as an ultimate expression of their masculinity, patriotism, and superb combat skills based on ruthlessness to an enemy.

Finally, some cultural activities, such as the KSP and KVN clubs described above, can also be counted as olim organizations as they usually rent public premises to meet and have a fairly permanent core of leaders and members. The common problems faced by all these organizations include conflicts over leadership and difficulty in fundraising and collecting dues from the members. In sum, over the past decade former Soviet immigrants have demonstrated their ability to build alliances for the pursuit of their mutual goals, although most such organizations proved to be short-lived and prone to conflicts. The bulk of community life still happens on the grapevine, that is, via informal personal networking.

Israeli Russian Youth and the Military Service

Military service after completion of high school (age eighteen) in Israel is mandatory for both genders; exemptions are given only to the Orthodox youth (who can choose instead the "national service" in hospitals, old-age homes, and schools), as well as to those married and/or having children, and suffering from serious physical and mental illnesses. New immigrants are exempt from the mandatory service if they arrived in Israel after age seventeen (girls) and twenty-two (boys), but can be called for reserve military duty in times of need. Thus, most Russian immigrant youths who made aliyah during their school years are enlisted for the regular service duty along with all other Israeli youths. The normal duration of the service is three years for boys and two years for girls, but many remain in the military for longer periods as officers or contract workers. The girls almost never serve in combat units and mostly do secretarial, teaching, computing, intelligence, and other office work for the army.

Many recent Soviet immigrants (parents and youths alike) had negative attitudes towards the military service as their ideas about the army life were based on the experiences with the Soviet Army, indeed the worst possible place to be for a young man (especially a Jew). Back in the FSU, Jewish parents made heroic efforts to save their sons from the army via false medical certificates, bribes, even placements in mental hospitals—anything to rid them of the humiliation, violence of fellow soldiers and officers, and mortal danger of combat operations in Afghanistan, the Caucasus, and any number of other campaigns the Soviet Army had always been engaged in. The impending danger of recruitment had been a major reason for desperate attempts of young Jews to be admitted to any available college before age eighteen (i.e., straight after high school and regardless of their true interests or talents) because students were exempt from the military duty until graduation and then had only a short time to serve. The impending draft of the sons was rather often the reason of hurried decisions of Soviet Jews to emigrate to Israel as the only country with rapid entry process. The lingering trauma of the Soviet Army explained the reluctance of many young immigrants (and mainly their parents and grandparents!) to join the Israeli military. An additional predicament was the loss of potential provider for the family (often a single mother with another small child to support) for three long years. At the same time, many young immigrants, who came of age among their native peers, volunteered for the elite combat units, despite parental objections (Azariya and Kimmerling, 1998).

Over time, most parents came to terms with the need to live through their children's service as part of normative Israeliness, and the central component of youth socialization in this country. The Israeli Army is perhaps the only true melting pot of this mosaic society, a meeting place for the immigrants and natives, Ashkenazim and Mizrahim, the wealthy and the poor, white and black (Ethiopian Jews). Besides its main functions, the army offers many additional benefits for soldiers with disadvantaged social background: recent immigrants learn Hebrew, school dropouts can complete their matriculation studies, and most can join different tracks of vocational training that would be useful in their civilian life. Above all, the army is the cradle of most important social networks that would support Israelis throughout their lives (Azarya and Kimmerling, 1998). The moral spirit of the Israeli military is usually high and the plagues of the Soviet military (bullying of beginners by old-timers, officer rudeness and violence, poor nutrition and living conditions, shooting accidents) are not unheard of, but much less prevalent. In stark contrast with the Soviet Army, Israeli soldiers can go home for two to four weekends per month, and those in non-combat units can actually live at home and return to their base every morning. Yet, Israeli army inevitably reflects the larger society and its political schisms: one recent problem is the refusal movement among recruits and soldiers declining to serve in certain problem-ridden locations: policing the controlled Palestinian territories (rejected by the left-wing youths) and, most recently, evacuation of the Jewish settlements from Gaza and Samaria (rejected by the nationalist and religious soldiers). These young refusniks prefer imprisonment to participation in the violent actions that go against their beliefs.

During fifteen years after the Great Aliyah, soldiers and officers of Russian origin have been found in every path of the military service, comprising over 25 percent of the soldiers on the regular duty. Some of them start upscale military careers after service in elite combat units and completion of officers' courses. Many others are found among the repeat deserters and discipline breakers who frequent military prisons. The social profile of the latter category often includes poor social integration, no or little Hebrew skills, non-Jewish origin (including those proudly wearing crosses), low education and severe economic problems among the parents. The clusters of trouble-prone Russian soldiers appeared after the late 1990s: they represent the most recent arrivals from the FSU who came to the country during the last years of high school, did poorly or dropped out, and soon found themselves in the ranks of the army they detest, torn between the demands of the military discipline and the needs of their parents and siblings. Facing this new problem, the army revealed flexibility and understanding, offering these difficult soldiers psychological counseling, financial support, allowing them to combine service with part-time work, or releasing them altogether if unfit for service. Not so few immigrant soldiers fell in combat, which compelled their grieving parents to join the Israeli identity and collectivity, with its rituals of loss and mourning, on its saddest (but most valid) common ground.

Despite the proclaimed role of the IDF as the nation's chief melting pot, ethnic boundaries between the soldiers of different background and tenure in the country are very tangible, with Ethiopians and former Soviets of Caucasian and Asian origin being the most excluded groups (Shamai and Ilatov, 2001). Recent in-depth study by Eisikovits (2006) has shown that military service often fails to become a major integrative experience for the immigrant youths; neither does it endow them with a useful social network for the advancement in the future, the way it does for the sabras. Most of her informants stressed the pragmatic benefits they received in the Army, mainly in the form of skills and training, and seldom referred to the themes of patriotism, Israeli identity, or self-sacrifice. As fewer immigrant men volunteer for elite combat units (and/or do not score high enough on the tests to be recruited there), they often end up in service roles (drivers, cooks, etc.) doing routine manual work and surrounded by Israeli youths with disadvantaged backgrounds. Often they opted for these mundane tasks in order to serve close to home and contribute to their families' income. Their attitude to the service (influenced by their parents' antagonism to the military) was often passive and formal; they seldom tried to improve their performance by asking to be moved to another job, if dissatisfied, the way their Israeli peers would do. Young women were often better at using the social and professional opportunities offered by the army (within positions allotted to women), and their level of satisfaction was generally higher (Eisikovits, 2006).

On the Diversity of Russian Immigrant Experience:
Gender, Age, and Ethnicity

Individuals and families who left the FSU to resettle in Israel and in the West are extremely diverse, representing a cross-section of the huge and heterogeneous Soviet society. Personal socio-demographic characteristics play at least as important role in immigrant adjustment as do the structural and economic conditions of the host society. Although differential experiences of men and women, younger and older immigrants from different parts of the FSU have surfaced throughout our previous discussion, the present chapter will briefly highlight the key findings regarding these specific categories of former Soviet immigrants.

Breadwinners, Caregivers, and Sluts:
Russian Immigrant Women in Israel

Many times over the last decade of my research among Russian immigrants in Israel I turned to gender differences in integration, and especially to the challenges faced by the immigrant women.[11] Several surveys and multiple qualitative studies addressed the issues of premarital sexuality and family planning among young women (Remennick et al., 1995), professional careers of male and female immigrants (Remennick and Shtarkshall, 1997; Remennick, 2002b, 2003b; Remennick and Shakhar, 2003), chronic diseases and preventive behavior (Remennick, 1999b); utilization of social and medical services (Remennick, 1999c; Gross et al., 2001); attitudes towards abortion and its emotional aftermath (Remennick and Segal, 2001); multiple roles and emotional burnout among middle-aged women (Remennick, 2001), cross-cultural dating (Remennick, 2005a), and more. When these facets of immigrant women's lives are collated together, it becomes obvious that beside the problems of physical and psychosocial adjustment in the new country, common to both genders, women face an additional set of constraints evolving from cultural and normative differences in gender roles, especially in sexuality, fertility, and family life, which are usually viewed as the essence of femininity. In Russia, Israel, U.S., and in most other societies, sexual and reproductive issues are also perceived as moral, which puts female immigrants (usually seen as different if not deviant) in public spotlight and often inspires critical discourse in the media and other vessels of public opinion.

When minority women form a large and visible group, they often become the target of sexist attitudes and attacks. Their very presence triggers outbursts of patriarchal sentiments, normally repressed and hidden in the mainstream politically correct discourse.

The image of a Russian woman as an alien and exotic Other, stressing her sex appeal as a threat to local male mores, emerged as a key element in the popular discourse on the post–1989 immigration wave. Russian women had a special sex appeal for local men due to their "European traits": fair skin, blond hair, and a more gentle and "feminine" demeanor vis-à-vis tough and assertive sabras (Lemish, 2000). Such attributes of immigrant families as high prevalence of divorce, single motherhood, use of abortion for birth control, and low number of children got wide critical coverage in the Israeli media of the early 1990s, as in the mainstream Israeli society, traditional, family and child centered, these phenomena are still uncommon. In a nutshell, the verdict was that the long-expected Russian aliyah turned out to be "The aliyah of frauds, sluts, and welfare mothers" (Lemish, 2000). Making things worse for the ex-Soviet women, the latest Jewish emigration has coincided with an influx of illegal sex workers from the FSU via international organized crime channels. Post-communist states became the major world exporters of sex workers, and Israel one of the major destination countries due to sustained demand in sex services, huge profits gained by the pimps, and relative ease of smuggling women via the Egyptian border and other channels. Thus ever since the early 1990s Russian, Ukrainian, Moldavian, and other Russian-speaking women with outdated tourist visas, traded and detained by force by their owners, fill the massage parlors and nightclubs of Israeli cities. By association, any bearer of a Russian accent was perceived by some Israeli men as sexually available and looking for a native "patron." During their first years in Israel, women with a Russian accent have often been approached with blatant sexual offers in the street markets, public gardens or buses, in apartments they rent (by the owners), and, of course, in their new workplaces. This is not to say that local women are never treated similarly, but many of them perceive men's "joshing" as a natural expression of masculinity, and those who wish to resist it have cultural tools to do so. The term sexual harassment as such appeared in the Israeli media and legal discourse only recently, mainly as a result of American influence. This problem has suddenly been "discovered" by Israeli society and, once being named, sexual harassment proved to be common (Israeli and Bejaui-Fogel, 1997).

Single motherhood was another cause for negative stereotyping of Russian-speaking women. Due to high divorce rates among ex-Soviets (before and after migration), over 17 percent of all Israeli-Russian families are single-parent (CBS, 2000). Most of these are mothers with young children, often living together with one or both grandparents, a household type considered an oddity by native Israelis. Since single-parent families are relatively few in Israel (6 to 8 percent) and single mothers often cannot work full-time, they are viewed as "social cases by default" in need of public aid (Toren, 2003). Hence, immigrant single mothers had been defined at the outset as an expected welfare burden. Yet, soon it turned out that over 70 percent of them work full-time and show economic mobility similar to or higher than that of married women, relying on their parent's help with childcare and household chores. Apparently the social profile and human capital of Russian-Jewish single mothers is rather different from that of native Israeli ones (Adva Center, 2002).

While younger immigrant women often faced a venomous mix of sexual harassment and moral criticism, middle-aged women had to struggle with their multiple role overload, working long hours and taking care of both their children and aging parents (Remennick, 1999b, 2001). Relegated to the manual tier of the workforce (mostly eldercare and cleaning), many of these educated women have been doing service and care-giving work around the clock, first for wages and then at home. Their male partners, who often worked fewer hours, were still rather marginal in the home and only provided periodic instrumental help to their wives, who bore chief responsibility for the smooth running of the household and meeting everyone's needs. Hard physical effort and emotional burnout often caused deterioration of women's health, but their tight time budgets did not allow them to engage in self-care (visit doctors, go to the gym or aerobics classes, etc.) as they perceived themselves as care providers for their close ones, not themselves. Low health motivation and lack of preventive care could result in delayed diagnosis of cancer, heart disease, and other age-related illnesses (Remennick, 1999c).

Let me now offer several highlights from my most recent research among 150 couples of former Soviet immigrants of working age (thirty-sixty), which explored gender differences in the psychosocial adjustment by using both questionnaires and personal interviews for data collection (Remennick, 2005b). The results shed some new light on the differential ways men and women adjust to the challenge of making a fresh start in a new economic and social context. First of all, immigrants bring with them the legacies of their socialization and former life experiences in the FSU, where most women were as educated and economically active as men (Ashwin, 2002). Often facing severe occupational downgrading on the host marketplace as immigrants, men and women respond to it in different ways. Women proved to be more ready than men to trade their higher occupational status for pragmatic benefits of employment and some financial security. Driven by responsibility for their families, they were ready at the outset to undergo occupational change in any direction that would bring in a steady income. Converting to white-pink-or blue-collar occupations demanded on the Israeli market, these women revealed flexibility, ability to learn rapidly, and successful social networking within their new milieu. Women's greater adaptive potential in the new economic context of Israel resembles the stories of women's initiative, courage and flexibility in the feverish post-communist economies of Russia, the Ukraine, and other places of origin in the FSU, where many men found themselves on the economic and social margins while women had to assume full financial and logistic responsibility for family well-being (Ashwin, 2002; Ashwin and Lytkina, 2004).

Our findings suggest that men's response to the economic novelty and uncertainty tends to be more protracted and conservative, whereby their main effort is directed at former status preservation and career continuity, rather than immediate adjustment and financial survival. In the context of resettlement and cultural gap with the mainstream society, as well as saturated marketplace, this strategy often proves to be a dead end, especially for older and more senior (in the FSU) professionals. It often takes men more time to find an alternative occupational track in the semi-skilled sector, giving up their professional ambitions in the face of a new economic reality. When they finally found work, men often focused on the status-related, instrumental, and technical aspects of their occupation (the key source of their job satisfaction), while women more often appreciated the chance to learn new things and the work content as such, for example, being able to support people in need (in helping occupations), and developing new relationships with co-workers. Similar differences in the ways in which men and women make sense of their new (lower status) occupations have been shown in our study among Russian immigrant physicians who converted to physiotherapy (Remennick and Shakhar, 2003). Although female immigrant professionals in Israel have suffered greater downgrading in their social status, job terms and content of work, women's overall perceptions of their new work experiences are at least as positive as men's, and in some aspects their satisfaction from work is even higher. These findings point to greater flexibility and resilience of women in the occupational realm, their ability to act upon the old wisdom: When life hands you lemons, make lemonade. My research confirmed some earlier findings that immigrant women suffer more often from mood disturbances and score lower on optimism than men; they are also more sensitive to social isolation and the loss of old friends as a result of resettlement (see the study by Aroian et al., 2003, among Russian immigrants in the U.S.).

Yet, at the same time, women are more active than men in trying to improve their social milieu and rebuild their informal networks in the new country—this finding is supported by most research on gender and social support, showing that women have denser personal networks and invest more energy in socializing and friendships, compared to men (Dion and Dion, 2001; Liebler and Sandefur, 2002). Despite heavier burdens carried by the women due to their multiple roles, general indicators of psychological well-being and satisfaction with various aspects of life were rather similar between male and female partners, and in some respects women's responses were even more positive (e.g., regarding satisfaction with human relations at work and general adaptation in Israel). The in-depth interviews have reinforced our earlier findings (Remennick, 1999b) that women often are more resilient and better at mobilizing social support in coping with various life adversities, as well as more energetic and inventive in exploring new opportunities. Men often tend to be trapped in their past, grieving the loss of their former status and clinging to it as a source of identity; they are usually reluctant to change their lifestyles and slow in building relationships with their new social milieu.

The 1.5 generation Shopping for New Identity:
Between Russian and Israeli

The research on the so-called 1.5 generation (i.e., immigrant children and adolescents born in the country of origin) is burgeoning, as the futures of immigrant youth will define the place and role of ethnic minorities in the multicultural societies. Socio-cultural and psychological experiences of the 1.5 generation are quite unique, and its members often face vexing questions of loyalty and affiliation, especially when the cultural gap between the immigrants and the hosts is vast enough (Portes and Rumbaut, 2001). In the early 2000s, I conducted an exploratory study of the integration process among the 1.5 generation of Russian immigrant students who moved from the FSU to Israel as teenagers, that is, between the ages of eleven and eighteen. This group of immigrants is of special interest due to its intermediate position on the generation scale and the fact that it belongs to the large and well-established ethno-cultural minority whose adult members cherish their language and cultural heritage. For immigrant adolescents the cultural conflict between past and present is the most potent, given that they have spent their initial formative years in the Russian school system, fluently read and write in Russian, and are accustomed to the cultural standards of the Russian-Jewish intellectual milieu (Lerner, 1999; Lomsky Feder and Rapoport, 2001). Many young immigrants, especially coming from the major urban centers of the FSU, strongly identify with the norms of academic excellence espoused by their parents and regard education as their chief path to upward mobility in Israel (Eisikovits, 2000; Rapoport and Lomsky Feder, 2002). They experience cultural transition in a complex way, marked by ambivalence and identity split, augmented by the common coming-of-age dramas. Psychosocial research among young Russian immigrants in Israel, U.S., Germany, Finland, and other host countries have shown that the intersection of personal and sexual maturation with challenges of resettlement and facing a different youth culture coalesce into a harsh experience for many youngsters (Mirsky and Kaushinski, 1989; Kraemer et al., 1995; Lerner, 1999; Jasinskaja-Lahti and Liebkind, 1999; Kasinitz et al., 2001; Steinbach, 2001).

The interested reader can find a detailed discussion of this issue in my article in *Diaspora* (Remennick, 2003e). The bottom line is that, by any measures of social integration, the locations of the 1.5 generation are where I expected them to be—in the middle between the Russian and Israeli axes. The key determinants of Israeliness vs. Russianness were younger age at migration (the cutoff point being around the age of fourteen), residence in a mixed rather than co-ethnic neighborhood, attending a better school, and socio-economic mobility of the parents. Those who came to Israel as older adolescents, often against their will, leaving behind friends and familiar milieu, typically made a slower transition towards Israeli youth culture and viewed it very critically. As with other young immigrants (Portes and Rumbaut, 2001), the integration process of Russian-speaking youth in Israel can be described as segmented: in some realms/segments of their lives young immigrants are well-adjusted and play by the local rules, while in others they stick to their Russian mentality and habits. Most young "Russians" successfully navigate various Israeli institutions (including the military and universities) and exhibit good adaptive skills necessary for their future upward mobility: Hebrew proficiency, understanding of local social codes, instrumental contacts with Israeli peers and supervisors.

However, in the private segment of their lives most stay firmly plugged into their co-ethnic circle, which serves as the key provider of social support and a safety net in case of trouble. Intimate relationships, romantic and friendly, arise mostly within immigrant social networks (Remennick, 2005a). Apparently, it is difficult to juxtapose the case of Russian speakers in Israel with host-immigrant relations in other countries due to the large size of this community and the existence of the thriving Russian subculture. It can be argued that such a critical mass of co-ethnic migrants in a small country may by itself lead to socio-cultural retention among immigrant youth. Yet, a similar tendency has been found among Russian immigrants in other host countries, where they comprise a much smaller minority. Some studies among young Soviet immigrants in the West (Gold, 1997; Zeltzer-Zubida, 2000; Jasinskaya-Lahti and Liebkind, 1999; Nauck, 2001; Steinbach, 2001; Kasinitz et al., 2001) have found a tendency to preferential social networking with co-ethnics among adolescents and young adults, regardless of their socio-economic adjustment in the new country.

Another common feature of the young immigrants' experiences in different national contexts is their gradual process of self-acceptance as "Other" along with psychosocial maturation. In their memoir-based study of the formation of ethnic identities among young Asian-American professionals Min and Kim (2000) have shown that their informants could socially assimilate without relinquishing their original culture. Most participants recounted that they tried to hide their minority affiliation during early school years in the new country, but later on—usually in college—they came to accept their distinct ethnic identity as an asset. This subjective perception is congruent with the objective data, showing that bilingual immigrant students are doing better at all levels of schooling than monolingual ones, including native English speakers (Feliciano, 2001). In my study, as well as in the earlier interviews with Russian students of the Hebrew University conducted by Lerner (1999), many immigrants recounted that during their initial school years in Israel they had practiced social mimicry, trying to imitate their local peers, only to discover later the value of their own cultural identity. Many respondents noted that they felt much better about their Russianness in college than they used to feel at school. This similarity points to the uneven and stepwise process of ethnic identity formation in young immigrants, whereby school years may be the most difficult stage of trial and error. Within immigrant youth, the integration potential is varied as a function of ethnicity (Jews, vs. partial Jews vs. non-Jews), venue of arrival to Israel (with the family or alone under a special youth program[12]), place of residence (a mixed neighborhood vs. Russian enclave), and the extent of social integration of their parents. Gender differences in the adjustment process have also been shown: while adolescent boys prefer to maintain exclusively co-ethnic ties regardless of their tenure in Israel (thus reinforcing their sense of competence and masculinity), the girls are better skilled at cultural border-crossing and more prone to befriend and date Israeli-born peers, along with other "Russians" (Eisikovits, 2000).

The aforementioned studies suggest that young Russian immigrants follow the hybridism script of acculturation, that is, develop their own distinct pathway between the home and host cultures, augmented by the new transnational opportunities. Adopting multiple elements of the local conduct, lifestyle and fashion, young immigrants retain the core mindset and outlook shaped during their formative years in the FSU. As a result, a new hybrid cultural realm is emerging, typified by hyphenated identities (Russian-Israeli, Russian-German, Russian-Finnish, Russian-American), lifestyles (e.g., Russian discos and clubs that feature popular Russian, local, and MTV-style music), and mixed lingoes such as "HebRush." These newly emerging immigrant cultures await their ethnographers, who would probably appear from their own ranks. It remains to be seen whether these hybrid-transnational cultures will survive (and thrive?) for a long time or dissolve with the advent of the second and third generations. We lean to the former option, at least in the Israeli context, where Russian speakers will be able to maintain their cultural autonomy and transnational networks in the near future.

Uprooted in Old Age or Taking a Fresh Start? Immigrant Elders

Among the newcomers, about 150,000 are of retirement age, that is, sixty or over for women and sixty-five or over for men, comprising some14 percent of the recent arrivals (vs. around 10 percent among Israeli Jews) (CBS, 2002). Most of these older migrants have moved along with their adult children and/or grandchildren, but about 25 percent have immigrated alone or with a spouse (CBS, 2002). Most former Soviets emigrated with little or no financial assets and had to rely on public aid in the host country. All new senior citizens are entitled to subsistence old-age benefit (around $400 in 2003) from Israeli Social Insurance Service, subsidized or free health care, and often also to a modest housing allowance. Yet, all these benefits are barely enough for daily living, and many retired immigrants work part time (usually in private services for cash) to supplement their income. Due to soaring housing costs in the 1990s and a paucity of public housing in Israel, most older immigrants had to rent apartments along with their children and grandchildren. In most cases, co-residence of three generations was a necessity rather than choice: lumping together scant economic resources helped many extended families to survive. Family members form a natural social support network, where younger ones help their elders to get around in the new country and receive in return hands-on help in childcare and domestic chores. Despite certain balance in the give and take relations in multigenerational families, their members often suffer from the lack of space and privacy (Naon et al, 1993; Lowenstein, 2002). Yet, those who arrived alone were especially disadvantaged, both materially and socially, and were often compelled to find roommates for joint rentals of living quarters.

Research on immigrant seniors has been scarce and mostly driven by a social work or geriatric agenda. Several studies addressed the issue of co-residence and its effects on family relations from the stand-point of emotional costs, solidarity, and conflict (Naon et al., 1993; Litwin, 1995; Lowenstein, 2002). Litwin (1995), Ron (2001), and Ritsner and Ponizovsky (2003) studied psychiatric/psychological out-comes among Russian-speaking elders and found high levels of emo-tional distress, reflecting material privations, loneliness, a cultural gap with Israelis, tense family relations in multigenerational households, and a general sense of insecurity. Another recent study explored the experiences of family caregivers of Russian immigrant elders—their daughters or daughters-in-law (Remennick, 2001). It has shown that, as a result of resettlement, the elders who used to be self-sufficient in the FSU became helpless and dependent on their children for most daily interactions with the host society due to their deteriorating health, poor Hebrew, and misunderstanding of the new social codes. Remennick and Ottenstein (1998b) have found that poor adjustment to the new environment and mental health problems may translate into high utilization of community health services by the immigrant elders, who often approach their general practitioners (especially Russian-speaking ones) as an outlet for both medical and non-medical psychosocial aid. Similar patterns of distress and utilization of health services were reported by Aroian et al. (2001) among older Russian immigrants in the U.S.

Fewer researchers were interested in older immigrants as active participants in the new society and their own agency in shaping their post-migration lives. To fill in this void, I conducted an ethnographic study based on focus groups and personal interviews with thirty-nine retired immigrants (mean age 69.2 years) centering on their socio-cultural adjustment in Israel. Among my informants, 60 percent were women, 45 percent had post-secondary education, and 70 percent came from the large Soviet cities. Two-thirds had moved to Israel with their children's families and about 50 percent shared with them housing and family budget at the time of study. Below I highlight some key findings.

Older generation of Soviet Jews, albeit mostly secular and subjected to the assimilative pressures of the Soviet regime for most of their adult lives, nevertheless have a stronger Jewish identity than younger cohorts of immigrants. Many of them are Holocaust survivors who grew up in the Jewish towns of provincial Ukraine, Belorussia, and other areas of the former Pale of Settlement, went to Jewish schools before their closure in the late 1930s, spoke Yiddish at home, and observed elements of Jewish tradition. Many of them lived with hidden Zionist sentiments throughout the years of anti-Israeli propaganda in the FSU and dreamed of seeing Israel. When the gates of the FSU finally opened in the late 1980s, the decision to emigrate to Israel came about rather naturally. For many of them, the push factors (problems in the deteriorating FSU) were as strong as the pull factors (the wish to live in the Jewish state). Among the latter, the expectation of higher living standards and better health care via entitlement for public benefits were of significant weight. Many older Jews who would not emigrate by themselves were compelled to join their children and their families, otherwise facing old age all alone in the FSU. Hence for the majority of older migrants the decision to make aliyah was a combination of ideological and pragmatic considerations.

Most older migrants, who had spent all their lives in the FSU, often in the same city, had never been abroad before emigrating to Israel and had no previous exposure to other cultures. They had hard time realizing that Israel is very different from Russia or Ukraine in most aspects of daily living. "Of course I knew that I was going to live abroad, in a country with language and traditions of its own, but I somehow denied this knowledge, hoping in my heart that things would be familiar and workable for me. . . . So it was kind of shocking that most people I met in Israel won't speak Russian and I couldn't make a thing of what they were saying. . . . The feeling of helplessness was overwhelming" (Vladimir, seventy-four). "The landscape, the climate, the calendar, the names of streets and people—all was new and puzzling for me. And you know, it's very unpleasant for old folks like us, educated and cultured, to feel like half-wits, not understanding the rules, being unable to express ourselves. Russian newspapers and radio were of great help for us to get oriented. On hindsight, my husband and I had a hard time getting settled in Israel" (Lydia, seventy).

The motivation for learning Hebrew and social incorporation depended on the general attitude towards the new country: those who felt more positive about Israel and Israelis were more willing to get to know them better. Those, who felt alienated by the locals or found them "primitive, uncultured, and Asian," typically preferred co-ethnic company and Russian-only cultural basket. Most participants have attended an Ulpan for at least a few months, but believed that they had no chance for mastering Hebrew in their lifetime and sufficed with a basic fifty-to-hundred-word lexicon. After five to seven years spent in Israel, most informants felt socially adjusted among other Russian immigrants and did not have much need for Hebrew. The initial cultural shock was behind them and they learned to navigate Israeli institutions and make the best of what Israel had to offer. "Israel is far from being heaven, but it is still worth it. This is the only place on

Earth where a Jew can feel a normal first-rate citizen, and for this I am ready to take up all the risks and problems" (Semyon, seventy-six). Many other informants endorsed this opinion, saying that they had a strong sense of community and the ability to be active citizens, despite their old age—a feeling they never experienced before emigration.

The most significant loss is permanent housing, perceived by most former Soviets as a great privation. Residential mobility in the FSU was rather low; many people had lived for decades in the same city and even the same house. Most former Soviets now in their sixties and seventies had suffered from meager housing conditions during their youth, living in small, crowded apartments, often shared with strangers (so-called "communal apartments"). It took them many years to get decent housing of their own, either from the state or via workplace coops. Being relatively settled and comfortable in their homes by the late 1980s, most pained at uprooting and venturing for the unknown place under sun. "If only we had hope to live in a home of our own one day, to shed this dependency from the caprices of the landlord [there is no rent control or long-term lease contracts in Israel]. But we know full well that we'll have to move from one shabby flat to the next till the end of our days. With our income, who can dream of buying a home in Israel?" (Yosef, seventy-seven). "I feel like a displaced person, always living on the suitcases and carton boxes. In my nine years in Israel, I have changed six flats, first sharing them with my daughter and then renting with strange roommates. It is so sad to always use other people's old beds and closets. . . . I don't have even a chair that is my own" (Vladimir, seventy-four). Another recurrent topic in the interviews was the need to manage on a very low budget in a country with high living costs. "Our salaries in Russia had always been low, but then we also had free housing, paid next to nothing for electricity, water, telephone, public transport, etc . . . and food was cheap, albeit hard to get. In principle we are used to living modestly and counting every ruble (or shekel), but it's hard to get used to the fact that what was cheap (and taken for granted) in Russia is expensive in Israel" (Maria, seventy-three). "The state benefit is totally unrealistic, as if the authorities don't know what the costs are out there. If my wife and I didn't make some extra money by taking whatever small job comes our way, we won't be able to rent a flat by ourselves" (Alexander, sixty-nine). Many educated immigrants were bitter about their inability to afford some "vital extras" as one woman put it, mainly cultural products such as books, musical records, and theater tickets. Yet, several informants pointed out that they were ready to cut down on food, telephone, and other basic expenses in order to save money for a concert or a show. On the other hand, some older immigrants enjoyed the financial support of their economically successful children, allowing them to travel and to consume cultural products they otherwise could not afford.

Older immigrants who are part of multi-generational households complained about gradually losing contact with their children and especially grandchildren, due to their immersion in Israeli life, new interests, and friends. "I often feel left out of their life. My daughter and her husband work very hard and I hardly ever see them. When we sit together at supper, they discuss matters I do not understand, using many Hebrew words. I don't dare asking to explain since I see how tired and irritated they often are . . . " (Faina, seventy-six). Drifting further apart from their children, Russian elders seek social support from each other, via both formal and informal community networks. Organizations established by the senior immigrants, with the aid of the local authorities, include the above-mentioned War Veterans' association, as well as classes for the study of Judaism and/or Hebrew, chess and card clubs, groups of nature lovers, and more. During election campaigns this picture is complemented by various support groups, lobbying for both "Russian" and national parties and politicians. Retired immigrants probably comprise the most politically active sector in the "Russian street," their voting rates and engagement with political campaigns being very high. "Because Israeli society is so small, every activist with brains and energy can really make a difference. It's exiting to see the results of your effort! As a Jew living in my own country I know I can change things for the better, and I never had this feeling in Russia" (Alexander, sixty-nine). Apart from community organizations, older immigrants are involved in multiple informal social networks of their own that spread around apartment blocks and neighborhood gardens where they often walk, alone or with the grandchildren. The involvement with various formal and informal groups fills the communication void that senior immigrants find themselves in due to the almost complete detachment from the host society.

The earlier survey research (Remennick, 2002a) has shown that Russian Jews in Israel form an integral part of the post-Soviet diaspora and manifest multiple signs of the emerging transnational lifestyle. It is expressed in their permanent social and cultural ties with the former places of origin in the FSU and with co-ethnics in other host countries of the West. Older age groups of Russian Israelis, free from permanent employment and often having some financial help from children, have been most active in actual physical movement across borders. Over half of the retired immigrants keep their Russian or Ukrainian passports and some also own apartments there (especially former residents of Moscow and St. Petersburg). It is estimated that over one-third of them travel to their home cities annually or every other year and many avoid Israeli heat by spending summer in their Russian country cottages. In addition, about 30 percent have close relatives and/or friends in the U.S., Canada, or Germany and visit them every now and then. Most informants told me that they were nostalgic about their past, cities and homes they left behind. "No day goes by without me thinking about my old street, my cozy flat, the neighborhood park. . . . I feel an urge to go there every now and then, although I know that this place is no longer mine, strange people live in my apartment. . . . Still I returned there three times since coming to Israel—to clean and plant flowers on my parents' grave, if not for anything else" (Elena, seventy-two). Although most informants admitted that they enjoyed their ability to travel back to the FSU, no one in my sample was ready to return there for good. When asked why not, the informants gave rather similar answers such as "My new home is already here in Israel, where my grandchildren are," "Although I like visiting Russia, I prefer to live among the Jews," and "You cannot survive on Russian pensions."

Thus, my findings depict a more positive general picture of older immigrants' lives in Israel than did some earlier studies by psychologists, geriatrists, and social workers (Litwin, 1995; Ron, 2001; Ritsner and Ponizovsky, 2003) that reported on the high levels of distress, loneliness, and lacking social support. This discrepancy may reflect my sampling scheme based on community centers and hence involving more active (and maybe also younger and healthier) sector of the retired immigrants with broader opportunities and social networks. Also, my methods of eliciting information were more open and holistic: I tried to capture the total subjective experience rather than measure specific psychological indicators by means of structured scales. My principal finding is that older Russian Jews, who had suffered from anti-Semitism for most of their lives in the FSU, have a strong affinity to Israel and largely do not regret making aliyah. Over 40 percent of the informants have attended classes of Hebrew and/or Jewish history currently or in the past. Besides, most pensioners often take advantage of various subsidized tours and cultural events offered to them by senior citizens' centers and other local organizations. Their cultural needs are met by a wide selection of Russian-language TV and radio programs, press, and books. Older immigrants are the most regular users of Russian-language libraries available in every Israeli town. At the same time, real Israel, with its Middle Eastern landscape, climate, and lifestyle, was rather shocking for those of them who had expected to find here a Jewish version of Europe. After the initial years of cultural shock and social orientation, older immigrants concluded that they had no chance of joining the Israeli mainstream; instead they built their social lives within the co-ethnic community. Over time, the informal social networks were complemented by a variety of community organizations, through which senior immigrants got more tangible involvement with social and political life of Israel. At the same time, many older immigrants use the advantages of globalization, open borders, and double citizenship that allow them to keep in touch with their places of origin in the FSU as well as travel to the West as tourists or guests. In this way, senior Russian-Jewish immigrants heralded the advent of transnational lifestyle in the post-Soviet global diaspora (more on this in Remennick, 2002a).

The major problems faced by older immigrants are found in two realms: material privations (low income and the lack of quality permanent housing) and weakening emotional ties with younger generations in the extended families. The financial problems are partly overcome by finding supplementary income from various cash jobs available to younger pensioners. The generation gap is much harder to narrow, since it inevitably ensues from a varying pace of social integration between various generations of immigrants. Adult children, and especially grandchildren, typically learn Hebrew fairly soon and often switch language codes at home, thus excluding older family members from the verbal exchange. The very range of interests, contacts, and pastimes grow very much apart between the younger and older relatives living under one roof or close by. As a result, the cultural common denominator, which sustained emotional ties and mutual interests between parents and children in the past, often tends to shrink to a bare minimum of mutual responsibility. Adult children and grandchildren continue to provide instrumental aid to their elderly parents (e.g., take them to a doctor, help with banking transactions, etc.), but since the elders have few favors to offer in return, this is increasingly perceived by caregivers as an unfair burden (Remennick, 2001). Reflecting these trends in family relations, many senior immigrants try to minimize the claims on their children's time and attention and seek alternative outlets of help and guidance from other seniors, who often become their equal or even primary sources of social support. The central role of co-ethnic peer social networks for older immigrants has also been shown in the earlier Israeli studies by Litwin (1995), and among senior Russian immigrants in the U.S. (Aroian et al., 2001) and Germany (Nauck, 2001).

In sum, this study has shown that many senior Russian immigrants lead active lives in their new country and are endowed by multiple personal resources underused by the receiving society. Given their high educational level, social energy, and flexibility with time, senior Russian immigrants could contribute a lot to the local communities, for example as paid workers (for symbolic wages) or volunteers in daycare and youth centers, hospitals, and rehabilitation units for the mentally ill. Given that former Soviet immigrants are found among all these populations receiving social services, the Russian-language skills of the volunteers would be an asset rather than a problem. Volunteering is rather common among old-time Israeli seniors, but recent immigrants are usually excluded from these venues of self-actualization, being seen largely as passive and helpless receivers of social services. This attitude of the Israeli social institutions needs to be changed, for the benefit of all parties involved.

When the West Meets the East:
European, Bukharan, and Caucasian Jews

The division between Ashkenazi and Mizrahi Jews on the mainstream ethno-cultural map of Israel is paralleled by a similar distinction between Jews of the European Soviet Union and Jews who have lived for centuries among the peoples of the Caucasian Mountains, Uzbekistan, and other Asian republics. Three main groups of non-Ashkenazi Jewry that lived in the southern and eastern Soviet territories have a rich history of their own dating back to Biblical and early Christian times. Georgian Jews are descendants of ancient Jewish tribes who had migrated to the Caucasus even before the Christian Georgians; they speak a dialect of Georgian with some inclusions of Hebrew and Russian. Tats or Mountain Jews had also populated the Northern Caucasus from pre-modern times, with their largest modern concentrations found in the towns of Derbent and Kuba. Bukharan Jews had settled in the ancient Oriental city of Bukhara (now in Uzbekistan) in the early centuries of A.D. after escaping from the Babylonian exile. The ethnic languages of Tats and Bukharan Jews belong to the Iranian group, distant derivatives of Farsi spoken in today's Iraq and Iran. All of the non-European Jewish groups in the south and east of the USSR comprised together about 8–10 percent of Soviet Jewry. They were culturally rather close to the surrounding titular nations (e.g., Georgian Jews are difficult to tell from other Georgians), with the only difference of keeping some key Jewish traditions and marrying strictly within the group. Indigenous Jews of the Caucasus and Soviet Asia were much less exposed to anti-Semitism than Ashkenazi Jews living in the European part of the USSR due to extreme ethnic diversity of these areas and the long-standing tradition of ethno-religious tolerance. It should be noted that many Jews of Ashkenazi origin had resettled in the capital cities of the Caucasus and Central Asia (especially Tashkent, Alma-Ata, and Baku) during the war evacuations or went there to work as specialists in the industry, education, medicine, and science in order to facilitate the advancement of these remote regions. Yet, despite their common religious background, European and indigenous Jews almost never mixed socially as the former deemed themselves to be culturally and educationally superior.

Indeed, the social and cultural makeup of the non-European Jewish groups is very different from that of Ashkenazi Soviet Jews. Georgian, Tat, and Bukharan Jews maintained a traditional lifestyle, with women doing housework and raising children, while men provided for the family. Relatively few of them went to the university or college, and their occupations were usually in trade, small business (even in Soviet times when this was illegal), and artisan occupations such as shoemakers and barbers. They usually lived in extended families or clans under one roof or nearby, and their close family ties resulted in the flows of mutual financial and hands-on help. As opposed to European Soviet Jews, most of their Caucasian and Asian distant cousins have kept Jewish traditions, go to synagogue, cook kosher meals, celebrate Jewish holidays, and circumcise their sons. Although all of these groups have ethnic languages of their own, during the Soviet era Russian was their second language as most went to Russian schools, and Russian was the lingua franca of the whole diverse area (Cooper, 2003).

During the 1970s, most Georgian and other Caucasian Jews left the USSR with the first postwar emigration wave. The majority resettled in Israel, while smaller groups arrived in the U.S. (e.g., forming Bukharan enclaves in New York and Los Angeles [Kandinov, 1996]), and yet others remained in Europe (e.g., a sizeable group of Tats managed to gain asylum in Vienna, where the transition camps had been located). After 1989, almost all the remaining Bukharan and Caucasian Jews emigrated, joining their relatives in Israel and in a few Western cities. Thus, although these groups had comprised a small minority within Soviet Jewry, their representation in the Israeli former Soviet community is disproportionately large—about 200,000 or 20 percent—as most of them have resettled in Israel (while many Ashkenazi Jews left for the West). Due to their preserved ties with Judaism and living in the Eastern cultural milieu, these groups have blended in extremely well with the traditional and religious segments of Israeli society. They settled in large co-ethnic enclaves established back in the 1970s (e.g., in Tel Aviv suburb of Or Yehuda, in Beer-Sheba and Ofakim in the South) and politically joined the Mizrahi social-religious movement SHAS. Older generations of Bukharan and Caucasian Jewry preserve their traditional lifestyle with strong family ties and frequent gatherings of relatives around an abundant table featuring pilaf, shashlyk, manty, and other Oriental delicacies. Many women had to join the labor market, but usually in part-time, low-skill jobs; the bulk of their time is still devoted to the family. Older Bukharan women dress in traditional long dresses and headscarves; younger women are recognizable by their flashy style of dress and abundant jewelry. Men continue to make a living in trade (salesmen of this origin are rife in most street bazaars), money changing, restaurants and catering, jewelry shops, and other small businesses.

In the 1990s, Caucasian Jewish teenagers were described as the most trouble-prone group among the immigrant youth, having high rates of school dropout and delinquency, including involvement in violent street gangs. They were also marked as a problematic group in the military, manifesting high rates of desertion and often initiating violent conflicts between soldiers of different ethnic origin (particularly bullying timid Ethiopians). This acting-out behavior probably reflects confusion at the face of the normative and cultural gap between their parental families (with their respect of the elders and strict hierarchy) and liberal conduct of their Israeli peers (Azarya and Kimmerling, 1998; Shamai & Ilatov, 2001). For the same reasons, Bukharan and Caucasian girls (who had been kept at home or chaperoned till their marriage was arranged by the parents) often rebel against their confinement, modesty, and early marriage by joining the army, or by hanging out with boys and staying out at night. This is a typical expression of the generational conflict and cultural transition from traditional to modern pluralist society and lifestyle (similar trends are found in Ethiopian immigrant families).

As virtually all Eastern Jews had lived in their enclaves in the Asian and Caucasian territories, few European Jews from the large cities of Russia and Ukraine had a chance to meet them before emigration. This encounter in Israel was somewhat of a cultural shock for the Russian-Jewish intelligentsia, who conceived of all Jews as highbrow professionals, readers of literary magazines, and listeners of classic music. Their fellow immigrants featuring Uzbek robes, golden teeth, and tacky outfits were a kind of Oriental bazaar exotica for them (Yelenevskaya and Fialkova, 2005; Lomsky-Feder et al., 2005). As former Soviets are prone to constructing social hierarchies within their social milieu (where Moscow and Leningrad intelligentsia is at the top and small-town provincial Jewry in the middle), the Caucasian and Bukharan Jews were rapidly placed at the bottom of this ladder (sharing this position with Moroccan and other Mizrahi Jews), with only Ethiopians and Arabs below them. In surveys, up to 30 percent of "white" (Ashkenazi) soviet Jews admit to their dislike of the "black" Jews, both of Soviet and Middle Eastern origin. The dislike is probably mutual, although in most surveys there are not enough Bukharan and Caucasian respondents to confirm this trend (Feldman, 2003). Given the emerging compliance with the norms of political correctness and self-censorship of public speech, the actual negative attitudes between members of different soviet Jewish communities are probably much more prevalent. Ashkenazi Soviet Jews try to keep social and residential distance from their Eastern cousins, although this is not always possible and many neighborhoods and schools are still mixed. It is noteworthy that former Soviet Mizrahi Jews have made a rapid linguistic transition and usually speak a mix of Hebrew and their ethnic languages, while European Soviet Jews are firmly attached to

Russian as their primary language. A fascinating case study of the interplay between ethnic, cultural, and linguistic factors shaping relations of work in an Israeli organization where sabras, Russian, and Georgian Jews work side by side is described in my recent organizational ethnographic study (Remennick, 2004b).

From the Other Side: Native Israelis' Attitudes Towards Russian Immigrants

A shock-anger-acceptance-indifference continuum probably describes concisely and accurately the dynamics of the mainstream Israeli discourse on the last-wave Russian immigration. As a popular saying goes, Israelis love aliyah but detest olim. Every historic wave of newcomers was met by the established community with a mix of hostility and disappointment and got its fair share of negative stereotyping in the mass media and popular lore (Weissbrod, 2002; Shifman & Katz, 2005). German Jews (*Jekim,* or Jews wearing jackets), who first sought refuge from the Nazi persecution in the late 1930s and after the war arrived as Holocaust survivors, were deemed arrogant, refined, and too highbrow for the brave new society of kibbutzniks and soldiers. Like Soviet Jews fifty years later, they were highly educated professionals, unwilling to trade the German language and culture for Hebrew and local gruffness and camaraderie. While many Jekim laid the foundation of Israeli professional education and practice in medicine, law, engineering, and science, many others were relegated to working-class occupations and never recovered from the cultural shock (Spolsky and Shohami, 1999). Conversely, the large influx of Moroccan and Yemenite Jews in the 1950s caused the upsurge of Ashkenazi white supremacy (if not sheer racism); so-called Arab Jews were labeled as savage, ignorant, a public health hazard, irresponsible parents, violent, and fit only for manual labor. In line with those views, they were settled in the remote development towns, employed in low-skill occupations, and steered towards vocational training rather than comprehensive schooling and universities. The results of these attitudes and policies are showing in the lingering socio-economic gaps between second-generation Ashkenazim and Mizrahim (Cohen and Haberfeld, 1998; Kimmerling, 2001).

The Great Russian Aliyah of the early 1990s was perceived by old-time Israelis as a mixed blessing. On one hand, the massive influx of the newcomers was a burden for a small and saturated housing and labor market, causing soaring rentals and plummeting wages for the natives, along with the olim themselves. On the other hand, many employers and homeowners ripped fat profits from cheap and skilled labor, as well as high housing demand; by the mid–1990s the rapid growth of the population and consumer market caused the largest economic boom in Israel's history. Throughout this time, the mainstream press was rife with stories about the Russian mafia, welfare fraud, olim who grabbed from the absorption basket and fled back to the FSU, high shares of non-Jews with forged documents, Russian prostitutes, pimps, and single mothers (Lemesh, 2000). This imagery has shaped popular attitudes of the natives towards Russian immigrants.[13] On the level of everyday conduct, the gap between the immigrants and the hosts was evident to both parties, and both considered their own culture superior. In several surveys that examined native Israelis' attitudes towards Russian olim, the repeated claims voiced by respondents included the lack of Zionist sentiment and commitment to chief Israeli values, detachment from Jewish traditions and no interest in learning them, the manipulation of the welfare system and getting too many benefits at the expense of veteran taxpayers, the lack of appreciation for the aid they were receiving, and (perhaps the gravest sin) the continued use of Russian and estrangement from the Hebrew-based collectivity. Immigrant children and youths entering en masse Israeli educational institutions and the military faced significant antagonism and exclusion by their Israeli-born peers (Ilatov and Shamai, 1999). Additionally, many Israelis raised the argument that former Soviets had been molded in the totalitarian and over-centralized society and were unfit for democracy and work in modern organizations (Remennick, 2004b). The demographic sectors which shared negative opinion about Russian immigrants included the less educated and Mizrahi Jews, the unemployed or working in unskilled labor force, and religious Israelis (Leshem and Lissak, 1998). The antagonism of the lower tiers of the Israel social pyramid towards Russian olim is understandable in the light of competition for scarce jobs and insecurity they felt vis-à-vis the wave of better-educated newcomers.

As part of my 2001 study of integration patterns among Russian Israelis (Remenick, 2003a), a "mirror survey" was conducted in a smaller but representative national sample of adult Hebrew-speaking Israelis (N=508, sex ratio 50:50). The Israeli sample was asked five questions, typifying their attitudes and conduct towards Russian immigrants. Here are brief results. 1. *Do you have friends or pals among Russian immigrants who arrived in 1990s?* 34 percent answered yes, many; 16 percent yes, some; and 50 percent said none. 2. *How many times during the last year did you attend concerts, shows or other cultural events by Russian or olim performers?* 12 percent said twice or more; 11 percent once; and 77 percent said never. 3. *Do you ever shop in Russian non-kosher delis and groceries?* 7 percent answered yes, often; 16 percent yes, sometimes; and 77 percent never. 4. *Would you like to learn the Russian language?* 26 percent said yes, definitely; 34 percent wouldn't mind; and 40 percent were not interested. 5. *Would you be interested in a romantic relationship and/or marriage to a Russian immigrant? (If this is irrelevant for you, then for your children).* 36 percent said definitely yes; 42 percent possibly; and 22 percent rejected this option.

Generally, these answers point to the remaining social and cultural gap between the hosts and the immigrants—after fifteen years of close coexistence—in terms of both social networking and consumption patterns. The only indication of the rising socio-economic status of Russian speakers (as perceived by the Hebrew majority) is rather high interest in them as romantic and marital partners. The analysis of variance confirmed Leshem and Lissak's (1998) findings that the extent of inclusion/exclusion of "Russians" depends on age and especially the level of education of Israeli respondents. Generally, younger and more educated Israelis have more contacts and friends among Russian speakers, probably via studies and work. Among those aged eighteen to twenty-four, 64 percent have Russian speakers in their social networks, vs. 43 percent in the age bracket fifty-five and over. Among Israelis with a postgraduate degree, 68 percent had Russian contacts and friends, vs. 41 percent among those with a high school education. Ashkenazi Israelis are more prone to contacts with Russian immigrants than are Mizrahi ones (66 percent vs.30 percent of positive answers), and religious Israelis are the least disposed to contacts with the olim (only 35 percent had any Russian contacts or friends). The bottom line is that Russian immigrants are best accepted by (and slowly blending with) their Israeli social and ethnic peers—secular educated Ashkenazi Jews. Yet, despite their constant mingling in the workplaces, universities, and other mainstream institutions, on many levels Russian immigrants and native Israelis keep separate social tracks, different cultural interests, and have little intimate acquaintance with each other.

Back to Mother Russia: The Return Phenomenon

With their emigration, Russian Jews discovered a freedom of movement unthinkable in Soviet times. As was already noted, many immigrants visit their cities of origin in the FSU and their relatives and friends in the West as often as their modest incomes allow. About one-third of all post–1989 olim keep Russian or Ukrainian passports (most other successor states ban double citizenship) and do not need visas; some also have apartments or country cottages in which to stay. It should be noted that after the economic and political pitfall of the early 1990s, living standards and consumer markets in Russia and Ukraine significantly improved. There is a thriving business culture and the winds of opportunity blow strong in the vast former Soviet territories. For creative and sociable individuals, especially endowed with some capital and business skills, the sky is ostensibly the limit in Moscow. Both day and night cultures of restaurants, clubs, and discos are thriving and suitable for any taste and wallet, the city is growing increasingly cosmopolitan and diverse. At the same time, the level of street anti-Semitism is much lower today than it was in the early post-Soviet years, and institutional anti-Semitism has all but vanished, judging by the visibility of Jewish politicians and businessmen.

Given that many immigrants still have dense social networks in large Russian cities, and thrive in the familiar language and culture, the idea of return is very appealing. After a number of shuttle visits, some olim may decide to stay there for good or, alternatively, to live in both countries. The Jewish organizations in Moscow estimated that the number of returnees who live and work in the city is around 35,000, and the number has been growing. At the same time, the statistical bureau of the Russian Federation reported that only about 14,000 immigrants who returned to all Russian cities from Israel have registered as permanent residents between 1997 and 2003 (Shapiro, 2005). Russian Jews who have lived in Israel and returned to Moscow established there various cultural and entertainment venues for their own ilk, such as Israeli club Darkon (passport in Hebrew) frequented by young programmers and IT designers who speak a mix of Russian and Hebrew. Restaurants of Israeli and Middle Eastern food, stores selling Israeli musical records and film DVDs, and other businesses owned by Russian Israelis in Moscow, St. Petersburg and Kiev serve as a mirror image of the Russian stores in Tel Aviv, Haifa, and other Israeli cities. Everything Israeli is no longer clandestine but, on the opposite, rather trendy, so Russian Jews who can speak Hebrew enjoy a high status in Moscow's inner crowd (personal communications).

The option of keeping two homes is more practical for the retired immigrants not tied to workplaces in either country; some of them continue to collect their modest pensions in both countries, spending winters in Israel and summers in Russia. Israeli old-age benefit of some $250 (an additional $150 are withdrawn after two-month absence) is still two to three times higher than an average Moscow pension, and these combined incomes allow older Jews to live comfortably in their home cities. Another category of potential returnees are entrepreneurs whose ventures draw on the supplies or partnerships in Russia and Ukraine. Speaking with the more successful olim business people, I heard a repeated complaint that growing Russian businesses are stifled and contained in Israel by local protectionism and nepotism; for outsiders and novices there is simply no access to low-interest bank loans, prestigious locations, and lucrative contracts. For some others, the internal Israeli market is just too small. Frustrated by these barriers, some of them moved their operations to a more dangerous, but familiar Russian capitalist jungle. The third category of returnees includes high-tech specialists, especially in IT and programming, who could gain higher incomes and better contracts in the booming Russian high-tech than in Israeli one. Yet, for most returnees this comeback is not final, but rather another stage in their cosmopolitan life cycle. Although "double return migrants" spend most of their time in Moscow or St. Petersburg (two main hubs of return), they never sever their ties with Israel; many keep apartments there and come quite often visit their parents and friends.

Throughout the last decade the policymakers and demographers have tried to measure the extent of out-migration of former Soviet olim from Israel. Mark Tolts (2005) reported that the highest rates of return to Russia (17 per 1,000 olim) were registered in 1992—the year when conditions for adjustment in Israel were still very harsh but the situation in Russia ostensibly started to improve—and consistently decreased ever since, to the level of 8–10 per 1,000 in the early 2000s. In 2004, the number of Russian Jews who left Israel and did not return for at least one year stood at 58,400. Juxtaposed with 908,200 immigrants from the FSU who resettled in Israel between 1990 and 2001, this means that out-migrants form around 6 percent of the total. This is a much lower level of exit compared to other immigrants to Israel from developed countries (e.g., 25 percent among North American Jews, 18 percent among Argentinean Jews, and 16 percent among the French Jews). The majority of ex-Soviet Jews who left Israel moved to Canada and the U.S., and some also to Russia, Ukraine or European countries. As all of these people keep Israeli passports and some of them will possibly return or come for prolonged visits, it is technically difficult to measure the fraction of final out-migrants (*yordim*, i.e., going down, in the Hebrew lore). In any case, the absolute majority of the post–1989 Russian immigrants remained in Israel, despite all the political turmoil, security problems, and economic ups and downs.

Israel as a Hub of Transnational Russian-Jewish Community

The concept of transnationalism, described as an integral part of the globalization process, is increasingly popular in social and political sciences (Glick Schiller et al., 1995; Guarnizo and Smith, 1998; Vertovec, 2004). Originally coined in international economics to describe flows of capital and labor across national borders, this concept was later applied to the study of international migration and ethnic diasporas (Safran, 1999). The transnational perspective became increasingly useful for exploring such issues as immigrant economic integration, identity, citizenship, and cultural retention. Transnationalism embraces a variety of social relations that are both embedded in and transcend two or more nation-states, crosscutting sociopolitical, territorial, and cultural borders. The ever-increasing flows of people, goods, ideas, fashions, and images between various parts of the world enhances the blending of cultures and lifestyles and leads to the formation of "hyphenated" social identities (e.g., Russian-Israeli or Chinese-American).

In the late twentieth century, efficient and relatively cheap means of communication and transportation (time- and space-compressing technologies) made the old dichotomy of immigration vs. return largely irrelevant. They allowed numerous diasporic migrants to live in two or more countries at a time, via maintaining close physical and social links with their places of origin. Transnational activities became widely spread, embracing large numbers of people and playing a significant role in economy, politics and social life of both sending and receiving countries (Van Hear, 1998). Guarnizo and Smith (1998) have introduced a useful distinction between two types of transnationalism: "from above" and "from below." The former refers to institutionalized economic and political activities of multinational corporations like Intel and organizations such as Amnesty International or Greenpeace, which propel large-scale global exchange of financial and human capital. On the other hand, an increasing role in these networks belongs to ordinary migrants—grassroots agents of transnationalism who run small businesses in their home countries, organize exchange of material goods (e.g., ethnic food) and cultural products (e.g., tours of co-ethnic performers) within the diaspora, pay regular visits to their homelands, and receive co-ethnic guests. All these activities typify the emerging transnational lifestyle. The full-time loyalty to one country and one culture is no longer self-evident: people may divide their physical presence, effort, and identity between several societies. Citizenship and political participation are also becoming bifocal or even multifocal, since some sending countries allow their expatriates to remain citizens, vote in national elections, and establish political movements. In this context, international migrants are becoming transmigrants, developing economic activities, enjoying cultural life and keeping dense informal networks not only with their home country, but also with other national branches of their diaspora. The split of economic, social and political loyalties among migrants, and gradual attenuation of loyalty to the nation-state as such, is seen as problematic by some receiving countries (Glick Schiller, 1995; Guarnizo and Smith, 1998). Yet some recent studies show that dual citizenship may in fact promote immigrants' legal and socio-political attachments to both their home and host country rather than reinforce the so-called post-nationalism (Bloemraad, 2004).

Due to its ethnic diversity (including both Jews and Slavs) and timing in the years of intense international exchange and growing openness of the former Soviet states to their expatriates, the Great Aliyah was prone to transnationalism at the very outset. As one can deduce from the aforementioned trends of return, or rather shuttle movements across the borders, many Russian Jews who made aliyah during the 1990s embraced a transnational script of adjustment, that is, keep two homes and a double set of attachments and loyalties. In my estimates, over 25 percent of all olim partake in different forms of transnational living, including regular trips to their former home cities (or living there part of the year), visits to the U.S. and other Western countries where their relatives and friends live, hosting co-ethnic guests from the FSU and Western countries in their homes, participating in transnational business ventures run by former Soviets, and voting in Russian and Ukrainian elections. Admittedly, olim of non-Jewish or mixed ethnicity are more prone to the ties with their homelands because most of them have parents, siblings and friends living there (while core Jews usually emigrated as whole families and have all or most of their relatives in Israel and in the West). The transnational activities of Israeli Russians grow "from below," that is, draw on personal initiative and social networks rather than institutional support. Immigrants' orientation towards local and global co-ethnic networks is intertwined with their socio-linguistic separatism and may play a dual role in their futures. On one hand, the "diasporic syndrome" is conducive to the cultural alienation from the host society and, therefore, to social marginality. On the positive side, co-ethnic community life serves as a potent source of social support and mental well-being for many immigrants, ameliorating the process of uprooting and hardships of resettlement (Remennick, 2002a).

Since Israel has hosted about 62 percent of all Jews who left the FSU after 1988, it has naturally become the demographic center of the global Russian-speaking Jewish diaspora. Given the relative geographic proximity of Israel to Europe (about a four-hour flight to most destinations), the transnational links established by Russian Israelis are especially dense with the European part of the FSU and with other European hubs of Russian community—major German cities, Prague, London, Greece, and Cyprus. The physical links with the U.S. and Canada are more difficult to maintain due to greater distances and more expensive travel, so the remote connections via telephone and e-mail are more common. The joint businesses of Russian speakers spanning the Mediterranean area include organizations of tours of artists and performers, import and export of food between the FSU, Israel, Germany, Greece, and Cyprus; manpower companies arranging for employment of Russian speakers across the region; entertainment and sex industries smuggling Russian women across borders and, naturally, operating in the shadows. On the other hand, the institutional links between Russian Jews living in Israel, U.S., and Canada are still rather weak.

Dr. Sam Kilger, a sociologist of Russian origin working for the American Jewish Committee and representing Russian New Yorkers, has cogently noted an almost exclusive orientation of Russian Jews in Israel towards their former homelands in the FSU rather than attempts to team up with Russian Jews in America for joint projects and mutual support. While Russian Jews in the U.S. express massive support for Israel (and endorse it by their monetary donations for Israeli causes), Russian Jews do not show much awareness or appreciation of these efforts. American Jewish organizations consider sponsoring more intense human exchange via joint projects to broker closer ties between former Soviet Jews separated by the Mediterranean Sea and Atlantic Ocean (S. Kliger, personal communication).

Links with the homeland and the global Russian-Jewish diaspora have emerged as one of the key sources of the apparent self-sufficiency of the Israeli-Russian community. The very availability of these networks, in both material and virtual terms, attenuates the newcomers' dependency on the host society and allows them to preserve their old identity or to invent a new, hyphenated one of "Russian Israeli." Global Russian-language press and electronic media (such as RTVi channel and Russian Internet) have a special role to play in sustaining bi-national or transnational identity among Russian speakers, enabling their mental and emotional, and sometimes actual, participation in the life of more than one country. Therefore, the Israeli-Russian version of transnationalism can be described as pertaining mainly to the socio-cultural and identity realm. To be sure, the extent of olim involvement with transnational networks strongly differs, mainly as a function of their age, ethnicity, personal and family history, and occupational success in Israel. There seems to be a core group of young-to-middle-aged successful professionals coming to Israel from the metropolitan centers of the FSU, who display more interest in transnational co-ethnic activities. These Israeli Russians are often well integrated in the host society (i.e., are bilingual and bicultural) and active in transnational exchange. Conversely, older Russian speakers and those disappointed in their professional ambitions often seek self-actualization and support on the Israeli "Russian street," while some of them may go back to Russia for good. The transnational opportunities are mainly open to more dynamic immigrants endowed with social and marketable skills applicable in the global economy. Despite the tacit resistance of the mainstream, the influence of Russian Jews on Israeli politics, legislation, and economic life is growing. This is conducive to both the incorporation of the immigrants into the existing institutions and to their successful lobbying for the cultural rights of Russian speakers. The gradual penetration of Russian Israelis into the national and local government may also enhance organized support for transnational activities, such as scientific and industrial cooperation with the FSU. Hence, a decade or so from now, grass-root transnational structures built by Russian Jews may also add a new institutional roof "from above."

Israeli Society and the Great Russian Aliyah: The Mutual Impact

In conclusion, let me cast a general glance on the social and economic impact made by Israelis with Russian accents on the receiving society, and the processes of their Israelization. All things considered, was this immigrant wave a burden or a blessing for the small and troubled country? Let us take a closer look at the dynamics of the principal domains of Israeli society by the early 2000s, after some fifteen years of close co-existence between Hebrew-and Russian-speaking Israelis.

The *demographic impact* of almost one million former Soviet Jews has been impressive in several respects. Fist and foremost, they have shifted the shaky balance between Jewish and Arab Israelis, fortifying the Jewish majority and bringing it to 80 percent (Della Pergola, 2004). As most Russian-speaking immigrants are secular and Ashkenazi, their presence has enhanced the respective segments of the Jewish population, with the ensuing changes in the electoral basis of different political forces. At the same time, ethnically mixed composition of former Soviet immigrants compelled the Israeli establishment to relax the definitions and broaden the boundaries of the Jewish affiliation for most purposes but religious rituals, but this will have to change too in the near future.

As total fertility rates of former Soviet Jews have been much lower than those of Israeli Jews (in the early 1990s, around 1.3 vs. 2.8, respectively), their increment in the population has contributed to the slow but tangible decrease of the Jewish fertility rates occurring in all sectors but the Orthodox. On the other hand, Russian Jews who moved to Israel tend to have more children than those who remained in the FSU, due to both their slowly improving living standards and the adoption of the local family standards with at least two to three children as a norm. Mark Tolts (2005) estimated that as a result of moving to Israel, Russian Jews experienced a positive vital balance (in 1999, 9.300 births vs. 6.300 deaths, with a population increment of 3.000). Had they stayed in Russia, the respective figured would have been 5.200 and 10.300, with the loss of 5.100 Jews for the next generation. In 1999, total fertility rates among Russian olim in Israel who arrived in 1990, 1991, and 1992 were, respectively, 1.78, 1.81, and 1.82, indicating slow but consistent growth in their family size, approaching the levels of secular Israelis (2–2.2 in the early 2000s). Over the last decade, life expectancy of former Soviets in Israel has improved significantly, virtually reaching the means for the general Jewish population (roughly 78 for men and 81 for women in 2002). Thus, in purely demographic terms, the community of former Soviet Jews has certainly improved its vital balance and prospects for physical continuity as a result of relocation.

Politics. During the 1990s, ethnic mobilization of former Soviet immigrants took the shape of Russian immigrant parties first emerging as political lobbies for olim rights (Israel be Aliyah) and increasingly involved in the national political agenda, splitting along the mainstream spectrum from the liberal left to the ultra-nationalist. The process of mainstreaming of Russian politicians and Knesset members resulted in their merger with the large parties by the early 2000s. Yet, politicians with Russian accents still form defined ethnic factions in Likud, Avoda, Meretz, Kadima, and Ehud Leumi, and with each new election campaign Russian immigrants are targeted as a separate voting entity, which due to its size often shapes the outcome. Since the mid–1990s, the overwhelming majority of Russian Jews has identified with the secular nationalist right-wing agenda, espousing hawkish anti-Arab ideology. (One cannot miss the analogy with the predominant Republican leanings of Russian Jews in the U.S.) At the local level, Russian immigrants increasingly promote their candidates for municipal administration, and in several Israeli towns their representatives became deputy majors and City Council members. Thus, although Russian Jews did not join the Israeli political elite in numbers congruent with their weight in the population, they have certainly delegated from their ranks a number of prominent leaders whose voice is heard in the corridors of power.

Economy. The Great Aliyah spearheaded the economic boom of the

1990s, due to its demographic size and significant human capital. The rates of unemployment among Russian immigrants of working age decreased from about 40 percent in 1991 to about 10 percent (the national average) in the early 2000s, so over 90 percent of them are in gainful employment. Although the majority could not pursue their original occupations, most olim make a decent living and do not rely on the welfare system any more than native Israelis. Professionals with Russian accents are densely present today in every economic niche, from medicine to education to high-tech, engineering, and military industry. Russian immigrants comprise over 20 percent of the consumer market in real estate, personal services, food and catering, tourism, and every other economic sector. Besides contributing to the mainstream manufacturing and consumption, they have also established a thriving ethnic economy catering to their specific needs, but also involving a range of untaxed cash flows and employing their undocumented co-ethnics from the FSU.

Culture and language. A thriving subculture has emerged on the Israeli "Russian Street," gradually crossing the community boundaries to attract general Israeli audiences, at least in the genres that are less dependent on language, such as music and dance. Russian performers who, besides their artistic talents, have mastered good Hebrew (exemplified by the Gesher Theater company) established themselves as national cultural celebrities; the Israeli-Russian TV channel (where all shows and films have Hebrew subtitles) is watched not only by Russian speakers but also in some Israeli homes. Reflecting the rising socioeconomic status of Soviet immigrants, Russian has, in fact, become the most common second language in Israel. Although a different language base still forms a barrier between the immigrant and mainstream cultural and media consumption, these borders are increasingly penetrable. The basket of cultural consumption of the former Soviets (especially younger ones) grows wider over time, incorporating many Hebrew and international elements into their reading and watching. In education, the national network of Mofet schools established by Russian immigrant teachers of math and sciences had upgraded Israel's educational standards, incorporating over time increasing numbers of native children and youth. Children of Russian Jews who grew up in Israel still manifest a high propensity for education, forming about 30 percent of all undergraduate students in universities and colleges and promising upward social mobility for the second generation.

In the Israeli Defense Forces, Russian youths comprise about 25 percent of the regular duty soldiers, including 20 percent of the staff in elite units and in officers' courses. On the other hand, due to their dislike of the military and recurrent disciplinary problems, about 30 percent of inmates in Israeli military prisons speak with a Russian accent. In other words, olim soldiers are found on both ends of the spectrum, among the best and among the most troubled ones. Many elite former Soviet engineers are working in the military and aviation industry, research and development, contributing to the national security on the technological side.

Besides these major domains of Israel life, Russian immigrants have also contributed to both amateur and professional sports, upgrading most local and national teams. Many of the best soccer and basketball players, swimmers and other athletes, as well as their coaches, are former Soviets; their efforts and traditions of excellence imported from the Soviet sport schools brought to Israel several Olympic medals (which seldom happened in the past). Finally, in the everyday life of Israeli neighborhoods (especially the less wealthy ones), Russian immigrants often upgraded the existing population profiles, adding facets of a more quiet and clean behavior respectful of the neighbors, trying to counter the littering and chutzpah common in the conduct of the Israeli society's lower tiers. In the open markets, shopping malls, public transport, medical clinics, and every other social venue the advent of Russian Jews has largely improved the general demeanor of the local crowd. This self-flattering opinion has been repeatedly expressed not only by Russian immigrants themselves, but also supported by many veteran Israelis, both in my own and other ethnographic research (see the work of Fialkova and Yelenevskaya, Zilberg, Leshem, Horowits, Lomsky-Feder, and others). On the other hand, the marginalized segments of Russian youth added new facets to the local youth culture in the streets, featuring beer cans and vodka bottles, chain smoking, Russian pop and disco music, Russian *mat* (curse lore) as their regular language, and outbursts of inter-group violence, for example, between youths from the Caucasus and other parts of the FSU.

Throughout their years of adjustment to Israeli society, Russian Jews managed to preserve many elements of their old lifestyle, buying familiar food in non-kosher Russian groceries, celebrating the New Year with a fir tree, attending shows by their favorite Russian performers, sending their children to Russian-style schools and enrichment activities. As the largest cultural and linguistic Jewish minority in the country, they could afford to cross the bridge to Israel slowly and on their own terms, picking from the mainstream cultural menu some items (e.g., new food and dress items) and rejecting others, pertaining to their core values (e.g., gender roles and parent-child relations). By the virtue of its mixed demographics and abundance of families with non-Jewish members, the Great Aliyah introduced new facets of diversity to the Israeli ethnic mosaic and compelled the host society to redefine the very boundaries of Jewish identity and collectivity. Despite consistent resistance of the Orthodox rabbinical establishment, Russian olim through their political and cultural activities are gradually reshaping the traditional religious understanding of Jewishness as such, showing by their own example that there is more than one way of being a Jew. By doing this, they redress the delicate balance between religious and secular sectors of the Israeli polity. The fortification of the secular society and secular forms of Jewish identity will hopefully increase the political pressure for separation between religion and the state and improve Israel's image as a viable democracy. This would probably be the most important contribution of the Russian aliyah to the future destiny of Israel.

Notes

1. Although I dislike this language as ideologically loaded, I will use the terms aliyah and olim because they are very typical of the Israeli discourse on immigration, constantly appear in the mass media, and are used by immigrants themselves.
2. Throughout this chapter, I will refer to former Soviet Jews, Russian Jews, Russian immigrants, and olim (repatriates) interchangeably, as synonyms. The word Russian is used to describe Russian-speakers, as language is the principal common ground for the otherwise diverse immigrants, coming from all the former Soviet republics.
3. Ashkenazi Jews (i.e., originating from East-Central Europe) had founded the state and still comprise a hegemonic group in the Israeli society, forming the backbone of the political, economic, and academic elites. Jews of South European and Middle Eastern origin (Mizrahim), although forming about half of the population, still manifest socio-economic disadvantage and educational gaps (Goldscheider, 1996; Cohen and Haberfeld, 1998). The majority of former Soviet Jews are of Ashkenazi origin and their influx over the 1990s significantly fortified the Ashkenazi ranks.
4. I am only touching upon Ethiopian immigration of the 1990s inasmuch as it crossed paths with the Russian Jews. For more detailed accounts on this very

unique wave of immigrants see the works of Shalva Weil, Malka Shabtai, Haim Rosen, and other Israeli anthropologists.

5. Israel is one of the most contested and troubled spots of the global geopolitical map. Whenever I have to relate to the political processes and current events, I will try to use the most neutral language possible and not to reveal my personal sympathies and opinions. My focus is not on the Israeli politics and government, but on Russian Jews in the context of given Israeli realities.

6. I keep a scrapbook of Hebrew newspaper articles and other citations from radio and TV news and talk shows that engage the topic of the proliferation of non-Jews in the current aliyah wave, and common forgery of Jewish documents in the FSU. Unfortunately, these allegations are not unfounded: while visiting different cities in the FSU, I heard stories about the black market of Jewish birth, marriage, and death certificates procured from elderly Jews or their young relatives in exchange for money, favors or under threat. As last names may change due to marriage, loss of documents, etc. –fabricating then a new "family history" is not so difficult.

7. Many problems faced by non-Jewish olim have to do with extreme difficulty of obtaining Israeli visas and residence permits for their non-Jewish relatives, especially elderly parents. Many informants in my fieldwork complained that they have been struggling for years with the Ministry of Interior to allow their siblings and parents even come visit them in Israel, let alone stay for good. Civil marriage is another insoluble problem: the persistent attempts of the Israeli Left, olim parties, and most recently Shinui to introduce alternative registration of marriage by municipal authorities have failed, meeting with fierce opposition of the Orthodoxy. Nearby Cyprus has been the most popular destination of "marriage tourism" for non-Jewish Israelis ineligible for religious ritual in Israel.

8. I am entering here a dangerous ground (largely avoided in the Israeli political discourse) of the ethnic and social composition of the latest wave of former Soviet immigrants, of whom two-thirds are non Jews, have lower levels of education and largely enter a manual labor sector of the Israeli economy, often from its "back door," that is, untaxed cash economy. Sochnut is interested in filling the plummeting quotas of aliyahh (Rubina, 2004), and the dispossessed people from the vast former Soviet periphery are willing to flee to any "abroad" to find sources of livelihood and help their relatives in the FSU by sending remittances. Driven by economic motives, most have little interest in learning Hebrew, serving in the IDF and becoming Jews. The young olim are increasingly involved in criminal behavior, drug use, alcoholism, and even anti-Semitic attacks. Yet the Israeli policymakers and brokers of aliyah are unwilling to examine the issues of "quality" and social capital of the immigrants, let alone alter the entry policies. The implicit rationale is: former Soviet olim help Israel maintain demographic balance vis-à-vis Moslems within and outside the country.

9. Thus, one informant told me how their Polish-born landlady first instructed them in the use of electricity and WC in her apartment (assuming they had never used them before) and later came weekly to check if the walls and furniture were still unharmed. When they hosted their close relatives just arrived from Russia for a week or so, helping them find a suitable flat in the vicinity, the landlady brought

a policeman to evict the relatives who had not been mentioned in the lease contract. Needless to say, she made a scene every time their rental check was late by half a day. My informant was deeply insulted by this "predator behavior," in her words, of fellow Jews towards poor and disoriented newcomers.

10. For the details of methodology, sample and findings see: Remennick, L. Language Acquisition as the Main Vehicle of Social Integration: The Case of Russian Jewish Immigrants in Israel. International Journal of the Sociology of Language 2003, 164: 83–105, and Remennick, L. What Does Integration Mean? Social Insertion of Russian Jewish Immigrants in Israel. Journal of International Migration and Integration 2003, 4(1): 23–48.

11. The reader will find more reflections about former Soviet immigrant women's paths to social integration in the West in Chapter IIIA describing their encounter with American ideas about femininity and feminism.

12. From the early 1990s on, the Sochnut has maintained several immigration programs for ex-Soviet Jewish adolescents (NAALE, SELA) coming to Israel alone to complete high school, learn Hebrew and, possibly, continue to the University, with the hope that the parents will joint them later on. These newcomers are settled in "youth villages" (boarding schools), where they experience many problems vis-à-vis their Israeli peers, miss their families, and often face harsh Israeli realities head-on (Mirsky, 1998). Some of them bridge the gap to the youth mainstream fairly soon (especially after the military service), while others lump together in Russian peer groups (or gangs) and live on the margins of the Israeli society. Despite all the challenges, few of them return to the FSU; the majority assumes Israeli citizenship and are later joined by the parents.

13. More recent media images of Russian immigrants on the Israeli TV include the puppets of olim politicians such as Natan Sharansky and Avigdor Liberman in the satiric puppet show of the late 1990s *Hartsufim*, and most recently a very popular image of supermarket cashier Luba from a weekend satiric show *Eretz Nehederet* (Wonderland)—a heavy middle-aged lady in a blond wig and large specs who is both tough and cunning with the clients. Apart from their thick Russian accent, all these characters are usually endowed with some traits reflecting Russian Jews' totalitarian past and current marginal place in Israeli society (e.g., cashier Luba had probably been some kind of boss back in Russia, judging by her tough manners and demeanor of hurt dignity). Many recent Israeli films feature small-role characters with a Russian accent, usually depicted as security guards, pizza delivery boys, salesgirls and street women, more seldom as doctors, and never as business managers. Yet, by and large, the images of Russian olim are not too common in the Israeli cinema and the media.

3

Soviet Jews in the U.S.:
Chasing the American Dream

"Centuries of persecution and oppression tend to develop extreme traits of character, some most commendable, others not so praiseworthy. These people possess all the faults of an oppressed people, but they have also the heroic virtues fostered by their oppression. The Russian Jew seems to be of a dual character; to be the best of men and the worst, to practice the meanest vices and the most exalted virtues."

"The records of the public schools show that the attendance of the Jewish children is more regular than that of the children of any other class, and that their standard of scholarship is higher. No sacrifice is considered too great by the Hebrew father and mother to keep their children at school as long as possible."

"A strong point in favor of the Russian Jewish immigrants is the fact that they come here with the intention of becoming permanent citizens of the United States. They alone, perhaps, of all the immigrants who come to America are free from any endearing ties and associations which would, at any future time, draw them back to the land of their birth."
—from Ida M. Van Etten's 1893 essay
"Russian Jews as Desirable Immigrants"

Introduction

America has always been perceived by Russian Jews as a country of unlimited opportunities, a safe haven free of ethnic prejudice and persecution, or *goldene medina* (Yiddish for golden land)—a belief that lay behind all the four waves of their migrations to the U.S.

169

(Simon, 1997; Gold, 1999). The first historic wave of about 3.2 million East European Jews came to American shores between the late 1870s and early 1920s on the tide of privations, persecution, and pogroms they had suffered in the Russian Empire and other Slavic countries. They were then the poorest and the least desirable group of immigrants in the eyes of the hegemonic Christian majority, which stereotyped them as people who are "dirty, cannot speak the English language, live closely crowded in unwholesome, ill-smelling tenement quarters . . . and do not assimilate with other people." (Van Etten, 1893). German Jews (who had arrived in the U.S. some thirty years earlier and by the late 1870s had become wealthy capitalists with affluent lifestyles and polished manners) also looked down upon their poor East European cousins and generously donated money for "civilizing" these "savages" (Simon, 1997).

In her essay written in defense of Russian Jews, a late nineteenth-century publicist, Ida Van Etten, challenged these negative images, stressing that Russian Jews manifested tremendous power "to rise above their miserable condition" and had potential for upward social mobility via hard work, propensity for education, and social activism. Jewish workers, students, and agitators had indeed been at the heart of the nascent labor movement in the New York garment industry, and their efforts ultimately led to mass improvement of labor conditions for all. Van Etten goes on to praise other Jewish virtues such as temperance and sobriety, low rates of criminal behavior, independent thinking and rejection of political demagoguery, and strong family values. She concluded her essay by predicting that Russian Jews would soon rise to prominence in the American economy and politics. Indeed, the children, and especially grandchildren, of the poor illiterate Jews who disembarked from the crowded boats, were frowned upon and checked for lice and trachoma on the Ellis Island, had already started mass entry into professions and the American middle class, becoming urban and secular at the same time. Abundant literature has been devoted to the acculturation and success story of the first two generations of Russian Jews in America (e.g., Simon, 1997; Gold, 1999; Sarna, 2003), and I will not go into it in detail. I began with this historical narrative and quoted Van Etten's cogent essay so as to underscore the intrinsic cultural coherence and continuity in the immigration narrative of all the consequent waves of Russian Jews who reached American shores from the turn of the twentieth century to the present (Gold, 1999).

Despite this historic and cultural continuity, every new wave of Jewish immigrants was more assimilated and less Jewish than the previous one, reflecting the major trends toward secularization and assimilation experienced by Jews in most sending societies.

The Second Wave was mainly composed of Holocaust survivors fleeing devastated Europe in the wake of the World War II (joining those few who had managed to escape before 1939); among them, Jews of Russian/Soviet origin were a small but prominent minority. Along with the descendants of the First Wave, these Jews from East-Central Europe became founders of the contemporary Jewish communities and residential enclaves such as those in Brighton Beach in New York and West Hollywood in California. The generation of Nazi camp survivors was multicultural and very heterogeneous, speaking a host of European languages along with Yiddish. Some of them were deeply religious and prayed in Hebrew, while others paid superficial dues to the Jewish traditions, and yet others (e.g., educated German Jews who fled Nazi Germany) were fully secular and positioned themselves as life-long European expatriates. By the late 1950s, this patchwork of European Jewish cultures made a deep imprint on the American urban landscape, creating many distinct neighborhoods with their own ethno-cultural landmarks: schools, synagogues, community centers, groceries, eateries, and other ethnic businesses. Over time, all these different groups of Jewish Americans, defined by their origin countries and time of immigration, as well as by education and achieved social status, have established complex relations with each other, often imbued with negative stereotypes and social exclusion. The established community met every new wave of arrivals with a mix of welcome and suspicion, as they were often perceived as the "wrong kind of Jews" (too secular, too religious, or simply weird), people of the dim past and dubious migration tracks (Simon, 1997; Orleck, 1999; Hoffman, 2001). (Let me note sadly that Jewish intolerance and prejudice towards their own brethren can at times exceed that shown by Gentiles). This was the social fabric of the American Jewish life, into which Soviet Jewish immigrants of the 1970s, and the following wave of the late 1980s and 1990s, were immersed by the will of fate and the directive hand of the Hebrew Immigrant Aid Society (HIAS).

The atmosphere that surrounded the arrival of the first wave of Jewish refugees from the "Soviet Egypt" was initially marked with genuine enthusiasm, as many American Jews had contributed their efforts and their dollars to the cause of "liberating Soviet Jews." The established Jewish communities that for years had lobbied for their emigration rights, and then sponsored the resettlement of Soviet Jews, expected to welcome to their ranks a group of people like themselves (or rather resembling their East European grandparents) who would invigorate and rejuvenate the community life. Although most American Jews had known about the destruction of Jewish life in the USSR and the secular ways of Russian Jews, they certainly expected that, after escaping the confines of atheism, they would seek to join their brothers in faith. In Rita Simon's words (1997:75), "Many American Jews expected the Soviet Jews to arrive hat in hand, head slightly bowed, and grateful." Reality brought bitter disappointment: the "New Russian Jews" of the 1970s were not only ignorant of the very basics of the Jewish observance, but were also unwilling to learn and get any closer to Jewish life, as it was understood by American Jews. Only the elderly and those coming from the Soviet periphery responded to the welcome of the synagogues and Yiddish cultural societies; the younger and better-educated ones were busy looking for well-paying jobs, advancing their careers, and improving their living standards. The majority stayed in touch with Jewish community organizations as long as they were useful in the resettlement process; when the time came to return the favors, to pay the fees, and volunteer their own time for the mutual causes most newcomers fell out of sight. This is the side of the story told by American Jewish activists; the newcomers saw this encounter in a different light, mainly as an attempt by their wealthy distant cousins to push on them a version of Jewish identity they could not accept. Soviet Jews had expected to be met as lost family members and partake in the community's wealth and social networks; not to be patronized but respected for their hardships and stoicism vis-à-vis the Soviet regime; accepted for the way they were, not judged for their lost Judaic observance. Moreover, they cherished their high European culture, were proud of their professional identities and many of them were unwilling to accept any jobs paying a minimum wage, as their forefathers did in the early twentieth century. They wanted to remain Jewish in America on their own terms, defined by the Soviet reality that had shaped their unique self-image as a "persecuted elite." But was it possible in the Golden Land?

I will try to cast some light on the acculturation of Russian Jews to life in America, and to American Judaism, drawing upon ethnographic material collected in three American urban areas with significant presences of Russian Jews: Metropolitan New York, Greater Boston, and the San Francisco Bay Area of California. First-person narratives, oral histories, observations of natural social interactions, and other methods of so-called unobtrusive social research are invaluable tools for an in-depth understanding of lived immigration experiences; these methods of data collection have gained increasing recognition and a firm place in the migration literature side by side with traditional survey research and statistical analysis (Agozino, 2000; Portes and DeWind, 2004, Morawska, 2004). In addition to my own data, I will also rely on the earlier social research on Soviet Jews in the U.S. by Fran Markowitz (1993), Rita J. Simon (1997), Barry Chiswick (2000), Zvi Gitelman (1997), Steven Gold (1997, 1999, 2003), and Annelise Orleck (1999), and Betty Hoffman (2001), as well as recent surveys by Sam Kliger (2004) and Dimitri Liakhovitski (2004, 2005) and ethnographic data collected by Vera Kishinevsky (2004), Philip Kasinitz et al. (2001), and a few other researchers. During the 1980s and 1990s only a handful of mainstream American social researchers were interested in Russian-Jewish immigration (most of them are listed above). American Jewish organizations were mainly focused on issues of Jewish observance and community participation among Russian Jews and did not fund research driven by a more general social integration agenda. Some statistical information on Soviet-Jewish immigrants can be drawn from the two recent Jewish Population Surveys of 1990 and 2000–1. However, most figures cited below are either expert estimates or come from modest local studies, often motivated by specific goals such as elections and voting patterns of Russian Jews. However, a new cohort of writers is emerging: most articles, dissertations, and books on the Russian-Jewish experience in the U.S. published in the 2000s have been written by researchers of former Soviet origin living in the U.S., and hence reflect a first-hand acquaintance with the reality they depict. These recent writings typically zoom in on ethnographic details and personal narratives, not on statistical trends. The paucity of valid population-based data on the geographic distribution and social condition of post-Soviet immigrants in the U.S. is a puzzle in itself; my modest goal is to review the available data as a backdrop, but mainly to explore and interpret some previously overlooked aspects of the encounter between former Soviet Jews and American society.

Soviet Jews on the American Jewish Landscape

For the last fifty years, demographers and sociologists have struggled with the thankless task of counting American Jews; the numbers may vary broadly as a function of the operational definition of who is a Jew and the wording of the survey items. (General population censuses are of little help as they usually do not include direct questions on religion and ethnicity is often coded by the country of birth rather than ancestry, for example, the response *Russian Jew* would be coded as *Russian* [Chiswick, 2000]). The discrepancies in the published data reflect the gap between understanding of Jewish-ness as religion, ethnicity, or ancestry. Many non-observant Jews do not identify themselves as such in surveys, but, rather, choose the "no religion" category. Some secular Jews who count many generations on American soil no longer see themselves as ethnic Jews, perceiving ethnicity as cultural practice or a set of customs that are alien to them. Thus the range of estimates of American Jewish population starts from 5.2 million on the lower end and goes all the way to an upper estimate of 6.7 million when using an extended definition of Jewish affiliation. Between 6.7 and 6.9 million Americans live in "Jewish households," that is, are Jews themselves and/or have Jewish spouses and/or observe some traditions. Some scholars assert that the U.S. Jewish population has grown by 18 percent since 1990, while the latest Jewish Population Survey of 2001 has shown that it has in fact declined by 5.5 percent (Singer and Grossman, 2004). The Survey further suggests that 15 percent of all American Jews are foreign born, among them the majority immigrated from the former Soviet Union since 1970 (NJPS, 2001; Kliger, 2004).

Estimating the size of the total Russian-Jewish population in the U.S. is even more difficult. According to official governmental statistics of legal immigration, between 1820 and 2001 the number of migrants and refugees from Russia, the USSR, and the FSU totaled about 3,962 million people, most of whom were Jewish; Armenian refugees formed a 5–8 percent minority and other non-Jews are estimated at 10 percent. The U.S. Department of State reported on 598,519 Jewish refugees from the USSR/FSU who immigrated between 1961 and 2001, and the Department of Justice published a much lower figure of 394,140 (Chiswick and Wenz, 2004). These discrepancies suggest that Soviet Jewish refugee program was controversial and politically charged and that federal authorities were unwilling to reveal the true size of this migrant wave, and probably downplayed it in the face of criticism of the "special treatment" Russian Jews were getting vis-à-vis other claimants of refugee status (Lazin, 2005). Expert estimates show that the first major post-war wave of Soviet Jewish emigration probably brought to American shores over 250,000 individuals between 1970 and 1981, with the majority arriving between 1975 and 1980. Another 350,000 (the Fourth Wave in the American count) have joined them about a decade later, in the wake of the USSR's demise (Gitelman, 1997; Tolts, 2004).

The majority, some 75–80 percent, of all former Soviet Jews now living in the U.S. came here as refugees, with the ensuing entitlement to governmental assistance programs. When counted together with other former Soviet Jews who moved to the U.S. under other legal statuses (with job visas, as winners of the Diversity, or Green Card, Lottery, spouses and other sponsored relatives of American citizens), the total size of the Russian-speaking Jewish population in this country is estimated at between 600 and 750 thousand. This is the second-largest population of Russian-speaking Jews after Israel and the largest one in the Diaspora. HIAS statistics and other estimates indicate that about 50 percent of all former Soviet Jews live in Metropolitan New York and the rest are scattered among several major metropolitan areas—Los Angeles, Chicago, Boston, San Francisco, Philadelphia, Cleveland, and a few others (Kliger, 2004).

According to the last Jewish Population Survey, among Soviet immigrants who live in the U.S. since 1980, fully 30 percent are older than sixty-five (compared to only 7 percent among Jewish immigrants from other countries) and only 12 percent have children below age eighteen (vs. 28 percent for other Jewish immigrants). Some alternative sources (HIAS, 2000) cite a much lower percentage of elderly immigrants (16 percent) and a higher share of children (23 percent). A large number of Soviet immigrants live below the official poverty line (27 percent vs. 11 percent among other immigrant Jews), and 46 percent report an annual household income of less than $15,000 (vs. 13 percent, respectively). The latter figures reflect high proportion of the elderly immigrants who are unemployed, have no pension savings of their own, and therefore qualify for Supplemental Social Security Income (SSI) and other welfare benefits. On the other hand, some Russian-Jewish households may underreport their real income in order to safeguard their SSI and other welfare benefits (NJPS, 2001). Comparison of the economic adjustment of Soviet refugees (of whom 80 percent were estimated to be Jews) vis-à-vis other immigrants according to the U.S. censuses of 1980 and 1990 has shown that older people with less education and poorer English skills continue to fare much worse after five to seven years in the country vis-à-vis their younger and more educated compatriots with better command of English. The latter category of former Soviet Jews has greatly improved their income over the first five years in America, and their economic advancement is comparable to that of Asian immigrants who have similar levels of education (Chiswick, 2000; Chiswick and Wenz, 2004).

I will argue in this chapter that there is no single and coherent migration narrative describing this stream of post-Soviet Jewish migrations to America. Both the immigrants' social characteristics and the conditions for their integration differed vastly between various hosting states and cities. As they say in the real estate business, location is everything; this is similarly true about social and economic fortunes of Soviet Jews in the diverse American society. As it is hardly possible to capture all the geographic diversity of Russian-American experience, I will limit my study to three selected metropolitan centers on the East and West Coast with significant presence of former Soviet Jews that represent different dimensions of this experience. I will start from a general description of the profile of the Russian Jewish communities in New York, Boston, and San-Francisco Bay Area, and then discuss the major thematic domains and issues that have emerged in my field work, illustrating them with individual examples and quotes from the interviews conducted in these cities. My empirical basis for the following analysis includes over 250 personal interviews with the immigrants, officials and case workers from HIAS, Jewish Community Centers, Jewish Family and Children's Services, Jewish Vocational Services, and other local organizations involved in the resettlement of Russian Jews, as well as observations made in various community settings, anecdotal evidence from personal encounters, the Russian-language press, websites, and other sources. Initial contact with the informants for this research was made in two ways: via Jewish resettlement services and other aid agencies and my personal social networks among Russian Americans, with subsequent snowballing, that is, consecutive referral from one informant to the next. Although the resulting samples are not representative in the statistical sense, I tried to diversify the sources and social networks from which my informants were drawn in terms of period and legal venue of arrival, education, employment type, material wealth, and places of origin in the FSU. Most interviews have been tape-recorded, transcribed, and analyzed by means of repeated scanning for common topics and subsequent thematic coding (Crabtree and Miller, 1992). Some of the spontaneous interactions were reflected in my field notes. The following analysis reflects a synthesis of all these encounters, interviews, and observations made during my repeated visits to the U.S. between 2003 and 2005, both as a researcher and a private traveler. The informants' names are pseudonyms, but other personal details (age, year of arrival, etc.) have been left intact. Before turning to specific themes that emerged in my analysis of Russian-Jewish experiences in the U.S., I will provide a general backdrop on the major city-based communities in question.

Russian Jews in New York

Fully 43 percent of American Jews live in the Northeast of the country, among them over 1.4 million in Greater New York. As the Jewish capital of America, New York has traditionally attracted Russian-Jewish immigrants. An estimated 350,000 of post–1970 immigrants live today in the New York Metropolitan Area, forming about half of all former Soviet Jews who resettled in the U.S. and about one quarter of New York Jewry (Kliger, 2004). Although today Russian speakers are scattered across Greater New York boroughs and in many parts of New Jersey and Long Island, their major concentrations are still found in the old Jewish neighborhoods: Brighton Beach, Kings Highway, Boro Park, and Midwood in Brooklyn; Rego Park and Forest Hills in Queens, Riverdale in the Bronx, and Washington Heights in Manhattan. The influx of Soviet Jews into these areas occurred during the 1970s and late 1980s, when many elderly East European Jews from the previous migration waves died or moved down to Florida, leaving behind multiple residential and commercial vacancies. Other family members and friends who arrived during the 1990s joined the already existing social and residential networks in these neighborhoods. The new residents rejuvenated the old and withering economies of these areas built during the first half of the twentieth century. They opened multiple restaurants, groceries, nightclubs, and bars with bright neon exteriors featuring Russian, Ukrainian, Georgian, Uzbek, and other culinary and cultural traditions varnished by the new American glamour. The few remaining elders who spoke Yiddish, went to synagogues, and voted for Democrats were shocked and intimidated by the pushy newcomers who ate pork and sushi, knew nothing about Jewish life, and professed hard-line conservative views.

Describing the relations between old East-European and new Soviet Jews, a native of New York Annelise Orleck (1999:86) cogently summarized the nature of this conflict:

These new neighbors fell into a strained sort of intimacy, like estranged cousins bound to one another by bloodlines in the distant part, related but uncomfortable. They had high expectations, for each had nurtured idealized images of the other during the long years of struggle to "free Soviet Jewry." And so there were inevitable disappointments, turf wars, and misunderstandings over new immigrants' relationship to Jewish religion and culture; over the traditionally left-wing politics of the old immigrant Jews and the "New Americans" conservatism; over the newcomers' flashy style of dress and non-kosher foods they lined up to buy; over the old-timers' jealousy of the financial subsidies that the new immigrants received; over the perceived gruffness and aggressiveness of the new immigrants; and over the small but visible numbers of gangsters and racketeers who slipped in among the masses of honest émigrés, bringing extortion, prostitution and gang-style killings to neighborhoods that had not been visited by these plagues before.

The social composition of Russian-accented New Yorkers is indeed very diverse, reflecting a cross-section of former Soviet Jewry in terms of origins in the USSR and social background. Due to the paucity of survey research in this population we know little about its socio-demographic profile and different aspects of the integration process. One of the few recent sources of data is the series of surveys among former Soviet immigrants sponsored by the American Jewish Committee of New York between 1998 and 2001 and conducted by the Research Institute for New Americans (RINA) headed by a sociologist of Soviet origin, Dr. Samuel Kliger (2004). The data collected in these surveys show that between 40 percent and 50 percent of Soviet Jews came from Ukraine (mainly large cities such as Kiev, Kharkov, Odessa, and Dnepropetrovsk, as well as smaller towns affected by the Chernobyl nuclear disaster) and 25–25 percent came from big Russian cities, among them about one third from Moscow and St. Petersburg. Another 10 percent came from Belarus and 6 percent from Uzbekistan, including a small but visible minority of Bukharan Jews. Only 20 percent of the sample were younger than thirty-five, while 16 percent were between the ages of fifty-five and sixty-four, and 18 percent were older than sixty-five. Thus over one third of the immigrants belonged to the age bracket when social and economic adaptation in the new country is extremely slow and difficult. Partly due to the advanced age composition, women outnumber men among the Russian Jews of New York (53 percent vs. 47 percent). Similar shares (25 percent) have lived in the city for less than three years and more than nine years; the remaining 50 percent arrived three to nine years ago (the median length of residence was about seven years). The downward economic mobility of recent Jewish immigrants reflects both their own structural features (older age, poor English command, skills incompatible with labor market demands) and the disadvantage many new immigrants experience in the New York economy due to fierce competition for jobs with other skilled immigrants, resulting in a lowering of wages for everyone. In cities with a smaller immigrant body and weaker competition for both blue- and white-collar jobs, Russian Jews reported higher wages than in New York. For example, in Philadelphia only 44 percent of Soviet Jews were in the lowest income bracket, while 19 percent were in the highest one (vs. 76 percent and 2.5 percent, respectively, in New York).

Although about 60 percent of respondents had a higher education in the USSR (which is somewhat higher than the share of people with five or more years of postsecondary education among general Jewish population of New York), their income lagged behind established U.S. Jews. While only 22 percent of American Jewry reported an annual income of less than $25,000 in 1998, this was true about 78 percent of Russian Jews in New York in 1999. Conversely, ten times as many U.S. Jews than Soviet Jews in New York (25 percent and 2.5 percent, respectively) reported being in the highest income bracket of $80,000 or more. The latest survey by RINA in 2004 has shown that only 41 percent of Russian Jews in New York were employed full time, 6 percent worked part time, and fully 53 percent were unemployed. About 67 percent of respondents reported annual family income below $30,000 (*Jewish Week*, October 15, 2004). Anecdotal evidence shows that these official reports fail to capture a vast number of economic activities going on in the co-ethnic sector, with payments made in cash

and unreported for taxation (e.g., private lessons, sublease of dwell-
ings, help in stores, etc.), so the real economic situation among poorer
Russian immigrants may be not as bad as it seems (Gold, 1999). New
York is a traditional hub of Russian-Jewish entrepreneurial activities,
followed by Los Angeles on the West Coast. The corps of Russian
entrepreneurs in the city was formed by the three main groups: former
shadow businessmen (so-called *tsekhoviki*) of the Soviet times; those
who started their business after the fall of the USSR, made some
capital, and moved operations to New York; and finally former Soviet
professionals who failed to find relevant skilled jobs and tried small
business as a way to make a living. Much of the late Soviet and post-
communist business culture based on shadowy informal networks rather
than formal institutions has been transferred to New York. Some niches
of the Russian ethnic business world merge with the criminal structures, using extortion, goods smuggling, money laundering, and white-
collar fraud (e.g., manipulating medical insurance), which reinforce
popular stereotypes of all Russian immigrants as cons and criminals
and feed media stories on the ruthless Russian Mafia (Finckenauer and
Waring, 2001). Russian-Jewish newly rich businessmen love to manifest their wealth and glamour by purchasing expensive real estate,
driving SUVs, wearing leather (and the women, sable furs, diamonds,
and stiletto heels) wherever they go (including the beach), and throw-
ing lavish parties is multiple Russian restaurants. A savvy and hilarious depiction of Russian-Jewish life in New York emerges from the
pages of *The Russian Debutante's Handbook* by a young writer Gary
Shteyngart, who emigrated from St. Petersburg as a boy in the early
1990s.

Between the 1970s and mid–1990s, the Russian enclave of Brighton
Beach has been described by social anthropologists as a thriving subculture of "Little Odessa," the heart of Russian-Jewish New York
(Markowitz, 1993; Orleck, 1999). This crowded stretch of seafront
became a haven for several cohorts of Soviet Jews who had dreamed
about being independent entrepreneurs in the USSR and had, in fact,
few marketable skills to succeed in the mainstream economy. Ethnic
businesses have thrived in Brighton Beach for the last three decades:
its many stores, restaurants, bars and disco clubs catered, until very
recently, solely to Russian-speakers and avoided outsiders by all possible means (such as blanking or camouflaging the entrances). Only
recently have the owners of Russian eateries and groceries discovered

the profits of ethnic tourism in New York and became much friendlier towards native English speakers. A corollary to business activities was crime: during the 1990s Brighton Beach became a safe haven for the global Russian Mafia and the incidence of racketeering, theft, pimping, and inter-group violence became so high that many old-time residents were compelled to move out. To enhance the vilification of Soviet Jews, several Hollywood movies (such as *Little Odessa*) and the popular television series *Law and Order* featured episodes with Russian-speaking émigrés as career gangsters in leather jackets, complete with gold teeth and oversize guns. By the early 2000s, most bosses of the Russian mob have been jailed, gone legal, or moved operations elsewhere, but most Russian businesses are still thriving.

The social landscape of today's Brighton Beach features four synagogues with Russian- and Yiddish-speaking rabbis, also offering classes in English, computing, and other "marketable skills"; a large number of Russian groceries and restaurants with their unique mix of Russian and American chic and glamour; several old age homes employing many Russian-speaking nurses and offering a broad range of cultural activities for the elders; a Russian-owned gymnasium with about 40 percent Russian-speaking members; and a colorful ethnic bathhouse (*bania*), combining a steam room (with heat reaching 120 degrees Fahrenheit, only Russians can survive that!), pool, Jacuzzi, café, and massage parlor, all staffed by Russian speakers. Bathhouses are a favorite social venue for the less sophisticated among former Soviets, often used to reinforce male bonding and strike business deals. American observers who depicted their field trip to the Russian hub of New York were impressed by the low English proficiency of most Brighton residents and visitors; among English-Russian bilinguals, speaking English with their co-ethnics was considered rude and arrogant, so almost no English was heard in the streets and shops (Palatnik and DeAngelis, 2001).

Until the late 1990s, the Brighton Beach Russian community of about 20,000 was typified by its old age, relative poverty and low rates of integration in the American mainstream. (Popular joke: An old lady speaks in Russian to a street cop and when he fails to understand her exclaims, "What a stupid nation, these Americans! We've been living here in Brighton for ten years now, and they still can't speak any Russian"). Over the last five to seven years, Brighton has witnessed a visible rejuvenation of it populace on account of recent arrivals from the FSU, both Jews and non-Jews (winners of the Green Card Lottery, job visa holders, undocumented workers, business visitors, etc.). Judging by the ongoing construction of expensive apartment complexes and renovations of the old buildings on Brighton and Coney Island, many of these New Russians belong to the business class and arrived with money. Many of them chose to live in the area because of proximity to their parents, with the ensuing bonus of free babysitting and domestic help. Yet, the majority of Brighton's residents are middle-aged and elderly of modest means, small-town Ukrainian, Belorussian, Moldavian, Georgian, and other provincial Jews who work in the ethnic economy and/or collect welfare checks. Professional-class and better-integrated immigrants from larger Soviet cities never wished to live there in the first place as it represented the lower tier of the immigrant life, a proverbial ethnic ghetto. Others had started their way in America from this safe haven of Brighton, where one could get by without speaking a word of English, but moved out to other parts of Brooklyn and Manhattan, or to suburban New Jersey and Long Island, as soon as their income and acculturation allowed. However, in many ways Brighton Beach retains its role as cultural home base for most Russian New Yorkers—a place they come to shop for familiar food, to celebrate birthdays, bar mitzvahs and weddings, and to visit older relatives. Both recent arrivals and seasoned New Yorkers need a sense of community, which is created in the groceries, eateries, and beaches of Brighton; many also enjoy the chance to show off their newly acquired wealth and style to their co-ethnics in large gatherings of family and friends. Despite its image as a somewhat provincial ethnic hub, the recent influx of a wealthier population with a concomitant "facelift" of the urban landscape will probably ensure a continued role for Brighton Beach as the ethnic heart of Russian-Jewish life on the East Coast.

At the other end of the Russian-Jewish social scene of New York we find a cluster of intellectual and artistic elite, represented by such international celebrities as sculptor Ernst Neizvestny, postmodern artists Vitaly Komar and Alexander Melamid, cellist and conductor Mstislav Rostropovich and singer Galina Vishnevskaya, and a host of other, more or less famous, writers, journalists, musicians, actors and free thinkers who struggle to make a living in the artistic and intellectual hub of the world. New York had been a spiritual center and a thematic backdrop of the emigrant literature that so much boosted the ripening of dissidence in the Soviet Union, when the outlawed writings by Sergei Dovlatov, Joseph Brodsky, Vasily Aksyonov, Peter Weil, Alexander Genis, and others were smuggled across the border and reached Soviet readers. For years, New York has also been one of the chief centers of Russian-language immigrant press with newspapers such as *Novoe Russkoe Slovo* and the Russian version of the Jewish *Forward*, the literary almanac *Slovo*, and a few other influential periodicals. By the mid–1990s the romantic halo of intellectual dissidence in exile has largely dimmed, as in Russia itself censorship disappeared, and all kinds of literature could thrive in the newly pluralist society. Along with the global spread of Russian-speaking immigrants, there was a mushrooming of Russian-language press and electronic media in many other U.S. cities as well as in Israel, Germany, Britain, and Canada, so that New York, again, lost its unique role within the immigrant media scene. Yet, by this time the Russian-Jewish artistic element has largely become an integral part of the New York cultural mainstream, especially in the art gallery life, music, dance, and other visual and performing arts.

Journalists, writers and other men and women of letters have a more difficult time finding their place in the New York cultural mosaic, but a few younger ones succeeded in attracting readership across ethnic lines: thus, the first novel (in English) by Gary Shteyngart *The Russian Debutante's Handbook*—a hilarious account of the mishaps and adventures experienced by a Russian-born, New York-raised young man—was read by both native and immigrant New Yorkers. Many other intellectuals, of course, could not reach beyond the ethnic press and small-time Russian publishers, but they also have their audience in the city where every fourth Jew speaks and reads in Russian. One of the outlets for their talents was the opening of multiple after-school educational and artistic venues for Russian-Jewish children and youth: Russian language and literature clubs, theater, ballet, and painting studios, gyms and athletic schools that helped transfer the cultural capital of this community to the next generation. The example of Russian ethnic cultural and educational industry in New York was later followed in Boston, Chicago, and other centers of immigrant life. Thus, instead of Jewish Sunday schools and Hebrew summer camps (which many of them had tried at the outset but rapidly left, disliking the religious or Zionist indoctrination) most Russian-Jewish youths found themselves in the rediscovered confines of the Russian cultural universe.

In between Russian grocers of Brighton and intellectuals, artists, and musicians of Manhattan, scattered across New York neighborhoods are thousands of rank-and-file immigrants, most of whom had to part with their old Soviet professions and find new ways of making a living. Some are driving taxis; others work in retail and services, still others retrained to become programmers and social workers. A significant share of Russian immigrants still lives in modest rented apartments in high-rise buildings as few could buy their own homes due to prohibitive costs. Others have prospered and purchased private houses and condominiums in many areas of Brooklyn, especially those near the ocean (e.g., Coney Island, Manhattan Beach, and Sheepshead Bay). Still others opted for larger private houses in the leafy suburbia and commute for work in the heavy New York traffic. Despite problems with affordable housing in Metropolitan New York, most elderly parents live separately from their adult children and grandchildren, often in Jewish community housing projects or in regular apartments subsidized by the federal programs for elderly refugees. In the major Russian-speaking enclaves of the city, a dense network of community organizations (educational, leisure, self-help, religious, etc.) are catering mainly to the needs of the youth and the retired immigrants with time to spare and limited financial resources. The cultural fabric of these organizations is a unique amalgam of Russian/Soviet, American, and Jewish topics and traditions.

Russian Jews in Greater Boston

There are few official sources on statistical patters and social characteristics of Russian Jews who settled in the Greater Boston area of Massachusetts, so this overview is a compilation of several small-scale surveys and databases maintained by the local chapters of the American Jewish organizations, as well as the bits of information and anecdotal evidence offered by my Bostonian informants. Greater Boston area is unique in terms of its high concentration of intellectual resources, perhaps the highest on the East Coast, featuring seven major research universities (Harvard, MIT, Boston University, Tufts, Brandeis, Northeastern, Suffolk), dozens of upscale colleges, major research and tertiary care hospitals, and a host of private companies in computing, information technology (IT), pharmacology, and biotechnology. It is hardly surprising that this city and its vicinity attracted the elite of educated former Soviet Jewry, especially those with backgrounds in education, laboratory science, medicine, and high technology. An estimated 70,000 former Soviets came to Boston after 1970 (but mainly after 1987) as Jewish refugees and have been resettled with the aid of Jewish community services of Greater Boston. Former Soviets are the largest immigrant/minority group in Greater Boston after Puerto Ricans and other Central American ethnics combined (Ena Fineberg, a former teacher of English in Moscow and currently director of the local Jewish Family and Children's Services). Since the mid–1990s, the ranks of Russian-speaking residents in the area have been fortified by many thousands of scientists, engineers, and high-technology specialists (plus their family members) who had come to the universities and industries located in this area on job visas, which were later converted into Green Cards and, in many cases, U.S. citizenship. The latter category of former Soviets is a mix of Jews, Russians, Ukrainians, and any number of other ethnic groups whose entry to the U.S. was due to their human capital rather than ethnic or religious affiliation.

About two-thirds of Russian-speaking Bostonians come from just two cities—Moscow and St. Petersburg, the scientific and educational capitals of the USSR, and over 25 percent have postgraduate degrees (Ena Fineberg). The migration of professionals to Bostonian universities and firms often followed a chain pattern, that is, senior professors, scientists or managers of Russian origin invited on purpose, or tended to hire from diverse applicant pools, the best and the brightest of their co-ethnics, whom they had often known back in the USSR. Thus by the mid–1990s it was not unusual to find a research laboratory at Harvard or Tufts staffed by a Russian-speaking professor and multiple former Soviet post-doctoral scholars, laboratory assistants, graduate and undergrad students. Anti-nepotism/ethnic preference policies of the employers were really beside the point as most of these workers and students arrived there on the basis of merit and achievement.

Thus, in the early and mid–1990s a large percentage of academic and research staff at math, physics, biology, chemistry and other science departments at Harvard, MIT and other elite universities spoke Russian among themselves and accented English with their American and international colleagues. By the late 1990s, many former Soviet professors on the faculty of Boston universities discovered the pitfalls of internal politics of promotion, tenure, research funding, and privilege, as only few could climb to the top of the academic ladder. Attracted by higher wages and guaranteed research funds, many relocated from universities to high-tech/bio-tech industries and other private companies. Yet, to this day many university-based research laboratories at Harvard, Tufts, Brandeis, and Boston University have numerous Russian-speaking scientists in both permanent and post-doctoral positions.

Judging by fragmented local data, over 85 percent of Russian Jews in Boston are employed full time, usually as professionals or white-collar workers. They typically put in anywhere between nine and sixteen hours of work every day; some also work on weekends and holidays or at home. Few of them can take more than a week of holiday at a time. (Russian immigrant anecdote: "How is life in America? –Great! It's like . . . a forced labor camp with fourteen-hour work day and enhanced nutrition"). In most families with children both husbands and wives work, but more wives work part time or with flexible hours. The average family income in this group of former Soviets is between 80,000 and 120,000 (guesstimates of my informants). Reflecting economic returns on their human capital, most Bostonian Russians achieved high living standards and relocated from the ethnic enclaves of Brighton and Lynn to wealthier Brookline and suburban Newton, Lexington, Natick, and other leafy and quiet suburban towns. Their children attend the best public and private schools and engage in multiple extra-curricular activities, which (along with parental wealth) promise their future admission to the upscale colleges and universities. The older generation typically stayed in the subsidized housing complexes of Brighton and other parts of downtown Boston where they have greater access to social services, Russian/Jewish community organizations and to each other, for company. Those who moved to the suburban houses with their children and grandchildren often face social isolation from other Russian-speakers and dependency on the younger family members for transportation and translation.

Like their co-ethnics in New York, Bostonian Russians have gradually established a network of cultural and educational institutions that serve their social and intellectual needs and help transfer Russian-Jewish cultural values and practices to their children, many of whom were born in the U.S. and never lived in a Russian-speaking milieu. The more prominent of these institutions include the Russian School of Mathematics that helps broaden and complement the limited American curriculum and cultivate young mathematical talents, the Russian Art and Music School (both located in Newton), and multiple small-scale and private classes of the Russian language and literature, where children from Russian families can meet each other, find common interests, and stay plugged into their parental culture. There are two Russian-Jewish amateur theaters in Greater Boston, one performing in Russian and the other in Yiddish. Reflecting Russian/Soviet tradition of excellence in chess, many students attend chess classes and some become high-level players and participate in various local and state-wide tournaments. Some of the educational initiatives catering for former Soviets gradually evolved to attract more diverse student body, and by now became English-based and open for everyone; one example is the above-mentioned Mathematical School in Newton, where one-third of the students are non-Russians, most often children of Chinese and Indian immigrants aspiring to a good knowledge of math.

Although Russian food and catering businesses are less prolific in Boston than in New York, both Brighton and suburban towns with significant Russian-speaking population have at least one (and usually more) Russian grocery. As elsewhere in the Russian-Jewish diaspora, these social spaces serve multiple purposes besides food shopping or eating: they sell Russian newspapers (sometimes also videos and CDs), tickets for shows and concerts, feature diverse personal ads in Russian, and provide a familiar ground for waiting in line and small talk with co-ethnics. Russian restaurants are far fewer in the Boston area than in New York, Chicago and other cities of Russian immigration, probably reflecting the peculiar social profile of its Russian-Jewish residents. Very high rates of full-time employment and long working hours in high-tech and research generally leave little spare time for outings and entertainment; when they do go out, Bostonian Russians usually choose from a variety of mainstream or ethnic restaurants like other middle-class Americans. Being secular and largely uninvolved in the Jewish community life they seldom throw bar mitzvah parties for their children (and those who do use American-Jewish venues), and are rather foreign to the show-offs of wealth and success Brighton Beach style. In brief they are busy people having no interest in the flashy and loud style of entertainment so typical of Russian restaurants in America.

Russian Jews in San Francisco Bay Area and Silicon Valley

The links between Russia and California date back to the early eighteenth century, when the Russian Fleet first reached San Francisco Bay and fur traders established a joint Russian-American company with a center in Fort Ross. A larger wave of immigration to Northern California was boosted by the Gold Rush of the mid–1800s, when traders, builders, and adventure-seekers from Russia's far east and north joined thousands of Americans stalking the riches of the El Dorado and Sierra Mountains. Some Jewish traders had also moved to California around that time to try their luck in gold mining or in retail trade providing food, drink, clothing and other supplies to gold-seekers. Some of the landmarks in today's San Francisco (such as the Russian Hill neighborhood erected on the site of an old Russian cemetery) and a few old Orthodox churches and synagogues date back to these days (www.consulrussia.org). San-Francisco has a large Russian Cultural Center opened in the early 1990s that hosts multiple cultural programs, classes of Russian, music and film festivals, and other activities. (www.russiancentersf.com).

Reflecting two recent migrant waves of the late twentieth century, today this area hosts the second largest Russian-Jewish community on the West Coast after Los Angeles. Bay Area Russian speakers fall into two different groups in terms of age and social background. The urban San Francisco immigrants residing in the Sunset and Richmond districts comprise a mix of backgrounds and cities of origin, but generally tend to be older and less integrated, not unlike their counterparts in Brooklyn on the East Coast. Catering to the Russian-speaking enclaves, these neighborhoods feature multiple Russian groceries, eateries, small businesses, and social venues. The other group, spread across the suburban towns of the Bay Area between Palo Alto and San Jose, lives in the so-called Silicon Valley (which is a brand name rather than geographic location)—the hub of the computing, information, and bio-technology world on the West Coast and globally. In this high-tech shrine engineers and software designers of Soviet origin work side by side with Indian, Chinese, European, and any other number or ethnics enjoying fourteen to sixteen hour workdays, six-figure incomes, and transnational lifestyles. While San Francisco's aging Russian community living in subsidized housing or in small rented flats is of modest means if not outright poor, the younger crowd in the Valley is perhaps the wealthiest sector of the American-Russian community, residing in beautiful large houses and driving their kids to private schools in SUVs. Of course, this opulence comes as a result of hard multi-hour labor and is often rather fluid: it can be lost overnight if a company folds up. On the other hand, many of the Russian-speaking owners of the large Valley properties have made significant revenues during the IT boom of the late 1990s and have enough "fat" to keep them going in between the jobs.

The Russian-speaking colony of the Valley is composed of similar numbers of those who had arrived in the U.S. as refugees back in Soviet era and those who relocated here from the FSU, Israel and other countries receiving job offers from the area companies during the 1990s and early 2000s. Some of the Valley's older talents were educated back in the USSR, while their increasing number belong to the 1.5 generation, that is, arrived as children or adolescents, and completed their education in the U.S. (Sergei Bryn, educated at Stanford and one of the two Google's founders and co-owners, belongs to this group). The Valley's population is typified by high mobility, as high-tech companies have their complex lifecycles, starting-up, thriving, going public (i.e., selling their stock on the Wall Street) and some-times also surviving or collapsing, or merging with other firms, or else "outsourcing" and moving their operations to the developing world. With all those changes, often occurring in the matter of a few years, the staff of these companies may rapidly grow or dwindle, workers (and their families) come and go, move abroad, etc. For all these reasons, it is hard to estimate the total number of Bay Area Russians (Jewish and other); I have heard estimates ranging from 50,000 to 100,000, depending on who is counted and how.

Regardless of the exact numbers, the presence of Russians is strongly felt and heard across the Valley towns and, as elsewhere, they have developed their own cultural and educational venues to engage them-selves and their children in Russian pastimes and cultural pursuits. Palo Alto, a town adjacent to Stanford University, serves as the cul-tural hub of this community, featuring not only traditional grocery stores, Russian language classes and chess clubs, but also hosting a peculiar Russian/Soviet tradition of adult intellectual games, humor festivals and amateur song groups.[1] Palo Alto is also a center of an-other large expatriate population—Israeli Jews who permanently moved to California for a variety of economic, political, and personal reasons.

As opposed to a very mixed social composition of Israelis living in their largest enclave outside Israel—Los Angeles—the Bay Area Israelis are also an overly educated crowd working mainly in academic and high-tech venues, as well as running small and large knowledge-intensive businesses. The Israeli-born Jews (sabras) and former Soviet Jews, who spent parts of their immigrant lives in Israel and then moved to the U.S., have quite a few common interests and Hebrew-based cultural attachments. They intersect socially in many Israel- and Jewish community-related events and charity activities, as well as in informal social networks (Gold, 2003). Thus, large numbers of Israelis, including those of Soviet origin, gather every year to celebrate Israel's Independence Day in city parks and other venues; these gatherings feature three languages (English, Hebrew, Russian) and a variety of music and food found in these three newly related cultures.

Russian Jews on the Two Coasts: Some Common Dimensions

Having briefly depicted the general social profile of these three regional Russian-Jewish communities, I will now turn to an analysis of the common themes that have emerged in the interviews, observations, and other components of my ethnographic research conducted on the two U.S. coasts in 2003–2005.

Being Jewish: There and Here

Although former Soviet immigrants are ethnically rather mixed, the predominant group of about two-thirds consists of Jews, full or partial. From my historic and social sketch on former Soviet Jews in chapter 1, the reader can easily infer that there are fundamental differences in the ways Soviet and American Jews perceive and represent their Jewish identity. Descendants of the "Ellis Island cohort" of nineteenth-century East-European Jewry, American Jews construct their ethno-religious heritage in the forms inherited from the pre-modern shtetl (Jewish town) in the Pale of Settlement, drawing on the intertwined components of religion, Yiddish-based cultural traditions, and small-town community life. The blueprint of the popular American imagery of Jews and Jewish life is the 1971 musical *Fiddler on the Roof*; most Americans probably expected their Russian/Soviet co-ethnics to resemble Tevye and his family, forgetting that for Soviet immigrants those times and places became remote history. The American sense of Jewish affiliation still rests on the shul (synagogue) attendance, making donations for Jewish and Israeli causes, celebration of Shabat, some kind of Jewish education for the children, rites of birth and coming of age (circumcision or brit for the boys, and bar/bat mitzvah for boys and girls), getting married under a chupah with rabbi, and celebrating high Jewish holidays. This is the "basic package" of Jewish observance common within the more liberal Judaic denominations (Reformists and Conservatives), in which Judaism is reconciled with modernity, for example, women can be ordained as rabbis and worship together with men. Orthodox Judaism implies rigorous observance of all the tenets of Judaic faith: three daily prayers, no driving or any work on Shabat, keeping kosher (dietary rules), and Ishut (rules of marital life and sexual hygiene). However, less than half of American Jews report in surveys that they are affiliated with any kind of denomination or synagogue, and those who are typically belong to Reform or Conservative congregations. The Jewish connections of most American Jews are often described as "cultural Judaism," when individuals pick and choose for themselves a few cultural practices (historically of religious origin) that symbolize their being Jewish (Dershowitz, 1997). Most often cited practices are celebrating in some form three High Holidays—the Jewish New Year Rosh ha Shana, Passover, and Chanukah; bar/bat mitzvah parties and some Jewish schooling for the children; interest in the Jewish topics in the press and literature; and having half or more close friends who are Jewish. A much smaller share of American Jews (between 10 and 20 percent) light Shabat candles, keep kosher, participate in adult Jewish education, visit Israel, and regularly contribute to Jewish causes (NJPR, 2001; Sarna, 2003).

Former Soviet Jews had been harshly separated from the shtetl life, Judaic practices, and the community spirit of their grandparents; for many decades, state-sponsored anti-Semitic propaganda and policy compelled them to downplay or disguise their Jewish-ness. Yet, Soviet Jews maintained a secular Jewish identity based on their common history (both ancient and modern, including the Second World War and the Holocaust) and mutual experiences of discrimination, prejudice, and adjustment to adversity. Another fundamental part in the Russians' self-perception as Jews is formed by multiple secular icons of Jewish genius and achievement throughout history—the images of great reformers such as Jesus, Marx, or Freud; scientists such as Einstein and Lev Landau, politicians such as Disraeli and Kissinger; chess champions such as Kasparov and Fischer; writers and poets such as Pasternak, Singer, and Brodsky, composers such as Mendelssohn and Mahler, musicians like Horowitz and Heifetz, and so on and so forth. This cultural gallery of their great co-ethnics in different countries and times formed a solid basis for Jewish pride, sense of superiority vis-à-vis non-Jewish majority, and consolation in the face of hardship. These role models served as an important incentive for hard effort, intellectualism and excellence that were so typical of the Jewish urban elite of the Soviet times. Besides, former Soviets dislike and mistrust any formal organizations and express their social affiliations via informal personal networks, which explains their self-distancing from various Jewish community institutions (Gold, 1997).

Russian Jews understand religion in a rather non-dogmatic way, as a spiritual, cultural, or philosophical concept rather than a set of practices or tenets guiding personal behavior. The relationship with God is private for them and faith is not necessarily related to temple attendance, or performing certain rites. Although about 40 percent of Moscow and St. Petersburg Jews in a 1993 survey believed in the existence of God (in a broad meaning of the word), only about 20 percent considered themselves religious in any way, more often Russian Orthodox rather than Judaic. A much higher share of former Soviet Jews than either non-Jewish Russians or U.S. Jews call themselves atheists or agnostics (Kliger, 2001). Perhaps, there are two common components in the Soviet and American ways of being Jewish. One is the central role of the Holocaust as consciousness-shaping event: every other Jew on the Soviet territory had been killed by the Nazis during the occupation, and almost no family was spared these losses. The other is the "social" nature of the Jewish identity, that is, the tendency to stick socially with other Jews, to befriend, date and marry Jews. Although in both FSU and U.S. over 50 percent of the Jews are intermarried (Sarna, 2003; Tolts, 2004), the residual proneness to Jewish sociality is still lingering in the current generations, but is perhaps destined to dwindle in the future diverse and cosmopolitan world. Given the gap in understanding of what it means to be Jewish, it is hardly surprising that Russian and American Jews were a disappointment to each other ever since the late 1970s when the first post-war immigrant wave reached the U.S. (Orleck, 1999). One of my informants, Alex (44), an advanced IT engineer from Moscow who lives in Boston since 1988, recounted his impressions from the Jewish Sunday school his son briefly attended in the early 1990s:

> In these years many of us believed that our kids should be better Jews than we had been, and so we sent them to get some Jewish education. But soon it turned out that our views of Jewish education were at odds with those of local Jewish schools, where our kids were taught to pray and keep kosher. That was it pretty much, their teachers were so ignorant of anything but religion . . . they never told the kids about the twentieth-century Jewish history, even in America itself, let alone Europe and Russia. . . . But religion hadn't been our goal at all; I wanted my son to know more about the Jewish people in the U.S., Russia and across the world, about life in Israel and in the Diaspora; about Jewish literature in Yiddish, about Shalom-Aleichem . . . this is what Jewish education means for me, but we were obviously at cross-purposes. So I guess my son will have to learn all this on his own, from books and travel . . .

Lena (forty), a biology teacher from New York, told a similar story of her brief and negative encounter with American Judaism:

> When my son was in junior high school, he was somewhat interested to learn more about his Jewish side, as were most of his Russian-Jewish classmates; they kind of thought that being Jewish (or different in any other way from the rest) was cool. He had even asked me to arrange for his bar-mitzvah ceremony in the local synagogue, but then he gave up this idea after seeing how much biblical text in Hebrew he'd have to recite, and that he'd have to be circumcised before his bar mitzvah. . . . All these religious rites are so tedious and outdated, so his interest in Jewish-ness evaporated rather soon.

Discouraged by this and similar encounters, most remain secular and detached from Jewish community life, but there is certainly a minority, which is seeking a new social framework for belonging and leans on the established community as a source of new identity and support. These New Americans send their kids to Jewish schools, have bar mitzvah ceremonies and parties, join a synagogue, and socialize with American Jews as role models for their own future success and achievement in America. Lydia, a forty-two-year-old engineer from Moscow retrained into programmer, told me,

> In this country everyone belongs to some community or framework, religious or ethnic; otherwise you don't have a social identity, you don't

know who you are. And we certainly wanted that our kids grew up as Jews, so we sent them to a good full-time Jewish school where they study Hebrew and religion along with the regular subjects. . . . We got a stipend for the first year, but now we pay full tuition ourselves, and it is worth it. Via this school we met many nice and influential people—the parents of our kids' classmates, we got invited to local Jewish homes, we became part of this group. So being Jewish gives you both spiritual content and practical benefits . . .

The last part of Lydia's quote is particularly telling of the sense of social benefit that many Soviet immigrants discovered upon joining Jewish community institutions and personal networks. Detached from their old pre-migration social safety net, they tried to establish new ties within local communities, discovering that affiliation with the Jewish network can bring about many direct and indirect benefits. In most American cities Jews are wealthy, well connected, and often inclined to charity towards the newcomers, so Russian immigrants can only win from joining this group and getting information, referrals, social life, and sometimes material aid. Some other informants told me that they joined Jewish community projects and/or volunteered for its causes out of the sense of gratitude to specific people who had helped them resettle and adjust. But when they did voluntary work, it was not any work but usually something related to their area of expertise. Victor (forty-two), scientist in a pharmacological company in the Bay Area, said,

I believe in reciprocity. Our case worker and a few other people from the Jewish Vocational Services had helped me a lot to find my way on the American labor market in my specialty and they also put my wife in touch with her first employer ten years ago. Since then I volunteer as their consultant trying to help the newcomers to prepare their resume, advice them about local companies, in brief give them a head start. It is time consuming, but you feel great satisfaction when you manage to help someone . . .

Victor's effort had in fact little to do with any Jewish causes, but rather was directed as a gesture of good will and solidarity towards his co-ethnics searching for professional adjustment. Similar stories were told by Tania (thirty-five) in New York, a clinical psychologist who volunteered a few hours each week to counsel immigrant parents on their family and children's problems in the NYANA (New York Association for New Americans, another local chapter of the Jewish Community Services); Dina (fifty) who could not find any paid work and volunteered as a babysitter for immigrants visiting advisors and case workers, and a few other informants. The common line between all these volunteering activities was that their beneficiaries were other immigrants, fresh and disoriented as they themselves were upon arrival. I heard no stories of participation by the last-wave immigrants in the voluntary projects of religious, educational, or any other non-immigrant content. Quite a few retired men and women receiving public aid and having much spare time and energy were involved in community projects seeing this as meaningful pastime for themselves and a chance to return past favors; younger individuals were seen volunteering only when unemployed or underemployed; when they found full-time jobs their participation in the community projects stopped. "We have to fight for our own survival and earn every dollar we can; we cannot afford to do work for free like these wealthy Jewish women married to lawyers and doctors," said Galina (50) a hairdresser from Brooklyn. Of the three cities that I visited, New York Jewish organizations engaged more immigrant volunteers than did those in Boston or San Francisco, reflecting perhaps the specific profile of Russian New Yorkers (high shares of the retired and unemployed with time to spare) as well as a highly developed Jewish organizational culture of New York.

Yet, since the mid-1990s the leadership of the American Jewish organizations such as HIAS and United Jewish Appeal has been determined to attract more Russian Jews to the cultural practices of Judaism American-style by sponsoring community leadership courses, subsidized Sunday schools, and Jewish summer camps for the children. These projects have some popularity within parts of the younger English-speaking immigrant generation, who see them as offering a new spiritual content to fill in the void of their Americanized lives and as a gateway to a new circle of friends and activities. Again, the same need for social belonging and peer company, rather than interest in Judaic practices as such, was the chief motivation for most participants. The young generation is also interested in the Israel-related projects, is willing to travel there, date Israeli partners, and establish other personal links (many already have them as many relatives and friends live in Israel). However, a recent survey in a national sample of younger Russian immigrants (mean age thirty), of whom 77 percent identified as Jewish, has again shown that most of them (about 70 percent) are remote from religion. Almost 37 percent described themselves as "Jewish, not practicing," 22 percent as atheists, and 10 percent as "agnostics" or "spiritual without specific faith" (Liakhovitski, 2004). When asked in focus group discussions what deters them from more active participation in Jewish community events in New York, many young immigrant professionals complained about the low intellectual level of these gatherings, the agenda that is too narrowly focused on religion, and the lack of charismatic leadership from the ranks of Russian Jews. The participants said they would be more attracted to discussions of important social issues (such as ethno-racial relations in New York), cultural programs, and entertainment with both Russian and Jewish "flavors" (Liakhovitski, 2005).

Another recent survey among Russian Jews in New York (Kliger, 2004) points to a slow drift from a negative basis of Jewish identity (i.e., drawing on anti-Semitism and discrimination) towards a more positive self-definition as a member of a respectable and successful American Jewry. Only 18 percent of the large (about 800 respondents) New York sample answered that being Jewish means for them "experiencing hostility from other people," 21 percent said that being a Jew means "feeling different from other nations," while the rest chose different positive aspects of the Jewish identity. As for the role of religion in their lives, the majority (over 80 percent) paid respect to Judaism as the religion of their ancestors but had little interest in theology or religious practice. In fact, few former Soviets of the middle generation even know the difference between the principal Jewish denominations, and their spiritual pursuits comprise an amalgam of ideas not fitting into any clear pattern. In Kliger's words, they can "simultaneously attend a Reform synagogue because it is close to home, invite an Orthodox rabbi to officiate at a bar-mitzvah ceremony, put up a Christmas tree [2], admire the Russian Orthodox architecture, and learn Buddhist meditation."

In sum, last-wave immigrants did not come to the U.S. in order to lead Jewish lives (if anything, those more inclined towards Zionist and Judaic values made aliyah to Israel); they stay in touch with the Jewish organizations only in so far as they help them to resettle and gain a new foothold. They consider it natural that their main preoccupation in the new country is economic survival and investment in future prosperity, as well as setting a firm economic basis and a head start for their children. When they adjust and can afford to pursue new intellectual and cultural interests, Judaism is again low on their priority list, which features travel, child education, entertainment, and communication with co-ethnics. Few Russian Jews, even relatively wealthy ones, would choose to pay $1,000 for local synagogue membership at the expense of going on a European vacation, or hiring a private tutor for a high school child (Liakhovitsky, 2005). At the same time some of them learn how to be Jewish in a new way, picking up certain American practices (such as bar mitzvah and Passover celebrations) and merging them with their own tastes and traditions. Some join Jewish organizations for the benefits of social networking and/or solidifying their children's Jewish identity, which is seen by them as an asset in America's diverse culture. When they volunteer for community projects, it is usually in their professional capacity and in favor of other new immigrants rather than for abstract "Jewish Causes." Yet, a surprising 66 percent have been shown to donate their dollars to Jewish charities (*Jewish Week*, 2004), again mainly to the immigration and social welfare related projects in the U.S. and in Israel. It can be concluded that over the last ten to fifteen years of their residence in the U.S. Russian Jews have not become any more religious but often drifted towards the accepted forms of American Jewish life.

Living on Welfare, but Voting Republican

Many observers have commented on this apparent paradox about former Soviet Jews living in the U.S., mainly their older part (Orleck, 1999; Shasha and Shron, 2002; Kliger, 2004). Despite their hatred for state socialism, most of them have developed the "entitlement" mentality reflecting their experience of living in a "cradle to grave" welfare state. Moreover, their diligence in "working the system" of socialist bureaucracy has trained them for getting the most out of the American welfare system, with few concomitant ethical qualms. For the initial resettlement period, Russian Jews heavily relied on the HIAS, NYANA, and other Jewish organizations for all their practical needs (perceiving them as a co-ethnic version of state social agencies), and later on those over the age of sixty-five switched to the federal welfare programs, for which they were entitled as elderly and as refugees. Receiving these invaluable benefits (SSI, Medicaid/Medicare with full medication coverage, housing subsidies, and food stamps), most immigrants perceived these allowances as their normal due in a country where they had not worked for a single day, and never paid taxes and social security fees. Few of them realized that many Americans, who had worked and contributed to the social welfare system for decades, do not receive any of these "free perks" and struggle hard to pay their rent, medical bills, or prescription drugs. One of my Bostonian informants, a hard-working single mother (ethnic Russian), told me about her work in the early 1990s as medical interpreter for the immigrant Jewish elders in one of the area hospitals:

> These old ladies would have a windowsill full of prescription meds that they got for free on their program, and they won't even take them, they kept them in store just in case. . . . Americans won't ever buy a prescription drug they don't need, as it is so expensive and there is no reimbursement in many health plans, let alone the uninsured ones. Often these drugs Russian ladies got for free would expire and be discarded—who cares, they can always get a refill. . . . They didn't pay a dollar for their treatment, would never receive a medical bill, but were often grouchy and critical of every aspect of their care . . . it wasn't good enough for them. . . . I think that access to all these services for free terribly spoiled Soviet refugees—they think that America is a socialist haven just like Russia, only better . . .

Thus, by way of paradox, a modest but safe existence with a few taken for granted privileges that typified the older generation's premigration lives continued for them in the U.S.[3] Moreover, while most Americans who apply for social assistance in their times of need, view this as humiliating and are reluctant to discuss it, the former Soviets are rather forthcoming and even proud of themselves when they manage to get approved for an additional benefit. This is what a NYANA worker Boris Kardimun meant when he said in his interview, "psychologically, Russian Jews never left Russia" (Shasha and Shron, 2002). Apparently, few elderly immigrants with poor English can make an independent living in the U.S., so SSI and Medicare are their basic survival necessity. The point is that many of them (not all of course) take these benefits too much for granted and do not bother to return the favor to the hosting society, for example via volunteering.

As mentioned above, over 50 percent of New York Russians (who comprise in turn about one-half of all Soviet Jews living in the U.S.) are unemployed and collecting SSI and other social benefits, such as home attendant services for the elderly, frail, and disabled. When their special privileges were endangered by President Clinton's immigration and welfare reforms of 1996, [4] older Russian Jews manifested an outburst of social activism in order to save their welfare benefits (Orleck, 1999: 187–189). Their political participation, if any, is usually driven by self-interest, for example, rallying in favor of continuing immigration to the U.S. while expecting their own family members to join them, and benefits to immigrants and refugees. In the late 1990s they even teamed up with Latino immigrants in southern California opposing the bill that suggested limitations on immigration (Orleck, 1999). At the same time, many Russian Jews are ready to contribute their time and dollars to Israeli causes, which reflects both solidarity with the Jewish state and multiple personal connections with the relatives and friends living there.

It is often argued that Russian Jews manifest a more conservative political stance than the rest of American Jewry and vote Republican more often. Indeed, in the last Presidential election in November 2004, the exit poll conducted by RINA among 802 Russian-speaking voters in four locations in New York and Philadelphia (Kliger, 2005) showed that 77 percent voted for President Bush, 22 percent for Senator Kerry, and 1 percent for no one; 80 percent of respondents who voted Bush had decided on this choice more than a month before the elections. No differences by gender or income level have been found in the distribution of the votes, but older voters more often voted Republican than younger ones: among those older than sixty-five, 82 percent voted Bush and 14 percent Kerry, while among those under age thirty-five the respective figures were 58 percent and 39 percent, with middle-aged respondents in the middle (73 percent and 26 percent). Among those who voted for Bush in Brooklyn, the most important political issues were Israel (53 percent), terror (21 percent), and strong military (11 percent). Among Kerry voters, the most important issues that guided their choice were economy (36 percent) and Iraq war (17 percent). "Strong leader" as the main candidate quality was cited by 40 percent of Bush voters and 18 percent of Kerry voters. Almost 96 percent of those who had voted for Bush in 2000 voted for him again in 2004. Of those who had voted for Gore in 2000, 64 percent voted for Bush in 2004, and 35 percent remained loyal to the Democratic candidate.

At the same time, Kliger's (2004) survey data on Russian Jews suggest that their political stance on domestic and international issues cannot be captured using the traditional liberal-conservative scale applied to mainstream Americans.[5] Many of his respondents do not understand these concepts the way most Americans do and often manifest an inconsistent amalgam outlook—a patchwork of ideas and beliefs borrowed from different doctrines. Thus, most Russian immigrants approve of a strong anti-terrorist campaign even at the expense of personal liberties (73 percent), support the death penalty for murder (77 percent), and object to gay marriage (81 percent), but at the same time believe that abortion must be elective and accessible under most circumstances (66 percent). The pro-choice stance of former Soviets reflects the long tradition of free access to abortion in the FSU as the only birth control option in the absence of reliable contraception; they cannot imagine women's lives without the option of pregnancy termination (Remennick et al., 1995).

Over 88 percent of Kliger's respondents agree that caring about Israel is a very important part of Jewish identity. Regarding the Middle Eastern conflict, Russian Jews take a definite right-wing stance: about 40 percent opposed Israel's withdrawal from Gaza, 51 percent were against Palestinian statehood, and over 80 percent were against any compromise on the status of Jerusalem as part of a permanent settlement (the respective figures for established U.S. Jews are 23 percent, 37 percent, and 53 percent). Many Russian Jews vote for Republicans for Presidents who, in their view, represent strong and consistent national leadership, but for Democrats as their local representatives, who can lobby for more immigrant rights, welfare benefits, and other "socialist" items. Commenting on the survey results, A. Brook-Krasny, representing the umbrella organization of Russian Jews in New York, said: "While Russians may express pro-Republican opinions, the fact is that a big part of our community relies on social services. If those programs are cut significantly by the Republicans, we could see a shift by Russians back toward the Democrats" (*Jewish Week*, 2004).

Kliger's data suggest that Russian Jews voted for Bush in 2004 for three main reasons: his perceived strong support of Israel and anti-Arab stance; successful anti-terrorist campaign, and intended tax reductions. The latter reason seems irrational as lower taxes mean cuts in welfare programs; but on the other hand, most Russian immigrant families of working age live on earned income and have few other assets (real estate, inheritance), so lower taxes simply means more net/expendable income—an important economic asset in their lives. Some

Russians believe that Republicans also make better use of public funds; they are ready to receive a lower pay or welfare check contributing some of their income to the important causes such as support of Israel or the war in Iraq that may change the balance of power in the Middle East. As many Russian immigrants have poor command of English and do not peruse the mainstream press and television, their political views are often shaped by the Russian-language media, which is extremely conservative and typically represents only the right-end spectrum of opinion, especially on international issues and Arab-Israeli conflict. Age, education, and extent of contact with the mainstream middle-class Americans (including American Jews) also influence the political outlook of Russian Jews. Although no survey data is available to vouch for this, my impression was that younger and more successful professionals in the Boston and San Francisco Bay Area are often in the Democratic camp, compared to their less integrated co-ethnics in New York, New Jersey, and Philadelphia.

On the one hand, middle-aged and older Soviet immigrants tend to resent all varieties of socialist ideology, support the free market, and low governmental interference as the opposite of the total state control of economic and private life in the USSR. At the same time, coming from a well-disciplined authoritarian society, they had been shocked by the general lack of order and "anarchy": rundown inner-city blocks with graffiti on the walls, the rampant behavior of American youth (especially its non-white segment), violence at schools, and street crime in large cities. Many saw a hard-line conservative government as the only force that can keep in check this ambient "lawlessness," the image that better fits Republican than Democratic rhetoric. As one of my interviewees commented on Bush vs. Kerry dilemma, "Who told you that Harvard-educated polished demagogues make good presidents? In my view, political will and strong guts are more valuable for a national leader these days than articulate speech and advanced degrees." Regardless of their stated attitudes, the voting behavior of Russian Jews over the past two decades has been rather flexible in line with their current self-interest as beneficiaries of the welfare state, as the above-cited examples on the protest campaigns against immigration and welfare cuts show. The majority voted against Bush the Senior after he had imposed limitations on the immigration of Soviet Jews in 1989, and against Clinton's second term in 1996, when he breached their hopes by his welfare reforms. I would therefore de-

scribe the political outlook of Russian Jews as pragmatically conservative, or conservatively pragmatic.

However, a younger, well-educated, and upwardly mobile segment
among Russian immigrants in the Internet-based survey by Liakhovitski
(2004) is much closer to established U.S. Jewry in its political outlook
than are New York immigrants in the Kliger's (2006) sample. Answering the question *"Which party in the U.S. comes closest to representing your views?"* 55 percent said Democrats (61 percent among
the women and 48 percent among the men); 24 percent said Republicans (18 percent and 30 percent, respectively); 9 percent chose Green
or Libertarian Parties, and 12 percent answered "None." Almost 64
percent (70 percent among the women and 57 percent among the men)
said they would vote for the Democrats, vs. 26 percent (22 percent and
32 percent) for the Republicans. A greater leaning of the young immigrant women towards the Democratic political agenda vis-à-vis their
male counterparts (although not manifest in de facto voting patterns in
New York, perhaps due to a lower turnout among women) is an interesting trend worth further study. Is it women's greater exposure to the
diverse and paradoxical U.S. realities that makes them more flexible,
socially responsive, and attentive to poverty and suffering next to
opulence and snobbery? Or is it that former Soviet men perceive hard-
line and hawkish views as synonymous with masculinity and self-
confidence? At the same time, more of these men had intended to vote
for Democrats than actually shared Democratic political outlook, perhaps reflecting the fear of Republican anti-welfare policies harming
their parents and grandparents. Only future in-depth studies can help
answer these questions.

Crossing the Bridge: Cultural Continuity and Americanization

Educated immigrants usually ascribe a high value to the possibility
to practice their pre-migration professions in the new country. Skilled
workplace is their main gateway to successful integration: at work, the
newcomers can meet their local social peers, improve their command
of the new language, perfect their professional skills, and receive decent remuneration to establish a new economic foothold. Yet, immigration is often accompanied by occupational downgrading, which for
some (younger and more dynamic ones) may be temporary, while for
many others proves to be permanent. Former Soviet immigrants of the

1990s in the major American cities with a large immigrant presence faced tough competition for skilled jobs, and many had to put up with manual or semi-skilled work unrelated to their training or expertise in order to make a living. One occupational group that experienced almost universal upward mobility in the U.S. economy embraces a variety of younger engineering, IT, and other high-tech professionals as well as advanced research scientists, who have been in high demand during the technology boom of the 1990s. Yet, many older engineering and scientific workers could not fit into this niche due to their poor English or a mismatch between their skills and the demands of the local industry. Immigrants with culturally and linguistically embedded professions in humanities, education, and culture (mostly women) also had to change occupational tracks. Unable to fit into the mainstream U.S. economy, many former professionals ventured into the unknown terrain of entrepreneurship. Soviet immigrants in large U.S. cities are typified by high rates of self-employment, reaching fully 33 percent for men in Los Angeles and 21 percent in New York (for women the respective rates are lower but still impressive: 17 percent and 8 percent [Gold, 1997]). However, the majority of Russian small businesses in catering, food sales, real estate, car dealerships, beauty salons, music and language lessons, etc. cater to the co-ethnic community and are not really conducive for acculturation in the American mainstream. Some converts to the small business world may be really content, having fulfilled their American dream of independence and relative economic security, while others may still mourn their lost professional identity. A few studies that looked into the psychosocial implications of occupational downgrading of Soviet immigrants in the U.S. (Vinokurov et al., 2000; Aroian et al., 2003) have shown that lower work status is related to poorer mental health outcomes (depression being the most common one), slower improvement of the English skills, and more negative general attitudes towards the host society.

Cultural shock is another common corollary of resettlement, especially for older migrants and those who had never traveled abroad before coming to the U.S. One bitter discovery most educated Russian immigrants made in America was the irrelevance of their old cultural capital in the new life. For members of Soviet intelligentsia, their cultural baggage—the books they had read, great Russian poetry they knew by heart since youth, the world of museums, thick literary almanacs, and intelligent conversations with kindred friends—was at the core of their self-concept and self-esteem in their old lives. The unique feature of the educated Soviet class was that even most technocrats and scientists whose professional expertise was very far from humanities, often had broad cultural and literary interests, read current novels, and knew world and Russian history rather well. Having fixed and not too busy work hours, free weekends, and long vacations, the Russian intelligentsia could also afford the luxury of long intellectual conversations with friends, prolific reading, and self-reflection as a lifestyle (especially for men who were spared the second shift of house chores). In America, this luxury—an important non-monetary bonus of state socialism—was gone, as everyone had to put long hours into hard work in order to make ends meet. Russian Jews realized that their broad erudition and elaborate tastes in reading and the arts were of little value and did not facilitate their labor market and social adjustments. As all their cultural riches were in the Russian language and impenetrable to outsiders, former Soviets faced the flipside of their taken-for-granted Russian mono-lingualism and the lack of facility with other languages and cultures. This sudden devaluation of their chief cultural currency, often juxtaposed with the inability to practice their former professions in the U.S., caused deep traumas and identity crises in many freshmen immigrants. Thus, Lena (thirty-five) a former high school teacher of Russian literature from Leningrad, recounted ten years after her resettlement in New York:

> I was totally lost during my first year in the city, feeling that I am a nobody, just this mute foreign person without identity or personality. I wandered between the high-rise buildings, looked at Americans bustling around me, not understanding a word of what they were saying (although I had believed that I knew English reasonably well!) and wondering: What would I do here? No one is interested in what I know and love, no one would appreciate that I can recite Akhmatova and Pasternak's verses for hours on end, this won't earn me a single dollar, not even a smile. Everything I had been prepared for in my old life proved to be useless. . . . I could keep this world of letters and ideas for my inner life of course, but then how would I ever adapt? I needed to cast off my old romantic heritage and become new, functional and rational person, an American.

Some newcomers discovered that even their good familiarity with classical American literature (in Russian translations) and music (especially jazz, a beloved genre of many Russian intellectuals) did not get them any closer to most Americans, many of whom did not read serious modern writers but mainly pulp fiction (if at all) and long forgot who Mark Twain, Ernest Hemingway and William Faulkner had been. And of course few younger Americans listened to Louis Armstrong and Billie Holiday, having more current musical tastes. "I was amazed to discover how ignorant many Americans were about their own recent cultural history. Like school and college education was totally lost on them. I guess we were more keen for anything American back in the USSR than these folks who grew up here and took it for granted," said Gene (forty-seven), a former Leningrad journalist. "But I stopped trying to discuss books with my American pals— instead we talk about baseball, kids, and the 'Sopranos' show," he added.

Over time, some immigrants realized that many old values and cultural codes of the Soviet intelligentsia were in fact counterproductive in American life. The attitudes towards money is one often cited example: discussions of money and overt show of financial self-interest were considered indecent and embarrassing for a "cultured person" in Russia; exchange of mutual services and favors (a peculiar Soviet form of barter) was indeed more important than direct monetary relations (Pesmen, 2000). In stark contrast to this money-squeamishness of the Russian intelligentsia, the American economy and lifestyle are all about in-your-face monetarism: making money, profiting, and economic success are central to the popular and media discourse. Moving from non-monetary values to the monetary-based assessments of success and personal achievement was a painful process for some immigrants. Irena (thirty-seven), who had majored in the English language in Russia and made a living as translator in New York, recounted:

In the beginning I used to help everyone who asked with translation of documents, official letters, etc.: by old Soviet habit I saw this as a favor to people in need provided out of kindness and belief that some day, in some form people would return kindness to you. But soon I was overwhelmed by the amount of work it required: the word was out about my good English and kind heart and many old women from Brighton and other parts of the city, let alone my own block, would seek my help. At some point, my boyfriend told me, "You are a kind-hearted idiot, a smarter person would have made a living out of this work!" This gave me an idea to start a translation business catering for Russian immigrants. But for a long time I felt guilty charging these old folks with low income (who

formed the bulk of my clients), and my fees were laughable. . . . Over time
I got used to the idea of working for profit and increased my fees.

Raised in a culture combining respect for intellectualism and spiritual pursuits with a disgust for sheer materialism and profiteering,
quite a few immigrants I met shunned their co-ethnics (usually old
timers who accumulated enough status and wealth) repelled by the
permanent show of financial success they made of their lives.

Thus, Olga (forty) teaching Russian literature in a Californian university town with a tangible Russian presence, mused:

> Most Russians here stick together, but I try to avoid their lavish parties
> and outings. I resent their self-demonstration of success and material wealth.
> Their large houses with manicured lawns yell at you: Look how affluent,
> how American I am! They discuss non-stop what elite colleges their kids
> are attending, what is the next ocean cruise they have booked, and how
> much they pay to their house maid. Their conversations became so shal-
> low, so American! I don't remember anyone discussing the book they
> read, a theater show, or even their political beliefs or elections. . . . It is
> amazing how much some people have changed here. I won't mind being
> financially comfortable myself, and of course you need a house and a
> car . . . these are basic commodities in America life. But they cannot be-
> come the center of your existence . . .

Like Olga, a few other informants noticed a persistent need of
former Soviet immigrants, when meeting socially one another, to rank
each other's standing and achievements in the new life on a scale that
includes several standard entries: the kind of job one has, their income, housing situation, the number and class of cars in the family,
schools/colleges their children attend, their English proficiency, and
the number of American friends they may have. Upon completion of
this inventory, your new acquaintance mentally ranks your social status below, above or at the same level as him/herself. This obsession
with social comparison is probably an early immigration-bound symp-
tom when the starting conditions had been similarly low, but the pace
of improvement vastly differed among individual immigrants and families. Partly this practice of socially ranking one's peers carries over
from the late Soviet times, when economic and social differentiation
had set in and people started comparing each other's success and
prestige by the location and size of their apartment, the possession of a
car and summer cottage, the institute of higher education that their

children attended, etc. With the advent of dramatic polarization of material wealth during post-communist times, the habit of building "status verticals" for one's social contacts only grew stronger. The goal of this comparison is to estimate one's own location on the social ladder and to try socializing with the people who are above you since this may help you or your children to improve social mobility. Many immigrants resented this culture of constant scrutiny and assessment by one's own co-ethnics.

The socializing and entertaining styles of former Soviets evolved over time, incorporating many American elements. For personal friendships and dating partners most former Soviets prefer their co-ethnics to other Americans, explaining it by their common mindset and many shared experiences, let alone the language. Those who are better off, often throw large parties, typically with a cultural agenda (e.g., a visiting performer or a book club discussion); those with modest means and smaller homes would invite close friends and family to celebrate birthdays and holidays (New Year's Day being a favorite one) or just to chat for no special reason. Several informants who are bilingual told me that they prefer to socialize with their Russian and American friends separately as the language, style, and content of these conversations would be very different, and misunderstandings or boredom can occur in a mixed company. "Certain types of anecdotes, comments and memories from our past would make no sense to most Americans and may even seem rude or racist to them—you know how outspoken we are on many matters silenced by polite Americans. So for everyone's peace of mind it's better to keep apples and oranges separately," said Marina (thirty-three), a New York art gallery keeper. Many informants also noted that they usually met with their American friends in cafes or shopping malls, while hosting their Russian friends at home. So, in a symbolic way, Americans still belong to the external or public realm of their lives, while fellow Russians are allowed into the inner chambers.

The style and content of socializing among new Americans have evolved as well. Heated kitchen debates on politics, philosophical or moral ideas, literature and film, psychological challenges and crises—forming a high-strung "life and death" discourse (Kardimun in Shash and Shron, 2002)—have turned into low-key discussions of the practical resettlement matters in America (jobs, house rentals, taxes, schools), and when a certain financial foothold has been achieved—drifted further towards the Americanized small talk on the trivia and trifles of everyday life. No more political or ethnic jokes are told in a mixed company: you don't know whom they can hurt. The intensity, aggressive style, and moral pitch are all gone; people coming together at parties try not to challenge each other by their opposing political views, seeking compromise, not dissent. As Simon (42), a biology researcher in a California university, told me,

In a decent immigrant company, everybody is doing their best censoring their speech not to sound racist or male chauvinist: the American culture of political correctness has taken its root in the Russian community. When I first came here I was shocked by this newly subdued talk culture of my old friends who used to be ardent debaters in Russia. But then I understood that in the diverse society this is the only way to respect other people's values and beliefs. As a result, you often end up doing small talk, not discussing the real things that matter and where you may disagree. I think Russians have learnt to discriminate between polite party-style small talk and the more personal and intense conversation between close friends.

Reflecting many decades of the "survival culture" of Soviet people, rich food is equated with wealth, and a full body—with health and wellness. Among American middle-class women, slimness not fullness is a measure of wealth, success, and savvy. Many middle-aged immigrant women had to find their way around this normative conflict. Meantime, food remains an indispensable element of Russian/ Soviet sociability: any get together between family and friends typically features lavish food (mainly of high-fat, high-cholesterol variety—cold cuts, meat and fish salads, caviar, cheeses etc.) and drink, often including vodka and other hard liquor. Psychologist Vera Kishinevsky (2004), herself a 1978 immigrant from Odessa, collected fascinating narratives of the three generations of Soviet immigrant women in New York (grandmother-mother-daughter triads) who told about their love affair with American food during their "freshman" immigrant years. After living through permanent food shortages in the USSR, they could not get enough of the high-calorie delicacies from Russian and American groceries, spent hours in the kitchen preparing lavish family parties, and of course gained much weight as a result. Their subsequent long-term preoccupation was to get rid of those extra pounds by engaging in simple but severe techniques such as fasting (no time or money for the gym, no mental energy to calculate calories, no culture of jogging, but starvation is familiar!). Over time the styles of eating and entertaining guests have changed, but mainly among the younger generations: they are no longer ready to spend hours food shopping and "slaving in the kitchen," preferring to eat in restaurants on the weekends and to order take-out food on weekdays. Older immigrants continue to cook and eat mostly at home, both due to financial limitations and lingering mistrust of public catering (who knows what they put in their soup and how they wash their lettuce?). The new "healthy food" tenet has entered many middle-class Russian immigrant homes; the cooking and eating patterns have drifted towards the low-fat, low-sugar, high-fiber dietary code of the U.S. middle class (Kishinevsky, 2004). The elderly and other residents of the Russian ethnic neighborhoods continue to savor high-fat sausages and pates, deep-fry their chicken in butter, and have rich cakes for the desert, with the results showing on their figures, blood counts, diabetes, and heart disease rates.

Thinking about cultural transitions that educated Soviet immigrants have experienced in the U.S. over ten to fifteen years of their residence here, I would delineate between the more superficial and outwardly oriented tiers of behavior and self-expression vis-à-vis the shifts in the intrinsic values and attitudes. The external drift towards American middle-class ways of dressing, housekeeping, eating, decorating houses, spending weekends and vacations, fitness and sports, some aspects of child rearing in line with the new schooling system—all these signs of acculturation and social mimicry have certainly set in. In the elegant leafy suburbs of New Jersey, Philadelphia, and the Bay Area, one cannot really tell a house, a front lawn, a child or a dog of former Soviet immigrants from any other house, child or dog. They have barbeque parties in their backyards, go hiking on weekends, and hire low-status women (usually other Russians) to clean their houses like other middle-class homeowners do. Newly wealthy Russian Jews often make a point of demonstrating their economic success (which in America is tangibly measured by house size, prestige of the neighborhood, number and class of the cars per household) to their co-ethnics and other onlookers as their main immigrant "ego trip." The visibility and cultural difference of Russian immigrants is much greater in the urban ethnic enclaves, such as parts of Brooklyn in New York and Sunset Boulevard in San Francisco, where they stick together for company and support, seldom learn good English or work in the mainstream economy. Apparently, age at migration is another crucial factor: younger men and women cross the bridge to American lifestyles much faster (Kasinitz et al., 2001). So one can argue, after Chiswick (2000) and other macro-level researchers, that acculturation is largely a function of economic success and occupational integration into the American mainstream. Or, more precisely, that the improving command of English, economic success, and acculturation feed and reinforce each other.

However, the micro-level picture is more complex: on a deeper level even the most externally Americanized former Soviets retain many salient differences from their American social peers. Polish-Australian sociologist Jerzy Smolitz (2001) has coined a notion of *core cultural values* that shape identity and collective boundaries of minority groups preventing their dissolution into the surrounding majority. Ewa Morawska (2004) speaks of the ethnic "cultural repertoires" in a similar sense. In the case of former Soviets, including the Jews, their repertoires and values rest on a clear distinction between the formal/public and informal/private spheres and behavior codes, reflecting their old survival tactics in the face of adversity and ubiquitous social control over private life. The family and close circle of trusted friends are one's safety net, while any type of local administration, let alone the government and all its institutions, are perceived as oppressive and need to be manipulated or bypassed. Chronic mistrust of any officialdom and authorities, including law enforcement officers, INS and IRS agents, and, by the same token, social workers, census takers, and other perceived agents of the state, is one common legacy of living under state socialism. Every pollster or social researcher who tried to interview older Russian immigrants knows how difficult it is to convince them to open their minds to strangers (Kishinevsky, 2004). The shadow of the controlling and punishing hand of the State lurks everywhere. Former Soviets find it hard to believe that researchers and poling companies can be independent, not in the service of the state and not reporting to INS about houseguests with dated visas or to IRS on any "side income." The mistrust of the state and the tendency to bypass its rules and regulations is paradoxically combined with the sense of entitlement to public benefits discussed above. Of course, the imprint of Soviet socialization is much deeper on the older and middle generations, but some of these influences spill over to the immigrant youth as well.

Let me turn now to the cultural values found in the private domain, specifically in gender roles and family relations, the concept of self-value among the women, and relations between parents and children. I picked these particular facets of Soviet culture as they are very much at odds with comparable American middle-class norms. All of them have historic and contextual explanations into which I cannot go, offering only the highlights and referring the reader to some additional sources (especially two recent ethnographies based on detailed oral histories of Soviet immigrants [Shasha and Shron, 2002 and Kishinevsky, 2004]).

Gender, Family, and Parent-Children Relations

Soviet women had been raised to be superwomen; they have surely been the stronger sex, the responsible sex, the nurturing sex, and the breadwinning sex (Ashwin, 2002). All but a few of them worked full time in a broad range of occupations, although they seldom achieved the high professional status reserved for their male coworkers. Trying to offset the state-imposed "gender equality-in-misery" at least in the private domain, many women paid symbolic dues to traditional gender roles by marrying young and calling their husbands family heads. Reflecting the chronic shortage of men throughout the Soviet regime (due to wars, political purges, mass imprisonment, and high male mortality) many Soviet families were matriarchal, consisting of three generations of women headed by a strong grandmother, both giving and controlling. Women usually gave birth to their one or two children young, between nineteen and twenty-seven, in between studies and full-time work. Grandmothers, still in their fifties and sixties, would often retire in order to take care of the grandchildren and tend to all the other house chores, thus setting their daughters free to pursue their studies, careers, and other personal goals. The self-value of middle-aged and older Soviet women, both before and after emigration, rested on their ability to be indispensable to their children, rather than on individualistic pursuits of career, eternal youth, perfect health and fitness, travel, and other "selfish" indulgences of Western women (Kishinevski, 2004). Men, if present in the picture, were rendered marginal and secondary in the domestic realm, with few expectations for participation in child- and elder care, shopping, and other mundane chores. Men's self-esteem rested entirely on their success as workers and providers, and if they failed to achieve economic mobility and respectable occupational status (which was common!) they often succumbed to depression and alcoholism (Ashwin and Lytkina, 2004).

In immigration, women often turned out to be more fit, adaptable, and faster learners than their male partners. I cannot refrain from citing here a rather lengthy first-person account by Boris Kardimun (in Shasha and Shron, 2002) that typifies the relations between marital partners soon upon resettlement:

> Here the master [which he ostensibly used to be in Russia] turned into zero. My wife was making rapid progress. I remained where I was. This created certain problems between us until, finally, our family collapsed. Many Soviet families don't survive immigration. And quite often the wives do much better than their husbands. While a Soviet-Russian husband spends his time reflecting on life, a wife keeps working. She has no time to suffer, to contemplate. She has responsibilities. In Russia it was taken for granted that a woman should endlessly stand in lines, cook, clean, take care of her husband and children, and yet go to work every day. But here you can't take it for granted. This is the West. The rules are different here. I'm ashamed to say I was a typical macho Russian husband. For a long time I was convinced it was her duty to take care of me and the family, while I sat and contemplated life and death issues. Now I can't believe I was so stupid. And it took me a very long time to realize that, and to admit that, despite all my hatred for the Soviet system, I was in fact a typical product of it.

Having achieved higher professional status in the USSR, men usually had greater stakes in their occupational readjustment, and if they could not continue their previous careers, or successfully launch new ones in the U.S., they often became dysfunctional. Women were psychologically prepared for any occupational change that would give them a stable income and promise family survival, and in many cases became principal income earners (see more on that in chapter 4 on immigrant women in Greater Boston). Thus, old matriarchal patterns, with or without presence of men slowly drifting from despair to adjustment while the women kept working, have often been reproduced in Soviet immigrant families (Gold, 2003).[6] Many women were divorced single parents, whose chances for occupational adjustment in the new country depended on having a *babushka* (grandmother in Russian) –babysitter and housekeeper at home. In this context, the identity of older women was based on self-sacrifice rather than self-care, on inner strength rather than external appearances. Their life satisfaction was a direct reflection of the perceived success of their children and grandchildren in their new lives. Of course, co-residence and deep involvement into children's lives comes with strings attached: grandmothers needed to extend their influence over the decisions and lifestyles of the younger ones in America. When the mid-generation and youth took affront at this control and drifted away from the elders (especially when they no longer wanted to live together), the older immigrants were deeply hurt and frustrated (psychologist Vera Kishinevsky [2004] and social worker Leonid Althausen [1993] relate many such stories).

The mid-generation now in its forties and early fifties, has inherited this culture of deep mutual involvement of parents and children and, although they no longer insist on co-residence, they certainly prefer their children to live nearby and visit often. The question of whether to go to a local college and live at home or to study in another city/state and live independently, like most American youths do, is a hard moral, not just practical, dilemma for many Russian immigrant youths. They know that their parents need them for support and hands-on help in the many challenges they face in the new country, and they feel bad about leaving them on their own. On the other hand, the supreme value for everyone in these families is getting the best possible education for the young generation to ensure its future career success, so the decisions are usually a compromise between these competing needs. Throughout their life cycle, adult parents and children keep intense emotional ties, financially support each other and share the burdens of hands-on care for the children, the sick, and the elderly. These multiple responsibilities inevitably take their toll on immigrant women's mental and physical health (Remennick, 1999b; Aroian et al., 2001; 2003).

The flipside of these close emotional and instrumental ties between parents and children is that parental control (becoming symbolic rather than real over time) never ends in the lives of former Soviets. These mutual dependencies are especially strong among Jews, with their greater emphasis on the family as one's primary safety net and high personal investment in children's upbringing and education (Althausen, 1993; Mirsky, 1998). For most Soviet Jews, the whole emigration endeavor had been motivated by the promise of a better future for their children, and they made multiple sacrifices in order to ensure this future. When their Americanized children fell short of the expectations of academic excellence and intellectual effort (the backbone of Russian-Jewish culture) these parents were deeply frustrated. Thus, Vladimir, a high-tech engineer from Leningrad and a father of three children, reflected on his youngest son (fifteen) born in the U.S.:

> We made all we could to put this boy in the best public school and as many enrichment activities as we could afford, but all seems to be in vain. He is bored at school, we have to pay tutors just to get him do his homework and pass the tests; and he never reads a book. All he ever thinks of is consumption and entertainment—he must get every new electronic game, all the expensive CDs, music systems, now also an IPod. . . . These new things make his eyes spark, not the ideas, books or conversations about the important things about life. . . . Hard work is not for him, he already told me that all he wants in his life is to get rich soon, but not through toiling twelve hours every day like his dad. What scares me most is his, and other youngsters', full detachment from the pool of world culture, history, intellectual achievement. . . . I don't know how he can get any moral education, just peering at the computer or TV screen, or listening to the hip-hop. . . . Is it the influence of shallow American life or has the time and generation simply changed everywhere? I honestly don't know, but I often see myself as a failed parent.

Vladimir's concerns about zealous consumption instead of intellectual and moral development were shared to some extent by many parents, sensing the divergence between their own and their children's basic beliefs and values. On the other hand, bookish and studious children and adolescents were often lonely and unpopular among their peers, unable to fit into the local youth culture—which also saddened immigrant parents. In Mila's (fifty) words "Children of émigrés are always split and fall in between parental expectations and the urges of their new life. I think they are having a more difficult time adjusting and finding their way in America than adults because we at least made a decision to move here ourselves and now face the consequences; they were drawn into this mess by us, nobody asked what they had wanted." One typical arena of conflict is the choice of vocation by the children, which had traditionally been guided by parental wisdom and social ties. Immigrant parents come from a society that, on one hand, set multiple limitations on their choice of occupation as Jews, and, on the other, defined professional choice made in youth as final (few former Soviets changed their occupation after completing higher education). Driven by their own experience, the parents try to push their children towards solid professions that promise good income and clear tracks of upward mobility, along with prestige and high social status. Most often these are computing and information technology, different kinds of engineering, biological and chemical technology, accountancy, the judicial and medical professions. From their mid-school years Russian immigrant children strive for high academic achievements in order to make their way to the best universities. By way of paradox, the sky-high tuition fees of the best colleges were less of a problem for new immigrant parents than for their American counterparts as many bright immigrant students received generous scholarships and other financial aid due to their parents' low income (as I was told more than once by these parents).

The problems arose when the children did not show any inclination towards the "solid" occupational tracks picked for them by the parents, of course "keeping their best interest at heart." A study at Brandeis University near Boston, where many Russian immigrant students—the children of high achievers working in the area's high-tech firms—were studying during the 1990s, has shown that some of these students were not doing well in their science and engineering programs, failing exams, and dropping the courses, but almost never approached academic advisors for aid and guidance. In-depth interviews with the students pointed to the deep conflict between their own and their parent's wishes regarding their education: quite often these youths found themselves studying disciplines they were not interested in and had no talent for. When advisors got involved, they would usually counsel the students to drop out of the programs they disliked and switch to another field, in other words, to pursue their true interests. The parents would, on the contrary, press the students to continue and complete their "hard-core" degrees instead of switching to history, fashion design or social sciences, which, of course, did not promise a solid "piece of bread on your table." Torn between the American freedom of choice and the parental pressure towards pragmatism, some young people teetered for a while and then dropped out of college altogether in order to make a fresh start (unpublished Brandeis study report by Dr. Jana Kaplan).

Many others, of course, did follow the path broken by their parents into medicine or electronics, and indeed succeeded on the labor market putting twelve to sixteen hours of daily work into their upscale high-tech or medical careers. The qualms of the young immigrants caught between the parental indoctrination and the culture of their new peers brings me to the next large focal point of my analysis: social and cultural locations of the second and the 1.5 generation, the latter term referring to the immigrants who moved to the new country as older children or adolescents, after having spent part of their formative years in the FSU.

The Second and the 1.5 Generation: Caught in the Middle

> *"What sort of Americans, and what sort of American Jews, will these immigrants become? Indeed , will they ever become 'Americans' at all? . . . Ultimately these questions will not be answered by the immigrants alone, but also by their ambivalently American children. . . . It is this second generation, now coming of age, who will negotiate new and different ways of 'being American,' 'being Russian,' and 'being Jewish.' These choices are not always explicit, nor they are mutually exclusive, and as with all young people, their identities may fluctuate over time"*
> (from Kasinitz et al., "The Next Generation: Russian Jewish Young Adults in Contemporary New York.")

American scholars of immigration are increasingly interested in the process of social incorporation of immigrants' children born in the U.S. or brought here as children and adolescents. Typically the research framed under the caption of the *New Second Generation* targets young immigrants belonging to the visible minorities (Asian, Latino, or black) whose experiences of assimilation are shaped by both parental social and financial resources and the racialized urban environments in which they come of age. The social dynamics experienced by young immigrants is often depicted as *segmented assimilation*, meaning that some segments of the immigrant youth experience upward mobility and join the white mainstream while other parts of it drop out of school and merge with the marginalized street-level youth groups of their U.S. co-ethnics (Rumbaut, 1996). The location of the Russian-Jewish youngsters in the multiethnic urban mosaic of New York or San Francisco is rather privileged as, phenotype-wise, they belong to the white mainstream and their parents are endowed with significant human capital, if not financial means. Although most of them are on an upward leading educational track, the dilemmas of ethnic identity and cultural affiliation are constantly present in their lives.

Although most immigrant parents are interested in transferring their language and core cultural values to the children, various minorities differ in their ability to develop and sustain the organizational framework necessary for this task (Smolitz, 2001). Russian immigrant parents are both strongly determined to pass on their cultural heritage to the next generation and have enough resources to do so. The two main arenas of this cultural transfer are the family and various educational and cultural institutions established by and for Russian-speakers in every American city and town with sizeable presence of Soviet immigrants. Take for example Newton, Massachusetts: a town with a population of about 90,000 (an estimated one-third of them Russian-Jewish immigrants), it has two mathematical and three chess schools established by Russian teachers, several musical and drama groups in Russian, a Russian choir, a "sports academy" in a nearby town run by Russian trainers, and any number of private teachers giving classes in the Russian language and literature, music, plastic arts, yoga and meditation (in Russian). You name it, it is there. Russian-Jewish parents are extremely wary of the American teenage culture of laziness and mindless pastime playing computer games, watching television or loitering in a nearby mall plaza (let alone more dangerous hobbies of sex and drugs). They are determined to keep their children occupied from the end of the school day till bedtime, and they invest their hard-earned dollars and a great effort chauffeuring them from one class to the next. If no grandparents are around to do the task, then mothers, who often work part time or have flexible hours, would take their kids to various classes; yet, Russian "soccer moms" should rather go by the name of "chess and math" moms. The goals of general intellectual and esthetic development, and Russian cultural continuity, merge in these prolific after-school activities. This is what good parenting, Russian-Jewish style, is all about.

When children become adolescents, they start making choices for themselves, dropping some activities and pursuing others. Their affinity with their Russian side also varies, and some may see no added value in speaking their parents' language and identifying as Russian. In my experience, the majority of the children who came to America under the age of ten saw themselves as Americans with an additional Russian streak (multiculturalism is cool these days!). By their mid—to late teens, most of these kids would speak limited Russian (with an accent) to their grandparents, a mix of Russian and English to their parents, and only English with their friends, regardless of their origin.

I observed a similar speech pattern among immigrant adolescents in Israel, representing a mix of Hebrew and Russian with rapid code-switching, depending on the identity of their contact (Remennick, 2004a). A few examples of symmetric bilingualism among immigrant youths (in the U.S., Canada, and Israel alike) are found among the families where parents made an iron rule of speaking only Russian at home, especially if these youths also visited Russia on a regular basis (e.g., during summer vacations), and read Russian books. Yet, all these components of language maintenance were seldom present together, so the youths who came of age in the U.S. typically combined some Russian oral proficiency with a limited literacy.

I was fascinated by these girls' and boys' reflections on their mixed linguistic and cultural identity. As most of my young informants lived comfortably, studied in good schools, and did well academically, their self-confidence and self-esteem were rather high, not in the least tainted by their immigrant background. On the contrary, it turned out that having an additional ethnic streak, especially speaking another language, carried an added value among their American peers. For example, Dasha (seventeen) in a prosperous California town said: "It's cool to be Russian, or Chinese, or French—anything different, non-mainstream adds to your aura and charm. When I meet my Russian pals in the presence of American kids, I make a point of speaking Russian with them, and everyone would envy my facility with the language and wonder what are we talking about . . . " Dasha looked and sounded a 100 percent American teenager to me, complete with a nose ring and tattoos, her main hangout being the global youth village of Berkeley, yet she greatly enjoyed her summer trips to Russia with her (ethnically Russian) mother, spoke fluent if heavily accented Russian, and even read contemporary Russian novels (under her mother's slight pressure).

Russian teenagers living in New York were somewhat more ambivalent about the meaning of their Russianness, given all the negative stereotyping of Russian Jews as gangsters, black market traders and pimps found in the media. For one thing, their families usually had a rather modest lifestyle, residing in small urban apartments and often hardly making ends meet on a single salary, as the other parent was either missing or unemployed. As in many parts of New York, Russian immigrants form the second largest ethnic minority after Hispanics, most public schools have significant numbers of Russian-speaking students, who lump together socially and hence retain their cultural boundaries for a longer time, compared to schools in other cities with few Russians present. At the same time, due to their solid knowledge base imported from their previous schooling in Russia, they easily master the American curriculum (especially in math and sciences) and can therefore concentrate on learning English. In a matter of year or two their English proficiency almost reaches the native-born level, but they would often continue to mix the two languages (code-switch) with other Russians. By and large, former Soviet students are usually catching up with the top of their U.S.-born peers, closing the language gap much faster than other immigrant students (Hispanics, Chinese, Korean, etc.). The dropout rates among them are also much lower (Palatnik and DeAngelis, 2001).

For the majority of former Soviet youths, coming of age in the multiracial social milieu of a large American metropolis (especially New York) has been both challenging and exciting. New York public schools became the arena of their first encounter with ethno-cultural diversity and often-hostile relations between different groups. Russian students had to define their stance vis-à-vis the African-American, Latino, Chinese and other minority groups, often comprising a majority of the student body. In the more problematic schools of Manhattan and Queens, the relations between the Russian-Jewish and the black "crowds" were often rather tense, as Russian immigrants represent all the social traits despised by the poorer black youth as part of "acting white" syndrome, that is, striving for academic achievement, keeping quiet in class, wearing dull mainstream clothes, and showing no interest in drugs and guns. For example, Genia, a fifteen year-old boy, who came with his single mother from Minsk four years ago, put it like this (in fluent English):

My school is a jungle, and every ethnic tribe tries to survive the best they can. We have a majority of Black students, all coming from the tough neighborhoods with a lot of drugs and guns going around. Another large group are Latinos; they used to be rather quiet when their English was still poor, but by now they tend to stick with the blacks and became more aggressive. There are seven Russian kids in my class, and we usually go together, just for the reasons of safety, not necessarily because we like each other. . . . The study is easy for me, I hardly do any homework and get straight A's, but it is not my main concern. . . . I wish I could switch to a private school, but my mum cannot even dream to afford it.

Other young informants, usually college students, emphasized that they actually enjoyed the multiracial and multicultural makeup of the city, finding this an exciting change from the homogeneous white human landscape of their Soviet cities. Tania, a seventeen year old from Tashkent, said that she disliked other Russians in her class as they were arrogant and often made fun of her clothes, hairdo, and "provincial" ways. "I befriended a group of Latina girls and a few times they "took care" of my Russian torturers, so that finally they left me alone. Since then I go out with Latinas and even learned some Spanish." Other informants told me that living, working and studying with other ethnics made them more liberal, open minded, and less prejudiced against any otherness than are their parents and than they themselves had been before coming to the U.S. In a recent survey, over two-thirds of respondents agreed (fully or to some extent) with the statement that immigrants made New York a better place to live. On the other hand, hostile encounters with racially different peers can reinforce the feelings of otherness and in-group preferences among young Russian immigrants (Kasnitz et al., 2001).

The above-mentioned study offers a snapshot on the lives of the 1.5 and second generation of Soviet Jewish immigrants as part of the larger research scheme called The Second Generation Project in New York. It examined in some detail the acculturation process of the youths and young adults (ages eighteen to thirty-two) belonging to several large immigrant groups of this "Gateway City" (Kasinitz et al., 2001; 2003). Data for the Russian component of this research was collected between 1998 and 2000 and included 300 structured telephone and forty in-depth personal interviews with young Russian-speaking immigrants, most of whom were Jewish. Both the informants and their parents were well educated; many were still in college or in graduate school and often worked full time as well to help their families financially and pay their tuition. The majority was single and lived with the parents, both for reasons of high rental costs and strong emotional ties with the family. The choice of college was often driven by proximity to home and expediency of getting a degree, with quality and prestige being secondary considerations. Not surprisingly, the study pointed to a strong negative association between age at arrival and the extent of acculturation, those born in New York to Russian parents being the most American and the most Jewish at the same time. The in-depth interviews tapped into several interesting tendencies among young Russian New Yorkers.

These youths witnessed the difficult plight of their parents in regaining their former occupational status and making their way back to the middle class, with varying degrees of success. Most fathers and all but a few mothers started their life in New York toiling in manual jobs among other multinational immigrants. Many families had lived for years on end on social assistance, although by the time of the study only the grandparents still received it as their only income. These struggles left deep impression on the young people and boosted their own strong drive for education and economic success, repeating the story of the previous generations of Jewish migrants (Simon, 1997). All but a few of them had started working part time in the catering industry and other services back in high school and knew rather well that money comes with a lot of sweat. In their own choice of education and career, most opted for the prestigious and well-paying occupations in finance, law, management, computing, and information technology. In the sample of 300, over a dozen worked as financial consultants and brokers on the Wall Street.

Over half of the sample (53 percent, including those born in the U.S.) continued speaking Russian at home and at least sometimes with their Russian friends. About 90 percent said their oral Russian was fluent but only 62 percent could also read well, and only 49 percent wrote well in Russian. Several informants reflected on the change in their attitude towards their Russian origin: while during the first years following resettlement they were driven by an impulse to conform to the mainstream American youth culture and spoke English in most settings, in their twenties many rediscovered the world of Russian literature, enjoyed their ability to speak Russian with family and friends, and generally reappraised their cultural heritage as an asset rather than a liability. Despite their fluent English and cultural competence in American urban living, over two-thirds (68 percent) said that most or all of their friends were of Soviet origin (not necessarily Jewish), while 22 percent had a mixed circle of friends, and only 10 percent befriended mainly non-Russians. The Russian-based social networks played important role in the lives of these youths: although only 18 percent said that most of their co-workers were other Russian Jews, over 40 percent found their current job via co-ethnic friends or contacts.

Many also met their dates and fiancés via co-ethnic grapevine or common hangouts and disco clubs (Zeltzer-Zubida, 2000; Kasinitz et al, 2001).

As expected, the questions about the participants' Russian, Jewish, and American identity revealed a rather dynamic and complex picture, endorsing the assertion that ethnic identity is always situational and elastic rather than essential and fixed (Castells, 1997). The Russian component was deeply carved in the self-concept of most young immigrants due to the linguistic practice in the family and frequent socializing with other Russian-speakers. An American/New York identity was also rather firm, as most perceived New York as their home, did not intend to leave the U.S., shared the basic American values of liberty, individualism, and respect for law; over 60 percent were already naturalized or in the process of gaining citizenship (this is a very high rate given that most were relatively recent arrivals). The Jewish segment of their identity was the most fluid and contradictory one; yet it was significantly more pronounced among young New Yorkers than among their counterparts in other U.S. cities with a smaller Jewish presence and fewer Jewish cultural institutions. About half of the sample had attended a full-time Jewish school (yeshiva) for at least one year, not because their parents wanted them to turn to religion but because they perceived these schools to be safer and having higher education standards than regular public schools (the tuition waiver for new immigrants was also enticing). In practice, most parents were disappointed by the amount of religious indoctrination and weak secular curriculum of these schools and soon removed their children from yeshivas, so that 83 percent completed public high schools. Yet, the yeshiva experience left an imprint on many Russian youths: they are more knowledgeable and often more observant of Jewish traditions than their peers outside New York. Eighty percent of the sample said that they had a strong sense of belonging to the Jewish people; 42 percent attended synagogue at least once a month, 44 percent had bar-bat mitzvahs, and 45 percent lived in the households where Shabat candles were lit and donations to Jewish charities were regularly made. A small minority of Yeshiva graduates became religiously observant Jews (*baalei tshuva*) (Kasinitz et al., 2001).

The young generation of Russian Jews manifests a greater propensity for self-organization and community life than their parents. Although their regular participation in the mainstream Jewish organizations and in the urban civic associations is relatively low (about 35 percent and 20 percent, respectively), in several large cities young Russian Jews established informal social groups of their own. The examples include the youth club called Mishpukha (family in Yiddish) in Greater Boston and the 79ers' Association in the San Francisco Bay Area. While the former was formed under the sponsorship of the Synagogue Association of Massachusetts and one of its goals is reinforcement of the Jewish identity among its members, the latter has a largely secular orientation and aims at creating a social network for the similarly minded co-ethnics. Its home page opens with the statement: "Generation-R: All American on the outside, Russian Jewish émigré on the inside. You emigrated as a kid or pre-adolescent and grew up here. Your Russian is rusty and your Judaism is. . . . God only knows. A generation of Russian-Jewish-American hybrid culture molders—Generation R" (www.tribe.net). The group's name reflects the initial intent to outreach for those who came to the U.S. with their parents around 1979—the peak year of the first Jewish emigration wave from the USSR, but later on came to include all members of the 1.5 generation regardless of the arrival time. Although this group has also been established with the aid of the local Jewish Federation, its agenda will be set by the members, including the discussions of cultural issues (e.g., the concept of love in Russia and America), trips to the FSU, and attempts to set up interesting cultural activities in Russian for the children of the 79ers.

Social Networks and Community Building

Former Soviet immigrants are known for their social apathy, low rates of civic and political participation, and distaste for formal organizations of any kind (Markowitz, 1993, Gold, 1997). This is hardly surprising as in the FSU officially approved politics were usually corrupt and oppositional politics were dangerous. Even apparently benign groups like sports clubs and literary groups were under the thumb of the local Communist Party bureaucrats. On the other hand, participation in some "voluntary" organizations, such as the Komsomol (Young Communists League) and trade unions was, in fact, mandatory, including attendance of long and boring meetings and ceremonies. Any unsanctioned gathering roused suspicion on the part of the local administration and police, and no premises could be rented for these goals. In brief people could not self-organize for discussing and solving their mutual problems or pursuing their mutual interests and hobbies without ideological supervision and intervention of the state (Mondak and Gearing, 2003). By the late 1960s, this atmosphere extinguished any civic initiatives, and the locus of social life was once and for all transferred to the kitchens of private homes, where likeminded friends could argue about politics, literature, and any other matters, albeit not always free from censorship thanks to planted informers.

In the U.S., informal social networks between immigrants continue to thrive, while voluntary groups of different kind are often short lived and fail to increase their membership. One major reason for the lack of efficient self-organization among recent arrivals is that Jewish community services in fact cater to most of their initial needs in the areas of housing, employment counseling, English language training, and so on. This failure also reflects the lack of experience in self-organization and conflicts over leadership, as few leaders are ever accepted by the majority of the voters. Self-proclaimed activists are also assumed to have some personal interest or profit and hence are mistrusted ("activist" is a negative and ironic label in the Soviet argot). Difficulty in reaching consensus on the agenda and leadership matters reflects extreme regional, ethnic, and socio-cultural heterogeneity of the former Soviets who all of a sudden found themselves "in the same boat" of immigration. I have already noted the great skill of former Soviets at building social hierarchies and the tendency to associate only with those on the same level or those above themselves. Thus, former residents of the capitals (Moscow and Leningrad) look down on immigrants from smaller provincial cities, those with higher education and academic degrees would not talk with the "simple" folks like hairdressers or sales clerks, Jews from Russia would never vote for a Georgian Jew as their leader, etc. Most former Soviets base the social ranking of their co-ethnics on both their former status (e.g., if a person had been a senior physician, or a chief engineer in the USSR) and current achievements as immigrants (the kind of job one holds, material wealth, command of English, etc.). In fact old, pre-migration social hierarchies reproduce themselves on the new soil, and most former Soviets socialize in the U.S. mainly with those who had been their social peers in the FSU (Gold, 1997). Hence they prefer to build their social networks on a pick-and-choose principle rather than enter organizations where they would have to deal with a variety of people, whom they may find uninteresting or uncultured.

Another guiding principle in the formation of social networks among former Soviets during the 1990s and early 2000s has been the venue of arrival in the US, which often correlates with ethnicity. Former refugees (largely Jews) socialize with their own kind, while those who came to the U.S. on job visas (largely non-Jews) keep company with each other, often via workplace or university networks. Men and women from the FSU, who came as labor migrants (legally and not) and work in blue-collar jobs, form yet another social circle of their own. The last line of social demarcation is the time of arrival: well-established and wealthy immigrants of the 1970s prefer the company of their own "generation" to those who arrived after the collapse of the USSR. Of course, these tribes intermingle under many circumstances (for example, when the less fortunate ones come to clean or baby-sit for their wealthier co-ethnics) and they often share cultural interests and venues, for example attending concerts and shows by touring artists from Russia or Israel. All Russian speakers form a loose social network when it comes to shopping in Russian stores, using various services (such as construction or real estate) or being "minority parents" to children attending American schools. Perhaps the best indicator of the intimacy of social liaisons of former Soviets is the list of guests invited to their homes for birthdays and New Year parties—these form the most proximate circle of the co-ethnic social web.

Despite the dislike of formalized associations and problems with leadership, over time some categories of immigrants were compelled to get together in order to solve common problems, to find business partners, borrow money, or simply to socialize, build client networks, and exchange useful information. The examples of such associations include various entrepreneur groups of former Soviets such as cab drivers or restaurateurs. These groups were especially valuable for the beginning businessmen as they lacked two central prerequisites for entrepreneurship—capital and business experience in a Western economy. These groups are especially active in Los Angeles, where fully 33 percent of former Soviet immigrant men and 17 percent of the women are self-employed, followed by New York (21 percent and 8 percent, respectively) (Gold, 1997). Another example of successful civic organization of former Soviets are doctors and dentists associations that emerged across the U.S. since the mid–1990s. Immigrant physicians who, upon examination and/or additional training, qualified for U.S. licenses typically opened their practices in or near Russian ethnic concentrations in large cities. They serve predominantly Russian-speaking clients, usually receiving payment via their publicly funded health plans (Medicaid and some others). By the system of mutual referrals Russian physicians enhance each other's client networks and as a by-product also support the businesses of Russian pharmacists, psychologists and counselors, physiotherapists, homeopaths, dentists, and finally Russian newspapers, which advertise their services. The R-AMA (Russian-American Medical Association—see their website at www.russiandoctors.org), as well as local Associations in different states, serve as clearing houses and information centers, and organize professional conferences with medical lectures and social events at least once a year. Some other organizations operating on the "Russian street" comprise a merger of social, commercial, and service-oriented goals; they are funded via both governmental programs (Medicare, Medicaid) and direct client payments. One typical example is Zabota (Care) Center in Boston, combining a kindergarten, day care for the elderly, various psychological and counseling services for Russian-speakers, plus a pharmacy selling imported drugs (produced in the FSU and in Europe) familiar to the former Soviets from their past.

Last but not least of the common social venues for Russian-Jewish immigrants are established American-Jewish organizations that never stopped their outreach efforts towards Russian Jews, striving to fortify their tenuous Jewish identity. The American Jewish Committee (AJC) has been the most active in this respect thanks to the enthusiasm of its executive director David A. Harris (partly of Russian origin himself); it has even established a Russian Division and an affiliated Research Institute for New Americans (RINA) headed by former Soviet social scientist Dr. Samuel Kliger. Acting upon Kliger's initiative, AJC has been running since 1997 a successful Leadership Training Program for Russian Jews in New York, Boston, and San-Francisco (www.ajc.org/russian). A similar project has been organized by the Russian Division of UJA-Federation of New York (see www.ujafedny.org). Besides their chief goal of reinforcing Jewish identity and participation in community life among Russian immigrants, these programs aim at fostering relations with Russian-speaking Jewish communities in Israel and in the world. As a result of this leadership training, several new associations have emerged on the Jewish scene of New York, for example a group called Russian Jews of America for Israel, whose leaders often comment on the current events in Israel, and Russian-Jewish responses to them, on the New York-based global Russian TV channel RTVi. On a smaller scale, educational programs on the Jewish religion and tradition, Israel, and other components of the "American Judaism package" are offered to the newcomers by Jewish Community Centers in many cities with a Russian immigrant presence.

However, as already noted, this kind of framing of Jewish identity is rather alien for most Soviet Jews; some of them (mainly older and unemployed ones) attend these classes for the sake of pastime and company rather than intellectual stimulation or religious practice. These programs are more successful when they are organized by Russian-speakers themselves and manage to recruit more erudite leaders and lecturers. Unfortunately, few communities went beyond religion and tradition, expanding their vision of Jewish civilization to include Jewish history and philosophy, literature by the Jewish writers and poets, courses on Jews in science and politics, and other more secular programs that would appeal also to younger and more educated and successful Jewish immigrants. Recent focus group research among young Russian Jewish professionals in New York (Liakhovitski, 2005) indicated that they are more interested in the intellectual content or, alternatively, quality of entertainment, offered by different Jewish events rather than their religious messages. On their scale of interests, a chess tournament or a jazz festival with participation of Jewish musicians is a much greater attraction than lectures about Halacha or Gmara. Some centers managed to attract Russian immigrant youth to the projects related to Israel, especially when they promise free travel (e.g. the Birthright Program) and other perks. The outreach efforts among younger Russian Jews seem to be more diverse and successful in New York vis-à-vis other cities. Finally, many immigrants use various facilities offered by Jewish community centers, such as swimming pools, gyms, subsidized meals, libraries, and cultural events. But this is probably a matter of socializing and convenience rather than Jewish affiliation.

Transnational Interests and Activities

The concept of transnationalism has already been introduced to the reader in chapter 2 on Russian Jews in Israel; in brief, it refers to the maintenance of intense and regular ties and commitments between immigrants and their significant others in the former homeland and other migration countries of this ethnic group, as well as economic and political activities of expatriates in these countries (Vertovec, 2004). After the collapse of Communism, the global Russian-Jewish diaspora (with the FSU as its historic homeland) has emerged in multiple centers, Israel being the largest of them, but U.S. certainly the wealthiest one. While Soviet émigrés of the 1970s had to sever any contact with the people and places they loved in the old country, the last-wave immigrants can enjoy relatively open borders, affordable airfares, fast and easy contact with the FSU via telephone, fax, and e-mail. The emigration does not have to be a one-way irreversible motion anymore; friends and relatives, colleagues and business partners living in different countries can visit each other and stay in touch easier than ever before. Are Russian-speaking Americans part of the transnational Russian-Jewish social space? Of course they are. Do we find a large amount of grass-root transnational activities "from below" (Guarnizo and Smith, 1998) directed at the home country (Russia, Ukraine, and other parts of the FSU), Israel, and other large isles of the co-ethnic presence? Probably not in general, but certainly yes in some segments of the Russian immigrant community.

To answer this question with greater confidence, we need a survey in a large nationally representative sample of post–1988 Soviet immigrants to the U.S., asking them about the actual amount of travel to the FSU, Israel, and other countries of co-ethnic presence with personal, business or political goals, as well as remote connections (phone, e-mail) with friends and relatives living there. Such a survey could also glean information on financial support Russian Americans may extend across borders to their parents, siblings, and friends living in the FSU or in Israel; on their interest in establishing joint business or scientific ventures with people in these countries; keeping Russian and Ukrainian citizenship and voting in these nation's elections; and their general interest in the political, economic, and cultural developments in these countries. This would give us an indication of whether the mind, heart, time schedules, and wallets of the former-Soviet-now-American Jews, indeed, incorporate co-ethnic people and projects beyond the U.S. borders. But no such survey has ever been conducted in the U.S., so at this time I can only offer some fragmented observations and smaller local studies.

Sociologist of ethnicity and migration Ewa Morawska (2004) reported on her comparative study of assimilation and transnationalism among Polish and Russian-Jewish immigrants in Philadelphia who arrived during the past twenty years, but no later than 1995. The Polish "colony" of the city numbers about 12,000, while the Russian-Jewish population is much more spread out and is in the range of 30–35,000 immigrants. Each sample included thirty informants (fifteen women and fifteen men); they were recruited by snowballing starting from community leaders and proceeding by informal referrals, and interviewed in their homes in their native language. A majority of the Russian sample was middle aged and older (44 percent were in fifty-six to sixty-nine age bracket); over 80 percent had a higher education; most of those still working were in managerial and professional occupations and had a higher than average income. The author found a high degree of assimilation among Russian Jews into American middle class, expressed in their economic success, good working knowledge of English, high naturalization rate (80 percent), respect for American civic and political values, and pride in educational and occupational success of their children. Polish immigrants were assimilating via what Morawska calls ethnic-adhesive path, that is, working mainly within their co-ethnic economy and identifying as Poles rather than Americans; 90 percent kept Polish passports regardless of naturalization in the U.S., and many expressed the hope of eventual return to their homeland. For both immigrant communities, the primary social circles have been co-ethnic, with an addition of some American-Jewish friends for the younger Russian informants. Explaining this pattern, both Russian Jews and Poles referred to a familiar argument of sharing a common frame of mind with their own kind while having little in common with native Americans. Many older informants from the FSU stressed their satisfaction in rediscovering their Jewishness, albeit in a new American framing. Coming from the former Socialist bloc with its forced collectivism, both Poles and Russian Jews shunned formal organizations and expressed their social engagements via personal networks and informal exchange of information and support.

In relation to transnational engagement with their homelands, Morawska found striking differences between the two immigrant groups. While the Poles manifested strong commitments to Poland, made a point of maintaining the Polish language and traditions at home, kept closely updated on current events in Poland, made regular remittances to their families and friends, traveled to Poland at least once a year, and received guests from Poland in their homes, few

Russian Jews pursued any of these activities regularly or often enough to become an important part of their life. While the majority of the Poles, regardless of age and socioeconomic status, said that their true emotional and spiritual home is Poland, none of the former Soviets said the same about Russia or Ukraine. Despite their active engagement with all things Russian while living in America (attending cultural venues, shopping in Russian groceries or having parties in Russian restaurants), none of that had to do with their nostalgia for Russia itself, but with habit and convenience of socializing in their native language. The economic activities and lifestyles of the Russian Jews were strongly oriented towards success and integration in their new homeland—America; few informants visited the FSU more than once after emigration and none felt obliged to Russia in any way, let alone wished to return there. If they had any nostalgia at all, it was about their youth and friends they left behind rather than the country itself. Most informants did not express any serious interest or attachment to Israel, except for those few who had close relatives living there; yet many informants supported Israel by making regular donations to the Jewish charities.

In her analysis, Morawska explains this "America-centered ethnic-path adaptation" for the former Soviets by the "group's outcast minority status in the home country," with the ensuing lack of positive sentiment or obligations to Russia and its people. She also notes that for a large part of former Soviets their reasons for emigration were civic-political, while most Poles emigrated in search of better economic fortunes. The reception of the two groups in the U.S. was also rather different: while Soviet Jews were generously supported by their wealthy American co-religionists, the Poles had to adapt by themselves and had a much harder time gaining a foothold. Finally, the upward socioeconomic mobility experienced in the U.S. by most Russian Jews and/or their children reinforced their positive identification with their new home and pride in being American. Other factors that discouraged transnational engagements of the former Soviets include the migration of full families and having few significant others still living in Russia or Ukraine. Finally, the newly acquired sense of security and opportunity in America (that is, not achievable either in Russia or in Israel) reinforced inwardly oriented rather than external interests and pursuits.

While generally agreeing with Morawska's findings and explanations, I would like to add a few observations of my own. Indeed, transnational interests and activities of the former Soviets are often defined by whether or not they have significant others living outside America—in Russia, Israel, or elsewhere. While many extended families immigrated to the U.S. together, many others could not exit at the same time or preferred other countries of emigration, and as a result quite a number of families are scattered between different hosting countries and the FSU itself. This is especially true of mixed or non-Jewish families that moved to the U.S. via work or study visas and whose residence here gradually turned from temporary to permanent. Most of them had not intended to stay in the U.S. to begin with, and hence kept their apartments, summer homes, and other property in the big Russian cities. Their parents, siblings, and friends are still living in the FSU, creating many reasons to travel there. Those having this current human link to the former Soviet countries travel there quite often, and support their relatives by direct remittances, expensive gifts, and inviting them for prolonged periods to their American homes. Here is a typical story told by Maria (forty-two), a former art librarian from Leningrad's Hermitage and an ethnic Russian, who moved to Boston with her Jewish husband in 1988. She was rather successful in her new work life and is currently a research librarian in one of Harvard's libraries. Maria's parents and brother are prominent physicians in St. Petersburg who have intense work lives and never intended to emigrate. Maria and her thirteen-year-old daughter Lika visit their family in St. Petersburg twice every year—during Christmas-New Year vacations and in summer. The girl spends at least two months each year with her grandparents and friends in their apartment in the old center of St. Petersburg or in the summer cottage near Finland. Every winter mother and daughter fly to the Northern Capital (as St. Petersburg is often called) to attend the Russian Winter Arts Festival with its rich offerings of the best theatrical and music events from all over Europe. In this way, they stay closely connected with Russian culture and current life; both mother and daughter are basically bicultural, symmetrically fluent in Russian and English. Lika regards herself as a Russian girl living in America; she is doing well at school and has many friends, most of whom are immigrants from different parts of the world. Besides Russian and English, she excels in French and wants to study in France some day. Maria reflected aloud:

Despite my work at Harvard and dealing with the best and most educated part of Americans, this country is still a desert for me. I cannot find much charm or appeal in the mainstream U.S. culture, entertainment and ways of living. I need Russia and more generally—European culture, literature, landscape, architecture . . . you know what I mean. And Lika grew up the same, although she actually enjoys the best of both worlds. My husband for many years berated me for taking her out to Russia for prolonged visits: he was afraid that she would never adapt to America and would have a split identity. But now he can see that she is doing fine: her life is twice as rich and she is twice as smart and sensitive as most of her American peers.

During my travels between different Russian-American hubs I met quite a number of former Soviets who share this truly transnational lifestyle because they have many human and sentimental attachments to their homeland. Indeed, most of them were non-Jews—typically Russian wives of Jews who wished that their children spoke fluent Russian, stayed in touch with their Russian grandparents, and had a first-hand knowledge of Russian life. Among job-visa immigrants, who were predominantly non-Jewish, this shuttle movement between their new American and old Russian homes was a rule rather than an exception. In the words of Alex, a New York based artist, "I don't want to choose between Moscow and New York, so I am trying to live in both countries, as far as my limited income allows." Like Alex, many with artistic or freelance occupations who had no permanent jobs (Russian and Jewish alike), traveled to Russia (mostly Moscow and St. Petersburg) as often as they could afford the airfare. Several artists had studios both in Moscow and in New York and exhibited their work in both cities. A few journalists and writers I met in New York published regular columns in both American and Russian press, worked on American, Russian, and international television and radio stations. Most of those who traveled to Russia a lot, and all ethnic Russians, usually kept Russian passports along with American ones.

Like ethnic Russians who kept permanent ties to their families in Russia, quite a few ethnic Jews had close friends, and often siblings or parents living in Israel. Leon (thirty-nine) a software designer with an MIT-related company, said: "I fly to Tel Aviv at least twice a year, for my mom's birthday and for the New Year. Although I can't speak Hebrew I feel pretty much at home there, as so many Israelis speak Russian today. I have more friends in Israel than in Cambridge; it is practically my second home. I mainly live in America because of my high-tech job, I won't be able to find such an interesting and well-paying work in Israel." In fact, most Jewish-Russian Americans had close friends or former colleagues, if not relatives, who had moved to Israel in the early 1990s, when virtually no other destinations were open to the emigrants. Those who could not travel to Israel in person, usually due to the demands of job and family, typically maintained regular telephone and e-mail contacts with their Israeli-Russian friends, sent gifts with other travelers, and invited Israelis to visit them in America. All this human exchange was found across the age span, differing mainly in its forms: while young and middle-aged individuals preferred personal visits and e-mails, older immigrants communicated with their contacts in Israel mainly on the telephone. Many American residents regularly visited Israeli and Israeli-Russian websites to update themselves on current events.

A significant share of Russian Americans watch Russian television channels, both transmitted from Russia itself via satellite and produced in America, including the New York Russian Channel and RTVi (former NTV) channel owned by Russian Jewish media magnate Vladimir Gusinsky. While TV programs made in Russia itself naturally reflect Russian politics, economy, and cultural life, the media channels produced in the U.S. cater to American, Israeli, and other diasporic Russian speakers, and have a broad comparative coverage of international matters of relevance and interest for the former Soviets. They include multiple reprints and digests of events from the FSU, Israel, North America, other diasporic countries, as well as personal profiles on the former Soviet artists, professionals, politicians and other former and current celebrities from across the Russian-speaking world. The role of the global Russian-language media in the shaping and cementing of the transnational social space inhabited by former Soviets in different corners of the world is growing more salient every year (Caspi et al., 2002). The same is true of the global Russian-language Internet, which serves as a meeting place for former Soviets spread across the globe (Fialkova, 2005). The popular web-portals such as www.russianny.com; www.russianboston.com; www.russianseattle.com; www.russiansf.com; www.gorodok.com, and other city-specific nodes feature a variety of news releases, information on community events, thematic forums, friends and dating services, and so on. These websites offer a comfortable option of staying plugged into co-ethnic community life (which typically occurs in the mixture of English and Russian, especially in the venues meant for younger people) while simultaneously enjoying a lifestyle of American middleclass. In other words, they both reflect and reinforce bicultural and bilingual identities of most Russian Americans.

Yet another important facet of transnationalism among former Soviets is found in the realm of scientific research in the work of scientists who share their time and labor between their laboratories in Russia and United States. Reflecting a deep crisis in both fundamental and applied science after the fall of state socialism, many of the brightest Soviet scientists (at least half of them Jewish) have moved abroad, mainly to the U.S. as the scientific superpower, to be able to continue their work. In only five years between 1989 and 1993, over 70,000 researchers in physics, chemistry, biology, and other laboratory-based sciences left the FSU (Simanovsky et al., 1996), and by the early 2000s their number had probably doubled. Quite a few renowned scientists, especially in physics, have managed to move their whole laboratories (or at least their core staff) to American soil, by chain reaction attracting young Russian doctoral and postdoctoral scholars, many of whom have families and spend part of the year in Russia. The story told by a leading Russian physicist Konstantin Likharev in Shasha and Shron's collection of oral histories (2002) is very informative in this respect. Likharev's Moscow laboratory working on cutting edge research in cryo-electronics lost its state funding in 1990, and, as his work had been well known in the West, he managed to secure university or industry R&D positions for himself and six of his chief co-workers. Since 1991 Likharev's laboratory is based at State University of New York in Stony Brook, but it draws mainly on the "human capital" produced by Moscow State University and a few other leading Russian institutions. Are they American scientists or rather Russian scholars working in America and funded by American research grants? Probably both.

To conclude, the integration narrative of the Russian-speaking Jews in America is complex and multifaceted, reflecting their diversity in terms of human capital and adaptive potential, let alone their demographics. Juxtaposed with different economic conditions in the cities and towns where these immigrants have resettled, this diversity defined the varying pace of their acculturation. Yet, the majority of Russian Jews manifested a remarkable "ability to raise above their miserable condition"(to quote Van Etten's late nineteenth-century essay) due to hard effort, mutual support, and an intense charge of "immigrant adrenaline" in their bloodstream—the internal drive for success and upward mobility that typified all the earlier migrant waves of Russian Jews in the U.S. The initial period upon arrival is often marked by identity crisis and reassessment of the old cultural values, along with labor market adjustments that often include retraining and occupational change. After three to five years, most immigrants get some economic foothold and learn enough English to start bridging the gap to the mainstream middle class, with the gradual Americanization of their everyday lifestyles. Yet, even after a decade or more of life in the U.S., the attitudes and practices pertaining to the private domain of immigrant's lives (e.g., relations between parents and children, choice of romantic partners and friends) show much less Americanization than instrumental adjustments they had made in the public domain (workplace, relations with social institutions) and in their daily lifestyles (housing, transportation, media consumption, leisure, etc.). To cite again psychologist Vera Kishinevsky, "the closer you get to the core of immigrants' personal life and intimate relations, the less their beliefs, priorities, and choices have been affected by life in America" (personal communication).

By this time, a tangible economic polarization is apparent between the high achievers and underachievers, expressed in the kind of the jobs they hold, success of their business ventures and expendable incomes, with the ensuing quality of housing and child education they can afford. Russian immigrants are found on both ends of the socio-economic spectrum, as "legally poor" beneficiaries of social assistance and as successful academics, upper middle-class physicians, financial consultants, and high-tech professionals. Although most have not become more religious, their tenuous Jewish identity slowly evolves from a negative Soviet to a proud American way of being Jewish. They gradually overcome their old prejudice against civic organizations and start community building, driven by their own current interests and the wish to transfer their cultural heritage to the children.

Educated women often manifest greater flexibility in occupational readjustment than men and embark on new "pragmatic" rather then status-oriented careers for the sake of their family well-being. In the meantime, the younger generation of Russian immigrants strives to define its social location in the American mosaic, within the axes set by the old parental values and those of the American youth mainstream. Being the most successful and wealthy among the branches of post-communist migrations, Russian-Jewish Americans often appear as rather arrogant rich cousins in the co-ethnic transnational networks, sponsoring the travel, sending remittances, and hosting the global Russian-language media. The orientation towards success and upward mobility in America apparently outweighs their interest in Russia, Israel, and other countries where Russian Jews live. The overwhelming majority see America as their one and only home and do not look back.

In Conclusion: Personal Vignettes

To illustrate some stories of immigration and adjustment to life in America, I am closing this chapter by several personal vignettes (or case studies) selected from my interview pools in New York, Boston, and San Francisco Bay Area. These stories highlight some of the themes discussed above, primarily those reflecting the qualms of Russian-Soviet cultural continuity versus acculturation to the American middle-class mainstream. All of the narratives, from which these vignettes have been extracted, belong to educated former Soviet professionals, who arrived in the U.S. after 1988 in the active working age between 30 and 55 years and had to take a fresh start on the new labor market. Probably none of these narrators can be called "typical Russian Jewish immigrants" in a statistical sense, but they certainly help us understand the lived experiences of resettlement among this particular segment of the newcomers.

Andrey (Andy) (forty-three), research physicist from Moscow, moved to a California University as a postdoctoral fellow in 1992, along with his wife (also an applied physicist) and a little son. Both he and his wife are partly Jewish by blood, but have no tangible traces of Jewish identity. After having worked in several research positions on "soft money" and having slim prospects for tenure, Andy gave up his ambitions as researcher and opted for a more secure consultancy job at the University's Patent Office. Besides his day job, Andy has also succeeded in a real estate market, riding the recent housing boom in California; after several increasingly profitable home purchases and sales, Andy's family has recently moved in a large, custom designed and decorated house in a prestigious college town. Andy speaks of his real estate deals as an engaging intellectual hobby, not unlike chess, where ability to see a few steps ahead is required for winning the game. His wife, Anna (forty-two), never sought research positions in the U.S., but after staying home with their second, American-born son, got a job in computer system maintenance at a large Californian hospital. Both Andy and Anna work normal eight-hour working days (a drastic change after the unlimited time Andy had spent earlier in physics labs!), and devote their evenings and weekends to the improvement and decoration of their large property. They also like to travel and proudly show to the guests (using a huge home cinema screen) numerous pictures from their ocean cruises to the Caribbean, Alaska, and Europe. The couple enjoys hosting large parties for friends in their backyard or spacious living room equipped with a professional bar.

An amazing feature of this family's lifestyle is an exclusively co-ethnic circle of friends and all-Russian oriented cultural interests. After thirteen years of life in the U.S. (and despite their good English proficiency and economic success), they are still firmly rooted in Russian culture, read recently published Russian fiction and popular magazines, watch Russian films and television serials on DVDs, follow Russian news via Internet sites, and so on. The only language spoken at home is pure Russian, with no "contamination" by English words and idioms allowed even to their U.S.-born younger son. Every year, both Andy and Anna spend their summer vacations in Moscow and at the family's county cottage (*dacha*) with their parents and siblings, usually taking their younger son (eleven) with them (the older one, now twenty-one, made several independent trips to Russia). They return from their Moscow vacations loaded with new books, CDs, and DVDs, and are happy to share these last highlights of the Russian cultural market with their multiple immigrant friends from several nearby suburban towns.

Andy and his wife seem to have found an optimal balance between the economic benefits of life in America and the ability to enjoy Russian culture and socializing Russian-style. "We could hardly have achieved such living standards and quality of life in Russia remaining in purely intellectual workforce, as science is no longer prestigious and it doesn't pay even a minimum living wage. But at the same time we will never become Americans despite having lived here for a long time; and our sons also have a big part of their identity set as Russian. I know that we are a weird kind of a tree: our branches are bathing in Californian sun, but our roots are still planted in the Russian soil. . . . We are seriously considering the option of returning to Moscow after retirement; there we can comfortably spend our old age in a familiar and dear place. Our children will probably choose America as their main home, but they will also be connected with Russia, maybe will go there to work for a few years, or find themselves girlfriends and wives in Moscow . . . " When asked about his social relations with Americans, Andy said that he gets along with his co-workers and bosses very well, and he appreciates some features of the American social relations of work, for example, respect for privacy, not mixing private matters with business, and dislike of nepotism and protectionism. Yet, at the same time he never tried to befriend any of his American colleagues or neighbors, seeing them as an alien species that cannot fit into his and his family's personal space. "I have enough Russian friends here, with whom I share common language and interests, why should I seek Americans? They are often real nice guys, but for me they are just a part of the local Californian scene; they blend into the landscape like exotic trees or nice houses. Socially I am not part of that landscape, and by the same token they have no interest in me. I am good at my job, but an alien in most other respects. I guess this status quo is suitable for both parties. We respect each other, but keep safe distance; we just live in parallel universes that will never intersect."

Lena (forty-four) emigrated from Kiev to San Francisco alone in 1990. As a Jewish woman, she had faced barriers to higher education, and after several attempts to study law at the Kiev State University she settled for the evening law college in the city. After graduation, Lena worked for a few years as labor relations consultant at a local enterprise—a dead-end job with no intellectual challenge or chances for promotion. She compensated for the boredom of her work life with ardent cultural activities, never missing a theater premiere, a new book, or a gathering in the city's Jewish underground for Simchat Torah, Purim, or a literary reading by Jewish authors. By the age of thirty, Lena was fed up with her job, still did not meet a right man to start a family, and decided to embark on emigration in search of new opportunities and new friends. As she had expected, none of her legal credentials had been recognized in California, and she went to school again to become a paralegal. While studying, Lena supported herself by cleaning work, waiting the tables, babysitting, and any odd jobs that came by. Meantime, Lena met and married an ex-compatriot from Odessa and they had two children (now aged nine and five). Due to

difficult pregnancies and childcare demands, Lena's studies extended
to a period of five years, and upon graduation from college she found
it difficult to find a job compatible with her interests and family roles.
Since the late 1990s, she has been working part-time as a legal secretary at the municipal administration and, in order to upgrade her job,
studied for paralegal bar exams, which she has failed twice. Lena had
a really hard time juggling her family life and the attempts to embark
on a new and demanding career; she was deeply frustrated by her
failures at the exams. Now she is studying for the third, and probably
last, attempt to pass the exam.

Meantime, Lena's husband has been in and out of different technical and low-grade engineering jobs, tried to switch to software design
during the high-the boom, but lost his job when the IT bubble burst in
2000. Since then he has been unemployed, but did not use his spare
time to take over some household and childcare tasks from Lena. For
the last few years, she had been responsible for both breadwinning and
running the household. The family hardly makes ends meet, and the
mortgage payments for their nice little townhouse are often late. Yet,
Lena never complains about her passive house-ridden husband who
hardly ever leaves the TV couch; she feels sorry for his bad luck (not
the lack of effort!) and quietly tolerates his mood swings and short
temper with the children. "He is depressed, poor guy, his self-esteem
fell as low as it gets, and I don't want to make it any worse by
scolding him. A woman has to be a backbone for the family during
bad times, and stand by her man no matter what. I am still glad that I
have a full family life, and I am prepared to wait for better times, for
myself and for my husband. Children should not feel that anything is
missing or going wrong." Lena admits that her life in California is in
many ways more tedious and routine than the one she had led in Kiev:
she splits her days between work, house chores, and tending to her
husband's and children's needs, seldom going out with her American
friends (acquired before marriage). Due to financial problems, Lena
and her husband cannot afford entertainment or travel and strive to
meet the educational needs of the children (like all Russian kids, they
attend several enrichment activities after school). Yet she says that she
is so exhausted from her two daily shifts that she is not really interested in anything but rest and a bit of TV or a book at bedtime. Lena
finds it difficult to define whether her life has improved or worsened
due to immigration; she just takes it by the day and tries to avoid big

questions. "I had been a merry city girl in Kiev and became a dull workhorse here; but this is probably what age and family life do to most women anyway. I don't think I would be much happier or freer had I stayed back there . . . "

Fania (fifty-seven) came to New York with her husband David and daughter Zhenia in 1988, from the West Ukrainian city of Lvov. At home, David had been a well-known senior physician (orthopedic surgeon) and had a very hard time leaving behind his job at the leading city hospital. Fania herself had a biological degree and worked in a medical laboratory as clinical researcher. During their initial years in New York, David invested all his time into preparing for the licensure exams, while Fania toiled in several manual jobs and in the evenings sold insurance policies to Russian-speaking immigrants to keep the family afloat. At the outset of their emigration saga, she gave up her ambitions as biomedical researcher, realizing that one of them had to downgrade for the sake of the other's success. After getting his license (from the second attempt, mainly due to his lacking English), David decided to try and open a back pain clinic in a Russian neighborhood of Brooklyn. As he had only been licensed for general practice and was not ready to start a new five-year residency after having over twenty years of experience in orthopedic surgery in Ukraine, David could advertise his practice as a GP and/or chiropractor. As he was really good and managed to help many patients with muscular-skeletal problems, his practice grew rather quickly by the word of mouth. Before the advent of managed care in the U.S., David had received direct fees for his services and was not dependent on insurance companies or HMOs for referrals and reimbursement. Most of his immigrant patients had been on Medicaid and Medicare, which refunded partly or fully their expenses at David's pain clinic. In 1992, Fania left her insurance company and started working as David's assistant and secretary at the clinic. For a few years things were running very smoothly for the couple: they bought a nice townhouse, could afford holidays abroad, and a good college for their daughter who went to study law at New York University.

However, after the managed care revolution in the mid–1990s, the stream of patients sharply dwindled as they no longer got reimbursed by their federal health plans, and most other HMOs also refused to cover pain treatments. David and Fania had to reduce their fees to the levels acceptable for thin immigrant wallets or lose most of their patients. The income they now got was hardly enough to pay for the office and equipment rentals, and by 1998 the couple made a hard decision to sell their beloved practice while still viable. Shaken by all the turmoil and the impeding loss of his clinic, David suffered a massive heart attack and died at the age of fifty-three. Fania was devastated by David's untimely death. At the same time, she had to make brave financial decisions and handle the sales of the clinic; she managed to find a reasonably good deal within one year. After selling the clinic, she found herself completely alone, with her husband dead and her daughter moving out to Washington for a legal job with the government. For a few years, she was depressed, did not work and lived on her savings, which soon came to an end. For a brief time, Fania was hospitalized to treat her clinical depression. In 2000, an old friend of hers from Boston insisted on introducing her to a neighbor, a Russian immigrant and recent widower himself. After a short period of courtship, Fania remarried and moved to Boston, where her second husband works as civil engineer. Now she works as a secretary/manager for another Russian immigrant doctor, and her past experience helped this young female physician to establish herself on the medical market of Boston and the suburbs. At the same time, by her mid-fifties Fania discovered a new interest in the Jewish life and joined several Jewish community projects targeting new immigrants. For example, she took active part in organization of the joint Passover seder celebrations for Russian—and American-Jewish women at the initiative of the Hadassah-Brandeis Institute in Waltham. Through this project Fania met several women who later became her friends in the new city. Fania impressed me by her optimism and fighting spirit in the face of many adversities she has encountered during her life in America, the last of which is her current struggle with breast cancer and the treatment's aftermath. She is the kind of person who never gives up and is ever ready to embark on new activities, relationships, and responsibilities.

Nick and Nina (both aged sixty-four) led a fulfilled life in Moscow as music professors at one of the leading music schools of Moscow, respected and loved by their many students and colleagues. Nina taught musical theory and earned a Ph.D. in musicology in the early 1980s. Nick, beside teaching, had also had a busy performance schedule playing viola, violin, and conducting a large student orchestra. He devoted his few spare hours to painting; his art was well liked by his friends and even brought a little extra income. Their daughter Katia was also a talented young musician, playing several instruments, teaching and performing. Like most Russian intellectuals, Nick and Nina were distressed by the rapid devaluation of all non-commercial artistic work in the post-communist years and strove to maintain decent living standards on their tiny academic salaries supplemented by Nick's performance fees. Like many of their friends and colleagues before them, they finally applied for emigration (with the help of a distant cousin in the U.S.) and found themselves in New York in 1993 as a Jewish refugee family. The musical labor market of New York is both extremely rich and saturated, making it very difficult for immigrant musicians to reestablish themselves. Nick and Nina were in their early fifties when they came to New York, with their divorced daughter (then twenty-six years old) and her five-year-old son; the older generation was represented by Nina's mother (seventy-five) and her sister (seventy-two). The extended family settled in three separate but closely located apartments in Washington Heights, thanks to the generous assistance of HIAS and NAYANA, covering virtually full rental cost for the old ladies and subsidizing the rent for Katia as a single mother, and for Nick and Nina as unemployed refugees. The adults received Medicaid health coverage as long as their income was below the poverty line, and the elders were covered by Medicaid, including daily home attendant services and free prescription medicines. Thus, the family's material survival had been ensured, and the struggle for professional recognition could now be started. Luckily, even a basic command of English (which both spouses had) was enough to teach and perform music. Drawing on his few old contacts in the musical world (mostly earlier Russian immigrants who had already gained some foothold), Nick started looking for teaching jobs in music schools, as well as for private students. He also attended multiple auditions for orchestra and ensemble vacancies, and soon work started flowing his way. Inspired by this success, he even went back to painting and exhibited his New York landscapes along with other Russian artists of the city.

By the end of his third year in New York, Nick had a dozen of private students, two part-time teaching jobs at colleges and played at least five concerts per month. The rising income was good news, but it had a flipside: Medicaid coverage was denied to the spouses, as they no longer fitted the poverty criteria. At the same time, Nina was diagnosed with a serious chronic condition requiring medical follow-up and possibly serious surgery in the future. The couple could not take the risk of living without health insurance, and ever since the mid–1990s a significant portion of their modest income (depleted by the need to pay full rent for a Manhattan apartment as all initial subsidies were gone) went to the purchase of private medical insurance. Due to her illness, and the theoretical nature of her musical specialty, Nina had slim chances of returning to her old occupation. Instead, she found several part-time jobs as musical accompanier for classic ballet classes in different parts of New York. Since then, she has typically worked four to eight hours a week, and her paychecks were hardly enough to pay utility bills, but she is glad to have at least this amount of work (for which she is clearly overqualified). In her spare time, Nina used to help her daughter, mother and aunt with various daily chores, and took her grandson to various after-school activities. Thus she drifted from being a full-time professional to being a free-lance "small gig" musician plus almost full-time homemaker and caregiver. Katia had ups and downs in her musical career in New York, but by and large she gained a foothold in the musical teaching world and also performed every now and then with different orchestras. During her twelve years in New York, she managed to marry and divorce an American man, to try her luck in Europe, travel back to Moscow, learn to play another instrument, and (most recently) dancing professional tango. Her son is finishing high school and considering a career in a restaurant business. The old women (now aged eighty-eight and eighty-five) attend a Russian daycare center, watch New York Russian television, and read Russian newspapers. They even managed to pass the citizenship exams in 1999 and can now understand a few words in English. They miss their youth and the old Moscow they used to know, but slowly came to accept New York as their final destination in this life. Although this extended family has had its share of troubles, professional and personal, after twelve years they are all firmly set in the Big Apple's artistic and social world and think of the city as their one and only home.

Notes

1. See more about KVN and KSP movements during the last decades of socialism and among Soviet immigrants in chapter 2 on Israel, where I discuss "transplantation" of these unique cultural genres. U.S. national KVN team stages periodic

contests with former Soviet and Israeli teams (shown by global Russian television channels); amateur song festivals featuring both old and new authors are organized twice a year in open-air venues on both U.S. coasts. See more on the American KVN website www.kabh.org and KSP website www.kspus.org.

2. For all Soviet people, Jews and non-Jews alike, New Year's Day was a secular holiday—a celebration of the fairy tale, magic, and time change, rather than Christmas as a religious holiday. A New Year Tree (rather than a Christmas tree) was an indispensable part of this annual ritual, as were loud and merry gatherings of family and friends around festive table. The friendly sparkle of New Year's Eve remained one bright spot on the bleak calendar of official Soviet holidays.

3. The generous benefits received by Russian Jewish elders did not go unnoticed by the conservative and anti-Semitic groups who accuse the U.S. Jewish lobby for bringing in these "parasites" living on account of good American taxpayers. See the article under a telling caption "Russian Jews Are Depleting American Workers SSI" on an ultra-right website: http://adlusa.com.

4. These reforms made collection of the refugee social aid package contingent on their naturalization within five years upon arrival. To become U.S. citizens, all refugees regardless of age had to pass exams on American history and government in English, and for many thousands of the Russian-Jewish elders this was an impossible task. At this time, United Jewish Appeal saved Russian Jews once again, offering generous training programs in most residential enclaves, and at the same time lobbying for the defeat or relaxation of these reforms. As a result, a reasonable compromise was achieved: most elderly refugees passed the test and saved their income, and those who had not retained at least some of the benefits.

5. By the same token, orthodox methods of social research often misfire when applied to the former Soviets. Thus, the pollsters hired by the American Jewish Committee to run a survey among New York Jewry with an adequate representation of former Soviet Jews (who are known to comprise about one-forth) were disappointed to find out that their carefully designed statistical sampling scheme has captured only about 8–10 percent. The failure could be easily explained by the method of the initial identification of the Jews used by the pollsters, a phone call to a randomly selected number opening with a "screening" question: "Are there Jewish people residing in this household?" The deeply entrenched instincts of former Soviet Jews make them say a firm *No* to this question, or simply hang up, just to be on the safe side. It was hardly possible to locate enough Russian Jewish households by this standard technique, perfectly normal for most Americans. Thus, drawing on residential and social networks and snowballing are the only practical way to reach out for Russian Jews in surveys (personal communication by S. Kliger).

6. Such constellations of roles were especially common among Russians in New York with its harsh market conditions for migrant male professionals; they often form the backdrop of Sergei Dovlatov's popular émigré stories of the late 1970s and 1980s.

4

"Being a Woman is Different Here": Changing Attitudes towards Femininity, Sexuality, and Gender Roles among Former Soviet Women Living in Greater Boston[1]

"When I realized that I won't be an engineer in America, I was relieved rather than distressed. This meant I would be able to take a fresh start . . ."

"I could never figure just what 'sexual harassment' means; isn't every woman flattered when men pay attention and show interest in her as a woman, not just a co-worker?"

"Russian men don't' have this American problem of 'making a commitment.' They want to get married and start a family, just like the women. That's why we date and marry the Russian Jewish guys."
—Quotations from interviews, Greater Boston, Fall 2004

Former Soviet Women as Immigrants

The goal of this chapter is to take a closer look at the experiences of Russian-speaking women as immigrants in America, drawing on ethnographic data collected in one area—Greater Boston. There is a surprising paucity of social research on women from the former socialist countries as immigrants in the West, and this ethnography offers some initial observations to start filling in this lacuna. Well over 350, 000 former Soviet immigrant women live today in the U.S., scattered between large and small urban centers. Most of them came with their families, nuclear or extended, but some migrated alone or as single parents. The overwhelming majority is employed full-time, usually in professional or white-collar occupations; about 10 percent are self-employed. As most of these women have made a successful transition to the American middle class, they did not attract much attention either from migration scholars or from feminist researchers interested in migration and gender (Gold, 2003). The scholarship on immigrant women has typically examined the lives of Asian, African, Latino, and other women from visible ethnic minorities, for whom immigration entails a dramatic change in traditional gender roles, moving from the domestic realm into paid employment (Simon, 2001; Hondagneu-Sotelo, 2003; Pessar and Mahler, 2003). Women from the FSU also undergo multiple economic and cultural transitions but of a very different kind, given their high educational achievement and universal employment in the FSU. Like other educated female immigrants (e.g., from China, [You Zhou, 2000]), they often cannot continue their former careers and must look for alternative ways of making a living. Immigrant women of any origin often face a double jeopardy of their gender and minority location in receiving Western societies, with an ensuing social marginalization (Pessar and Mahler, 2003).

Russian-Jewish immigrant women have been at the center of my research since the mid–1990s. Over the past decade of my life in Israel, I conducted several surveys and multiple qualitative studies that addressed the issues of sexuality and family planning (Remennick et al., 1995), professional careers of male and female immigrants (Remennick and Shtarkshall, 1997; Remennick, 2002b; Remennick and Shakhar, 2003), chronic diseases and preventive behavior (Remennick, 1999b; 2003); utilization of social and medical services (Remennick, 1999a, b; Gross et al., 2001); attitudes towards abortion and its emotional aftermath (Remennick and Segal, 2001); multiple roles and emotional burnout among middle-aged women (Remennick, 2001), cross-cultural dating among young Russian women (Remennick, 2005a), and more. When these facets of immigrant women's lives are collated together, it becomes obvious that besides the problems of physical and psychosocial adjustment in the new country, common to both genders, women face an additional set of constraints evolving from cultural and normative differences in gender roles, especially in sexuality, fertility, and family life, which are usually viewed as the essence of femininity. In Russia, the U.S., Israel, and in most other cultures, sexual and reproductive issues are also perceived as moral, which puts female immigrants (usually seen as different vis-à-vis local women) in the public spotlight and often inspires critical discourse in the media and other vessels of public opinion. When minority women form a large and visible group, they often become the target of sexist attitudes and attacks. Their very presence triggers outbursts of patriarchal sentiments, normally repressed and hidden in the mainstream politically correct discourse. Opinions that would not be tolerated if expressed towards the majority women in the host society may be openly voiced regarding immigrant women (Lemish, 2000). Feeling observed and criticized, former Soviet women often feel the need to redefine their identity as professionals (e.g., being unable to regain their careers as engineers, doctors and in other male-dominated occupations), as well as redress their sexuality and reproductive conduct (e.g., to use the pills and not abortions for birth control) in the new normative context (Remennick, 1999a).

My interest in former Soviet women as immigrants informed a comparative study of these issues in America. In relative terms, former Soviets comprise a much smaller minority group in the U.S. than in Israel, but this group is rather unusual in terms of human capital, with well over half among men and women alike having postsecondary education and professional experience in the FSU. These highly skilled immigrants coming from a non-Western economy face the problems of occupational readjustment, as skills incompatibility is usually aggravated by limited English proficiency among most former Soviets. Another aspect of the integration experiences of Russian Jews generally and women specifically reflects their relations with the established American Jewish community that sponsored their immigration and resettlement. The ultimate goal of this comparative study is to follow the transformation of the former Soviet identity generally and the notions of gender roles, masculinity and femininity specifically in different socioeconomic and cultural contexts of Israel, U.S., Canada, and Germany—the main countries of immigration of former Soviet Jews.

Research Questions and Methodology

This research was guided by one general question about the influence of the dominant (and permanently contested) American notions of femininity, on one hand, and the exposure to Western feminist ideas and practices, on the other, on the attitudes and lifestyles of former Soviet women in the family, intimate relationships, and in the workplace. My approach to this study was feminist (i.e., taking as my point of departure the voices and interests of the women participating in the study) and ethnographic (i.e., drawing on observations and interaction with my informants in various natural contexts, supplemented by a number of more formal in-depth interviews). Relying on the qualitative-interpretative sociological paradigm means that I did not set my theoretical framework in advance but rather built on the insights and explanations arising from my fieldwork, i.e. interviews, observations, and the analysis of texts and other cultural products. Using these unobtrusive methods of social inquiry (that I believe to be epistemologically superior to studies using structured tools in formalized settings), I explored the lives of Russian immigrant women who moved from the FSU to the U.S. since the late 1980s.

There is no such a thing as a monolith Russian Jewish community in America, but rather a series of local communities in specific cities that broadly vary in their size and socio-economic profile. Greater Boston hosts the third largest Russian-Jewish community in the U.S. (after Metropolitan New York and Los Angeles) in terms of size (around 70, 000) and is perhaps a number one in terms of human capital. Three quarters of Bostonian Russian Jews come from Moscow and St. Petersburg and about 70 percent have postsecondary education, among them about 40 percent hold graduate degrees (Orleck, 2001:135). Women are as educated as men, but their occupational accommodation is usually more difficult due to work/family conflict and a less favorable occupational profile, compared to men. Massachusetts is a popular destination for many Russian-Jewish professionals due to its high concentration of universities, high-tech and biotechnology companies, and medical facilities. Reflecting their occupational success, Bostonian Russians have largely joined the American middle class; many of them moved out of the old inner city neighborhoods to suburban houses in Newton and other surrounding towns. My access to the Russian-speaking immigrant women was made possible by my own ethnic and cultural origins in the same community and having a number of personal contacts in the Russian-Jewish circles of Greater Boston. These initial contacts led me to other members of the Russian-speaking community via the so-called consecutive referral or snowballing. I also contacted local Jewish organizations and community service providers, who both shared their own experiences of working with Russian-Jewish clients and suggested useful leads to continuing my fieldwork.

My empirical observations pertain to the three main arenas of women's lives—individual, family, and workplace or community. To gain insight into these women's lives, I accompanied them in their daily routines such as shopping and taking children to various after-school activities; joined them at parties and family celebrations; I observed the ways these women interacted with their children, husbands and parents, and participated in communal and cultural events. I also conducted twenty-four in-depth interviews in Russian with former Soviet women (mostly Jewish or married to Jews) that focused on the ways immigration to America changed their lives. Interviews were semi-structured and usually opened with the general question, such as *"How has your life as a woman changed after immigration to America?"* or *"What are the differences between former Soviet and American women of similar social class?"* or *"Do you think that your Russian/ Soviet experiences make your better equipped for adjustment in America or are they counter-productive? In what ways?"* After the initial flow of free expression, I carefully stirred my informants towards the specific issues that interested me, or asked for clarifications and details. The interviews lasted from one and a half to three hours and most were tape recorded upon informants' permission. In a few cases when women felt uncomfortable about recording, I took brief notes and documented my impressions soon after the interview.

My informants were in the age range twenty-seven to fifty-six, with the mean age of forty-one. All of them came to the U.S. after 1987 (the majority between 1988 and 1995), usually as refugees or under family reunification clauses of the immigration law. All these women came to the U.S. from the major Soviet cities—Moscow, St. Petersburg, Kiev and Minsk. All had academic degrees in different scientific disciplines, humanities or teaching and had worked full time before emigration. Three women came to the U.S. following their husbands who received job visas as postdoctoral or research fellows, and subsequently stayed on shifting from temporary to permanent residency. Their average length of residence in the U.S. was around twelve years; most women have lived all these years in Greater Boston, but four of them had moved there from New York, Chicago, Columbus and a few other cities, usually for work-related reasons. Out of twenty-four women, seventeen were married or cohabiting with a male partner and seven were divorced or single (including two lesbians). All but the latter two women had children; among those having adult unmarried children, about one-third lived with them in the same household. All but four women were employed, mostly full time, some as freelancers (e.g., in journalism and translation). Out of those unemployed, three were looking for work and one was a stay-at-home mother of two small children.

Among other informants, I have interviewed four Russian women married to American men, exploring the cross-cultural encounter between different gender norms and the modes of their reconciliation in these mixed families. I have also interviewed two young Russian lesbian women, discussing their identity, participation in community life, and prospects for motherhood. As part of my fieldwork I also examined the Russian immigrant press, read fiction written by recent Russian-Jewish female immigrants, and explored other cultural phenomena reflective of the old and new ideas about gender, femininity, and masculinity. At the same time, I tried to follow cultural representations of Russian immigrants in the mainstream American media.

Below I report and discuss some of my findings, arranged by the principal themes that surfaced in women's narratives and illustrated by typical interview quotes. The names of my informants have been changed for ethical reasons, but other personal details (age, occupation, duration of life in the U.S.) have been kept intact.

Findings

Between Work and Family Roles

As mentioned previously, all my informants had been educated and employed full-time in professional or white-collar occupations in the FSU. For most of them, their profession was a significant part of their personal identity and they had wished for career continuity in the U.S. At the same time, most were aware of the difficulty and perhaps impossibility of continuing their working lives in America in exactly the same professional capacity. In fact, only six out of 24 women followed in the same career track in the U.S. (all six were research scientists), while eighteen women have changed their occupations completely or to some extent. Most women I spoke with never considered quitting their employment altogether and becoming homemakers, for both economic reasons and the need for self-actualization. In the words of Anna (forty-eight, a former engineer with twelve years in the U.S.), "I cannot imagine myself secluded in the four walls of my house and I don't know of anyone else, at least in my close social circle, who dreamed of becoming a 'lady of the house', even if their husband could earn a family wage. You need to be a somebody, to find outlets for your talents and energy. And besides that, how would you ever learn English and American customs if you stay at home? I think for fresh immigrants workplace is especially important as a road into the new society." Tania (fifty, a former physician with seven years in the U.S., works as medical social worker) said along similar lines: "Our generation of Soviet women was raised by working parents and everybody we knew got higher education and worked in some professional field. Maybe younger women who grew up in post-Soviet Russia are looking for a rich husband who would provide for them, but we have always counted on ourselves." This last quotation points to a strong tradition of self-reliance and economic independence shared by most middle-aged ex-Soviet women.

Women's decisions about their working future in the U.S. depended on their age, English proficiency, former occupation and experience, earning potential of their male partner (if any), number of dependents, and multiple other factors. Many younger women had a period of ambivalence and doubt about whether to try and regain their former occupation in the new context or retrain and start a new career from scratch. Their decisions were often informed by the extent of commitment to their former occupation, which quite often had been chosen for these women by their parents or reflected multiple barriers in career choice for Soviet Jews. Specifically, many Soviet-Jewish youths of either gender, like their parents, had been steered into various technology—and industry-related occupations as these were abundant in Soviet economy and relatively more open to the Jews, promising stable income and upward occupational mobility. In the FSU, the choice of occupation was usually once and for all as few people could risk losing their livelihood and venture into a new occupational track. In America, greater occupational flexibility and lower ageism towards late starters of new careers were a pleasant discovery for these women. For example, Anna (forty-five with twelve years in the U.S.) recounted:

In fact I never wanted to be a civil engineer and design roads and bridges. My parents were both engineers and they had decided that this would be the most safe and pragmatic choice for me as a Jewish woman. I never enjoyed my years of study, and then work was a daily drudgery. . . . I've always wanted to deal with people, to counsel, to help . . . *So for me the ability to shed a technical occupation and try something else was a relief rather than a loss* [my emphasis—LR]. I was thirty-six when we came here, in the Soviet terms I was almost half-way to my retirement age, but in America mid-thirties is not considered old, you can go to school again in this age. So I signed for youth worker classes at community college and also took courses in social work. . . . In brief, I became youth counselor for disadvantaged and immigrant youth. It's not an easy job, but I enjoy it and know that I really make a difference in these kids' lives . . .

For Anna, and other women who could not or did not wish to find work as engineers, community work and human services became a viable and attractive alternative. Several informants who arrived in the U.S. relatively young, had studied for a degree or certificate in social work, school counseling, youth programs, social geriatrics, home care, and other helping occupations. Although human services jobs are usually in a low-pay range, most women who had made this choice were satisfied with their work lives, stressing the interpersonal skills and multicultural competence it requires as well as flexible work schedule, allowing for family roles. Galina, forty-nine, a senior geriatric worker for a major day care center in Boston, said,

I have truly found myself in my second career here. Although I work with the elderly, including my own co-ethnics (who are not always easy to deal with!), I find a lot of satisfaction in what I do. In Russia old folks were treated as a society's burden if not human waste, but here the attitude is so different . . . . Everybody has a right to spend their last years in comfort and receive all possible support from society, even if they are not rich . . . . I hear so many incredible life stories from the Jewish elders—they had been through so much during the twentieth century . . . . I always try to invent some new forms of activity to spark their interest, to help them enjoy living . . .

Some women made occupational adjustments within their old specialty: engineers, mathematicians, and physicists retrained as programmers and other information technology (IT) specialists; two MDs and one pharmacist became biomedical researchers; three teachers shifted to special education or student counseling. Three musicians and two artists opened private art classes catering mostly (but not solely) to Russian immigrant children. Seven informants out of twenty-four (who arrived in their late forties) decided not to look for a professional occupation at all and found work in several Russian businesses near Boston (three worked in grocery stores, three in a realty agency, and one in a Russian printing shop producing a weekly newspaper).

Whatever they used to do in their old lives and whatever new jobs they were having in America, most women were satisfied with their occupational lives and emphasized their positive aspects. Women who worked in high technology or research stressed the intellectual challenge, good pay, and interesting circle of colleagues. Women who worked in human services spoke about their helping ethos and making a difference in the lives of their clients. Women working in sales and other unskilled occupations said they were glad to be employed and meet their co-workers and clients every day, while so many other women (especially older ones) could find no jobs at all and had to live on welfare. It seems that after several years of trial and error most immigrant women have managed to reinvent their professional identity and find meaning in their new work roles. Although most married women had a lower income than their husbands, they usually perceived this gap as "natural" as it was compatible with both their former Soviet experiences and current U.S. reality of gendered occupational and income tiers.

As for the work-family divide, juggling multiple roles was a typical situation for most former Soviet women, and this did not change in the U.S. Ten women had school-age children, and in most cases had to shoulder the responsibility for childcare as their husbands typically worked longer hours. Different women found different solutions, depending on availability of help from their own parents, their work schedules, and financial resources. If grandparents were living far away or were unwell and could not pick up children from school, feed them and take them to various after-school activities, most families hired paid help, usually from the ranks of their co-ethnics. Yet, most mothers of smaller children chose part-time or time-flexible jobs allowing them to have free afternoons and evenings. Only one woman in my group, Genia (thirty-six), a wife of a well-established MIT professor and a mother of two young children, decided to drop out of her own graduate program for the time being and become a full time home maker. She explained this choice by her personal priorities and the wish to raise her children herself rather than rely on hired nannies. Like many children growing up in Russian Jewish immigrant families, Genia's son and daughter attend a large number of extracurricular learning activities (music and art classes, Russian-language class, gymnasium, etc.), and chauffeuring them to all the different locations is time consuming. On top of that, Genia must often tend to her unhealthy mother in law living in a neighboring town. "Altogether, these tasks amount to a full time job and perhaps even some overtime. . . . I definitely prefer knowing that all my loved ones are taken care of and the family is running as smoothly as possible to getting my Ph.D. First things first." Genia also added that she has never really liked her original area of research (the physics of metals), and when and if she goes back to graduate school or the labor market she would probably opt for an altogether different occupation. She has several intellectual hobbies (writing and illustrating children's books, teaching Russian to immigrant children) that help her retain her identity as an educated and thinking person. Another woman in her mid-forties left her prior teaching career in art history for the sake of her nine-year-old son who is a musical prodigy and a home schooling student. She continues to work on her scholarly publications and supplements the family income giving piano lessons to the neighborhood children. Both women who decided to become full-time mothers underscored the importance of continuing some intellectual activities in order "not to let their brains get rusty" and to preserve a positive self-image as intelligent and creative persons.

Thus, the solutions to work-family conflict among Russian immigrants were basically similar to those found by most working women in the U.S., but with greater cultural emphasis on intergenerational solidarity and hands-on help. Several women who could economically afford it opted for quitting their careers, or at least took an indefinite time off, for the sake of giving hands-on care to their children and elders. Regardless of their current employment type and content, virtually all women in my study emphasized their need for self-actualization, either in the context of paid work or unpaid creative or social activities they pursued. Women who were compelled by the American labor market situation to switch from a more prestigious and professional occupation they had in the FSU to a less ambitious one (e.g., from engineering or medicine to social work or geriatric care) usually appreciated their new work roles and emphasized the ethical meaning of their new work in human services. None of the women I spoke with regretted the loss of their earlier social and professional status—in stark contrast to the men in this immigrant population (of whom I learned indirectly from the women's narratives). Many, in fact, spoke of their occupational change as liberating and were grateful to America for the chance at a fresh start.

The Family Sandwich: Relations with Parents and Children

Most Soviet immigrants of the late 1980s and 1990s resettled in the U.S. as entire families, bringing an unusually high percentage of the elderly compared to other immigrant groups (about 40 percent being over age sixty). At the same time, Soviet Jews have had low fertility, with the average family having about 1.4 children. Thus, a typical three-generational family coming to the U.S. included a couple with one or two children and their own elderly parents. Initially these families settled together, usually in old immigrant neighborhoods of Greater Boston, such as Brighton, Allston, and Lynn, in order to pool together scant resources and aid each other. However, as soon as adults found well-paying jobs they often preferred to move from these immigrant enclaves to middle-class suburban towns, while the elders often remained in their Brighton apartments or moved into communal projects for the elderly, where they had a better chance for social life and available geriatric services. Some immigrant families moved to the suburban homes together, which on the one hand preserved a natural family safety net but on the other resulted in greater social isolation of the elders and their dependency on the children for everyday help and transportation. Regardless of the type of residence (separately or together with the elders), women of the middle generation are the main providers of both instrumental and emotional support to their parents and in-laws (Remennick, 1999b).

In my small group of informants, two-thirds of the women had one or both parents living with them or nearby, some others had in-laws or other elderly relatives to take care of. Vera (thirty-eight, an art teacher) told about her mother (aged sixty-six and living with her own eighty-seven-year-old mother in a rented flat in Allston):

My mom and grandma try their best to live independently, but it is hard for them to get around without English. My mom has mastered some minimal number of words and phrases to explain herself but she usually cannot understand people's answers, and my grandma has no English at all. So I have to help them with the doctors, banks, social services, shopping—virtually everything that includes contact with the outside world. Often I have to drive them to different places in the afternoon or evening, so I get back home really late. My kids (ages fifteen and twelve) are not so little anymore, but they still need their mom, especially as they don't drive yet. So I am pretty torn between the old and the young ones—I am the family's caregiver and chauffeur.

While in the early years of resettlement the parents are a source of support and hands-on help with small children, over time the balance of aid reverses and aging parents become consumers rather than providers of care. Daughters and daughters-in-law also feel responsible for the emotional support of the elders who are often overwhelmed by the sense of loss of their past and the lack of a meaningful place in the new society. Another cause of loneliness for the elders is gradual attrition of the bonds with their Americanized grandchildren (whom they often cared for in their younger years). As their cultural expectations are those of authority over their children and grandchildren, active participation in family decision making and being providers rather than consumers of support, the process of marginalization and dependency is highly traumatic for many Russian-Jewish elders. In this respect, the stories told by my informants about their parents and intergenerational dynamics confirmed earlier observations in the Russian-Jewish communities across U.S. made by Annelise Orleck, (1999) and Vera Kishinevsky (2004).

In the Russian/Soviet cultural order, menopause signified the coming of old age and also overlapped with the official women's retirement age of fifty-five. Regardless of how they looked and felt, middle-aged women were expected to retire from both their working and feminine lives and to become subservient to their adult children's needs, helping them with childcare, schooling, and domestic chores. Menopausal women were not expected to want anything for themselves anymore, and those, who continued to pursue their individual careers and hobbies rather than becoming full-time grandmothers, were often perceived as selfish. As no menopausal counseling or therapy was available in Soviet gynecology (designed mainly for sexually active and fertile younger women) and the word menopause itself was unmentionable in decent society, most ageing women had to suffer quietly through the hot flashes, sleep disturbances, mood fluctuations, and other menopausal symptoms, not showing any distress on the outside. In a similar way, during their young years they quietly endured their menstrual problems (washing rags or using cotton wool as pads or tampons were unheard of), postpartum blues, post-abortion inflammations, and other ramifications of their feminine physiology without any hope of professional help or even friendly advice (as these subjects were hardly mentionable between "decent women").

This Soviet version of Puritan ethics regarding "feminine ailments" and aging was initially transferred by the Soviet immigrant families to the U.S., but rather soon middle-aged grandmothers discovered that menopause does not mean old age and decay for most American women. Conversely, menopause and freedom from the confines of monthly bleeding denote a fresh start, a new freedom when the children have left the nest and a woman can at last live for herself, to pursue the wishes and interests she had long kept on hold in favor of family responsibilities. The accounts of my older informants (seven women were above age fifty) suggest that some of them were glad to redefine themselves as "newly young" and use the freedoms of post-reproductive age, while others kept the old routine of devoting themselves to their children's families. Of course, all of these women were working, usually full-time, and did not have too much spare time on their hands; the question was how they used their evenings, weekends and holidays. Those who had young grandchildren would often spend every free hour they had babysitting, or taking older children from school and to different after-school classes. They explained it by both the wish to be with their "little ones" and to free their hard-working children for some time out, the way their own parents helped them out while they were young parents. Many women saw this hands-on help as an essential part of the intergenerational solidarity and were rather critical of American women who see their grandchildren a few times a year and limit their participation to sending occasional gifts. Two women who had no grandchildren spent their leisure hiking in nature, gardening, and traveling abroad—almost like their U.S.-raised peers. At the same time, all my informants were paying more time and attention to their health, trying to eat well and exercise from time to time, seeing their doctors regularly and taking replacement hormones to ease the symptoms. In that sense, they have made a cultural transition to female middle age American style.

Many younger informants who had teenage or young adult children spoke about the need to redefine their mothering attitudes and practices in America. Russian-Jewish parenting culture is very much about controlling children, setting the goals and limits for them, and generally intense involvement in their lives till adulthood and often beyond; the American parental license and alleged "carelessness" is perceived by Russian parents as irresponsible and dangerous. They are quite torn between the old and new social norms regarding parent-child relations and the extent of freedom given to offspring. Mothers (and fathers too) were deeply concerned about low educational standards in most U.S. schools and made multiple sacrifices in order to place their child in a better school, public or private. They also made special efforts to fill children's free time with meaningful and educational activities, taking them to various after school art, sports, math, chess, and other classes and groups. Many parents were scared by the risks of the "street Americanization" of their children and their joining the urban culture of "sex, drugs and hard rock" that valorizes "fun" and "having a good time" (or just "killing time") instead of hard work and achievement. In the words of one mother, "what came naturally in St Petersburg became a constant effort and swimming against the stream in America." So when and if the children did not adopt their parents' values of education, intellectualism and achievement, it was a severe disappointment putting into question their whole effort invested in migration (as most Soviet parents had asserted that they embarked on emigration for the sake of their children!). During college years, many parents tried to steer their children toward the familiar occupational tracks of science and technology, regardless of the children's interests and wishes, because of the future possibilities on the labor market. When children resisted parental pragmatism and made their own "nonpractical" educational choices (e.g., opting for the liberal arts), many mothers were frustrated and felt that they failed as parents.

Another source of tension had to do with children's sexual conduct. Like their U.S.-born peers, Russian-Jewish adolescents start dating and relationships with the opposite sex rather early by Russian standards, and without any clear marital intentions. For many former Soviet parents it is difficult to accept the detachment of sexuality from marriage, as in their own youth they often married their first serious date, and this usually happened in their early twenties (especially among the girls). Middle-class American youths often start active sexual lives long before they intend to start a family, trying to avoid pregnancy by means of effective contraception. Russian mothers still expect their daughters to find the right man and marry young (soon after getting their undergraduate degree is a preferred deadline), and they are ready to help them with future childcare like their parents used to help them. Yet, in many cases their daughters and sons follow a different scenario, dating and cohabiting with their partners and not thinking of marriage and children any time soon. Many informants believed that if not married by their mid-twenties, their daughters will stay single for life. "If you don't marry young all the good men will be taken and you'll have no partners to choose from," Men are looking for younger women, and after thirty your chances dwindle"—these and similar opinions were often reiterated by my informants. Young men's marital prospects were of lesser concern for their mothers, although some disapproved of their son's lifestyle either because they changed girlfriends too often or, on the contrary, never went out and had few female contacts. In any case, having a stable partner and a family life was seen as a universal human need and a sign of maturity by most of my informants. They saw themselves as responsible for their children's happiness and could not let go of the habit to shape and influence their lives, at the same time feeling that they do not have this power anymore.

Sisters or Strangers: Relations with American Jewish Women

As most former Soviet immigrants entered the U.S. on the "Jewish ticket," they had to define their place vis-à-vis the established Jewish community, especially in view of the significant assistance they received from the Jewish-American organizations at all stages of their resettlement process. Women often had a greater personal stake in these relations than their male partners for several reasons. First, due to the matrilineal principles of Judaism women are the backbone of the family and they define whether their children will be Jews by birth and by education. Second, women often served as social agents for their families during resettlement and were more in touch with the Jewish organizations that assisted them in housing, English studies, employment, child education, eldercare, arranging for immigration of a family member, etc. Men were typically more focused on finding jobs and making an income, while women took care of everything else, making a broader range of contacts in the new society. Most former Soviet-Jewish women (like their male counterparts) were secular and had very limited prior familiarity with Judaism, or none at all. Some experienced the remnants of the Jewish tradition in their families via Seder parties, Jewish cuisine, grandparents speaking Yiddish, rare (and dangerous due to the KGB surveillance) visits to the synagogue on Simchat Torah; many others grew up without even that, as regular Soviet youths. Some women were born of mixed marriages between Jews and non-Jews, or were in a mixed marriage themselves. Partly Jewish or non-Jewish wives of Jews felt that they did not belong to the Jewish world and could not connect with the receiving society on the Jewish grounds. Moreover, many women of Jewish origin but of secular orientation were uninterested in religious life and Jewish customs and also felt estranged from their mainstream co-ethnics in the U.S.

Most women followed one of two possible scenarios in relation to their Judaism: adoption or distancing. The first group, albeit remaining secular, chose to get closer to the mainstream "cultural Judaism" usually by making their children familiar with Jewish history, language, and religion. These parents sent their children to Jewish schools, summer camps, and trips to Israel; celebrated their bar—and bat mitzvahs; teamed up with American-Jewish parents in various extracurricular activities, thus getting socially accepted into Jewish circles. Some others also adopted elements of the Jewish lifestyle in their own practice (e.g., celebrating Jewish holidays, making donations to Jewish and Israeli causes, traveling to Israel, lighting candles on Shabat, not eating pork, trying to keep kosher). The other group, on the contrary, chose to distance themselves from any Jewish activities, refrained from giving any Jewish education to their children and generally preserved their neutral non-sectarian stance, trying to join the mainstream American middle class.

Women whom I observed and interviewed belonged to both categories, but most Jewish women have drifted over time towards adopting some Jewish traits, reflecting their wish to belong to some defined community in the large and plural American society. For most of these women, their acquaintance with Judaism occurred through American-Jewish women they met via work, study, or contact with the Jewish resettlement agencies and activist groups. For example, Rita (forty-three) a former engineer and current IT worker, said,

I was very impressed by my caseworker in the Jewish Family and Children's Services, and I guess deep inside I wanted to be like her—amicable, confident, connected with others in her community. She advised me about the Jewish history and religion group studying together at one of the centers, I went once just out of curiosity and stayed on. I am not always interested in the contents of each class but I like the atmosphere. About half of the women are truly religious, others are secular but interested, just like me. Religious Jewish women strike me as having integrity and a strong sense of purpose and meaning in their lives. I am afraid I cannot find faith and become observant at this time of my life, but I would like to enjoy at least some light that this tradition casts around us.

For many others, like Rita, the goals of joining Jewish activities were mainly social. Nina (forty-seven, a music teacher) told about her experiences with the mixed group of Jewish women who took part in the initiative to celebrate Passover Seders together in order to cross cultural barriers and get to know each other better.

I think for a fresh immigrant it is good to join some existing group, to belong somewhere. This is how you can make new friends, improve your English, have an interesting pastime . . . and also get back to your own historic roots. I found several good female friends in the group that organized Russian-American Seders—it was fun to plan for this event, to cook, to get dressed . . . and then the evening itself was so merry. I learned a lot about Jewish history—better late than never . . . Since then I kept reading books about Judaism, even went for a Hebrew class a few times (laughs). I am still in touch with several American and Russian women from these Seder parties—they taught me how to be Jewish in America without becoming Orthodox . . .

Some other Jewish women—a minority in my experience—did not see any added value in becoming more Jewish in America than they were in Russia. Their primary community of reference was usually other Russian immigrants; in some other cases they were well integrated in the American middle class via their workplace and did not need Judaism as a source of identity. Olga (forty-two), biomedical researcher:

I don't understand this mimicry of many Russian Jews here. All of a sudden they become "real Jews," recover their "true self," change their life habits in order to conform to these strange rules and rituals. . . . If you did not grow up with Jewish religion and tradition it's very hard to adopt it sincerely as an adult. I don't believe them—it's all a facade they put on in order to pass as good Jews among Americans. You know, in this country you must have "an identity," to be someone, of some group, of some faith. For me, my faith is my profession, it is enough for my self-identity to be a scientist, to do important research that can affect human lives in the future. On top of that, I am also a woman and a mother—isn't it just about enough?

Some others stressed incompatibility of Jewish faith with modernity: "For me, Jewish customs belong to the Middle Ages, or at least to the shtetl culture that my grandparents left in the early twentieth century in order to join the urban professional class. It would be weird if I went back to these rituals at the dawn of the twenty-first century— what do I need this for? I will not play these games even if it makes me accepted by the local Jews" (Vera, fifty, artist and arts teacher). "We came to America as Jews because we suffered from anti-Semitism, and we will remain Jewish in any country. But being a Jew means different things for different people; for me it is much beyond religion: it is the way you raise your children, relate to your husband, do your work . . . . I am Jewish in my own way and nobody will tell me how to be the right kind of Jew" (Clara, thirty-nine, mortgage broker).

Thus, immigrant women chose different locations on the scale between full secularism and Jewish religious observance, but most who developed an interest in Judaism subscribed to its moderate "cultural" version. For those who chose to live more Jewish lives than before emigration, the change was often triggered by encounters with American-Jewish women who set an attractive example of a more spiritual and meaningful living. In most cases, though, motivations for joining the American-Jewish mainstream reflected women's search for social inclusion and belonging to a significant and influential co-ethnic community. Yet for others it reflected social conformism and the wish to meet the expectations of the hosts and sponsors of their immigration. Whatever the underlying cause, the result was an increasing participation of Russian immigrant women in the informal Jewish social networks, often more prominent than that on the male side of Russian immigration.

Marriage, Sexuality, and Family Planning

As a preliminary to this theme, I should note a clear difference in the socio-cultural context shaping immigrant women's femininity and sexuality in the U.S. versus Israel. From the early 1990s on, women with Russian accents in Israel were surrounded by a cloud of negative sexual stereotypes that emerged due to several interlinked events of that time. The major reason for this reputation was an influx of Russian-speaking sex workers from the impoverished areas of the FSU to Israel in the years of mass aliyah of former Soviet Jews. The Israeli male "street," as well as the mainstream Hebrew media, usually did not distinguish between different ethnic and social categories of Russian women and attributed sexual license to all of them alike. On the other hand, marginalization of some young female immigrants and problems of economic adjustment made them comply with sexual advances of Israeli men they depended on in finding work, housing, and social orientation. Reflecting the rather sexist culture of native Israeli men (especially among the Mizrahim), popular Israeli discourse of the 1990s was imbued with sexual innuendo featuring stories on "seductive and accessible Russian blonds," massage parlors where they worked, and Russian single mothers in search of "protection." Such attitudes have for many years colored gender relations between former Soviet immigrants and the hosts, poisoning the air around all immigrant women regardless of their sexual lifestyles (Remennick, 1999a; Lemish, 2000).

Nothing of this has happened with Russian-speaking immigrant women in the U.S. and Canada, because Russian prostitution has never reached American shores on a mass scale, and hence never affected popular imagery of Russian women. At the same time, legal and cultural restraints on blatant expressions of sexual interest in the contexts of male power and female dependency, in the form of sexual harassment laws, made overt sexual advances toward immigrant women rather uncommon. The third reason for this difference was that, compared with Soviet immigrants to the U.S. who typically resettled as full nuclear families, many women arrived in Israel alone or with children, with the ensuing economic vulnerability and the need to find a new male partner for support and security.

During the interviews in suburban Boston homes, few women made detailed comments about sexual issues as these are still highly charged and difficult to verbalize in the Russian culture. Yet, some topics have emerged indirectly, especially in the narratives of younger women who were in their sexually formative years, that is, alone and/or dating, engaged in a relationship, or recently married and starting a family. Most were with male partners of the same ethic origin, that is, former Soviet Jews; a few young women were dating Americans, Jewish or not. None of the women spoke of any kind of perceived negative or offensive attitudes they experienced from American men; on the contrary, Americans were described as nice, polite, polished . . . but distant. Some women mentioned having short-term relationships with their American fellow students and other men, but few women were ready to start a family with an American partner. The main stated reasons against this option revolved around perceived cultural differences in the very concept of family life, relationships, and intimacy, especially in terms of making a firm commitment to marriage. These young women often voiced opinions suggesting strong influence of their mothers' values and attitudes regarding early marriage and the choice of the right partner.

Thus, when asked to explain their strong co-ethnic preference in partner choice, several women said that, apart from cultural similarity and common first language, Russian-Jewish men shared with them similar ideas about relationships and marriage. "I do not understand what the point is in prolonged dating or being in a relationship that doesn't end in marriage. If you cannot make up your mind about this man, then he is probably not right for you and you shouldn't waste your time. Most young men of Soviet origin I know also wish to marry relatively young because they believe in the importance of having your own family and they are not afraid of making the famous 'commitment' . . . they just don't have this issue like most American men do." (Marina, twenty-five, a married graduate student). "I think Russians, men and women alike, have a more realistic attitude towards relationships and as soon as they found a partner they like they don't wish to delay marriage, because everyone wants to get married eventually. I think young Russians assess prospective partners in a more pragmatic way too, i.e., what is their education, occupation, job prospects, income, parental family—all these things are at least as important as love" (Tina, twenty-eight, a programmer and married mother of two sons, ages five and three).

Most young women did not see their family and work roles as

conflicting and believed that succeeding in both is possible when you mobilize all possible help, either from older relatives or hired nannies and domestics. They asserted that investing first in education and career and then starting a family in your late thirties (the way many middle class Americans do) was a wrong strategy for a woman, reducing her chances for finding a right partner and having children. "I know a few American colleagues of mine who were on several boyfriends one after another, and ended up alone while approaching forty. Even if they have a man in their life, they cannot get pregnant anymore, or have problems with their pregnancies. Yes, they have achieved some status in their profession, but I am sure deep inside they are unhappy. A lonely woman in her forties is a miserable sight . . . . Like your work career, it is important to start your career as a woman early if you wish to succeed" (Inga, twenty-seven, graphic designer).

At the same time, all these women took for granted premarital sexual experience in both men and women and underscored the need to know your partner intimately before embarking on a marital relationship. Although premarital sex was abundant in the FSU it was never legitimized, admitted, or discussed in the open, so this change of attitude among young Russian women in America was quite remarkable, and similar to that among Russian immigrants in Israel (Remennick et al., 1995). As for the means of birth control, all my informants advocated the use of contraception and considered abortion only as a last resort. Most young women were aware of the ongoing political and moral controversy around abortion in the U.S. and believed that all effort should be made to prevent an unwanted pregnancy. Yet, at the same time all of them believed in a woman's basic right to decide if she wanted to carry or terminate a pregnancy at least during the first trimester; no one questioned the need to keep all abortions legal, including late ones in special circumstances. "We come from the country were access to abortion is perhaps all too easy, discouraging both women and men from being careful and using contraception. But you cannot rule out the chance for failure of birth control, so abortion should be there as your back-up. I can't imagine how in a democratic country the legal system can pressure a woman to carry pregnancy and give birth to a child she doesn't want or cannot raise" (Dina, thirty-six, accountant, a divorced mother of two). "In sexual matters not everything depends on a woman, she often has no control over her body, especially among the poor and minority groups in this country. Women often get pregnant against their will and you cannot punish them further by denying the right to abortion" (Lena, thirty-two, single, medical researcher). Thus, all my informants were convinced proponents of a woman's choice in sexual and pregnancy-related matters.

At the same time, these women's personal practices in matters of birth control still reflected their lingering discomfort about sexuality and difficulty of negotiating sexual practices with their partners. Over half of the informants experienced unwanted pregnancies while in the U.S., mostly due to their reticence in broaching contraceptive use with men. Irena (thirty-nine), primary school teacher, mused: "We still suffer from our Russian schooling as 'nice girls' who cannot insist that a guy put on a condom, or explain to him about unsafe days for sex. Folk wisdom tells you that if you are too demanding he can always find a more easygoing woman. . . . As most women try to keep a man they like, they often have to take risks and sometimes pay the price for pleasing him. With your husband you can be more assertive, of course, but go find a husband first . . . " Many women were reluctant to take oral contraceptives, which they considered more dangerous than abortion—an outlook not untypical of many Soviet gynecologists and older women they had influenced. Zhanna (thirty-eight), geriatric worker, said: "I've heard that the pills give you good protection from pregnancy, but they may cause many complications in the future . . . many women gain weight and have headaches. . . . I think it is very unhealthy to take hormonal preparations every day—I'd rather rely on more traditional methods and hope for good luck." Younger women who came of age in the U.S. had a more relaxed view of these matters, expected greater sexual responsibility from their male partners, and were less cautious of modern hormonal contraceptives. "I know that most men dislike using condoms, which, they say, is like eating candy in its wrapper. But why should I care for their pleasure before my own well-being? This is simple: if he doesn't care about me he is not the right man to count on in the future, so I won't bother if he quits the relationship" (Inga, twenty-seven). "I never take chances in the bed, especially with a new man. I am on the pill, but if I am not fully sure about his past (and who can be sure?) I also ask to put on a condom. In my experience, most men don't mind—it serves for their protection too" (Natasha, student, twenty-four).

As for an ideal age for having children, most women believed that long delays are problematic as your "biological clock" keeps ticking, and it is much healthier to bear children while young. "I am not for rushing with the first baby as a 'validity proof' of your marriage, but long delays are also dangerous. You know, the timing is almost never right—either you are in graduate school, or looking for a job, or having no money to buy a house . . . children always call for amendments and compromises, and the woman is usually the one to make them." "For most young Russian women I know becoming a mother is at least as important as finishing their education or getting a good job. You are not a complete woman as long as you don't have a child" (Nina, twenty-nine, marketing agent, mother of a five year old).

No woman I spoke with was ready to delay marriage to her late thirties and/or remain childless as many educated American women do. Despite their strong education and career orientations, marriage and children remained a priority on their personal agenda. Even lesbian women voiced their wish for motherhood in the future. "You have a wish for a child regardless of your sexual tastes, this is completely unrelated. Lesbians are as good (or as bad) in mothering as are the straights; it depends on your personality, your feelings about children, your educational beliefs, etc. So yes, I plan to have a child in a few years' time—by whatever technical means are available, or maybe via adoption" (Lisa, twenty-seven, an architect, lives with a female partner).

In terms of the number of children they wished for, most women said two, but some said that three kids would be ideal for them, and a few women said one child would suffice. Several women said that having siblings is important for the children, and a single child is often lonely and unsocial. As for the childcare roles of the parents, most women said that they were prepared to carry out the bulk of the parenting tasks, as their work lives were usually less demanding than these of their husbands. No one expected their male partners to sacrifice their careers or incomes for the sake of childcare; quite a few expected to get help from their parents or hire nannies. In sum, young women of Russian-Jewish origin expressed opinions and attitudes rather similar to those of American middle-class youth, with the exception of their emphasis on a relatively early marriage and motherhood and the expectation of help in childcare from the parents. They strongly opt for Russian-Jewish men as their boyfriends and marital partners believing that they share common values about the importance of family life, gender roles, children's education, and the normality of "commitment" for both men and women.

Attitudes towards Western Feminism and American Sexual Mores

Most former Soviet women share uneasy feelings towards third-wave Western feminism, at least at the level of ideology (not necessarily practice). Coming from a society where the "woman question" had been "solved" by the regime by eliminating gender differentials by decree, these women have a deep seated mistrust for any kind of gender equality rhetoric. In the times of "real socialism" this equality meant that women were exploited by the state as badly as men, employed in physically demanding "male" jobs and paid similarly miserable wages for their eight-hour work days, supplemented by the payless second shift at home. Under socialism, the state gave women free but miserable health care insensitive to their special needs, as well as cheap but low quality childcare facilities that resulted in frequent sickness and slow development of their children. Whoever could afford it, preferred to have a nanny or stay-at-home grandparents as private child minders. Despite the rhetoric of equal opportunities, actual occupational mobility of educated women was slow and even in the feminized occupations such as health care and education women rarely reached senior positions. Regardless of their initial aspirations and years of study, many women ended up making their living in dead-end semi-clerical or technical jobs. Being male, non-Jewish, and a Communist Party member were important prerequisites for occupational mobility in virtually any branch of the Soviet economy up until the late 1980s. Human sexuality and the needs in sex education and family planning services have been for decades ignored by the state, resulting in millions of abortions, abandoned children, infertility, and sexually transmitted diseases. By way of black irony, the Soviet society that officially denounced sex differences and sexuality itself, was perhaps one of the most sexist and misogynistic societies ever known (Kon, 1995).

Coercion always causes resistance of similar strength. Precisely because the state undermined femininity and tried to mould all citizens as sexless Soviet people, many women resisted this reality by finding multiple ways to underscore and valorize their feminine side. Deprived of most normal means of caring for their bodies, health and beauty taken for granted by Western women, many Soviet women invested great effort and spent their last cash on fashionable clothes and cosmetics (thanks to the thriving black market), sewed and knitted clothes themselves, exchanged fashion magazines smuggled from abroad, and against all odds managed to dress and look well. The harder to get these feminine commodities were the more desirable they became for the struggling, overworked, and underpaid Soviet woman (Kay, 1997).

In brief, seven decades of allegedly genderless state socialism made many former Soviet women yearn for a more traditional role division whereby they could devote more time and resources to their perceived "natural role" of beauty ideals, caregivers, child educators and home-makers, while men would regain their due place in the economy, with the ensuing authority, upward mobility and the ability to earn a family wage. On the domestic front, men are expected to "help" women when they can with domestic chores and childrearing. These unattainable bourgeois ideals of femininity and masculinity had lingered in the minds and hearts of Soviet women for decades, coloring their negative perceptions of Western feminism, that (on the surface of its rhetoric) pushed women back to the "equality labor camp" which they so ardently wished to escape. Unable to distinguish between various streams within modern feminist thought, many Soviet women identified feminist ideology with hatred of men, negation of marriage and mother-hood, undermining physiological and psychological differentials between men and women, pushing women into competitive and harsh male occupational niches where they do not belong, disproval of feminine beauty, sexual appeal and self-care, and a butch-lesbian lifestyle as its logical ending. This line of ideological attributions has been repeatedly voiced by former Soviet women when asked to describe how they understand feminism and why even the most educated, independent, and successful of them would never call themselves feminists (Kay, 1997).

However, life in America has somewhat redressed these negative attitudes. To begin with, many immigrant women have realized that the option of single male breadwinner and female homemaker has largely dwindled in the American middle class (let alone more disadvantaged groups), and the majority of women have to work outside the home in order to ensure decent living standards for their families. Secondly, many women have realized that feminism encompasses a broad range of ideas, and its liberal stream is very much in line with their own beliefs and practices as educated, working women. In the words of Rita, thirty-eight (married and mother of a teenage son, former engineer, now interior designer):

I think that the chief message of liberal feminists is that men and women are different but equal and should have equal opportunities in education and careers. How women use these opportunities is up to them, not everybody has an ambition to become a solid professional, many women have modest aspirations of just making a decent living and having a good family, and that's perfectly OK. So do many men, by the way. Your lifestyle should be a matter of choice: if you wish to be a homemaker and can afford it—that's great, but if you want to be a corporal lawyer—it is also your right to go out there and try it, and no one can stop you. People should be judged by merit not by sex. This is how I understand the message of feminism as part of a general liberal worldview.

Some other informants opined that the feminist ideology stripes women of their attractiveness, femininity and sex appeal—which is their main naturally coming "human capital." To explain this view, they often cited the exaggerations in the implementation of sexual harassment laws in the workplace. The following accounts were typical:

Americans are taking this principle way overboard—you cannot desexualize human beings, this is ridiculous. If these laws are taken to their logical end, all employees should become neuter, sexless beings, or at least become blind to each other, not to notice how others look, what they wear, etc. Judging by the instructions disseminated in my firm by the human resources office, any wrong glance, playful comment or a joke told in the elevator can be interpreted as sexual claims and be punished. This sterilization of human contact reeks of communism in some tricky way—everybody should be the same, wearing uniform plain clothes, not causing attention of the opposite sex . . . (Dina).

I am not saying that bosses should compel their secretaries to sleep with them, this is repulsive, but you cannot stop all and any sexually charged dialog between co-workers. This is the place where people spend most of their time, meet others, including potential dates . . . how can you ban sexual innuendo between people by decree? Again, I am against using sexuality as a form of payment for a job or promotion, but current rules are taking this too far. Almost anyone can sue or be sued for sexual harassment these days, and some people can use this to get even with their rivals or foes (Veronika, forty, IT officer in a large corporation).

Others had a slightly different take on the sexual harassment issue. Tanya, a forty-three-year old medical imaging technician, shared her thoughts:

In my lab in Russia I always remembered that I was a woman—my male co-workers made a point of reminding me: they noticed my new hairdo, would never miss a chance to pay a compliment . . . they simply meant to be nice and friendly most of the time—this was how a man was supposed to relate to a woman. Kind of being a gentleman . . . . But of course other things also happened—when your boss, say, invited you to his dacha [country cottage—LR] while his wife was in the city, and when you rejected his advances he got cross and denied your salary raise or put you on the least wanted night shift . . . this is indeed a shame. It happened quite a lot in Russia, at least in medical settings, where senior doctors were so powerful and nurses, medical interns, and technicians were kind of in their service . . . . But you had no power to resist the rules of the game, if you did not comply . . . you won't be fired probably but you would pay the price in your work terms. Now, here the very climate is very different. At my first American job I was struck by this atmosphere, I couldn't even name this feeling for a while . . . you are treated as a genderless colleague, nobody makes a point of your being a female. At first I felt uneasy about this—no one seemed to notice how I looked, what I wore—and I used to think of myself as an attractive woman, this indifference kind of offended me at first . . . but over time I realized that this kind of attitude is much healthier. It keeps people's lower instincts in check and does not allow men (and women too sometimes!) to use their administrative power to procure sexual favors from the weaker employees. And in general, a sex-neutral workplace is more pleasant, you don't feel constantly evaluated and judged as a woman. Over time I put aside my high heels and silk blouses and started wearing old jeans and trainers to work like everyone else.

Tanya's reflections underscore several important themes in the normative transition made by Soviet women: realization in hindsight of how perverted were the Soviet "rules of the game" where women's inferiority and submission in the workplace were often taken for granted; the advantages of " checking lower instincts" of the bosses by clear regulations; and the actual liberating potential of unisex style in dress and relations when both high heels and sexually colored compliments become irrelevant.

Discussing sexual conduct of American youth, some women mentioned their own adolescent or young adult children as an example of a more relaxed and accepting sexual attitudes than they themselves had had as young women in the FSU. "Today young people know so much more about sex and intimacy than we did, and I think this is very good for them. Ignorance in these matters brings so much misery, especially for the girls. . . . Today's young women are much more assertive, they know how to protect themselves, how to say no to a guy. . . . No sex without condom! (laughs). I think the AIDS epidemic in a way did a good service to American sexual practices, people became more cautious . . . " Some women brought up the subject of sex education, a very difficult topic in the former Soviet culture. "I think that mothers must talk about sex with their children, daughters and sons alike. Americans are more open in this regard than are Russian parents . . . we tend to shy away from these delicate topics till it's too late and your kid gets into trouble. Children must be given some basic knowledge of sexuality from their preschool years on. . . . I find it difficult to discuss these matters with my kids, but I have always found good readings for them, so I hope I have helped them glean some useful knowledge for their future private lives . . . " (Inna, fifty-six, a community worker).

Some informants reflected on the differences between former Soviet and American sexual cultures in general. For example, Vera (fifty-two) a former teacher, now eldercare worker, said,

> I think that most Americans are actually quite conservative in their sexual attitudes and conduct, this was a surprising discovery for me after all the Soviet propaganda about American sexual license, pornography industry, strip clubs, etc. In fact, after the end of socialism, Russia itself has been swept by the wave of commercial erotica and sex for sale of all possible kinds. . . . The amount of graphic sexual material on television, in the movies and in video shops in Russia is just outrageous, and it is not sold in special discrete places but is on display in every subway crosswalk. In Europe too, especially in Germany and Sweden, I've seen many images that would never pass on American TV, beach nudity is common. . . . Here in the U.S. Howard Stern's shows are among the only sexual teasers remaining in broad circulation, and everything else is strictly X-rated and kept away from the eyes of youth . . . "

> It seems to me that sexual freedoms in this country exist only on the two coasts, but not in the real heart of America. . . . The debates about access to abortion, gay marriage, sex education at schools are overlaid with conservatism and religious indoctrination. Even unmarried mothers are frowned at in many places, while in Europe, and in big Russian cities too, single mothering is becoming normal. You cannot even dream of telling a sexually charged joke to your colleagues at work. . . . I have lived in England for some time, so it is difficult for me to get used to American prudery (Lena, thirty-seven, a journalist and a single mother of a ten-year-old girl).

Other women, on the contrary, found similarities between Russian and American sex cultures. "In many ways Russians and Americans are similar in their values. At least in my own social circle, most men and women still believe in marriage and family life, and devote much time to their spouses and children. Or maybe these are just universal Jewish values, because most of my American friends are Jewish too . . . " (Inna, fifty-six). Irena (thirty-four), a nurse and a mother of two, said,

> I think that people's basic wishes and instincts are the same everywhere, in America they are just filtered through the culture of political correctness, so people are more restrained in their expression. Another factor here is fear of lawsuits, sexual harassment is a scarecrow for many men . . . as a result people's conduct becomes more polite if not to say sterile . . . and you can seldom guess what they really think or feel. I think that Russians in America are still more spontaneous and tend to speak out their mind, pursue women they like more openly, tell sexual (and sexist!) jokes and laugh at them . . . . I think most Americans would consider us very rude if they could understand our internal chats in Russian . . .

Thinking aloud about the ways in which their lives as women have changed in America, several women mentioned the evolution of their clothing style from hyper-feminine and flashy to more subdued, simple and driven by comfort rather than looks.

Olga, a forty-nine-year-old accountant in an investment company, said,

> When I first saw American women—you know, my neighbors, co-workers, etc.—I was taken aback by the plainness and lack of style in their dress . . . they did not seem to care how they looked, just picking up any clean items from the dryer, not coordinating colors, wearing outdated models. . . . And look at the abundance in the stores—you can dress like a queen, and it doesn't even cost so much. American women have no zest for clothes. In Moscow I would spend quite some time dressing and making up my face and hair before going to work, and here women hardly bother to put any makeup. . . . Well, after ten years, look at me now: I dress in plain trousers and flat shoes like everyone else, I don't remember when I last plucked my eyebrows or made up my eyes . . . . Does it mean that I became sloppy? Old and uninteresting for anyone? I don't know, it surely makes life easier, but at the same time I often feel like I lost some important part of who I am and my old life as a woman.

It took me time to figure out how to relate to my good-looking and friendly American boss. He seemed to like me a lot, paid more attention to me than to other women in the office. My first instinct would tell me to smile back and flirt, to show that I liked him too, to make him feel good about his manhood. In these first months I tried to dress my best, went to a hairdresser every week . . . . But soon a senior female colleague let me know indirectly that I was overplaying it, that my flirtation can get me into trouble. She was the first one to tell me about sexual harassment laws (I never heard the term before) and I understood that if I wished to keep my job I have to play it sexless, like other women. So I turned down my light bulb and became invisible. This guy, my boss, seemed sad at this change of mood at first, but probably the wise ladies spoke with him too and he withdrew. Until this day I think that maybe I lost the romance of my life . . . (Marina, thirty-five, computer company employee).

It seems so unfair, even absurd—this ban on flirting and relationships with men whom you work with. We spend 8–9 hours every day at work and don't really have much of a chance for meeting new people outside the workplace. Then, almost every man in the office is senior to me, so when and if he pays attention it is labeled sexual harassment and he is at risk. Tell me, where else can I meet a potential partner? (Tania, twenty-nine, secretary in an investment firm).

Thus, women whom I interviewed expressed a range of opinions as to American sexual culture and the role of feminism and political correctness in its regulation. Most perceived their own moral education and sexual expression to be quite different from those of their American peers, although they could not always define these differences. Some women were appreciative of the restraints on open expressions of sexism and male chauvinism instilled by the feminist movement in most American institutions, while others regarded them as excessive and stifling. Most women admitted that their own attitudes and lifestyles have evolved over time to embrace many American notions and rules of self-expression at least in the public domain (workplace, school, etc.). These included changed styles of clothing, hairdo and makeup (from flashy and hyper-feminine to more subdued and unisex) and keeping a neutral demeanor with the male bosses at work instead of former flirtatiousness. At the same time, most women grew more tolerant of the sexual expression in their adolescent children, accepting their girl/boy friends and trying to discuss with them condom use rather than marital prospects.

At the same time, Russian women still feel uncomfortable discussing sexually related subjects and have clear difficulty formulating their ideas in a polite and "cultured" way. As the Russian language is rather limited in its sexual lexicon (which is either blatantly rude or dryly medical), many women who touched upon these subjects included English words and expressions in their Russian speech. Younger women were considerably more at ease in this domain of discussion than older women, regardless of their formal education and the length of life in America. However, most women agreed with the idea that being a woman in America is different from being a woman in Russia or Ukraine. Most women, though, believed that their feminine lives had taken a positive turn in America, both due to material factors (better living conditions, access to better health and social services, rich consumer choice) and a less sexually charged social environment.

Conclusion

This ethnographic study sheds some new light on the process of social adjustment of former Soviet women as immigrants in the U.S. and in this way contributes to contemporary feminist scholarship on immigrant women and social transformations of femininity after socialism. It shows that, as in other immigrant and minority groups, the culture of Russian-Jewish immigrants is a result of the interplay between continuity and change, a hybrid of their homeland and American values and lifestyles. Most Jewish women from the FSU remain secular in their outlook and practices, but over time they adopt elements of mainstream American cultural Judaism, which helps them join the informal networks of their local co-ethnics. While more Jewish immigrant women in the U.S. than in Israel, Canada and most European countries can afford to leave paid employment and become full-time homemakers (due to the high earning capacity of their husbands), rather few of them choose that option. The need for an occupational life and self-actualization, as well as economic independence, is deeply ingrained in the Russian/Soviet cultural tradition spanning at least two generations of women. At the same time, most women had to reinvent themselves in order to adjust to the American labor market and trade their former "masculine" technology-related occupations for more "feminine" ones in human services, sales, clerking, and so on. Quite often women believed that this change was for the better, did not define it in terms of downgrading and loss of former social status, and found meaning and satisfaction in their new jobs. A similar tendency towards acceptance and adjustment to the new work roles among Russian immigrant women (much more than in their male counterparts) was shown in my earlier research among different occupational groups of immigrants in Israel (Remennick, 2001, 2002b, 2003b, 2005b).

While preserving many of their old ideas about marriage, childbearing, and the work-family divide, most immigrant women have adopted more liberal attitudes towards premarital sex and non-marital relationships. They also developed a new propensity for self-care and adopted more positive attitudes towards aging and active lifestyles after the menopause, not necessarily limited to the care of their grandchildren (although they still underscored their role as grandmothers). The latter may also reflect gradual adoption by older women of American values of individualism. Most Russian speakers strongly prefer their co-ethnics as intimate partners for themselves and their children; mixed marriages with Americans are rare even among the 1.5-generation women, who spent many years in the U.S. and speak fluent English. A similar tendency towards ethno-cultural endogamy is apparent among Russian-speaking immigrants in Israel and in other host countries (Remennick, 2005a, b). One possible explanation of this tendency is preservation of strong intergenerational ties in Russian immigrant families and parental influence on their children's partner choice. Another lies in a strong belief of cultural gap between themselves and their American peers. After forming their own families, most young Russian-Jewish women preserve a mutual support network with their parents, although they no longer live with them in the same household.

Entering American society with strong negative attitudes towards Western feminist ideology, many immigrants came to appreciate over time the gains it brought to women, especially in the workplace. At the same time, many Russian immigrants find legal campaigns against male chauvinism (in the form of sexual harassment) excessive and "sterilizing" gender relations in the public domain. Despite their critical perceptions of the legal implications of feminism in the workplace and politics, most working immigrant women have adopted a pragmatic stance towards local "rules of the game" and altered their style of dress and general demeanor to conform to the American norms of feminine self-presentation. It is difficult to directly juxtapose sexual aspects of immigrant women's adjustment in Israel and the U.S. as gender relations in the public domain are much less regulated in the former than in the latter, and sexual harassment complaints and lawsuits in Israel remain an exception rather than a norm. In that sense there is a much less cultural change in gender attitudes for Russian women to embrace in Israel than in the U.S., although the exposure of these women to actual sexual harassment and exploitation in Israel is probably much higher (Remennick, 1999a). Reflecting different social contexts of the two host countries, Russian immigrant women in the U.S. were largely spared the tainted sexual reputation they have faced in Israel. Yet, despite a favorable social context of integration and regular contacts with American men via work and studies, relatively few Russian women embarked on intimate relationships with them due to perceived cultural differences.

In sum, former Soviet women as immigrants in the U.S. manifested a remarkable adaptive potential, resilience, and strength in their new lives, combining new modes of self-actualization with the on-going responsibility for their loved ones. Similar conclusions were made in my earlier research in Israel (Remennick, 2001, 2005b) and in other host countries, such as Canada. Other American scholars who wrote about former Soviet-Jewish women have also underscored their good adjustment skills (often superior to those of their male partners), ability to shoulder work and family roles, and develop multiple social ties with the new society (Orleck, 2001:164; Kishinevsky, 2004). Future scholars of immigration and gender will follow and document the further processes of Americanization (versus lingering Russianness) among young immigrant women of Soviet origin, especially those born in the U.S. of Russian parents. Comparative research on former Soviet women and the evolution of femininity in the context of immigration to different Western societies is another prospective development of this research stream.

Note

1. The field work described in this chapter was conducted during my stay as a Resident Scholar at Hadassah Institute for Research on Jewish Women at Brandeis University in Waltham, MA in the fall and winter of 2004–5. I am grateful to the Institute's Director Professor Shula Reinharz for her support and interest in this research.

5

Former Soviet Jews in Toronto, Canada

Introduction

Throughout the 1990s and early 2000s, Canada has been one of the most active centers of former Soviet-Jewish immigration. Apart from the country's high living standards, this has been due to several factors, including the relative lenience of Canadian immigration policy towards skilled migrants and high human capital of former Soviet Jews reflected in their eligibility under the Point System.[1] The Greater Toronto area (GTA) with its thriving multiethnic economy and rapid urban sprawl has attracted disproportionate numbers of immigrants: over 47 percent of all new arrivals to Canada have settled in the GTA in the late 1990s (Jansen and Lam, 2003). Amongst other old and new ethnic minorities, the size of the Russian Jewish community in this area grew quickly from several thousand in the late 1970s to approximately 60 to 70 thousand of today. About 70 percent of former Soviet Jewish immigrants to Canada reside in the GTA (Brym, 2001). The continuing influx of Russian-speaking Jews comprises the principal demographic source of growth for the city's Jewish community typified by advanced middle age, growing rates of intermarriage, and low fertility (Cohen, 2001).

According to the 1996 Canadian census, nationally there were about 16,000 Jews born of Russian/Soviet parents, mostly refugees—arrivals of the 1970s and early 1980s (Brym, 2001). These Canadian-born children of Soviet immigrants (the second generation) must be fairly well integrated in the general or Canadian-Jewish mainstream (Basok, 1991), and will be left outside the scope of my current analysis. Within the stream of more recent Russian-speaking migrants, who arrived in the GTA during the 1990s and early 2000s, there are two major groups: those who resettled directly from Russia, Ukraine and other countries of the former Soviet Union (FSU) and those who re-migrated from Israel. Although the exact size of these latter groups is unknown, the secondary migrants from Israel are estimated at 50 to 70 percent of all post-1990 arrivals (Anisef et al., 2002). Despite their common background, these two immigrant groups may significantly differ in terms of their recent experiences preceding entry to Canada: one spent their pre-migration years in the tumultuous and corrupt social and economic milieu of late Soviet and transitional countries, while the other has had an experience of living under the imperfect but still more efficient democracy and market economy of Israel. The two groups can also differ in terms of their Jewish identity and family composition (of Jewish or mixed ethnicity) that had informed their initial decisions to immigrate to Israel or move straight to the West. Finally, the group or secondary migrants from Israel have experienced an additional set of challenges and traumas in the course of socio-economic, linguistic, and cultural readjustment for the second time—in Canada.

In this chapter, I present and discuss the findings of my exploratory qualitative study that aimed at comparison between the two subgroups described above of recent Russian-speaking Jewish immigrants in the GTA in terms of their integration experiences and the role of co-ethnic networks versus mainstream Canadian institutions (such as the Jewish community, workplaces and social services) in the process of social incorporation of these recent migrants. Before describing the study, I will provide a concise background on the two subgroups of Russian Jews in the GTA.

Former Soviet Jews and How They Arrived in Canada

On the Sending End: The FSU

The last immigration wave of Russian Jews (from 1988 on) was rather unique in its scope and socio-economic profile. Under the Soviet regime that from its very inception had proclaimed atheism as state policy, Jews were considered an ethnic rather than a religious minority. Indeed, their overwhelming majority was secular and had lost ties with the Jewish religious tradition, the Yiddish language, and system of education. After their initial emancipation and "mainstreaming" during the first three decades of state socialism, from the late 1940s on Soviet Jews experienced the rising tide of institutional and popular anti-Semitism that included barriers to higher education and a tacit ban on their entry into certain occupations and/or promotion (Brym, 1994; Remennick, 1998). The first wave of Jewish emigration in the recent Soviet history (over 250,000 people) took place between 1971 and 1981; an estimated 60 percent of these émigrés went to North America and 40 percent to Israel. The period between 1981 and 1988 was a political dead-time zone, when almost no one could leave the USSR.[2] In the years of glasnost and the subsequent post-communist transition the borders were opened again, with concomitant socio-economic turmoil and the rise of Slavic nationalism and anti-Semitism. These processes prompted mass exodus of the Jews: over 1,600,000 have left the FSU after 1988; of those about 62 percent resettled in Israel and over 30 percent moved to the U.S. and Canada (the remaining fraction resettled in Germany, Australia, and other western countries). By the end of the twentieth century, the pool of potential Jewish émigrés in the FSU has largely drained out, and today Israel and a few Western countries host roughly between 5 and 15 thousand of such immigrants per year (Remennick, 2003a; Tolts, 2004).

While immigration of former Soviet Jews to Israel and Germany was framed under ethnic criteria (i.e., as a privilege of return to their historic homelands, in the German case with an additional goal of redeeming the historic crimes against the Jewish people [Joppke, 2005]), and entry to the U.S. was usually under religious refugee status [Gitelman, 1997]), most immigrants from the FSU to Canada were granted visas via the Point System as economic immigrants (Cohen, 2001). This reflects their high human capital, specifically very high levels of post-secondary education (about 60 percent). Most former Soviet Jews of either gender had been professionals or white-collar workers, which on the one hand made them desirable immigrants with eligible occupations and work experience, but on the other posed questions of occupational readjustment in the hosting countries (Remennick, 1998, 2003b).

On the Receiving End: Israel

In Israel, despite the established system of public aid to educated immigrants (free Hebrew courses, fellowships to scientists, assistance in the licensure process, etc.), only under one-third of educated new-comers of the 1990s could find jobs compatible with their former training and experience. This is usually explained by both objective economic predicaments (small and saturated skilled marketplace, competition with local professionals) and the lack of relevant skills among Soviet-trained professionals: limited Hebrew and English proficiency, poor computer literacy, no experience in job search and self-marketing. For the members of culturally dependent professions in human services (health care, education), the media and cultural production (journalism, the arts etc.) linguistic deficiency posed a special barrier, but cultural differences in professional practice made it worse (Remennick, 2002b). Some younger immigrants made a successful occupational switch, retraining for a range of information technology jobs (especially during the high-tech boom of the late 1990s); others moved into demanded human services (mainly eldercare). Yet, the majority of last-wave immigrants to Israel had to make their living in semi-skilled manufacturing, sales or personal services; women and older immigrants have experienced especially dramatic occupational and social downgrading. The failure to continue their careers and join their social peers in Israel caused disappointment and identity crisis, with the ensuing poor progress in Hebrew proficiency and general social alienation from the Israeli mainstream among many immigrant professionals (Remennick, 2002b, 2003a,b).

Another set of tensions experienced by former Soviets in Israel resulted from the ethno-religious divisions of the country and ethnic definition of immigration. As the Jewish religious establishment is not separated from the state, most matters of civil status (marriage, divorce, burial) are regulated by rabbinic authorities who base their decisions on the traditional Jewish legal code—Halacha. Under religious law, only children born of Jewish mothers or those who underwent full Orthodox conversion (*giyur*) are recognized as Jews. Reflecting high rates of intermarriage at least in two generations of Soviet Jews, many arrivals of the 1990s were half Jewish (on the paternal side), quarter Jewish, or non-Jews married to Jews. All these immigrants were legally admitted to Israel according to the Law of Return, but could not enjoy full civil rights in several important domains, and hence often felt themselves second-rate citizens. For many non-Jews (as well as secular Jews) it was also difficult to identify with the Jewish values and traditions that form the bedrock of lifestyle for most

Israelis: Jewish calendar and holidays, *kashrut* (compliance with Judaic dietary rules) in all public settings, the break in public transportation and many forms of entertainment on the weekends (*Shabat*), the proliferation of synagogues, yeshivas, and other religious institutions, and the significant influence of religious parties on the national politics. Many former Soviets raised in the atheist mindset rejected this culture as backward and incompatible with modern democracy (Shumsky, 2002). Juxtaposed with economic hardships and occupational downgrading, this rejection prompted a decision to move to the West for not a few Russian-speaking families. As Canada is among the few Western countries receiving independent economic migrants, a steady stream of applicants has been stalking the offices of Canadian Embassy in Tel Aviv since the mid–1990s, and an estimated 3,000 to 7,000 left Israel for Canada every year (Canadian Embassy, personal communication).

On the Receiving End: Canada

Arriving in Canada (mainly Toronto), these secondary migrants faced a new set of problems in their occupational and social adjustment. On the one hand, they had already lived in a Westernized society and had acquired some salient skills that their counterparts arriving directly from the FSU lacked. They were used to a systematic job search, had some experience in Western-type organizations (if they were in a skilled occupation in Israel), many had improved their English as an international professional language. On the other hand, in Ontario these immigrants faced a tight regulation of most professional occupations and the need to undergo yet another reassessment and licensure, if at all possible for foreign graduates. Thus, Soviet-trained physicians (even with Israeli experience) had few opportunities for licensure and practice (Basok, 1997), and many were compelled to seek retraining into paramedical and nursing occupations. Many categories of engineers, regardless of their seniority and work experience in the two countries of prior residence, had to sit for extensive professional exams in order to join engineering associations and find qualified posts. Few teachers and other education professionals with Russian (and Israeli) diplomas could be licensed for similar jobs in the GTA schools and colleges. The system of recognition of foreign credentials in Canada generally, and in Ontario specifically, is very cumbersome and erects multiple barriers for qualified immigrants. On the other hand, it creates an artificial shortage of practitioners in many occupations (e.g., physicians, especially in the remote areas) along with the abundance of qualified candidates trained abroad. The resulting paradox is that, while selecting immigrants by occupational skills, Canada is unwilling to utilize their economic potential (PROMPT, 2004).

Making things worse, the demographic composition of Russian-speaking immigrants was not particularly conducive to economic success: they were on the average nine years older than Canadians (mean age of 46.3 in 1996), women outnumbered men by 8–10 percent, and as many as 25–30 percent arrived as single-parent families (Brym, 2001; Anisef et al., 2002). Surveys of the late 1990 and early 2000s have shown that about 70 percent of households of former Soviet Jews had below-median income and about 30 percent lived around the official poverty line (Anisef et al., 2002; Jansen and Lam, 2003). By comparison, less than 10 percent of native Canadian Jews live in poverty. The employment opportunities for all immigrants dwindled further after the mid–1990s with economic recession. Relegated once again to the economic (and hence social) margins, many families had to lower their expectations and living standards, at least for the time being. Yet, over time many immigrants in their prime working years tend to improve their occupational status and manage to gain higher returns on their education. By the early 2000s, clear economic polarization has emerged in the Jewish-Russian community of the GTA: the successful upwardly mobile immigrants (usually younger and with in-demand technology-related occupations) have moved out of the high-rise apartment blocks of the North Bathurst corridor Between Finch and Steels (known as the Russian residential enclave) to private houses in Richmond Hill and other affluent suburbs. Older immigrants, single-parent families, and the rest of their less successful co-ethnics have remained in the high-rise buildings, often renting and unable to purchase their apartments (Anisef et al., 2002).

Social Research on Soviet Jews in Canada

There is a surprising paucity of literature exploring migration experiences of the recent wave of former Soviet Jews in Canada, especially in relation to differences between direct FSU migrants and the "second lap" newcomers from Israel. Several Canadian authors who write about Jewish life have mainly addressed the issues of Jewish identity and relations between the established Canadian-Jewish community and the newcomers (Glikman, 1996; Basok and Brym, 2000; Cohen, 2001). Thus, Basok and Brym (2000) conducted a semi-structured (i.e., including a number of open-ended questions) survey in a residential sample of Russian-speaking Jews, in which they tried to compare various expressions of Russian/Soviet and Jewish identity between direct arrivals and former Israelis. They report a complex and contradictory pattern of identity change as a result of living in the Jewish state: although initially driven by Zionist sentiments and the wish to live among Jews, upon arrival many informants rejected the pressure towards rapid "Israelization" and distanced themselves from Jewish traditions and culture (hence their decision to re-migrate). Those who emigrated directly from the FSU often lacked any interest whatsoever in the Jewish religion and traditions and defined their Jewish identity either as "coercive" (i.e., reflecting ambient anti-Semitism in the FSU) or "social" (i.e., mainly expressed in the wish to socialize with other Jews).

In Canada, both subgroups have failed to find common ground with the Jewish mainstream, which they perceived as arrogant, universally wealthy, and indifferent to their hardships. Few newcomers were willing to participate in religious services and classes or volunteer their time for community causes, but most eagerly utilized any kind of material aid and services provided by the Jewish resettlement agency (JIAS) and a few other philanthropies. As a result, the mainstream community has grown more skeptical as to the ability of the newcomers to contribute to Canadian-Jewish life. In the words of director of the GTA Immigrant Services at JIAS Mila Voihanski, "the Russian community doesn't feel accepted and the established community doesn't feel appreciated" (cited by Anisef et al., 2002: 22). Some Canadian authors (Cohen, 2001) point to a gradual drift towards the mainstream forms of Jewish life among Russian Jews (e.g., sending their children to Jewish day schools and summer camps), while other scholars (Basok and Brym, 2000) did not identify this trend.

Another recent study (Anisef et al., 2002) looked into social adjustment of Russian-speaking immigrant youths (ages fifteen to twenty-five), also taking into account their migration history (direct or via Israel). The authors cogently assert that the negative labor market experiences of their parents and the resulting low living standards cast a long shadow on the integration experiences of the 1.5-generation (i.e., those who migrated as older children or adolescents). Additional problems ensue from the fact that many immigrant youths live in households headed by women struggling to make ends meet; the absence of father often means the lack of support and parental supervision. The Russian-Jewish community's dense residential concentration in a rather bleak high-rise apartment area has served to intensify youth anomie, and the absence of accessible recreational and social programs has further decreased their chances for social integration. Those who were (often against their will) moved from Israel to Canada by their parents often define Hebrew as their main language and miss their friends and the familiar environment they left behind. Some young men even enlisted to serve in the Israeli army, again going against their parents' wishes. Conversely, young people who moved to Toronto straight from the FSU underscored their attachment to Russian culture and felt deep alienation from their Canadian peers. Both groups of young immigrants manifested "fragmented identities they struggle to reconcile in the face of the minimal and shallow ties they have so far been able to forge in their newest homeland" (Anisef et al., 2002:23).

Drawing on this background, the current study tried to embrace different facets of the social incorporation process experienced by the two groups of recent Russian Jewish immigrants in the GTA, with the emphasis on their occupational adjustment, perceived living standards, family issues, and relations with the hosting society.

Study Participants and Methods

This research can best be described as multi-tiered ethnography, combining observations of immigrants in different social settings, personal interviews, focus groups, and critical reading of immigrant press and other written materials. As I share a common ethnic and linguistic background with my informants, I have cultural access to the Russian-speaking immigrant community. Materials for this study have been collected during my three recent trips to the GTA, during which I visited the homes of my informants, observed their family interactions, followed them to Russian grocery stores, schools, community centers, and cultural events. In a more formal way, I conducted sixteen in-depth interviews with recent immigrants, of whom ten were re-migrants from Israel (their average length of residence there was 5.7 years, ranging between three and ten) and six arrived directly from the

FSU. Interviewees were located by consecutive personal referrals (snow-balling) with the starting point in my own informal social networks among Russian-speakers and Israelis living in the GTA. Interviews were conducted in the immigrants' homes or in public places chosen by informants (parks, cafes, etc.). The socio-demographic profile of my informants is described in table 1. All of them were of working age (the mean of 42.4) and were employed at the time of the study, either part or full time; only three persons received welfare benefits. Most informants lived in the Russian ethnic enclave in the north of Toronto: about one-third still lived in rented apartments, one third owned their condos and the remaining third (usually with longer residence in Canada) lived in private homes in Richmond Hill and other suburbs. Most informants were married and had adolescent or young adult children living with them.

I also mediated two focus groups formed on the basis of entry route, that is, one with direct arrivals and the other with former Israelis (six and eight participants, respectively). Participants from these groups were invited via ads placed in the local Russian press and community

Table 1
Socio-Demographics of the Interviewees

Name	Age	Occupation former/current	Tenure in GTA (years)	Family composition
Natasha*	39	accountant/realtor	8	Divorced + 1 (17)**
Igor*	44	engineer/engineer	10	Married + 2 (16 & 20)
Galina*	36	nurse/nurse	7	Married + 1 (8)
Irene*	29	student/IT worker	6	Single + sister (17)
Gregory*	34	banking/banking	5	Married+ 2 (7 & 10)
Alex*	40	computing/computing	9	Married + 1 (17)
Vera	46	teacher/soc. worker	7	Divorced + 2 (19 & 22)
Maxim	39	auto mechanic/same	8	Married + 1 (16)
Olga	44	physician/paramedic	5	Divorced + 1 (18)
Michael	50	skilled technician/same	10	Married + 2 (25 & 16)
Jacob	47	sales manager/realtor	4	Divorced + 1 (22)
Lisa	42	hairdresser/ same	6	Married + 2 (16 & 10)
Josef	52	engineer/skilled worker	7	Married + 2 (22 & 18)
Dina	39	psychologist/counselor	8	Divorced + 1 (15)
Vladimir	46	graphic designer/same	5	Married, no children
Tania	50	nursery teacher/ same	9	Single, no children

* —Direct arrivals from the FSU; the rest have re-migrated from Israel

** —Ages of the children

centers; discussions were held in a community center in the evening hours. All the interviews and group discussions have been tape-recorded, transcribed verbatim, and analyzed using code-book technique described by Crabtree and Miller (1992). Analysis was based on repeated scanning of the transcripts and constant updating of analytical categories; it ascended from topical to thematic and conceptual levels. At the final stage, all materials (interviews, focus group discussions, observations, and press excerpts) have been integrated and structured according to the key themes. The resulting data pool comprises hundreds of pages of text as well as photo materials, newspaper articles, etc. Below I present the highlights from my findings arranged by the key topics that emerged in the informants' narratives on their new lives in Canada. To preserve the anonymity of the speakers, I have changed their names, but kept intact other personal details (age, occupation, length of residence in Canada, etc.).

Findings

The interview and focus group materials pertained to the five general realms: causes of immigration to Canada; labor market choices and limitations (occupational continuity vs. change), relations with Canadian mainstream (including the established Jewish community), living standards (including perceived quality of life as a result of migration to Canada) and family adjustment process (including marital quality, the problems faced by the youths and the elders). Below, I discuss each realm, illustrating them with the quotes from informants' accounts.

Causes of Immigration to Canada

Most informants stated economic reasons as primary in their decision to move to Canada, perceived as a country of opportunity and high living standards. Some informants admitted that their preferred destination was the U.S., but as economic immigration there is almost impossible, they decided on Canada as its next-door neighbor. Many of these informants also noted that they had insufficient or spurious information about the full range of differences between the U.S. and Canada in terms of labor market, political system, and culture. Important additional motives for both groups of migrants included high personal security and "quiet life" in Canada, relatively inexpensive higher education, universal access to health care, and a developed welfare system. Secondary migrants from Israel cited additional motives reflecting their wish to leave Israel due to its overly religious character and Middle Eastern cultural flavor; limited employment opportunities; ongoing military conflict and growing insecurity; the wish to keep their children from the military draft; having a non-Jewish spouse who feels uncomfortable in the Jewish state; inability to master the Hebrew language; dislike of native Israelis; hot climate, and more. Being one of the few Western countries still receiving independent migrants, Canada became their destination of choice. An additional argument in favor of moving to Canada was the promise of initial help from relatives or friends already living there (so-called chain migration). The period of time between the initial application and getting immigrant visa varied for different families from eight months to 2.5 years.

The Work Realm: Continuity vs. Change

All my informants had been admitted to Canada as independent economic migrants on the point system, meaning that their education and occupational skills had been recognized as eligible. However, upon landing in the GTA they had learned that decisions of immigration authorities had little in common with the actual labor market situation and their ability to practice their former professions. Barriers to career continuity were the highest for members of the so-called regulated occupations (physicians and other health care workers, psychologists, counselors and social workers, schoolteachers, many categories of engineers, lawyers, and others). Most newcomers had known that they would have to undergo some form of Canadian notification, but did not realize how complex and cumbersome were the existing regulations. Professionals who re-migrated from Israel (where many had already sat for professional exams and other forms of licensure) often had a belief that in Canada they would not need much of a reassessment as they were coming from a country with high "Western" standards of practice. Thus, Olga (forty-four) who had worked as a pediatrician in Kiev and then (after licensure) as a general practitioner (GP) in Israel (finally becoming an imaging technician in Toronto), recounted:

I knew too little about Canadian medical regulations when I made a decision to come here. In Israel, I could only be licensed as a GP and had to go back to a long residency training if I wanted to work in pediatrics. I naively thought that in Canada they would recognize my past experience in the Ukraine and also years of practice in Israel. But upon arrival I learned that in Ontario foreign-trained physicians had a tiny number of slots to enter residency each year, and the rest had no chance to practice medicine at all.

Josef (fifty-two) who had worked as civil engineer both in Russia and in Israel encountered a similar problem:

In order to find work in civil engineering in Ontario I had to join the local Association, which meant sitting for a huge exam in English, including large chapters on engineering ethics and legal regulations. When I saw the book that I had to learn by heart, I said goodbye to my engineering career in Canada. Since then I work as a foreman on an electronics plant; the work is routine and uninspiring but gives me a stable livelihood.

For Josef, as well as most other immigrants, their limited command of English posed an additional barrier to getting Canadian accreditation in their specialty. Although most of them had attended linguistic classes (sponsored by JIAS), their English proficiency was insufficient for passing complex examinations in accounting, law, psychology, or medical specialties. In that respect, direct immigrants from the FSU were often in a worse position as they had not been ready for the very concept of obtaining Canadian credentials, and their English was often poorer than that of former Israeli residents. Thus, Natasha (thirty-nine), a former accountant in a small commercial firm in Tashkent, said:

I had believed that my knowledge of accountancy was fairly standard and applicable anywhere—debits and credits are the same, aren't they? But it turned out that in Canadian conditions my knowledge was not enough and I had to go back to college. But on my second year I broke down—accounting science in English was too hard on me . . . I made a switch to real estate where my best friend had worked—and since then I sell houses . . . . My basic English is enough for that as most of my clients are Russian immigrants.

Many informants admitted in hindsight that their expectations about future work opportunities in Canada had been unrealistic, partly because the points they had scored on their applications made them believe that their specific skills were in demand. Thus, Olga, the former MD cited above, said,

> It's a paradox, in small Israel my experience was wanted more than in huge Canada; first they don't allow you to practice your profession as an immigrant and then they complain about shortage of doctors, nurses, counselors, almost every one in human services is lacking. I would be ready to move out of Toronto and practice in a small town, but even this is impossible.

Direct immigrants from the FSU had lower career expectations at the outset and were more ready to retrain to any locally demanded occupations to make a living. Gregory (thirty-four), former director of a small bank in St. Petersburg currently working as a regular banking clerk, said:

> I had reached a high status there but still had to leave my post due to financial and legal problems of my bank. . . . I had no illusions about my work in Canada: I consider myself lucky to have found a white-collar job; in fact I was prepared to work as a janitor or construction worker, or any other manual work. . . . When you are a new migrant, you usually have to start from the bottom.

In fact, just several specific categories of professionals experienced a relatively smooth transition from the FSU or Israel to the Canadian market, namely programmers, electronics engineers, and other computing/IT specialists (who comprised a significant part of the male immigrants). Members of most other occupations had to downgrade to lower-level positions (e.g., MDs became paramedics like Olga) or go back to college in order to obtain a similar Canadian degree. Several younger female informants took the second option and invested two to four years in order to become locally certified counselors, nurses, or social workers. Some women with former occupations in the humanities (e.g., teachers of English, journalists, social scientists, etc.) discovered a large occupational niche of legal firms: some took a year-long course to become legal secretaries or embarked on a three-year study to become a paralegal. Still others chose less demanding (in terms of formal training) occupations of real estate agent or mortgage broker, which at the same time is highly uneven in terms of income and hence feasible only with a second stable earner in the family.

Generally, female immigrants in my sample were more flexible and ready to re-launch their occupational life on new terms than were men, who more often opted for lower-level jobs in their old occupation (e.g., downgrading from engineer to foreman in the same industry). Out of sixteen interviewees, seven women and only three men went back to college or got other forms of retraining in order to start a new occupational track or improve their chances for finding a better job. For example, Vera (forty-six), former teacher of English, took two years of college to become social worker; Dina (thirty-nine), who had worked as clinical psychologist in Russia and in Israel, retrained into high school counselor, and Tania (fifty) had to study for a Canadian diploma to work as a nursery teacher, despite her twenty-five years of experience in two other countries. Partly this reflects the fact that men more often were in technology-related occupations in demand on the Canadian market and did not have to seek retraining. But several male informants in both interviews and focus groups expressed their explicit dislike of continued schooling at their relatively advanced age and career stage. Jacob (forty-seven), a senior sales manager in Israel, said that in order to find a managerial position in Canada he had to improve his English and study for an MBA degree: "I couldn't imagine myself becoming a student again, sitting in class next to the local kids in their twenties. . . . That was too high a price to pay. I decided to use my experience in real estate, for which it is easy to get licensed."

In fact, immigrants with former professional careers had a harder time trying to get a fair return on their education and experience than did immigrants in skilled technical or manual occupations. Examples include Maxim (thirty-nine), auto mechanic, and Lisa (forty-two) hairdresser, both of whom opened small businesses of their own and soon got back on their feet, serving mainly co-ethnic clientele in the north of Toronto. This is explained both by higher demands for English proficiency placed on professional vs. manual occupations and by the need to overcome tight regulations at the entry to the professional marketplace.

Overall, it is hard to say which group of the newcomers (direct arrivals or former Israelis) had an easier time readjusting to the new occupational situation. Re-migrants from Israel often had a higher skill level and stronger professional record but also carried unrealistically high expectations of rapid success and recognition. Migrants from the FSU were perhaps less equipped with marketable skills but their mindset was more flexible and ready to make a new start from a low position. Women often had less demanded and more culturally dependent occupations (e.g., in social services and the humanities) but were more ready for additional study and/or retraining into an entirely new occupational track. In sum, success or stagnation in the new economic marketplace could only be explained by multiple intersections of the demographics, professional credentials, and psychological traits of the newcomers as well as the local policies towards specific occupational groups.

Relations with Canadian Mainstream

In agreement with the earlier findings by Glikman (1996) and Basok and Brym (2000), my research has shown that former Soviet Jews often fail to find common ground with mainstream Canadian society generally and the established Jewish community specifically. Most participants in this research underscored their appreciation of Canadians' open attitude towards other cultures and languages. Most said that they never felt discriminated against or denigrated in any way on the basis of their Jewish origins or immigrant status. At the same time, none of the informants mentioned ever having informal relationships with native Canadians outside workplace, school, or any other institutional context. The following quotations from focus group discussions were typical:

Canadians are very polite, they smile a lot and even can strike a small talk with you, but they are not really interested in you as "other." This is all very superficial, yet another expression of political correctness. "You should be nice to immigrants" kind of attitude (Boris, forty-seven, a former surgeon, works in a chiropractic clinic).

I have many Canadian-born co-workers, and they are fairly pleasant to deal with at work, but I would never ask them for any favor, or advice in practical matters, let alone invite them to my small flat . . . they seem to live on another planet. I don't think they could understand us [recent immigrants] even if they wanted to . . . (Vera, thirty-nine, a former teacher, works in a post office).

At my community college there are both Canadian-born and immigrant students, and I would say that those two categories seldom interact. It's much easier for me to find common language with a newcomer from India or China (despite our similarly poor English!) than with a native Canadian classmate (Lena, thirty-four, a former chemical technologist, retraining for social worker).

When asked to explain this lack of communication, most informants stated more than one cause, including their limited proficiency in English, the perceived cold and uninterested demeanor of Canadians (mainly their WASP part), cultural differences in self-presentation and communication style, Canadians' perceived wealth (relative to recent immigrants), and arrogance. Yet, when I asked the participants if they ever tried to befriend their Canadian co-workers, neighbors, etc. (e.g., by inviting them to a party, joint outing, etc.) virtually all of them answered negatively, adding that they were sure it could never work. My impression was that many Russian immigrants tended to exaggerate the cultural differences and their advance negative attitude towards possible informal contacts with Canadians worked as a self-fulfilling prophecy.

As for relations with the members of Canadian Jewry, the reactions of Russian speakers were more variable and ambivalent. Many informants believed that Canadian Jews were universally religiously observant and expected the same from the former Soviet Jews. As most newcomers were rather alien even to the Jewish cultural traditions and holidays (let alone religious rites), they felt being unable to meet the expectations of the Canadian "hosting" community and believed that they would be disliked and excluded from its networks. But some informants also appreciated the elements of the Jewish traditional practice as a basis for developing a meaningful Jewish identity. A middle-aged female participant in a focus group put it this way:

We are not Jewish enough for Canadian Jews. But this perception is so false! It is just that for me being Jewish means something else than for a Canadian-Jewish woman. I may not light candles every Shabat and I don't have a kosher kitchen, but I know first hand what it means to live among anti-Semites who never treat you as an equal. Being a Jew for me is a negative label, and it's not easy to dismiss it and to develop a "positive" Jewish identity. But I hope to be able to do this over time. That's why I am also trying to learn from the local Jewish women. I hope that my daughter will feel better about being Jewish that I did as a young woman in Ukraine (Ada, forty-six).

Like this informant, many others connected their expectations of a greater Jewish affiliation with the next generation. Many felt rather positive about coming of age rituals (bar/bat-mitzvahs) for Jewish teenagers and Sunday Jewish schools. Although they did not expect their children to join in full-fledged Jewish religious life, most wanted them to be aware of their ethnic background and to gain some knowledge about Jewish historic and cultural heritage. In that sense, they subscribed to the mild version of "cultural Judaism" that is predominant among North American Jewry (Dershowitz, 1997).

The extent of interest and involvement with Jewish life in the GTA depended on the ethnic composition of the family: Jews with non-Jewish spouses were typically less inclined to participate in the community life, seldom had bar/bat mitzvah ceremonies for their children or sent them to the Jewish schools and camps. Jewish immigrants from smaller provincial towns of the FSU (especially in Ukraine, Moldova, Central Asia, and the Caucasus) were usually more connected to their Jewish side and sought affiliation with the local Jewish institutions. Conversely, arrivals from Moscow, St. Petersburg, Kiev, and some other major cities, where Jews had been almost totally assimilated, did not express interest in becoming more Jewish in Canada. Some immigrants had been familiar with the Jewish organizations while still in the FSU (mainly as recipients of their services and aid); quite a few had sent their children to the Jewish schools, mainly because they were perceived as having higher educational standards and better physical conditions than regular schools. Reflecting this pre-migration experience, many perceived Jewish organizations mainly as philanthropic outlets or a co-ethnic corollary of social work agencies (lacking in the FSU). Most informants related in the same way to JIAS and other resettlement agencies, which helped them during initial years in the GTA. Fewer informants regarded Jewish institutions as sites of activism, voluntary work for community causes, and an expression of their Jewish identity detached from any self-interest. Many informants pointed out (often with irony) that they would volunteer their time for community work when they become as wealthy and as confident in their future as long-standing Canadian Jews.

Arrival history also played some role: by and large, Russian Jews who had lived for some time in Israel were more inclined to partake in Jewish life and participate in community activities, which they saw as a way to maintain their symbolic connection to Israel. These immigrants more often established social connections with members of the Israeli community living in the GTA. Often this happened thanks to the children whose identity was at least partly Israeli, who often continued speaking Hebrew, communicated with their friends in Israel, and closely followed Israeli events. Dina (thirty-nine) said,

> My sixteen-year-old daughter took it very hard when I decided to move to Canada. She spoke fluent Hebrew, had many friends and did well at school. . . . Up until this day she enjoys speaking Hebrew, often e-mails her Israeli classmates, and one of them even came to visit recently. In brief she is an Israeli girl living in Toronto. We often go to the Israeli community center, celebrate Israeli holidays, listen to Israeli records . . .

Josef (fifty-two) offered thoughts along similar lines:

> It's a paradox: in Israel we resisted pressure to become more Jewish, but here in Toronto we find it attractive to be part of the Jewish life, at least at the symbolic level. I even went to a synagogue a few times for high holidays—mainly out of curiosity and social reasons, to meet my Russian and Canadian peers. . . . I never did that in Israel. When being a Jew is voluntary, it can be fun.

When I asked if his children (aged eighteen and twenty-two) felt the same way, he said that their identity was Israeli rather then Jewish: "My children keep speaking Hebrew to each other, read Israeli books. . . . They'd love to go back there for a visit or even to work for some time, but cannot afford the trip. They grew up in Israel and it will always remain their country in a way . . . "

Thus, the interest in the Jewish life appeared (if at all) in different forms among the newcomers, depending on their social and ethnic background, age, prior exposure to the Jewish activities, and the country of former residence. Arrivals from the FSU more often related to the Jewish organizations and established Canadian Jews as sources of help they felt entitled to and were often disappointed when denied this help. Former Israelis felt on a more equal footing with Canadian Jews because they spoke good Hebrew and were well familiar with Israeli reality and Jewish daily practices. Yet, they often felt closer to Israelis living in the GTA than to Canadian-born Jews. Both groups of newcomers spoke of a broad social and cultural distance between themselves and members of the Canadian white mainstream.

Perceived Material Well-Being and Quality of Life

Virtually all Russian-speaking immigrants, who participated in this study, admitted that their resettlement in Canada generally and the GTA specifically were driven by the wish to improve their living standards and provide a better quality of life and future prospects to their children. In the course of the interviews and group discussions, participants were asked to define in principle the chief components of the notion *quality of life* (QOL). The most commonly cited aspects (in the receding order of prevalence) included: material well-being (high income, good standards of housing, nutrition, leisure, etc.); quality of employment (relevance of the job to the skill level and self-actualization at the workplace); personal security, safe environment; high standards of schooling and higher education for the children; fulfilling social ties and inclusion in the hosting society; rich and accessible cultural life; developed urban infrastructures and public transportation; and moderate climate. In the course of interviews and focus groups, all informants (N=30) were asked to reflect on the direction of the overall change of their lives in Canada in each of these respects, compared to their prior country of residence. The answers are summarized in table 2.

It is apparent that the attitudes of direct arrivals from the FSU differ in several respects from those of the former Israeli residents. Informants, who compared their life in Canada and in the FSU, more often asserted improvement in various aspects of the QOL than did re-migrants from Israel (particularly in living standards, employment, and social ties). At the same time, arrivals from Israel were more satisfied with education, cultural life, urban infrastructure, and climate in the GTA. In both groups, there were significant shares of informants who believed that their lives have worsened in terms of employment quality, social ties and inclusion, and cultural consumption. One aspect where both groups fully agreed was the improvement in personal security and a safe environment, which is not surprising given that both FSU and Israel have been suffering from ongoing military conflicts and terrorist attacks, and former Soviet states also have high crime rates, along with corrupt and ineffective police forces.

When I asked my informants to name the three most positive aspects of their life in Canada, the most common answers could be categorized in the following way: (1) the perception of Canada generally and Toronto specifically as a highly civilized and well-managed

Table 2
Perceived Change in the Main Aspects of the Quality of Life (QOL)
Compared with the Prior Country of Residence (FSU or Israel)
as Percentage of All Answers

Aspects of the QOL	Direction of change in Canada		
	Improved	Did not change	Deteriorated
Material well-being			
FSU	82	18	0
Israel	63	32	5
Employment quality			
FSU	41	30	29
Israel	30	44	26
Personal security			
FSU	92	8	0
Israel	89	11	0
Education			
FSU	48	34	18
Israel	54	37	9
Social ties and inclusion			
FSU	31	24	45
Israel	22	38	40
Cultural life			
FSU	28	18	54
Israel	49	10	41
Urban infrastructure			
FSU	45	34	21
Israel	63	18	19
Climate			
FSU	20	65	15
Israel	51	5	44

society; (2) politeness and amicability of people to each other, including minorities and foreigners; well-organized social and medical services (direct arrivals from the FSU praised the Canadian health care system more often than former Israelis); (3) perceived low level of corruption and rarity of political scandals; (4) availability of a reasonable QOL even with a modest income (impossible neither in the FSU nor in Israel); (5) moderate climate (excluding a few winter months) and the abundance of green areas in the city; (6) rich consumer choice (especially praised by the direct arrivals from the FSU).

The list of three most unpleasant aspects of new immigrants' lives in Canada included the following most cited categories: (1) feeling excluded from the mainstream society, living on the social margins (especially common among adolescents and older immigrants, as well as residents of high-rise blocks of Northern Bathurst); (2) tight income and inability to afford many desirable things, including private housing and travel; (3) communication barrier due to poor English; (4) jobs below one's qualification and abilities; (5) detachment from the mainstream cultural life (again due to low income, poor English and social isolation); (6) overly bureaucratized health and social services; and (7) long, cold winters. However, on balance the majority of informants (twenty-two out of thirty) felt that their lives have improved as a result of migration to Canada.

Family Adjustment Process

Marital conflict. Immigration experience is often conducive to marital conflict reflecting multiple challenges of adjustment in the new society and the related stress (Sluzki, 1979). Former Soviet immigrants in Israel often experienced marital distress that in many cases led to divorce. The common reasons for conflict included disagreement about immigration to Israel as such; differential pace of adjustment of husbands and wives; poor housing and involuntary co-residence of three generations; and conflicts over child education in the new context (e.g., religious or secular schooling) (Ben-David and Lavee, 1994). Although no such research has been done in the Canadian context, my findings from the interviews and focus groups point to many similarities perhaps reflecting generic features of the immigrant experience juxtaposed with the Soviet socialization, values and lifestyle. To begin with, all five divorced informants in my sample of thirty (18 percent) got divorced after migration to Israel (2) or Canada (3) and all of them explained their marital dissolution by the hardships of adaptation. In the words of one informant, "Immigration is a trial, it puts your relationship to test: harmonic couples get even stronger but those, who had had cracks in their relationship when they embarked on this trip, often fall apart."

The most common causes of tension and conflict in the Canadian context are failed expectations of rapid success, economic difficulties, and differential pace of integration and occupational adjustment among husbands and wives. This was especially the case among dual career couples rather common among former Soviet intelligentsia. In the harsh conditions of a new marketplace, demanding of the newcomers to improve their English, get licensed for practice, retrain altogether or start a job as a volunteer, much depends on the flexibility and support of one's life partner and his/her readiness to take over as primary breadwinner during the transitional period. Although in most cases women gave up their own ambitions (if any) for the sake of their husbands, some couples could not reach agreement about how to proceed with occupational readjustment. When a wife was more successful or, alternatively, was not ready to give up her own professional aspirations in favor of her husband, the undermining of his masculine role damaged the relationship, often to the point of separation. Two of the three Canadian divorce stories among my informants followed this scenario. Alternative scenarios involved women who expected their husbands to find well-paying jobs or prosper in their own small businesses soon upon arrival; when neither of this happened these women left the "losers" and found themselves higher achievers for partners. Finally, being on the move and meeting new people in the process of resettlement could in itself serve as a trigger for new romances and the demise of old relationships.

Older Generation (the Parents). As opposed to the Israeli context of immigration, whereby most extended families migrated together or in chain, migrants to Canada seldom brought along their elderly parents from the outset. Yet, later on, when they received Canadian citizenship and could sponsor migration of family members, some young and middle-aged immigrants invited their parents to join them from the FSU (more seldom from Israel). Among my informants, about one third had one or both parents living in the GTA, either in the same household or nearby.

Many elderly immigrants felt lonely and isolated, being unable to master English and gain freedom of movement at least within city bounds. Without a working knowledge of English, they were dependent on their children and grandchildren for all contacts with Canadian organizations and service providers. On the other hand, Russian-speaking senior communities living in high-rise buildings along Bathurst gradually formed informal social networks of their own, offering each other support and aid in everyday matters. One focus group participant told about her mother: "At first she was lost in this new place where she knew no one but us. But when she moved to the subsidized flat near Finch, her life has changed for the better. She met many other older immigrants like herself and struck up new friendships. Now she is as active as she was in Moscow." Another participant added: "It helps that in their neighborhood they have all the groceries and many services owned by Russian-speakers. Now even medical offices in the North have Russian-speaking doctors, nurses and secretaries."

Since the mid–1990s, Toronto's Russian-speaking community has been building various social and cultural institutions, ranging from a religiously oriented Russian-Jewish Community Center (sponsored by Chabad) to chess and handcraft clubs, a World War II veteran's association, and companies organizing tours of musicians and theaters from the FSU and Israel.[3] Over a dozen of Russian-language newspapers and magazines are published in Toronto. Electronic media include about six Russian television programs transmitted from the FSU and New York. Having more spare time on their hands, immigrant elders take full advantage of the opportunities offered by the community's cultural life. One of my informants, who runs a small business combining the import of Russian videos and CDs with organization of artistic tours, said,

> I would say that over half of my clients are retired immigrants. They are very active in the pursuit of cultural life in the new country: they buy new books in Russian, rent newly released movies, come to the concerts and shows of Russian and Israeli celebrities when they tour in Toronto . . . I am always puzzled about how they can afford these luxuries given their tiny personal budget. They must be saving for months to be able to buy a new book or attend a show.

Although on the average they received good social services from Canadian welfare system (including home attendants and nursing care when needed), many older immigrants suffered from insufficient support and contact with their own children and especially grandchildren. While helpful with routine errands and medical care, younger family members did not show much interest in sharing their current lives with the elderly. Many elders complained that they did not see their grandchildren often enough, and when they came to visit they could hardly find topics for conversation (many younger adolescents had also limited Russian proficiency for such conversations as English became their main language). For instance, Ida (seventy-two) sadly mused,

> I moved to Canada from an established life and a good apartment in Moscow in order to be close to my children and grandchildren, but in fact

I saw them more when they came to visit me in Russia. Now that I live here, I hardly so much as receive a phone call once or twice a week. I understand that I have little to offer them in their new life, but I am still very disappointed.

Many of aspects of older immigrants' lives in Toronto were similar to these among elderly Russian immigrants in Israel (Remennick, 2003c) as they reflect common problems of uprooting and readjustment to a foreign culture in old age. There is, though, one important difference between Russian-speaking elders in the GTA and in Israel: many older Jews had strong Zionist feelings and found their resettlement to the Jewish state meaningful in a spiritual and moral sense, despite all privations and losses they had faced on this way. Many of them were deeply connected to the country, interested in the current events and active in local politics. Most Russian immigrants in Israel found it normal to say: "This is my country, I belong here." Russian-Jewish elders, who followed their children to Canada, do not have a similar sense of home and motivation to integrate into what they perceive as a completely alien society. They will always remain on its margins, economically and socially, their only social network being their children (increasingly distant) and other immigrants like themselves.

Children and adolescents. As mentioned above, concern for their children's future was one of the main driving forces behind the immigration decisions of my informants. In practice, the adjustment of the 1.5 generation to life in Canada was not easy. In this research, I learned about children's experiences from their parents' accounts, so my data was indirect. Yet, in many respects it confirms and expands the observations made by Anisef et al. (2002) in their focus group research among Russian-speaking youths in the GTA. Most young immigrants faced a broad linguistic and cultural gap between themselves and mainstream Canadian society, including their peers at school and other frameworks. Social and learning problems were especially common among adolescent boys (vs. girls) and in older vs. younger teenagers. Youths who came straight from the FSU had more severe adjustment problems (both academically and socially) than those who re-migrated from Israel and were familiar with schooling systems other than Soviet, had better knowledge of English and were generally more secure and "seasoned" as repeat migrants.

Several important themes have emerged from parental stories about their children's adjustment. Many parents who arrived to the GTA from the FSU were ambivalent as to the old vs. new norms of youth lifestyle and parent-child relations. Often coming from conservative Russian/Soviet notions of discipline and parental authority, many parents entered a permanent conflict zone with their adolescent children fighting over their dress style, late night curfew, going out with their girl- and boyfriends, etc. At the same time, young immigrants found it difficult, if nor impossible, to get included into local peer groups and instead were compelled to form informal groups of their own. Lisa (forty-two) said, "During his first two years of high school my son did not make a single Canadian friend, he barely knew the names of his classmates. After school he only spoke and hang out with his Russian pals, so his English improved very slowly." This was especially prominent in the northern Bathurst corridor neighborhoods, where most local high schools received sizeable groups of Russian-speaking immigrant students. Joining together, these students pooled their intellectual resources in order to master the new curriculum in English and pass all the necessary tests. Given that most had been good students both in the FSU and in Israel, they soon excelled in the parts of the school curriculum that are less language-dependent (math and the sciences).

After linguistic readjustment, further differentiation between immigrant students set in, with some reaching the top of their classes and others barely making it or even dropping out. Having limited English skills, these weaker students also could not find work. Given the scarcity of their family resources, most youths could not pay for after-school educational and social activities, and local community centers offered few free of charge programs. Natasha (thirty-nine), a single mother who emigrated in 1995 with her son Tim from St. Petersburg, recounted:

In Russia, Tim was always a good student and had lots of additional interests, like sports, playing in a rock band. . . . Here in Toronto his life became duller because for many years I was living on the verge of an economic fall, having several part-time jobs that were still not enough to survive. I could hardly help him in anything because I was not at home for fourteen to sixteen hours a day. Paying for a sports club was out of the question, and his school offered nothing much outside the classes. So his choices for leisure were basically between playing computer games and hanging out with other teens like himself in the mall plaza, if it wasn't too cold.

With fewer ambitions and more spare time, the less-successful youths spent afternoons and evenings loitering in the streets and public parks drinking beer, listening to music, and challenging each other. Street-bound pastimes were often conducive to inter-group violence between different Russian-speaking groups and between them and other local immigrant youths, mostly Chinese. One sad result of this violence was the vicious murder of teenager Dimitri Baranovski in 1999 by a group including at least two of his co-ethnics—an incident that turned public attention to the Russian community and stirred discussion of immigrant youth problems more generally (Anisef et al., 2002). In recent years, the range of opportunities for education and active social life for immigrant youths has grown considerably, reflecting both the improvement of the financial status of parents and the emergence of new after-school activities and clubs geared for Russian-speaking children and youth in the north of the city (e.g., a large arts and music school that also offers classes in the Russian language and literature).

As a result, Russian immigrant youths display a whole range of social profiles, from high achievers who excel in high school and enter good universities to marginal and alienated youths hanging out in the streets. Although no direct statistics are available, the stories told by my informants pointed to the higher numbers of troubled and maladjusted youths among those who came from Russia and Ukraine vs. those who spent some years in Israel. Another social correlate of poor adjustment included being raised by a hard-working single mother, with the resulting lack of supervision and support, and coming from working-class families of Russian or Ukrainian (as opposed to Jewish) ethnic origin. Although my informants (who were predominantly Jewish) mainly told stories of success about their own children, almost every one knew of their immigrant co-workers or neighbors whose children experienced problems and lived on the social and economic margins. On the other hand, many informants made a point that over time these coming-of-age problems have subsided. Compelled to make a living, most former troublemakers have settled in all kinds of semi-skilled jobs and some even improved their education at community colleges. Although time certainly has its healing power, there is clear room for culturally sensitive youth policies and specially targeted interventions that could ameliorate the initial experiences of young immigrants in the GTA and improve their chances for upward social mobility.

Transnational Identity and Lifestyle

In all of their new homelands, former Soviet-Jewish immigrants manifest multiple signs of transnational identity and lifestyle, feeling as part of a global Russian-speaking community stretching between the FSU, Israel, and the West. The main social glue connecting Jews, Russians, Ukrainians, and other former Soviets dispersed across the globe after the fall of communism is their affinity with the Russian language and culture, their common Soviet past, and recent emigration and readjustment in the host countries. The expressions of this grass-roots transnationalism are mainly found in the cultural and psychosocial, rather than economic and business, realm (see more on the transnational theory generally and transnational lifestyle of Russian Israelis in Remennick, 2002a). In my focus group discussions and the analysis of the Russian-language media I tried to follow the local signs of the universal phenomenon of fortification of ethnic diasporas and transnational speech communities (Guarnizo and Smith, 1998). Russians in Toronto are both producers and consumers of global Russian-language press and electronic media with headquarters in New York, Moscow, and Tel Aviv (exemplified by the *RTVi* TV channel catering for Russian-speakers in fifteen different countries). The Russian press in Toronto features multiple reprints and citations from similar publications in Russia, Israel, the U.S., and even Germany (which hosts a sizeable Russian-Jewish community since the 1990s). As a result of daily follow-up of current events in the FSU, Israel, and other branches of the international Russian-Jewish community, many immigrants (especially older ones) were more interested and updated on the global political and cultural issues than on the events inside GTA, Ontario, and Canada. Many of my informants perceived the internal politics and the news releases as uninteresting, uneventful or hard to understand due to their poor English. Another example of the transnational media embracing Canadian and global Russian-language community are bilingual web-portals catering to Russian immigrants in Canada, such as www.russiantoronto.com and www.torontovka.com (Russian ending *–vka* in the latter title referring to a village-like character of

Toronto's Russian enclave). These portals feature multiple rubrics of both universal interest (e.g., *Life in Toronto* and *Canadian News*) and of specific interest for the former Soviet immigrants (e.g., under the heading *Interest Clubs* we find *Brain Club, KVN*,[4] *Literature,* and *Camping*—the areas that capture their most common intellectual hobbies and favorite pastimes). Both sites also have dating services where Russian-speakers of any national origin looking for a Canadian partner can post their ads. Younger Russian immigrants in Toronto are ardent surfers in the Russian-language cyberspace (the so-called "ru.net") embracing thousands of websites maintained in Russia, Israel, the U.S., and other countries.

Many immigrants of all ages also kept close personal ties with their relatives, friends and former colleagues in the FSU, Israel and the U.S. With the advent of cheap and accessible communications (international calling cards, e-mail, relatively cheap air fares) more immigrants are involved in these ties and they become more regular. "I call my parents and friends in Israel a few times a week, as if we live in the same city. . . . It's amazing how cheap it has become. One can no longer refer to high expenses—if you wish to stay in touch with your folks in other countries you certainly can." This trend was more prominent among former residents of Israel, who were used to intense transnational connections and frequent travel, and among younger immigrants vs. older ones. To cite another focus group participant, David, in his early thirties, a former Israeli,

> I'd say over half of my friends still live in Israel, some in Moscow, and a few others are in the US. We e-mail and speak on the phone very often. One friend of mine who got rich during the high-tech boom and lives in a large house in Chicago offered his place for our reunion and we plan to get together from all the different countries around the New Year.

Nadia, a former Moscow resident in her mid-fifties, related,

> I love to travel and I could never do this living in the FSU, first because of political limitations and after Socialism due to the lack of money. Now I can visit so many countries where my friends and former colleagues live— France, Germany, Israel, Australia—at least I will stay there for free, and I can save for airfares. I am enjoying this immensely.

The majority of participants have traveled to their former countries of residence at least once since resettlement in Canada and received in their homes co-ethnic guests from the FSU, Israel, and other Western countries. A few informants were considering a joint business venture with their former co-workers or friends living in Israel or the FSU. "I think there is a good market here for some Israeli products in the Russian language—new books and literary magazines, some videos and DVDs related to Russian-Israeli topics, and such. Many folks I know who moved here from Israel still miss the country and would like to be more connected to it via these cultural products." A young woman from the Ukraine said, "I am about to open a small store selling Russian crafts and jewelry in Toronto. A friend of mine in Kiev has such business and she could broker for me very inexpensive and good stuff for sale. I hope it will be popular both among Russians and other Canadians—our tradition in the handcrafts is rather unique, you don't find such fine work in Canada."

Thus, many signs of what is called "transnationalism from below" (i.e., social and cultural ties on the individual level between co-ethnics across national borders [Guarnizo and Smith, 1998]) are apparent in the life of the Toronto Russian-Jewish community, rather similar to those found among Russian immigrants in Israel (Remennick, 2002a). In that respect, my observations are in disagreement with the recent findings by Morawska (2004) among Russian Jews in Philadelphia who displayed strong host-country orientations and few transnational engagements with either the FSU or Israel. This difference can be explained by the specific composition of former Soviet community in Toronto with a higher share of ethnically mixed families parts of which still live in the FSU, as well as strong cultural bonds many re-migrants had developed with Israel. Another possible explanation of greater involvement in transnational ties with co-ethnics among Toronto Russians is their relative marginalization in Canada: unlike their American counterparts, few of them can call themselves proud Canadians. Regardless of the reasons, though, Russian Toronto is certainly becoming an important isle on the expanding map of the Russian-speaking post-communist diaspora.

Conclusion

This qualitative study explored several aspects of the integration process of former Soviet immigrants (mainly of Jewish origin) who moved to Toronto during the 1990s either from the FSU or as secondary migrants from Israel. While some earlier studies were largely focused on the issues of identity transformation among Russian-speaking Jewish immigrants in Canada (Glikman, 1996; Basok and Brym, 2000; Anisef et al., 2002), this research addressed the more practical aspects of economic and social integration in the mainstream Canadian society, including the Jewish community. As was expected, my findings point to some tangible differences in the adaptation process between direct migrants from the FSU and those who had lived for several years in Israel. Although ethnographic data collected in this research do not allow for describing statistical patterns, some observations about these differences can still be offered to the reader.

Generally speaking, repeat migrants from Israel were better equipped for the Canadian experience of resettlement and socio-economic adjustment than were former citizens of the Soviet successor states. Although both groups were carriers of high human capital (which allowed them to gain enough points for the entry visa), former Israeli residents had had an important experience of adjustment to a Western-type labor market and developed some necessary skills for job search and self-promotion (better command of English, experience of job interviews, familiarity with advanced technologies, etc.). Immigrants from the FSU experienced a different type of chaotic socio-economic transition that may have enriched their occupational flexibility and general survival skills but did little to improve their odds for success in a western labor market. On the other hand, former Israelis often came to Canada with expectations of rapid professional success and economic prosperity they could not grasp in Israel and were disappointed by the tight regulation of their entry into most professions, the need to retrain or get licensed once again, and the generally slow pace of their rise to desirable living standards. Conversely, former Soviets were usually ready to start from the bottom regardless of their formal credentials, and this down-to-earth attitude was more conducive to both incremental economic mobility and psychosocial well-being. In both groups of immigrants, women have experienced greater employment problems due to their more culturally dependent and less demanded former occupations, but at the same time they were usually more ready for retraining and occupational change.

Although all former Soviets spoke of their great social and cultural distance from mainstream Canadian society (especially its white non-immigrant part), former Israelis found it less difficult to build bridges towards the established Jewish community due to their better familiarity with Judaism and Hebrew. Another social anchor for some of these newcomers (especially younger ones) became members of the Israeli community living in Toronto, with whom they shared attachment to Israel and Hebrew-based culture. Jewish immigrant youths often adopted the lifestyle features of cultural Judaism North-American style (bar/ bat mitzvah ceremonies, Jewish summer camps, trips to Israel) that helped them integrate among their Canadian Jewish peers. Direct arrivals from the FSU usually felt socially estranged from Canadian Jews, despite their readiness to utilize multiple social services offered by the established community. Some of them saw the lacunae in their Jewish identity as an unfortunate outcome of their life in the FSU and hoped that their children would be "better Jews" than they could be themselves.

In the family realm, both groups of newcomers often experienced marital and parenting conflicts as part of their adaptation process to the new economic and social reality. Meantime, their adolescent children were going through a double drama of immigration and coming of age in a new social setting. Immigrant youths had to struggle against parental authority in their wish to adopt the more liberal lifestyle of Canadian youth, and at the same time to face their inability to join the young Canadian mainstream as "others." Again, adolescents, who had already been through a similar adjustment drama in Israel, often managed their new role more aptly and made the transition faster than their former Soviet peers. Despite their difficult starting conditions, the majority of Russian immigrant youths have entered the upward mobility track by going to universities and colleges. Their grandparents, who moved to Canada via family sponsorship, are also getting adjusted to the life on the margins of the Canadian society, in the cultural and social framework of the Toronto's "Russian North." All three generations of Russian immigrants in the GTA manifest their interest in maintaining social and cultural ties with their co-ethnics in the FSU, in Israel and in other countries of post-communist Russian-speaking diaspora.

To conclude, the former Soviet immigrant community in Canada deserves more attention from social scholars and policymakers than it has received so far. This study points to important internal differentials in the integration process between immigrant generations and by the entry route. Direct arrivals from Russia, Ukraine, and other post-communist states usually have more scant personal resources and face higher barriers in their attempts to make it economically and integrate socially. Within this community, the 1.5-generation and the elders are especially vulnerable and could certainly benefit from specially tailored and culturally competent social services (such as labor market skills development, subsidized recreation and sports facilities, and matching newcomers with volunteer Canadian "siblings" and friends for companionship and guidance). In the absence of such services, the young and the old living in Russian enclaves have to rely solely on co-ethnic networks for information and support, which is not always sufficient and adequate. Another cost-effective form of assistance to former Soviets would be courses in leadership and civil organization that would help them lump together intellectual and financial resources to solve their common adjustment problems on their own. Finally, the experiences of skilled Russian-Jewish immigrants struggling to find their place on the Canadian labor market underscore the need to relax bureaucratic procedures for licensure and accreditation of foreign professionals on the federal and provincial levels—facilitating speedier integration of the newcomers and fuller utilization of their human capital, with the ensuing benefits for Canadian economy.

Notes

1. Immigration to Canada is regulated by the Immigration and Refugee Protection Act, the latest revision of which took effect on June 28, 2002 (see the overview on the website www.cic.gc.ca/english/irpa). The eligibility for independent economic immigration in the "skilled worker" category is assessed by means of the Point System, whereby the applicants and their adult family members are ascribed points for their age, education, occupation and work experience, proficiency in the state languages (English and French), close relatives living in Canada, and proof of authorized employment. Only those who accumulate a certain threshold sum of points can qualify for a visa. The criteria for assigning points (especially the list of in-demand occupations) are constantly revised in line with the needs of Canadian economy, with the goal of gaining maximum utility from international labor migration. Yet, in most provinces the recognition of foreign education and practice credentials is laborious and slow, comprehensive exams are often demanded for licensure, and for some professionals (e.g., physicians) it is virtually impossible to be licensed for practice in Canada without partial or full retraining. As a result, the much-praised "human capital" of the immigrants often remains untapped, and meantime most of them have to make a living by unskilled work. Some steps at the federal level have recently been taken to ease the accreditation process for professionals, but provinces have been slow

to adjust their legislation and practice, partly due to the resistance of the local professional associations (see the discussion of these issues on: www. promptinfo.ca).

2. In 1980, Soviet authorities stopped emigration of Jews (and anyone else) reflecting the end of the détente period and growing tension between the USSR and the West after the Soviet invasion of Afghanistan and the subsequent international boycott of the Moscow Olympics.

3. Many of these Russian-language cultural institutions cater to all former Soviet immigrants, regardless of their ethnic origin. Jews and non-Jews are as mixed socially in Toronto as they had been in their Soviet cities of origin. Separation occurs only in religious settings (for those few who practice religion): Jews go to synagogues and Jewish community centers, while Russians and Ukrainians attend their different churches. The dynamics of common ex-Soviet socialization vis-à-vis ethnic differences and the legacy of Slavic anti-Semitism shape the complex relations between Jews and non-Jews in their new immigrant locales.

4. KVN—transliterated acronym for *Klub Veselyh I Nahodchivyh* (The Club of the Merry and Savvy, in my free translation)—is a popular game in a form of stage show featuring competition of two teams, often representing universities or colleges. It includes both prepared and improvised jokes, stand-up, musical and dramatic vignettes, usually revolving around current events. The winning team (defined by the jury) must show the greatest artistic talent and the sense of humor; the KVN competitions are structured like sports events starting from the local teams and competitions and going all the way up to the national league. The latter are often broadcast on Russian-language TV networks, both in the FSU and in the post-communist diaspora countries, most of which have established their KVN leagues back in the 1990s. The first Canadian-Russian KVN team was established in 2001 and now there are three competing teams playing in the national league. For more information see: www.torotovka.com/kvn

6

The Promised Land in the Heart of Europe: Identity and Social Incorporation among Former Soviet Jews in Germany

"As for me, I emigrated to Western Europe. Germany was just the venue of entrance, not the goal in itself. With today's open borders, European citizens can live and work anywhere."—Berlin, August, 2003, interview with a forty-year-old man, electronic engineer from St. Petersburg

"You would be surprised to hear this, but I do feel that I have returned to my historic homeland. For Ashkenazi Jews, Germany, and especially the streets of Berlin, feel like home."—Berlin, October, 2005, interview with a fifty-seven-year-old man, architect from Moscow

"I rarely venture out of the house alone, with my poor German I feel uneasy among local residents, especially the youth. As a Jew you have to be cautious, you know . . . When I need to go downtown for shopping, I usually ask my husband or one of my Russian friends to go with me."
—Duisburg, September, 2003, interview with a sixty-eight-year-old former teacher, pensioner from Kiev

"Once a month or so, when I feel lonely and want to meet other Russian-speakers, I go to the central synagogue. There is a small group of us who meet there, although we don't really understand the religious service. . . . Sometimes local Jews offer us tea and cookies, or a beer in summer; before major holidays they give us small gifts . . . This is better than sitting alone in the four walls every day."—Krefeld, September, 2003, interview with a sixty-two-year-old man, former clerk from a small Ukrainian town

Jews in Postwar Germany and the Advent of "Russians"

After the Second World War, few people could imagine that Jews would ever again settle on German soil, establish roots and survive (Stern, 2001). The thriving Jewish community of Germany counted over 500,000 before the war, and only about 15,000 German Jews survived the Holocaust. Few of them intended to remain in Germany: most emigrated to Palestine/Israel, North America, and Australia. The core of postwar German Jewry was in fact formed by East European Jews (mostly from Poland, Romania, and Hungary) who found themselves as displaced persons in Germany and feared returning to their origin countries, as anti-Semitism there was even worse. Most found refuge in the American sector of the divided Germany and later became citizens of the Federal Republic, gradually reconstructing Jewish life and institutions among some 30,000 Jews. Traumatized and deeply insecure in the land of the perpetrators, for two postwar decades Jews sat on metaphorically packed suitcases hoping that they were in transit, on their way to a safer life elsewhere. Few Holocaust survivors told their children about horrors they had lived through, but the second generation was raised with a basic mistrust towards the surrounding majority, constantly negotiating their place in New Germany and alert for the signs of lingering anti-Semitism (Stern, 2001). Trying to keep a unified front vis-à-vis the state, the East European majority of the new Jewish community (*Judisches Gemeinde*, from now on JG) renounced Jewish pluralism and declared Orthodox Judaism as its only official denomination (most progressive congregations of native German Jews had left for the U.S.). The Central Council of Jews in Germany, and its long-standing Chairman Heinz Galinski, emerged as an umbrella organization representing Jewish associations of sixteen German states (*Lands*) and serving, in the eyes of the Christian population, the voice of all declared (i.e., paying church tax) Jews in Germany. Around the mid–1970s, several small non-Orthodox communities united into the Union of Progressive Jews in Germany, but their voice is not really heard in the German-Jewish dialogue. Despite their affiliation with the JG and declared Orthodoxy, the majority of Jews in Germany are not religious; they pay respect to some basic traditions and attend the synagogue on high holidays, but their lifestyle is mostly secular. Due to the advanced age of the postwar generation and its low fertility, the size of the German Jewish community has been shrinking over the years, standing at about 28,000 by the late 1980s (Stern, 2001; Peck, 2005).

To set the stage for the last Soviet-Jewish immigration in Germany, let me briefly describe the dynamics of mainstream German attitudes towards Jews (see more on that in Bodemann, 1996, Bensimon, 2003, and Peck, 2005). After decades of deep silence and repressed memories about the Nazi crimes, in the late 1970s the young generation of Germans discovered their terrible national past, influenced, among other events, by a powerful American television series *Holocaust* watched in virtually every German home in 1978–79 (in Susan Stern's words "what had not been accepted as reality before suddenly hit home"). From the early 1980s on, Holocaust education became an indispensable part of every school curriculum, the topic of multiple films, books, and intellectual discussions. The journey of deep collective guilt towards the Jews has been unwinding ever since, on both personal and institutional levels, recasting Jews as the country's most cherished minority. The historic pendulum has swung from traditional if hidden anti-Semitism to explicit philo-Semitism celebrating any thing and symbol Jewish, from klezmer music to bagel shops and Yiddish theater festivals. Multiple Holocaust memorials and museums opened across Germany (aside from the "natural" Holocaust sites such as former concentration camps). Public expression of anti-Jewish sentiments became obscene, and the new politically correct discourse by German politicians and intellectuals carefully avoided any negative messages about Jews both in the past and presently. On the global political arena, Germany has emerged as the most consistent supporter of Israel of all European nations; the German government has for decades been paying reparations and individual compensations to the Holocaust survivors and other victims of the war (e.g., those evacuated from Nazi-occupied territories), sending volunteers to Israeli kibbutzim and old age homes, and showing multiple other signs of good will.

Although a handful of Soviet refugees had managed to defect to West Berlin during the 1970 and early 1980s, more significant emigration of Soviet Jews to Germany started during the transition period surrounding German reunification. In the spirit of democratic reforms and old historic guilt, the last GDR government allowed several hundred Soviet tourists of Jewish origin to apply for asylum in Berlin. Soon the GDR became history, but the first government of united Germany decided to continue with the practice of granting asylum to

Soviet Jews, responding to pressure from the German-Jewish community leadership (and a personal promise made by Chancellor Kohl to JG Chairman Galinski) and not wishing to compromise its international reputation on the minefield of the German-Jewish relations. Granting former Soviet Jews a status of special refugees met with the double goal of paying the historic debt for wartime grievances and replenishing the country's small and aging Jewish community. Starting as a trickle, the flow of "special refugees" (*Kontingentfluchtlinge*) soon became a wide river: the proportion of Jewish émigrés who opted for Germany out of their total emigrant flow from the FSU increased from 8 percent in 1992–3 to 26 percent in 1998 (Tolts, 2004).

The German government found itself in a harsh dilemma, facing the rising tide of Soviet-Jewish immigration juxtaposed with severe Israeli reproaches for its open-door policy toward Soviet Jews. According to the Zionist ethos, seeking "refuge" in Germany is an oxymoron: there can be no Jewish refugees as long as Israel exists as a sovereign state, and the only place where Jews can live in dignity. The conflicting value is of course the freedom of choice: no one, not even Israel, can tell Soviet Jews where to live. Germany's wish to replenish its Jewish community and improve its international image by supporting Jewish immigrants was also seen as legitimate by some Israeli politicians. Yet, throughout the 1990s the issue of Soviet-Jewish influx into Germany put a significant strain on Israeli-German relations (Primor, 2003). The conflict culminated in the early 2000s, when the number of Russian Jews entering Germany significantly exceeded the number of olim to Israel (in 2003, 15,442 and 12,383, respectively, with the trend continued in 2004–5). In the light of the mounting criticism that Germany lures Russian Jews from their historic homeland and skyrocketing costs of their support (as about 85 percent rely fully or partly on welfare), the rules of refugee approval are being revised now. During 2005, a heated debate between German immigration authorities and JG leaders revolved around new criteria for the Jewish refugee status. The proposal defended by the state could drastically curb the influx of ex-Soviet Jews, as only those younger than forty-five, with a working knowledge of German, and an ability to find gainful employment in Germany (so-called positive integration potential) would be granted visas. The need to demonstrate proof of Jewish identity beyond passport registration or birth certificate (which can be forged) is negotiated between immigration authorities and the JG, frustrated by the high numbers of non-Jews among the newcomers. At the same time the Union of Progressive Jews in Germany resist the strictly Halachic criterion for establishing Jewish identity of the newcomers and is ready to embrace the half-Jews on the paternal side too. It seems that the final version of the new law will reflect a compromise between all these conflicting ideological and economic pressures; by late 2005 when I am writing these lines, the age limit of forty-five has already been revoked to accommodate older Holocaust survivors, and the test of German would be demanded only from younger applicants. In any case, after January 2006, the rules of entry will become stricter and some 27,000 of applicants awaiting their visas may need to reapply (Axelrod, 2005).

According to the data provided by the German authorities, nearly 200,000 of former Soviet Jews have migrated to Germany after 1989, mainly resettling in the wealthier Western Lands (Jasper, 2005). Berlin, especially its former Western sector, hosted a large share of the arrivals (an estimated 40,000). The process of resettlement of former Soviet Jews was managed by local chapters of the JG and funded by the federal government, Lands, and municipalities in par with the numbers of the new arrivals in every city and town. In the early 1990s, the immigrants could resettle in any German city of their choice, but from the mid–1990s the policy changed so that the burden of supporting the newcomers would be more evenly distributed between eastern and westerns Lands and different municipalities. The approved refugees were now allocated to the towns and communities that were ready to absorb them and they had to stay there for at least two to three years, if they wished to receive welfare aid. As opposed to the ethnic German repatriates—*Aussiedler*—who received German citizenship soon upon arrival, Jewish refugees were entitled only to a residence permit, and could apply for the citizenship after eight years of life in Germany. The definition of who is a Jew for the purpose of a refugee visa adopted by the German immigration authorities in the early 1990s was rather loose and also included half-Jews and their next of kin, not demanding proofs of Jewish origin beyond registration of "nationality" in Soviet documents. On the other hand, the Central Council of Jews in Germany and local communities adopted a stringent religious definition, accepting in its ranks only those born of a Jewish mother. As former Soviet Jews had experienced decades of assimilation and mixed marriage, a large number of new arrivals were not recognized as Jews and could not join the local JG. Due to these conflicting definitions, in the early 2000s the actual numbers of refugees who entered Germany via Jewish channel (according to the Foreign Office statistics) was roughly twice as large as the number registered by the Central Jewish Council as new members—95,000 and 190,000 respectively (Dietz et al., 2002; Schoeps, 2003).

Although the reader can find a detailed profile of Soviet Jewry in chapter 1, I will highlight several aspects relevant to the following discussion. Ashkenazi Jews under Soviet rule have gradually lost connection with their religion and language (Yiddish), moved in great numbers from small Jewish towns of the former Pale of Settlement to the major urban centers of the USSR, and manifested increasing rates of intermarriage from one generation to the next, so that today about 65 percent of Jews are married to non-Jews and among Jewish youth only about 25 percent have two Jewish parents (Tolts, 2003). As a result of their strong drive for upward social mobility (and despite state anti-Semitism), over 60 percent of former Soviet Jews received postsecondary education and worked in professional and white-collar occupations. Many of them have achieved relatively high professional status, with resulting economic and social gains. Most Soviet Jews of the older generation lost relatives in ghettos and in mass executions of Jews during the Nazi occupation of the western parts of the USSR in 1941–43; the death toll among Jews who lived on Soviet territory during the war is estimated at 1.5—2.0 million. Thousands of Jewish women and children survived the war thanks to the organized evacuation of citizens from Moscow and Leningrad when Hitler's armies were approaching those cities. Tens of thousands of Jewish men were recruited to the Soviet Army and fought the Nazis, were killed or wounded along with other soldiers; many received medals and high Soviet honors for courage (Altshuler, 1998). Thus the collective memory of the war and hatred for the Nazis (and lingering distrust of Germans as a nation) form an important part of the Soviet-Jewish identity, especially for the older generations. The indirect repercussions of this historic animosity spilled over to the younger generations of former Soviets via popular culture channels: literature and cinema depicting the Nazi atrocities, suffering of the populace, the heroic struggle of the Soviet Army, the partisans, and Soviet secret agents working in the heart of Hitler's political machine (Merridale, 1999).

The postwar relations between USSR and the two German states were complex and uneven, but after reunification they evolved into growing economic cooperation and political alliance, pragmatism taking over old historic accounts. Yet, the history of the Great War is still a factor coloring the bilateral relations and collective memory of both nations (Merridale, 1999; Fussell, 2000; Levy and Sznaider, 2002). It is easy to see from this brief account that Russian, Ukrainian, and other former Soviet Jews had rather mixed feelings toward Germany and Germans, and for many moving there as immigrants (formally as refugees, an even more socially loaded status) comprised a clear cognitive dissonance. In this respect, Jews were different from some 2.5 million Russian-speaking ethnic Germans (Aussiedler)—return immigrants who repatriated to Germany during the same period, driven by the promise of a better future in their historic homeland. Before turning to the context of social integration of Russian Jews in Germany, let me offer a brief reflection on the issues of ethnicity generally and Jewish ethnic identity specifically.

Jewish Identity and Immigration

The research described below was of an exploratory nature and did not seek to endorse or refute any specific theoretical constructs. Rather, my goal was to stimulate the initial empirical insights for further research and theoretical reflections by providing an ethnographic narrative account or "thick description" (Geertz, 1973) of the social encounter between Jewish immigrants and various segments of German society. However, the concept of ethnic identity is a useful lens for viewing my empirical data. There is little doubt that ethnicity and ethnic identity are socially constructed, context-bound, and constantly reshaped by both personal circumstances and historic processes. Despite this contingency, the main pillars of ethnic identity include language, cultural symbols (embodied in music, literature, cuisine, costume, etc.) and collective memory, with the adjacent mythology (Bell, 2003). Jewish ethnicity is even more complex, given thousands of years of Diaspora existence and cultural assimilation in various hosting societies, which along with secularization and dilution by mixed marriage turns current Jewish identity into both virtual and vanishing (Dershowitz, 1997; Sharot, 1998). Indeed, the Jewish identity of former Soviet and other East-European Jews has mainly been preserved through the twentieth century thanks to three forces: institutional and popular anti-Semitism with the ensuing limitations for Jews in education and careers, as well as exposure to prejudice and insults; the collective memory of the Holocaust; and the establishment of Israel, with the subsequent anti-Israeli propaganda across Eastern bloc countries (Remennick, 1998).

Being Jewish is defined by former Soviets as an ethnic rather than religious affiliation, as over 90 percent of them are secular, speak Russian as mother tongue, and know little about Judaism. Historically, both the persecution of Jews under Nazi regime and the 1950 Law of Return regulating immigration to Israel stem from the ethnic definition of Jews rather than religious observance, reflecting the predominantly secular lifestyle of most Jews in Europe and in the USSR after the 1920s. The ethnic concept of Jewishness has been further reinforced by the late twentieth-century immigration criteria adopted by Israel and Western countries (for Jewish refugees) based on ancestry and official documents stating '*natsionalnost*' (equivalent of ethnic origin in Russian) (Joppke and Rosenheik, 2002). Similar to other Diaspora Jews, ethnic identity of former Soviet Jews is split or two-tiered including both Jewish and Russian/Soviet components; they can underscore one or the other as more salient, depending on the context. Educated Soviet Jews living in large cities were both active creators and consumers of Russian culture and saw themselves as belonging to its very core, as many key cultural figures of the twentieth century—poets, composers, artists, journalists, etc.—were Jewish. Some preservation of the Jewish traditions, language, and religiosity was only found among older small-town Jews from Western parts of the former Pale of Settlement and in the small Jewish communities of the Caucasus and Central Asia.

Immigration transforms ethnic identity in a complex way. Migration itself is often caused by the wish to join one's ethnic group in its historic homeland, but reverse causality is also common: ethnic roots may be "rediscovered" with the emergence of opportunity of return migration to a wealthier country. Yet, upon resettlement the expressions of ethnicity are again reshaped in the light of majority-minority relations in the receiving society. In fact, immigrant ethnic identity is always situational and often reactive: it is crystallized and inflated as a reaction to discrimination or social exclusion by the hegemonic majority, and even more so in reaction to ethnic violence (Fearon and Laitin, 2000; Capo Zmegac, 2005). Immigrants typically express their ethnic and social identity via using their native language and reproducing various forms of their "authentic" cultural life in the new country (ethnic press, clubs and societies, language classes for the children, etc.), which is often perceived by the mainstream as their lack of interest in integration and further enhances majority-minority frictions (Roosen, 1989; Tong et al., 1999; Remennick, 2004c).

The ethnic consciousness of Russian Jews in Germany is augmented by the collective memory of the Holocaust and present-day expressions of anti-Semitism and anti-immigrant sentiment in the right-wing media and political movements (Levy and Weiss, 2002). The main venue of ethnic mobilization for all Jews in Germany is organized community (JG) that is called to settle the complex relations between this small but special minority (comprising slightly over 0.1 percent of the total population) and the German nation at large. At the same time, the identity dilemma of Soviet Jews in Germany must be rather intense, revolving around the eternal vexing question—to be or not to be Jewish? On the one hand, Jewish migrants have to pay their moral tribute to the JG that facilitated their immigration and helped them resettle, yet on the other being openly Jewish in Germany may be still seen by many as too risky and stirring conflict with the hosts. Hence, many former Soviets (especially those who are only partly Jewish) may choose to distance themselves from anything Jewish and rely instead on the Russian/Ukrainian/ Soviet component of their origins and identity.

Social Research on Russian Jews in Germany

Several German scholars took issue with the social integration of post–1989 Soviet-Jewish immigrants, often in comparison with a much larger Aussiedler population (over 2.5 million) that largely has rural or small-town origin and lower rates of postsecondary education. Most published studies were of a statistical or survey type, examining patterns of employment, social dependence, language proficiency, and other related issues (Schoeps et al., 1999; Dietz, 2000; Dietz et al., 2002; Nauck, 2001; Jasper, 2005). The 2002 volume edited by Daniel Levy and Yifat Weiss explored comparative aspects of citizenship among immigrants to Germany and Israel. Several anthropologists, including both Germans (e.g., Doomernik, 1997; Kapphan, 2000) and former Soviets living in Germany (e.g., Darieva, 2000) looked into the issues of immigrant press, cultural institutions, and adaptation strategies. More recently, several young researchers of Russian-Israeli origin conducted studies comparing the modes of social integration of Russian Jews in Israel and in Germany (Elias, 2003, 2005; Bernstein, 2004; Cohen and Kogan, 2005). While integration of ethnic Germans is understood by German scholars and policymakers rather straightforwardly as socio-economic incorporation in the nation's mainstream, integration of Jewish immigrants usually implies a double meaning: an inclusion in the existing Jewish communities (JG) and in the German society and culture generally. There is little doubt that both facets of social insertion have been rife with problems for both the immigrants and the hosts (Tress, 1997; Jasper and Vogt, 2000).

First and foremost, despite their high levels of education and professional experience, Jews have poor chances to find qualified work on the German market due to three main reasons: incompatibility of credentials and skills gained in the FSU with the local standards (and difficulty of their formal recognition); poor command of the German language (only 15 percent of respondents in a survey by Schoeps et al. (1999) self-rated their proficiency as good or excellent); and recession and structural changes in the German economy since the mid–1990s curbing the demand for workers in traditional skilled occupations (engineering, medicine, and others) and causing high unemployment. Augmenting these structural problems, the German labor market is very rigid due to strict bureaucratic regulations of all sectors (especially the public one), high unionization, tenured jobs, and low share of contract workers. German citizenship is required for most public sector jobs (including teaching), which barred Jewish refugees from getting these jobs even if their qualifications had been recognized. As a result, well over half of Jewish immigrants of working age have been unemployed for most of the years they spent in Germany. In similar circumstances, educated immigrants in North America and in Israel were compelled to lower their ambitions and take jobs in the semi-skilled or service sector, but Russian Jews in Germany did not have to sweep the streets or toil in old age homes for a minimal wage. Their main source of livelihood has been the welfare benefit (*Sozialhilfe*), modest by German standards[1] but rather generous by the Soviet ones, especially because it covers not only basic living expenses but also housing and medical care. Of those educated immigrants who rejected life on welfare, only some 20 percent could return to their original occupations, usually after years of diligent search and learning German (Cohen and Kogan, 2005).

A minority ventured into small businesses of their own, risky and complicated in light of legal hurdles for non-citizens, lack of capital and networks, and poor knowledge of the local market. The majority of small entrepreneurs targeted their co-ethnics, mainly in retail sales of "Russian" products, tours of artists and performers, and servicing other needs of the Russian community. The ethnic German returnees faced similar challenges on the labor market, although their status as citizens improved their chances to find permanent jobs. It is estimated that at any given time during the 1990s between 40 percent and 50 percent of all working-age immigrants from the FSU were receiving Sozialhilfe as their major source of livelihood; another 20 percent received unemployment benefit after losing their temporary jobs. Thus, despite a wide gap in their pre-migration education and occupational record, economic mobility of both Jews and Aussiedler has been similarly contained. Alternatively, one can argue that both groups of former Soviets have been similarly "spoiled" by the generosity of the German public aid system that allowed them to avoid manual labor,[2] either investing time in the search of proper job or becoming permanent "welfare junkies" (Guseinov, 1997; Schoeps et al., 1999; Jasper, 2005).

Another factor precluding the improvement of German and social inclusion is the formation of residential ethnic enclaves in most German cities and towns, whereby whole buildings and neighborhoods are gradually inhabited by Russian-speaking immigrants forming informal social networks of their own (exemplified by Charlottenburg area of Berlin jokingly called by veteran Berliners Charlottengrad). Although many middle-aged and older Jewish migrants have enough spare time (being unemployed or retired) and opportunities for studying German in free or subsidized classes, relatively few of them are engaged in regular study, probably because of low economic motivation, that is, slim chances for upward occupational mobility. At the same time, the Jewish immigrant children and youths grasp the German language and adopt elements of everyday German culture much more rapidly than their parents via schooling and other youth activities. Soon upon resettlement, they start speaking a mixture of Russian and German and over time move to pure German while keeping Russian mainly for "kitchen use." Many adult immigrants, too, mix German idioms and bureaucratic vernacular (e.g., related to welfare rules and benefits) into their Russian speech, Russify German words, but seldom learn to speak fluent German (Guseinov, 1997; Gladilina and

Brovkine, 2005). German proficiency combined with the traditional Jewish values of hard work and excellence in education facilitate mass entry of young Jewish immigrants to elite gymnasiums and universities thus promising the expedient social mobility of the 1.5 generation (Schoeps et al, 1999). This is in contrast to young Aussiedler, who often go into vocational training and remain bound in the blue-collar workforce like their parents (Dietz, 2000).

The second tier of the integration process—the insertion of new members in the local Jewish communities (JG)—caused multiple problems of growth due to the rapid expansion of Jewish ranks both locally and nationally, from about 28,000 in the late 1980s to about 95,000 today. Since the JG assumed the key role in the organization of resettlement of former Soviet Jews, they had to redefine and expand their functions from mainly religious congregations to civic associations delivering social services to the newcomers (German classes, housing aid, running old age homes and kindergartens, vocational and social counseling, and more). Although federal and municipal budgets allocated to the JG have also grown (in par with the numbers of new members), they were insufficient for hiring paid staff and meeting many other practical needs ensuing from these new functions (Jasper and Vogt, 2000). Before the influx of ex-Soviet Jews, most local JG in Germany counted from several hundred members in smaller towns to several thousand in larger cities, most being of advanced age. The incorporation of newly arrived Jews has drastically changed the demographic and political balance in most JG, rejuvenating them on one hand but redressing power relations on the other. Even in larger JG, such as those of Berlin, Frankfurt, and Munich, new Russian-speaking members now form over half of the total membership, while in many small towns (especially in the eastern Lands) JG almost totally consist of "Russians." At the same time, the organizational power and financial control of the JG still belong to the old timers, who vehemently oppose the entry of the newcomers to the elective councils, arguing that they are unequipped to deal with the tasks at hand, such as maintaining good relations with the mainstream German politicians, and lobbying for more funds. Yet, the voting power of the newcomers gradually shifts the balance towards their greater representation, and it is clear that the veterans will have to give in and share both their privileges and duties. Many old timers feel disenfranchised and alienated by this new challenge, resist the dominance of the Russian language at the meetings and the proliferation of Russian cultural activities sponsored by the JG (Stern, 2001; Jasper and Vogt, 2000; Jasper, 2005).

Another serious cause of tension between the old and new (Russian-speaking) members of the JG is the latter's lack of interest in religious learning and activities. Although most veteran members of the JG had been only moderately observant themselves, now they felt the need to juxtapose themselves against secular "Russians" and underscore their belonging to Orthodox Judaism. Complying with the expectations of the hosts, during the initial months after joining the JG some immigrants took classes in Hebrew and Jewish tradition and participated in religious services, but over time they tended to diminish or quit these activities and distance themselves from the JG. Many others simply never tried to join the local chapters of the JG. In fact, the continuous attendance of social and religious events is mainly typical of older Soviet Jews, while younger members show reluctance to reshape their Jewish identity along religious lines. As a result, new members are reproducing the age-related activity pattern that had existed in the JG before their arrival, thus calling into question the very purpose of their recruitment—rejuvenation of membership and ensuring the community's future (Jasper and Vogt, 2000; Dietz et al., 2002). The vital balance among Jews living in Germany after a decade or Russian immigration was even worse than before its onset: in 2001, deaths exceeded births by 873,000 (990,000 and 117,000, respectively). Between 1990 and 2001 the annual number of births to couples including at least one Jew did not increase, but mortality continued to soar (2.3 times increase) due to the old age structure of both the veteran and newly added JG members (Tolts, 2005).

An important background factor shaping the integration process of former Soviet immigrants is public atmosphere surrounding their arrival and the attitudes of Germans towards immigrants generally, former Soviets as a group, and Jews specifically. The total number of immigrants (or foreigners—*Auslanders*) in Germany is about 6.5 million (without Aussiedler, who are citizens and hence not counted as foreigners) and around nine million with Aussiedler, in the total population of 82 million (i.e., about 8 percent and 11 percent, respectively). Although the majority of Germans show high tolerance of other cultures and languages, the right wing and anti-immigrant sentiment has been on the rise in Germany, as elsewhere in Europe, in recent decades. This trend is especially clear in its former East German Lands, where some 17 percent express extremist views and vote for the radical right (vs. some 12 percent in the West), with the slogans such as "Germany for the Germans." On a daily basis, many Germans cannot distinguish between the two ethnic groups of former Soviet immigrants (Aussiedler and Jews) and perceive them on the basis of the spoken language, appearance, and conduct as "Russians" or "Soviets." On the other hand, the mainstream public discourse on Jews, German-Jewish relations, and the Holocaust is cautious and politically correct, underscoring the current pluralistic and democratic face of the New Germany. During the 1990s, German media extensively covered the arrival of Russian Jews, who "became the offering of choice on Germany's multi-cultural platter" (Jasper and Vogt, 2000). Yet, after the initial enthusiasm about return of Jews to German lands, the discussions shifted focus to the contested issues such as doubtful Jewish identity of many newcomers (and ensuing conflicts within the JG), their high unemployment and economic dependence on German taxpayer. This unflattering portrayal in the media further increased the alienation between the immigrants and the hosts (Schoeps et al., 1999).

Drawing on this background, my current study addressed several related questions about the integration process of former Soviet Jews in Germany. First, I wanted to explore identity dilemmas experienced by adult Russian Jews as a result of their resettlement in Germany, in light of historic legacies and current relations with the members of the mainstream German public. Specifically, I was interested in the perceived identity conflict as it surfaced while answering the uneasy question: Why Germany and not Israel? Secondly, I explored the ways in which Jewish immigrants perceive and present their relations with their principal counterparts in the hosting German society (the JG, Aussiedler, and mainstream Germans), as well as their own place and prospects in the new country. As my focus was on the subjective experiences of the cross-cultural encounter and their interpretation by the immigrants (and in some cases also the hosts), the best way to elicit this kind of data was qualitative ethnographic study based on observations and semi-structured personal interviews.

Participants and Methods

The study was informed by the qualitative research paradigm and drew on my observations and in-depth interviews with the immigrants and staff or activists of the local JG conducted in August-September 2003 and then revisited in October 2005. In order to compile a more comprehensive picture of the way Russian Jews adjust to life in Germany, I made field visits to six cities of different size with significant shares of new arrivals in the local JG—Berlin, Bonn, Dortmund/ Duisburg, Krefeld, Dusseldorf, and Munich. In every city, I met with JG representatives, who often provided the initial list of contacts among the immigrants, who further referred me to their friends and acquaintances, that is, the so-called snowballing method was used for the recruitment of informants. I conducted most interviews in Russian— my own native language. Two of the JG officials who spoke only German were interviewed with the help of interpreters. All interviews were tape recorded, transcribed verbatim, and analyzed by repeated scanning for the key topical and conceptual categories using the codebook method (Crabtree and Miller, 1992). Besides interviews, I also read the Russian immigrant press, and attended community meetings and religious services in the synagogues, taking field notes. Finally, in parts of this discussion I incorporated some findings of field research by the young Israeli sociologists Nelly Elias and Julia Bernstein.

The researcher-informant relationship is of paramount importance in gathering qualitative data, as it directly affects the quality and depth of the ensuing narratives. The studies of ethnic relations in multiethnic or border locations (Roosen, 1989; Galasinska and Galasinski, 2003) point to a wide gap between the public and private discursive styles people use while discussing sensitive topics of the "Other," depending on the context and identities of the speakers. Private exchange is usually less censored and may be fraught with negative stereotyping and referrals to the "Other" as a threat. My own location as a researcher was rather beneficial: on the one hand, I was perceived by the Jewish immigrants as a co-ethnic and spoke in their mother tongue, but on the other, I do not live in Germany, represent German official institutions, or belong to the immigrant social networks. As a result, I was not seen as a threat or a rival, and most informants were pleased to confide their innermost feelings and thoughts with me. After living several years in Europe, most former Soviets got used to censoring their speech and relating to sensitive topics in a relatively politically correct manner. Yet, with me they felt free to speak their mind on their own terms and in a more spontaneous language too, something they would hardly do with a German researcher. Although some of the remarks I heard during the interviews are rather straightforward and opinionated, I am conveying these accounts uncensored, changing only the names in the quotations.

Altogether I have interviewed eight representatives of the Jewish communities who work with the recent arrivals and forty-two immigrants who arrived in Germany after 1990 and have lived there for at least three years. Among these immigrants, eighteen were men and twenty-four women, their ages were between twenty-five and sixty-five; all but four had academic degrees from the USSR. The majority of interviewees were middle-aged people, because younger immigrants were usually busy at work or studies and were generally less available for interviews. However, many informants told me about the adjustment process of their children. Most informants came to Germany from Russia or Ukraine and have resided in the country for twelve years or more (30 percent), seven to eleven years (35 percent), and three to six years (35 percent). At the time of the study, less than half of all informants (43 percent) were working or had worked previously in Germany. The majority received social welfare aid as their principle or supplementary source of income.

Findings

Below, I present and discuss my chief findings, illustrating them with typical quotations from the interviewees. All names of informants have been changed to ensure anonymity, but other essential details (age, occupation) have been preserved.

Identity Dilemmas

The attitudes of informants towards their Jewish origin and possible Jewish lifestyle in Germany varied reflecting their own ethnic origin (i.e., having one or two Jewish parents), that of their spouse, and pre-migration proximity to Jewish life. Out of forty-two informants, about 30 percent had non-Jewish spouses and 40 percent had only one Jewish parent. Generally, all informants but three described themselves as secular and most have kept only a minor and symbolic (if any) attachment to Jewish traditions and lifestyle for at least two generations. Given this ethno-cultural ambiguity, for most informants identifying as Jewish or Russian/Ukrainian/ Soviet was a matter of choice rather than necessity. Several informants expressed their unease about the very rout of entry to Germany on a "Jewish ticket" and the definition of their status in Germany as refugees. Eugene (forty-eight) said "Everybody knows that this refugee status is just a pretense, we are in fact economic migrants from the deteriorating post-Soviet countries. State anti-Semitism in Russia was no longer there by the early 1990s, and popular dislike of Jews is probably the same everywhere, including Germany. German government offered us a comfortable shelter and we were happy to accept it."

Maya (fifty-one) added along the same lines: "Soviet Jews failed to live up to the expectations of the Germans: they wanted to 'import' real Jews, who observe the religious rules and contribute to the Jewish community life, but in fact received a bunch of regular immigrants who are eager to use German welfare and comforts of life in Europe." Vladimir (sixty-two): "I am rather torn between the two instincts: on the one hand, I came here as a Jew and must show some commitment to the Jewish causes, but on the other I have never lived as a Jew in Kiev and it's too late to start it here in my age. I feel rather foreign in the synagogue, and Jewish holidays do not interest me too much, but I still have to participate in this 'game' in order to justify my living here." Alexander (forty-four): "Who am I? I see myself as a member of Russian intelligentsia of a Jewish descent. My language and culture are Russian, the only Jewish trait I have is the record in my Soviet passport, and endless troubles that ensued from that during Soviet times. Thank God, Germany is part of Europe and a free country, so I can identify as I wish; I'd rather be a Russian immigrant than a Jewish one." David, forty-three: "For Germans, all speakers of Russian are the same, and I am no better or worse for them than any Aussiedler. And you know what—I don't mind being seen as Russian, or Soviet, it's unwise to underscore your Jewish origins in this country."

At the same time, some middle aged and older informants, in my own and in Elias (2005) sample, stressed that in Germany they had far greater chances to develop their Jewish identity and participate in different Jewish activities than they had in Russia or Ukraine. The majority of informants regularly read the Russian-Jewish newspaper *Evreiskaya Gazeta* published in Berlin, and some also contributed materials to it or wrote letters to the editors. On the other hand, for some informants their growing involvement with Jewish matters was an unintended byproduct of their search for new social networks and meaningful modes of spending their time (for those many who did not work), which most of them found within various frameworks established by the local JG—such as various cultural societies, Russian libraries, and German classes. Many older informants had apprehensions of explicit manifestations of their Jewish identity outside the "safe Jewish territory" such as the synagogue, Jewish clubs or their own homes; they refrained from participation in street festivals on Hanukkah or Purim and men never wore skullcaps (*kipa*) in public, even if they put them on during synagogue services. Some found it difficult to believe in German benevolence and were acutely aware of anti-immigrant sentiment generally. Thus, Gregory (sixty-one) from Elias (2005) sample said,

> I think it is not clever to speak Russian in public: one should remember that five percent of the German population are right-wing extremists. That's four million people! A man who sits on the bus next to me could be a neo-Nazi . . . . If they would see anybody who looks like an Arab or black, they could beat him. But if you are a white, they wouldn't know that you are a foreigner until you start talking. Recently there was a bomb here, in the Turks' neighborhood. Now the attack is against the Turks, next time it could be Jews.

Apprehensions of Anti-Semitism

The last quotation brings forward another facet of Russian-Jewish identity in Germany—tacit or explicit apprehension of the anti-Jewish sentiments on the part of native Germans. Jacob, fifty-three, said,

> You know, every German I met always made a point of his or her neutral or friendly attitude towards Jews; they have been conditioned from young age to atone for the sins of their fathers and censor their speech. But for some reason I don't believe them. If you scratch deep down, every German dislikes Jews to this or that extent. Today they repress and conceal this dislike, but tomorrow things can change drastically, especially as more Jews will become visible in the economy, politics, and the media.

Lydia, sixty, offered this along similar lines:

> You can see yourself that I don't look very Jewish. When I talk with the natives (which doesn't happen often!) I never say that I am Jewish from the "special refugee contingent," I say I am Russian, or come from the

FSU. I am never sure about how a simple German woman from a super-market or hairdresser's would react to meeting a Jew.

When I hear on the news about yet another neo-Nazi attack on a syna-gogue or a Jewish cemetery I shudder and feel really miserable and help-less—the past terrors my family had lived through come back to me, and I start brooding on the same damned question: what I am doing here in Germany as a Jew? But then I remind myself that in Russia the neo-Nazis and skinheads are even more numerous and violent, so this is the world we have to live in anyway (Galina, seventy-two).

I have noticed that older women like myself [i.e., Russian-Jewish immi-grants] seldom venture to go out into the city for some business or shop-ping alone, they always seek company of one or more other women. Maybe we do not realize it, but we feel insecure alone in the streets full of Germans, including these hideous youth groups in black leather and metal all over their bodies. Not knowing the language and being a Jewish woman is a double risk (Fania, sixty-four).

Several informants mentioned that the mere fact that every Jewish site in the city (community centers, synagogues, Jewish kindergartens, etc.) had to be safeguarded by armed police forces signaled the possi-bility of attack at any time. By way of paradox, the presence of police reinforced both tension and a sense of security.

Conversely, many other informants, mostly younger and working ones (who are more familiar with their German peers), believed that middle and younger generations of Germans were generally open-minded and free of racist feelings or prejudice towards minorities, including Jews. Some of them said they would like to befriend native Germans but feel embarrassed by their imperfect language. "I think it's all in the past. Younger Germans were raised like other Europeans in the atmosphere of tolerance and democracy. There are some right-wing and extremist elements here, but I think that their share is not higher than in other parts of Europe" (Sasha, thirty-eight, software designer). "My being of Russian-Jewish origin is irrelevant: We live in a cosmopolitan world, Europe is full of immigrants and visitors from every corner of the globe, and I am one of them. The important things are to learn German well, to find a good job, to find your own place in this society! You are judged by your achievements, and not by your origin or the blood running in your veins" (Michael, twenty-nine, chemist). Thus, the opinions ranged from the most apprehensive of potential anti-Semitism among Germans (largely among older im-migrants) to the most relaxed, denying any special problem for Jews, and assuming the amicability and meritocracy of the hosts (expressed by younger newcomers more involved with German society). It is interesting that those prone to denial of anti-Semitism among modern-day Germans often made reference to Germany as part of Europe, or the EU, or global Western society, while those, who believed that negative sentiments towards the Jews were still in place, spoke of Germany as a special country with unique history, without referring to a wider geopolitical framework. Yet other Jewish immigrants were concerned by their close proximity to Turkish residents, with whom they often shared subsidized housing projects. "Muslims are a greater threat to the Jews than are native Germans. Some young Turks turn to fundamental Islam these days and you don't know what they can do to us one day. It may be a ticking bomb here as elsewhere in Europe" (Eddy, fifty-five).

The Loss of Professional Identity and Welfare Dependence

A large part of identity crisis experienced by older Jewish immi-grants reflected their loss of social status and professional identity as a result of resettlement. Soviet-trained professionals often perceived their occupational role as the core of their self-image and self-esteem (Epstein and Kheimets, 2000). During the Soviet era, occupational change was rare among educated citizens: most remained in the same occupational track for life and very few embarked on drastic shifts in their careers. Hence the need to redefine one's professional identity on the new market and to find alternative ways of using one's skills and talents is a tightrope for most middle-aged ex-Soviet professionals. Many infor-mants who could not get their credentials recognized and/or find skilled work in Germany were nevertheless not ready to downgrade to manual work for low pay and preferred to remain for years on welfare. "I prefer to remain a former research scientist to becoming a current cleaner or caregiver for the elderly. I have modest needs and can survive on the unemployment benefit. This way, I am kind of frozen in my past and avoid a degrading experience" (Oleg, fifty-one). Dur-ing the last year or so the availability of "free lunch" at the expense of German taxpayers has been shrinking, and local labor offices adopt a new policy towards chronic welfare recipients—sending them to pub-lic works such as street cleaning for a symbolic payment (one to three

Euros per hour) if they wish to keep their welfare checks. Most educated immigrants are resentful of this new policy interpreting it as an attack on their dignity and civil rights, although some admitted that they understood its economic rationale.

Those who kept trying to find skilled jobs faced growing insecurity as to their actual ability to work under new conditions. "My papers say, 'N.N., Professor of Chemical Technology.' Ha! Big Deal! It's *there* that I was a professor, and *here* I am dog shit!"—was the punch line offered by one informant. The feeling of social displacement makes it difficult for educated immigrants to find proper ways of referring to Germans of ostensibly similar social status. Mark, forty-seven, a metallurgic engineer, recounted,

I once went for a job interview in an engineering firm in my old line of work, after being unemployed for over two years. Although the man who interviewed me was of middle rank, younger, and probably less experienced than me, I felt highly uncomfortable when he tried to examine my past work and knowledge. On one hand, I am almost sure that my professional expertise was greater than his, but on the other, I had a hard time proving it . . . all because of my humble immigrant condition, lack of current employment, and limited German or English. So I am no longer sure who I am and what I have to offer as a worker.

Anatoly, fifty-nine, a former surgeon: "I feel so useless, and, indeed, a nobody here in Germany—just another recipient of social benefits from good German taxpayers. In Odessa, we lived very modestly but at least I knew who I was, and people respected me and sought my advice. Here I became a shade of my former self." Several middle-aged informants who were unemployed for several years spoke about their need to utilize lots of spare time by finding some new hobbies, taking long walks, watching German television to learn the language, and reading. "I used to work like a horse all my life and now I feel so irrelevant and lost . . . . I invent things to do around the house, I help my teenage son with the math lessons, I go shopping with my wife . . . but the days are still too long for me. This forced leisure is demoralizing . . . . If I can't find engineering work in the near future, I will go and surrender . . . I'll take any job they will offer." (Igor, forty-eight, former power plant engineer). A good summary of these reflections was offered by Lydia (forty-nine), a former energy-systems engineer from St. Petersburg:

Living in Germany is good for the young, who adapt quickly, and for the old, who don't need to adapt and can just enjoy relative safety and welfare. The middle generation, that is, the people who interrupted their careers in Russia and hoped to regain them in Germany, are the ones who lost it all. It is very hard to make a decent living with the kinds of jobs that are available to people with unrecognized credentials and poor German. Many guys I know—doctors, musicians, scientists—have tried and failed, ending up among the recipients of welfare. Some see it as normal, others as degrading, but few have a choice of rejecting this option.

Limited proficiency in German was another common predicament damaging immigrants' identity and dignity. "Being unable to express yourself in a meaningful way is so humiliating! You feel like a halfwit, or a retarded child . . . muteness makes you professionally disabled. Because of this language problem I stopped even trying to find qualified work." (Vera, forty-eight, former social worker). "Germans are not really tolerant of accents and mistakes in German that immigrants make. When you come for a job interview, the boss is not sympathetic to the fact that you are new in the country and never spoke German before. If you language is less than fluent, you are automatically discarded, regardless of your qualifications and experience" (Rina, thirty-nine, a former school teacher, looking for work in a kindergarten). Some others expressed an opinion that regardless of their professional skills and German proficiency former Soviet immigrants have slim chances for good jobs even in the private sector, and the public offices are off limits for them as foreigners. "Regardless of how good you are, they would always prefer a German candidate, these days there is no lack of educated Germans without jobs. I realized that my attempts to apply for engineering openings are pointless, so I stopped altogether. Now I work in a printing shop and even this is temporary" (Josef, forty).

Altogether in my sub-sample of twenty-four working age informants only six were employed in skilled jobs, one as a dentist and the rest as programmers and electronic engineers in the largest German company, Siemens. All five immigrated in the early 1990s, managed to complete retraining courses sponsored by Siemens in the days of high-tech boom, and subsequently moved into the company's jobs. Siemens employees were highly satisfied with their work conditions and pay, but were usually alienated from their German co-workers. Many informants pointed out that all the later arrivals were disadvantaged vis-à-vis earlier ones as high-tech and IT jobs in Germany ran out by the late 1990s and many immigrants (as well as locals) lost their jobs in the early 2000s when the bubble burst. Since then, even a software design degree—formerly a secure meal ticket—does not promise solid income in today's Germany. Thirteen out of twenty-four informants were living on Sozialhilfe, five received unemployment, and six were working.

Many older informants believed that there is nothing wrong with being supported for years by the money of German taxpayers, seeing this aid as a form of historic retribution for the Nazi crimes. "I am not feeling guilty living on welfare. Firstly, if German bureaucracy doesn't recognize my professional experience as a doctor, then it is responsible for the fact that I cannot make a living with my profession. I am not ready to clean the streets for the same money I get as a living allowance. And I'd tell you more: I think they should pay the historic price for destroying Jewish lives not so many years ago. If they want Jews to come back and live here, they should pay" (Herman, fifty-two, a former physician). "Germans killed most of my relatives during the war, so they should at list compensate for their crimes by making my old age more comfortable. I see this pension as a kind of historic due" (Rosa, seventy-seven). Quite a few middle-aged and older recipients of welfare, free housing, and medical care have voiced an argument (apparently rather popular in the Jewish immigrant circles) that the funds allocated for their support actually come from outside Germany (e.g., special accounts in Swiss banks, the U.S., global Jewish organizations, and such) rather than from German taxpayers and therefore can be accepted without moral qualms. Another version of this myth asserts that there is a secret agreement between Israel and Germany that the latter accommodates Jewish immigrants in exchange for writing off some of the remaining reparations or other remittances to Israel. In either case, the bottom line is—they (the Germans) owe us this financial aid, and may even get some revenues from hosting Soviet Jews. Many former Soviets find it hard to believe that the benefits they get for free are hard to come by for rank-and-file working Germans, who pay the full price for their health insurance, housing, transportation, and subsidize the idle immigrants by their income taxes approaching 40–45 percent.

Thus, the combination of ambiguous ethnic identity, lack of trust in the alleged German tolerance of Jews, the loss of professional identity, economic dependence, and linguistic handicap created multiple points of ambivalence among Russian-Jewish immigrants as to their new identity and place in German society. To mitigate their basic insecurity and keep some moral integrity, the immigrants create and disseminate a "home ideology" of entitlement. On a daily level, most of them try to get all possible benefits from the German welfare bureaucracy showing great savvy in navigating the system, manipulating their caseworkers, withholding information on their additional income (e.g., Soviet pensions)—in brief, making good use of their skills acquired under state socialism and still handy under German social democracy.[3] When they meet with refusals and the emerging limitations in the system of free handouts, they deploy their most powerful weapon—sweeping accusations of anti-Semitism, a harsh blow for politicians and officials at all levels and a stigma for most native Germans that immediately puts them in a defensive mode and often leads to concessions.

"Idealists Headed for Israel, Pragmatics Chose Europe"

Given my identity as an Israeli scholar of Russian-Jewish descent interested in post-communist immigrants, many interviews came to touch on the vexing question of the destination country. Some informants mentioned in passing or even made a point of their reasons for choosing Germany rather than Israel, and I have asked some others myself by the end of the interview (unless they clearly avoided discussing this topic). The answers largely depended on age and the strength of informants' Jewish identity. Nikolai, forty-four, a former journalist, said, "I emigrated to Europe, not so much to Germany. Europe is becoming one entity with open borders, A European passport allows you to live and work anywhere in the region. . . . Why not Israel? I can't really imagine myself living in the Middle East—it's a different civilization, very far from my own. I grew up as a Russian intelligentsia member, which means being European in your outlook, values, interests . . . hence my place is in Europe."

Diana, thirty-six: " Israel was out of the question. To move from one troubled country to another, from chaos and instability in Russia to the war and terror in Israel? What would be the point in moving there? Besides their security problems, I have heard from my friends that there is no work for educated immigrants anymore, all the places are taken. What would I do there with my diploma as a music teacher? . . . On the other hand, neither do I practice my profession here in Germany. But at least it's quiet and you can ride the buses without fear."

Felix, sixty-five: "My wife and I had thought about Israel in the mid 1990s, but decided against it mainly because of a very hot climate. My wife has hypertension and I have heart disease . . . . Moderate European climate is better for older folks like us. It's not that we were seduced by higher pensions and free flats! I swear, health is the main reason why we moved to Germany."

Marina, forty-three: "We did not consider Israel because I have two sons who would be recruited in the military right away. I am not so much of a Jewish patriot to sacrifice my children to the endless war with the Arabs. I have also heard that veteran Israelis dislike Russian immigrants because they are too educated and took many qualified jobs that Israelis wanted for themselves, so the Zionist welcome is a myth."

A few informants opined that their moving to Germany was actually beneficial for Israel from a geopolitical standpoint. For example, Galina, sixty-seven, a former engineer and patent expert from St. Petersburg, said: "I think that Israel already has too many people and too little place to settle. It does not need more unemployed immigrants, especially older folks like myself. Living in Europe or America, we can lobby for Israeli causes, send money for Israeli projects, and influence public opinion in favor of Israel. This is more useful for the Jewish state than our physical presence there." A few others expressed their feelings of cultural and historic affinity with Germany, making them feel at home in the historic cradle of Ashkenazi Jewry. "My historic motherland is not in Palestine; ancient Jewish history is all too far from me. My actual roots are in Europe, where many generations of Ashkenazi Jews spoke Yiddish and German, advanced in German society and gradually became its elite. We all know what happened to them in the middle of the last century, but this cannot erase earlier historic legacies," reflected Eugene, a fifty-seven-year-old Moscow architect and journalist.

The image of Israel in the minds of my informants was skewed towards negative features such as rampant ethnic violence, insecurity, harsh climate, unemployment, and unwelcoming reception of the immigrants. Most informants drew on the images of Israel they saw on television (which focus on the military conflict and terror attacks and almost never show the images of everyday life, nature, cultural events, etc.), but were at the same time aware of the negative bias that the media coverage inevitably entails. Many had relatives and friends in Israel and stayed in touch with them by means of telephone and e-mail; fewer informants had actually visited Israel and had some first-hand impressions of the country, usually more positive if not excited. Regardless of their actual familiarity with Israel and Israelis, most informants felt tangible discomfort when confronted with the question, *Why not in Israel?*, and many went into a defensive mode while giving explanations (probably augmented by my own identity as Israeli researcher). Yuri (forty), a sound technician working at a Berlin radio station, expressed the opinion probably shared by many of his fellows:

> You know, there are idealists and there are pragmatics. Then there are more Jewish Jews and less Jewish ones. . . . Take myself: I was never interested in Jewish issues and would've probably totally ignored this birthmark (i.e., being born a Jew) if not for state anti-Semitism in the FSU. People who have moved to Israel are either idealists or have a strong link to their Jewish side, that's why they are ready to compromise their well-being for the Jewish cause. Pragmatics like me do not believe in the Zionist ideals and we opted for the civilized and yes! wealthy—Europe. I don't see any fault with the human wish to find a better place for yourself and your children.

Informants with a stronger Jewish identity were even more defensive in their attempt to justify their immigration to Germany instead of Israel. Alex, fifty-three, a television operator in Cologne, said,

> Not a day passes by without my asking myself—what the hell am I doing here? I found myself in Germany mainly for family reasons (my ex-wife insisted on Germany, not Israel), and now that we got divorced I am free to move wherever I wish. My fears about Israel are not related to Arab suicide bombers or political turmoil, they are about learning Hebrew and adapting to this new culture and work environment. I have invested so much energy in learning German and finding work, so it's scary to start again from scratch. But I am sure that I'll move there one day.

Mira, fifty, a JG activist in Munich:

> I am a convinced Zionist and have been active in the Jewish community for many years, both before emigration and in Germany. Most of my family lives in Israel and I visited there several times. I feel rather guilty about having to stay in Germany, and this is mainly because of my own

and my husband's poor health—a hot climate would kill us in no time. So I do what I can for the Jewish causes: teach classes on the Jewish tradition, raise money for Israel, host Israeli kids on vacation in my home. . . . This makes me feel better about myself.

There was one informant, an Orthodox religious man in his mid-forties and a teacher of Hebrew, who perceived his living in Germany as a national and religious mission of reinstating Jewish community there. "I see this as a moral debt to my German-Jewish forefathers who perished in the Holocaust. The German state gave us a chance to make a comeback to this part of Europe and it was my duty to oblige. In several decades Germany will have a small but thriving community of believing Jews." Perhaps in a weaker form, a similar idea was expressed by a few other informants, who saw their living in Germany as returning historical dues to the Holocaust victims and as a proof of vitality and resilience of the Jewish people. "Zionists say: You are winning by building Jewish state and making it thrive. I agree, but add: You can also prove your worth and win as a Jew by repopulating Western Europe where you had once been exterminated" (Evgeny, forty-eight). Similar motives of a mission fulfilled by the Jews who chose to live in Germany surfaced in the narratives quoted in the ethnographies by Elias (2005) and Bernstein (2004). Like Galina cited above, some informants referred to the vital role that Diaspora Jewry plays in support of Israel by providing political lobby and economic aid. Some informants noted that they often donate money to Israeli causes despite their modest income and participate in pro-Israeli demonstrations at critical moments of the Arab-Israeli conflict.

In her fieldwork with the Russian-Jewish elders who participated in the activities of the Nash Dom (Our Home) club in Cologne, Nelly Elias as a young Russian-Israeli researcher was showered with expressions of love and commitment to Israel as their "spiritual home." One woman, an eighty-nine-year-old Holocaust survivor, told her,

We live in Germany and we do not complain. Our living conditions are good; Germany treats us well. But it is a foreign country and it always will be. Jews will always be strangers here. What else do we have? Ukraine? I have no nostalgia for Ukraine, and no family there anymore. Actually, the strongest feeling that I have today for any country is for Israel. We live in Germany, but our hearts are in Israel. It is a homeland of all Jews and it is our homeland too.

Another elderly man told her how happy he was to visit Israel a few years ago, how he explored every stone and every building in Jerusalem, feeling elated and moved.

"I felt for the first time that I am at home. I felt completely free. I wasn't afraid that somebody would insult me because I am a Jew." Thus, although the Israeli identity of the researcher probably augmented the enthusiasm of the informants, some older Jews living in Germany as "displaced persons" who lost their old home in the FSU and never gained a new one in Germany, do imagine Israel as their alternative home or potential shelter, which gives them a sense of connection and security. Speaking about Israeli politics, all informants expressed strong right-wing opinions, insisting on hard-line suppression of Palestinian protest movements and against any territorial compromises. The majority strongly resented the pro-Palestinian stance they ascribed to most European countries in the Arab-Israeli conflict and lamented anti-Israeli biases of the European mass media. These informants relied mainly on Israeli sources (reprinted by the German-Jewish press) and Jewish websites in the Russian language for the coverage of Israeli politics and society (Elias, 2005).

"New Russian Jews" in the Social Landscape of Germany

I will now turn to social relations between Russian-Jewish newcomers and their main counterparts during the resettlement process—veteran members of the Jewish community (JG), ethnic Germans from the FSU (Aussiedler), and other Germans belonging to the host majority. These social relations form the context of the immigrants' new lives, whereby their ethnic identity is expressed, reinforced, or reshaped. It is in these interactions that they have to decide if they want to be perceived and treated as Jews, or rather switch to their alternative identity as Russian/Soviet immigrants.

Tense Relations within Jewish Communities. While in some Lands the newcomers need to get in touch with the local JG upon arrival to receive local residence permits and housing subsidies, the subsequent extent of participation in JG activities is voluntary, and for most younger immigrants it decreases over time. Many immigrants, who are not recognized as Jews by the religious criteria (i.e., those having a Jewish father, not mother), or those having non-Jewish spouses are often annoyed by the JG's policy to check the "purity" of the Jewish blood among the new applicants. All of them must submit their birth certificates and other documents for inspection, sometimes also undergo a long interview, in order to prove their Jewish origin. Veronica (fifty-two) said,

> My husband is Russian, so I was accepted and he wasn't. This means he cannot attend German classes or receive any other aid from the community, for which our daughter and myself are entitled as Jews. Of course he feels excluded! For example, when we come to a concert or lecture subsidized by the JG, I pay a symbolic low fee and he has to pay the full cost of the ticket. Since we are close and don't want anyone to split our relationship, we just stopped going there altogether.

Some informants told even more emotionally charged stories of suspicion and maltreatment by JG staff of the new members, whose Jewish-ness caused even the slightest doubt. Tanya (forty-five) depicted how her elderly parents were denied membership and had to appeal twice because their Soviet documents issued in the mid–1920s did not state their *natsionalnost* (there were several years in the early Soviet history when this paragraph was omitted from personal documents, to be latter reinstated).

> My parents are as Jewish as it gets, it's enough to look at their faces, their names, to hear their Yiddish accent. . . . Yet, this social worker at the JG (herself a former Soviet) was fixed only of their papers, not on them as people. . . . My old and disabled father even suggested to open his pants for her to see that he is circumcised . . . what a shame! After this prolonged agony, all our family has decided that we don't want to have anything is common with these bureaucrats, and we never crossed their doorstep ever since. Never mind that we have lost all possible subsidies and services.

Several informants defined these practices as openly racist and totally unacceptable in an enlightened European country. "Have we escaped anti-Semites in the Ukraine in order to be abused here by our fellow Jews? The German community had known in advance that Jews from the FSU have had mixed marriages for decades and many spouses are non-Jewish. Why even let us immigrate if we were not kosher enough for them?" (Leonid, forty-six). "The JG folks check our Jewishness four generations back like the Nazis had done back in the 1930s and 1940s. Shouldn't they be more sensitive and reasonable, after all the hideous history of racism and blood purity assessments? In my view, if you identify willingly as a Jew you *are* a Jew, no matter who your mother was" (Boris, thirty-nine). Some informants said that, due to these repeated humiliations, they felt greater hostility towards the established German Jews and JG officials than towards native Germans, with whom they have little contact and hence no basis for conflicts over identity or privileges. After unpleasant initial encounters with the JG officials, many Jews decided to quit any contact with the Jewish networks and live in Germany on ethnically neutral immigrant terms. It is estimated that even among Halachic Jews entitled to membership in JG, less than 60 percent pay the fees and participate in any Jewish activities. The membership is almost universal among the retired Russian Jews (whose fees are waved or very low) and is below 40 percent among younger Jewish immigrants who work or study and have to pay relatively high membership fees (*Evreiskaya Gazeta*, September 2005).

Apparently, the JG officials have a different perspective on this matter, arguing that by abandoning the religious definition of a Jew and accepting everyone in its ranks, the JG will soon lose its role and meaning as a religious Jewish congregation and will evolve into yet another social welfare office or an ethnic society. They realized that mixed couples of whom only one partner is entitled to join the JG often reject membership altogether, but still could not compromise. They also asserted that many Russian immigrants are trying to get their way into the JG solely to partake in all the material benefits that it bestows on its members, especially the elected representatives. "It is known that over one-third of the current immigration wave are not really Jewish, they are just seeking a better life in Germany, often using false identities or forged papers. How can we screen these people out without checking who they are?" (Hilda, social worker). She later added: "These Russian Jews are a great disappointment for us. They come with demands and want to grab as much as possible of our free services, but few of them are ready to offer their time and work in return. It's hard to find volunteers for our projects, they only look for paid jobs . . . the very idea of voluntary work for common causes is alien to them."

In response to this common allegation, several immigrant informants opined that it was unfair to expect that recent immigrants would do unpaid work. "Veteran members are established and wealthy Germans and we are immigrants from an impoverished country, and we have totally different resources and abilities" (Vera, fifty-four). "The old JG members and staff want us to work for community causes without pay, but how can we do this having no decent income? They see the world through their own lens of affluence and solid footing in Germany, while we are still nobody here and have to struggle for every Euro. Of course we seek jobs, not volunteering. If they could switch shoes with us for a few days, they would have done the same" (Maria, forty-three). Lydia, fifty-six, said,

> We need a few years to get some foothold in Germany before we start giving rather than receiving services. It's not true that Russian Jews do not volunteer: I know several psychologists and a lawyer who started helping here soon after getting their German licenses. Of course not every one is ready to invest their time with no direct remuneration; but then you can benefit from your community activism in many other ways, for example via meeting new people, building connections and such. . . . It may be even more important than money.

Other informants have pointed out that the very way of being Jewish is different for the veterans and the novices. "Although we are all Jews, but we are far from equals. Being Jews for us means something different than for them, it has little to do with synagogue attendance or keeping kosher. It's more about striving for education and a better future for our children, keeping some cultural standards, reading books. . . . Perhaps the only common ground for us is the lingering threat of anti-Semitic attacks, both in Russia and in Germany" (Victor, forty-one). Several informants said that they tried to take active part in the JG but were repelled by the internal power fights. Victor, forty-seven:

> We have become a majority in most local communities, but still have almost no representation in the elective organs. This is both because old timers still control the elections and because Russian Jews have little solidarity and don't vote for each other . . . . You know, a Bukhara Jew won't vote for an Ashkenazi one, and both would vote against a Georgian Jew—that kind of petty old prejudice. I know some activists who take part in these political fights that boil down to greater access to money and control . . . but for me it is repulsive. The more I know about the political kitchen of the JG, the less I want to take any part in it.

Time and again I heard the opinion that Russian Jews were driven away from the Jewish community life by the conflict-ridden atmosphere in the local JGs, power struggles between old and new elected council members, quarrels over budget allocation and privileges. One middle-aged couple, both volunteers at a Russian library affiliated with a local synagogue, told about the repeated attempts of a senior member of the Jewish Council to control the modest funds donated by the library members for purchase of new books.

This man, a former Communist bureaucrat who turned into a kosher Jew, could not forego his control even over these peanuts. When we opposed his demand to forward him all the donations (several hundred Euros altogether), he raised hell at the Council's meeting accusing us of buying secular books instead of Judaic literature. What a hypocrite! The budgets allocated by the State and Land to the JG are rather substantial, and former Soviet functionaries want to stay close to the feeder, as we used to say in Russia. It is hard to believe they do not gain personal financial benefits from their Gemeinde activism.

Some informants of mixed ethnicity said that the selective policy of the JG compelled them to look for spiritual life and self-expression as Jews in progressive congregations, which accept also half-Jews on the paternal side and non-Jewish spouses. "Our Reform temple is small and has no public funding from the state like the Orthodox Gemeinde, we only have what we raise among our members. So we do not have social workers or free excursions, but instead we have warm welcome for everyone who wants to be Jewish. We can hold religious services in Russian and women sit together with men. Our local members offer free language consultations, they invite us, newcomers, to their homes— in brief we are treated as equals, not suspects. I will never set foot in the Orthodox Gemeinde again" (Genia, fifty-four, musician). Yet others found comfort and social support in the Christian congregations, like a fifty-year-old woman from the Elias (2005) sample:

You know, it is much more difficult to be accepted here in the Gemeinde than to receive a visa to Germany. They check your documents, your parents' names, and if you don't seem Jewish enough, then you won't be accepted. . . . It hurts very much. And another problem is that these rules separate between family members: parents and children, husbands and wives. There is no such problem in Christianity. They would accept anyone who is looking for God.

On the positive side, JG premises and funds in the large cities have been sometimes conducive to creative activities initiated by former Soviet professionals, giving an outlet for their intellectual resources and energy in the context of unemployment and much free time to spare. One such example is the Scientific Society established by older Jewish immigrants with academic backgrounds (many of them with advanced degrees) in affiliation with the JG of former East Berlin, which holds its meetings in the premises of the Old Synagogue on Oranienburger Strasse. The Society holds a series of scientific seminars where its members present and discuss their research projects (mostly belonging to the Soviet past, but some on-going), publishes an annual collection of working papers in Russian and German, and runs individual and group consultations for Russian-Jewish youths with scientific talent or, conversely, having problems with math, physics, chemistry, and biology at high school. This society numbers over 100 members and allows older immigrant intellectuals to remain active and transfer their expertise and enthusiasm to the young generation, improving its chances for success in the contemporary knowledge-based economy. Other cultural activities adjacent to the JG centers include chess clubs, libraries, clubs for Russian-Jewish students and events featuring writers, poets, and musicians from Germany, the FSU, and elsewhere—admittedly, all of them Russian-based and not really conducive to social integration into the German mainstream.

Thus, the relations between the veterans and the newcomers in the JG are constructed around a give-and-take discourse reflecting inequality in their status and personal resources. The conflicts around membership and rights often reflect the clash between the ethnic and religious definitions of Judaism: the compromised reputation of Russian Jews and their blocked access to power in the community are often justified by their detachment from religion. Some newcomers also strive to gain more control over the JG's far from negligible funds and other resources, posing as ardent proponents of Jewish purity and barring the access for their "suspect" co-ethnics. Feeling mistreated, immigrants of mixed origin or married to non-Jews leave the formal Jewish networks altogether or else seek support in more liberal religious frameworks. At the same time, JG-sponsored activities comprise an important social and cultural outlet for the older segment of the immigrants, allowing them to lead meaningful lives and contribute to the cultural continuity in the younger generation of Russian speakers.

Russian Jews, Aussiedler, and Germany's "Russian Street." As is often the case with "ethnic return migrants," both groups of former Soviets in Germany found themselves at a wide social and cultural distance from the segments of the mainstream society that brokered and sponsored their migration: Russian Germans are as far from native Germans as Russian Jews are from German Jews. In this sense, they share the destiny and marginal social status of all foreigners in German lands. They are also perceived by the native Germans as members of a single group coming from Russland—social misfits speaking broken German and career welfare recipients—although these attitudes seldom find their way into politically correct mainstream discourse (Darieva, 2000). However insulting such an indiscriminate stance may seem to both Aussiedler (who often think of themselves as proud Germans) and Jews (who deem themselves intellectuals whose education and finesse are unappreciated by the hosts), in many ways they find themselves in the same camp. In Berlin and a few other major cities, the "Russian Street" is becoming increasingly diverse, including, besides Aussiedler and the Jews, also Russian, Ukrainian, and Kazakh spouses of these ethnic migrants (reflecting high rates of intermarriage), legal and illegal guest workers, Russian spouses of native Germans, and students from the FSU. In Berlin—the chief hub of Russian life in Germany, the Russian-speaking population is estimated at 200,000 (Gladilina and Brovkine, 2005). All segments of the former Soviet enclave strive to make it economically in a difficult economic climate of the former Eastern Lands, with unemployment rates in Berlin being twice the national average and approaching 20 percent. Due to their marginal social location, most Russian speakers often cross paths with another large minority living in Berlin—Turkish guest workers (over 300,000), three generations of whom make an indispensable part of the German urban landscape.

Of all the former Soviets, Aussiedler typically try to pass as legitimate Germans and improve their German proficiency. As their declared aspiration is to join the mainstream, they did not invest into formal community networks of their own. Conversely, Jews who openly assert their alienation from German society and define themselves as "invited guests of the German welfare state" (Guseinov, 2005) have actively created formal and informal ethnic networks and institutions, such as cultural centers, libraries, kindergartens, after-school enrichment activities for children, senior clubs—all of them functioning in

Russian, often drawing on the JG premises and budgets, and catering mainly to Russian Jews, with the growing inclusion of other "Russians." In the words of one informant, a middle-aged teacher living on welfare, "I can only survive in Berlin thanks to our rich cultural life in Russian: I never miss new Russian films, go to all interesting tour shows from Russia, take books in the Russian library . . . this is my oxygen, otherwise the city would be a desert for me." The so-called Russkii Dom (Russian House) in East Berlin, a huge community center established back in Soviet times and affiliated with the Russian Embassy, serves as a hub of cultural activities, Russian language classes for the children, adult classes of German, travel with Russian guides, and other activities targeting all former Soviets alike.

Russian Jews have also been more active than Germans in entrepreneurial activities: among sixty small businesses run by former Soviets in Berlin in the late 1990s (book and grocery stores, disco and music bars, car garages, real estate and tourist agencies, etc.) only a handful belonged to Aussiedler and the rest were owned by Russian or Ukrainian Jews. Most Russian stores are located in Charlottenburg area of West Berlin, and are frequented by Russian Berliners from all parts of the city, who travel there to buy familiar groceries, new books and CDs/DVDs from Russia. This can be explained by either greater historic proneness of Jews to entrepreneurial initiative or their higher occupational ambitions at the outset and unwillingness to take semi-skilled or manual jobs the way Aussiedler did. Having failed to find relevant professional posts but rejecting welfare-only lifestyle, some Jews switched to small business as a viable alternative saving their face and dignity. Although most lacked prior business experience, they could rely on their broad social networks in Germany and FSU for business partnerships and supplies, as well as on Homo Sovieticus type business smarts and cheap "Russian" labor available in German cities (Kapphan, 2000). As Russian Germans are still very much on the "Russian side" of the street but lack community networks of their own, they often come to use the services developed by Russian Jews (Darieva, 2000; Elias, 2003).

Endowed with educational advantages and journalistic experience, Jewish immigrants also initiated the establishment of the Russian-language media (several newspapers, radio and a TV station) in Berlin and other large cities (Dusseldorf, Hamburg, Munich) that caters to the information needs of all Russian-speakers in these cities. All the major German newspapers in Russian (*Evreiskaya Gazeta, Evropa-Express*, and even *Russkii Berlin* catering mainly to Aussiedler) have Jewish editors, producers, and core staff journalists. Moreover, the key media figures of the "Russian street" serve as de facto mediators or ethnic brokers vis-à-vis the native German majority, shaping the attitudes and behaviors of the newcomers and offering "cultural interpretation" of the Russian/Soviet mentality and lifestyle to the hosts, whenever misunderstanding or conflicts arise. Germany's most popular "Russian" writer—Vladimir Kaminer—has also emerged from the Jewish ranks. Born in Moscow in 1967, Kaminer moved to Berlin in 1990 and by 2004 has published three volumes of hilarious prose in German, depicting the encounter between former Soviet immigrants with German society and bureaucracy through the eyes of a newcomer. As the most able and funny cultural interpreter of Homo Sovieticus for the broad German public, Kaminer soon became a household name for many German readers, his books staying on bestseller lists for a few years.

Despite their constant mingling in different corners of Germany's "Russian street," the relations between Russian Germans and Jews are far from idyllic. The different social background of these groups has already been mentioned: the Jews are educated urban professionals or white-collar workers and the Germans are predominantly small-town or rural residents with blue-collar occupations (the respective shares of academic degree holders among them are roughly 65 percent and 25 percent). In Germany, Aussiedler as return migrants receive full citizenship with all the ensuing entitlements soon upon arrival, while the Jews only get residence permit, have no voting rights and fewer legal privileges. For instance, Aussiedler with academic degrees from Soviet universities and colleges are entitled by law to recognition as having comparable German degrees while applying for jobs or setting wage level, while the Jews with similar Soviet degrees are not entitled for their automatic recognition. This puts Jews in an unfavorable position vs. Aussiedler while competing for positions on the German job market (Jasper and Vogt, 2000). On the other hand, as a result of the federal resettlement policy, more Aussiedler than the Jews found themselves in the economically less developed Eastern lands with higher unemployment and poorer housing quality (e.g., living in former Soviet military townships). In most other respects, though, the starting conditions for economic and social integration of the two groups were rather similar: both were entitled for subsidized housing and free German instruction, welfare benefits, and health care insurance. German proficiency among Aussiedler had been preserved mainly among the older generation (who speak an obsolete German dialect of their forefathers barely comprehensible for today's Germans), while for younger Soviet Germans Russian had been their first and only language (Dietz, 2000). Hence the linguistic challenges were also rather similar. Both groups had high levels of unemployment in the initial years, but the pace of occupational mobility (i.e., finding jobs commensurate with one's education and prior experience) were higher among the Jews due to their higher human capital. More Jews are working in private companies (where citizenship is not required), whereas more Aussiedler got jobs in the public sector, with lower wages but greater job security (Jasper, 2005).

The two communities of former Soviets have developed a certain animosity toward one another and kept residential and social distance from the very outset of their lives in Germany. Both parties have had sad memories and historic claims about each other's conduct in Soviet times: older Germans remember too well the Jewish names of the NKVD/KGB officers who often organized their persecution and deportations from the Ukraine and Volga region (where Russian Germans once had their Autonomous Republic) to Siberia and Kazakhstan during the war with Nazi Germany. The Jews, in turn, accuse ethnic Germans of intrinsic anti-Semitism and generally consider them rough and uncultured. Aussiedler youth is often portrayed by the mainstream German media as inclined to heavy drinking, violence, and petty crime—the sad legacy of their coming of age in the deteriorating Soviet empire (Elias, 2003). Some Aussiedler are annoyed by the economic success of Russian-Jewish businesses and their own need to rely on "Jewish" services in many everyday matters. The current relations between the two communities of Soviet migrants are exacerbated by the explicitly anti-Semitic tone and messages of the ethnic press and a few cultural societies established by Russian Germans. These messages reinforce the antagonism between young Russian and Jewish immigrants, who prefer separate hangouts and entertainment venues in Berlin and in other cities (Elias, 2003).

Matvei, a sixty-year-old freelance journalist from a Russian-Jewish newspaper, reflected,

Russian Germans who came in the 1990s strongly contribute to the new wave of anti-Semitism via their newspapers, radio talk shows, and all kinds of cultural venues like youth clubs. They say and write things unimaginable in the mainstream German media: deny the Holocaust or accuse Jews themselves in what had happened to them; implicate Jews in all the crimes of the Stalin's regime; circulate obsolete ideas of the global Jewish plot, etc. After you read such materials, how can you keep speaking to these people?

Some informants expressed strong negative opinions about their German neighbors: "I declined good housing offers several times just because these buildings were populated by Aussiedler families. Why? Because they are anti-Semites and primitive rural people. Look at their youth—they don't study, don't work, just hang around in public gardens and drink beer. It's important for me to have good neighbors and not to be scared entering the house lobby at night" (Tamara, fifty-three). Others were more moderate and fair, but still had their reservations: "I don't have anything against Aussiedler, and I disagree with the stereotype that they are rude, uneducated, and criminal. I have met many of them here in Germany and I know that most are decent, hard-working people trying to take a fresh start, just like us. But I also know that Jews and Germans are indeed very different in their everyday culture and mentality. So I won't be happy if my daughter decided to marry a German guy . . . " (Pavel, forty-eight).

Unfortunately, I could not juxtapose these attitudes with those of Aussiedler themselves, since none of several persons I approached agreed to be interviewed by an Israeli researcher, and even if they did they would probably have refrained from expressing their true thoughts and feelings because of my identity. I have found indirect confirmation of anti-Semitic attitudes among Aussiedler from reading a bilingual newspaper, several magazines and websites published by Russian Germans in Berlin, Frankfurt, and Dresden, which were indeed full of tacit and explicit allegations against the Jews (and Israel) in many articles, memoirs, and political commentaries. Hence, the current former Soviet immigrant community in Germany has become a scene where mutual historical animosity between ethnic Germans and Jews is augmented by the ongoing economic competition for scarce jobs, and old motifs are replayed in new forms using modern electronic media. On the other hand, being part of the same speech community (Russian), immigrants of Jewish and German origin come together in different social venues (e.g., taking their children to the same classes of Russian and drama groups in Berlin's Russian House; studying together in German gymnasiums and universities). Over time, mutual prejudice is often attenuated by personal contact (especially between social peers, i.e., educated Aussiedler and Jews) and I have also heard stories of inter-group friendship and dating; thus a young Jewish woman in Bonn told me that she often takes her Aussiedler girlfriend to the dance party at the synagogue and nobody there objects to her presence.

In the Land of Former Nemesis: Relations with Native Germans

Gasan Guseinov, a Moscow linguist and journalist living in Germany from 1990, wrote the following in his 1997 article about the patterns of speech behavior of Russian immigrants:

> Most Jewish refugees are convinced that they can never penetrate the invisible wall between themselves and the surrounding German society. In this sense, the Russian-Jewish community is living on a self-constructed cultural isle: in their perception, Germany and Germans are not their next-door neighbors but a boundless foreign ocean, from which an occasional ship may sometimes visit their quarters. It is certainly quite ominous that the only Russian literary magazine established by the New Émigrés of the 1990s is called *Ostrov* (The Isle). This title resonates with a paradoxical sense of superiority expressed by many Russian Jews vis-à-vis other immigrant groups, and sometimes over native Germans as well.

Older Soviet Jews (age fifty-five+, comprising about 25 percent of the recent arrivals) living in Germany experience serious moral discomfort, if not full-fledged cognitive dissonance, which they try to mitigate in different ways. The majority of the retired immigrants fought against the Germans during World War II, some had been wounded and had long-lasting disabilities. Those who had not been drafted to the front, experienced the hardships of evacuation, toiled in the military industry, witnessed the destruction, famine, and loss of loved ones in the Great War. In their turn, older Germans remember the harsh months of 1945 when many German cities were totally destroyed by the air raids of the Allies, with the subsequent occupation and division of Germany. As of today, the veterans of the Soviet Army are entitled to the same benefits as the veterans of the Wehrmacht who had fought on the opposite side: higher pensions, subsidized health resorts, membership in special clubs, etc. Thus, by way of bitter historic irony, the former deadly enemies often have to spend their old age side by side. On May 8 and 9 the two groups of veterans hold their two separate parades in the streets of Berlin: the ex-soldiers of Wehrmacht express their grief over the losses of the war, while former Soviets demonstrate the pride of the victory. Instead of downplaying the old animosities, given their current status of dependents of the German state, many older immigrants, on the contrary, underscore their pride as soldiers who helped crush the Nazi regime and "freed the German people from the Nazis." Nelly Elias (2005) showed in her ethnographic study among elderly Russian Jews in Cologne that they repeatedly use this argument as leverage in their conflict with the established Jewish community. Thus, one eighty-two-year-old man told her, "It's not our fault that nobody taught us how to be Jews. We fought against the Nazis when they learned the Torah. Without us they won't be here. When I tell them this, they have no argument, they have to agree." Many of them believed that their role as fighters against fascism was also appreciated by the younger generation of the Germans. Another informant in the Elias sample, an organizer of the Russian-Jewish club in Cologne, a war veteran in his eighties, told her about the Victory Day celebration in the club:

> Just imagine this: what does it mean to organize here, in Germany, Victory Day over Nazi Germany! More than 100 people took part in the celebrations. All the local Jewish administration came over . . . [he goes on to describe the program of the evening]. . . . All the people in the hall just cried. After that we drank *Le-Haim* of course. . . . What else. . . . Eight German police officers secured the celebrations. *They saw all of our war medals and gave us a lot of respect* (emphasis mine).

Another elderly man told her about his stay at the special health resort for veterans where during dinner he was seated next to a German man who had served in the military police during the war. "I told him, with a translator's help: "I apologize, but I won't sit near a Polizei, because they killed many of my people during the war." And they [dinner organizers] immediately took him away. They found another table for him so I could sit in my place." These twisted and morally charged situations (being generously hosted by a German institution and making personal demands reflecting old historic animosities) were interpreted by the elders in a self-righteous way, with solid conviction of their rights and entitlements on German soil. Moreover, many also attributed similar interpretations of the situation to their German hosts (who typically keep politically correct silence and show no feeling or preference). This defense mechanism probably helped these elderly Jews attenuate the internal conflict between their past and present.

Some other older immigrants in my research used the opposite strategy to solve the moral conflict of their living in Germany: they asserted that the past grievances are history and the younger generations of Germans have fully repented for the deeds of their fathers. "The war ended sixty years ago, and we should stop living in its shadow. Both Russians and Germans were sent to the front by their governments; not all Germans were villains, and not all Russians were saints. . . . Blame Stalin and Hitler, not ordinary Germans. . . . We live in the twenty-first century and should simply learn the lessons of how to reduce animosity and try to understand one another" (Arkady, seventy, former economist from Leningrad). "I wish that Russian government would be as generous and considerate of its own War veterans as the German government is of us, foreigners and former enemies. . . . We can only thank the German people, it is simply indecent to complain" (Dmitri, seventy-five, a former engineer from Odessa).

The lingering memories of the war were a common motif in the accounts of many informants, including younger ones, but they always made a distinction between older Germans who lived during Nazi regime and the postwar generation. Oleg (forty-six), a storeowner from Minsk, said,

> When I see an older German man, I can't help thinking: he could have been an SS officer or a camp official during the war, he could have fought against my dad at the front . . . . It is largely a generation matter: younger Germans have no direct responsibility for the Nazi crimes, but most elders had been involved with the regime in some way. On the other hand, I realize that Germans had been drafted to this war just like Russians, having no choice and often paying with their lives, so one should be fair.

Younger informants typically said that their contacts with indigenous Germans were limited to workplaces (if they worked) and bureaucratic structures such as the Sozialamt (Social Welfare Office) or Arbeitamt (Work Bureau) they needed to visit for settling their financial, residential, and other matters. Few working informants have developed informal friendly relations with their coworkers. Yefim (forty-three, a working engineer) said,

It is not common in Germany to become friends with your fellow workers, let alone the bosses. Every one minds their business, although on the surface Germans are very amicable, smile a lot, ask how you are, etc. The moment the workday ends, they just shut down everything and everyone that comes from this part of their life and switch gears to their family roles, personal business, etc. Work and personal lives are kept separately. So no, I don't have friends whom I met via work, despite my full-time employment with the same firm for five years.

Sara (fifty), an unemployed former journalist:

We are aliens in Germany and we will never become real friends with the locals, our mentality and lifestyles are so different. . . . We moved here for the sake of our children and they will surely make it in the future. They can gain most of the German education system, they can travel around Europe; for them the sky is the limit. But our generation is lost—this is the price we have to pay.

Some informants mentioned being friendly with their German neighbors or volunteers whom they met during their initial hard months upon arrival and who kept helping them to this day. Irena (thirty-five) said,

I can only say the best about Germans who gave us hand in hard times, and for no reason or benefit of their own. . . . You sort of don't expect this openness and generosity from a German . . . . Some of them just wanted to help, especially after learning that we were Jewish. In fact, we found this apartment and I got my first job with the help of Gustav, an older man whom I just met in the street a week after landing in Germany. He approached me and asked if I needed help, seeing that I was lost and helpless, my eyes red from crying. . . . Since then we remained friends . . . .You cannot generalize, all Germans are different, like Russians or Jews . . . . But most people I met here are relaxed and amicable, not like us former Soviets, always tense and alert, always prepared for some mischief or blow from others . . . . Perhaps years of good life in security and affluence make people kinder. What's amazing, they are ready to share their wealth with total strangers like us . . .

Another informant in Berlin—sixty-seven-year-old Galina, a former engineer and a life-long poet, told me about her intimate friendship with a German Jewish lady of similar age who also writes poetry and knows Russian. As Galina has become fairly proficient in German after nine years of life in Berlin (few immigrants of her age can do it!), the two poets have published several bilingual books of poetry in mutual parallel translation. "She is my most intimate friend and counsel in Germany. With her aid I could slowly understand the intricacies of German mentality that is so different from out own," says Galina.

Many informants noticed that Germans' attitudes towards immigrants, including former Soviets, were related to their social status and prosperity. "I guess the locals are more against us when they themselves have no jobs and live in what they think is poverty (all is relative!). This is why most acts of violence against immigrants are in the Eastern lands, and in poorer city quarters. Germans who are educated, working and live in good conditions, especially in small country towns where there are few immigrants, they are much more friendly and accepting" (Victor, fifty-one, Berlin).

Yet, even in cases when Germans tried to be friendly and include the newcomers in their circles, there was some discomfort and tension in this encounter ensuing from the gap in statuses and personal resources. Nina (fifty-three) recounted:

> I am often invited to this ladies group run by a local woman, who hosts everyone in her large and beautiful house—to play bridge, talk about the books and films, drink sherry, etc. As I am the only immigrant in our wealthy neighborhood and can speak some German, they love me as a token object of their benevolence and charity. Some would bring me their used clothes or kitchen utensils, others would just show interest and give advice . . . but I still feel alien there and often try to find excuses not to come.

In sum, most adult and older immigrants limited their contacts to the German majority to instrumental contacts via workplace or social institutions and did not include natives in their personal networks. In most cases their opinions and attitudes about Germans and German culture draw on rather secondary or superficial sources such as the Russian press and other people's stories as their limited command of German does not allow them to have meaningful communication with the Germans they met in different contexts. Those who had a better German proficiency and a wider circle of German acquaintances often expressed more positive attitudes about the mainstream society.

Experiences of Younger Immigrants

Although I have mentioned the difficulty of outreach for younger informants, I managed to interview eleven immigrants aged between seventeen and thirty-two; the account offered below stems mainly from their narratives, complemented by an analysis of the Russian-language media. Like their counterparts in Israel and North America, children and youths who migrated to Germany with their families made a more rapid transition towards the hosting majority than did their parents, let alone grandparents. However their initial years of immersion in the German school system were far from smooth, reflecting the need to study in German, gaps in the curriculum, and a different school culture. In order to ease the accommodation and lower the language barrier, some parents decided to place their children one or two classes below their actual age group, which in fact slowed down their progress and graduation. Full secondary school in Germany embraces three levels and thirteen years of study (from age seven to twenty); of these only ten or eleven years are mandatory and the last years of high school (gymnasium) called the *abitur* are only necessary for university admission. This lengthy school track had two implications for former Soviet immigrants: many of them completed German gymnasiums by the age of twenty-one to twenty-two (at this time their U.S. peers have got their BAs), and those who had arrived with Soviet school diploma had to complement the last two years of the *abitur* and pass state exams in order to study at the university.

Yet, the protracted road towards academic education was compensated for by the ability to study free of charge at all German universities. As most German students work part time, it takes them anywhere between five and eight years to complete a BA or professional degree in accountancy or law, and for a medical degree it can be as long as fifteen years. As opposed to most Aussiedler youngsters, who completed vocational schools and went to work in the blue-collar sector at the age of eighteen to nineteen, the majority of the Jewish students completed the *abitur* with good grades and continued their higher education, often supporting themselves with part-time jobs. Being non-citizens, they were not drafted for the military (or social) service like their native peers, so their educational timeline was roughly similar to the local standards, with BA diploma received by the age of twenty-seven to twenty-eight. The most popular disciplines among Russian-Jewish students in Germany were the same as in other immigration countries—computing and IT, engineering, finance, law, and medicine. Although the German professional labor market has been rather slow and shrinking over the last decade, these occupations still promise higher chances for prosperity than most others, and Jewish students (like their parents) are mostly driven by pragmatic considerations. Young immigrants, who arrived in Germany with several years of college completed in Russia or Ukraine, could usually start their university degree from scratch (after passing a German test) as these years were equivalent to their missing *abitur*. Even those, who held full college or university diplomas from the FSU, often started their German degrees anew, foreseeing the problems with recognition of a foreign diploma in the German labor market.

In any event, the young generation of Russian-Jewish Germans shows clear signs of upward socio-economic mobility vis-à-vis their welfare-ridden parents. Although I cannot cite the relevant German statistics, I have never heard about a Russian-Jewish offspring who avoided the university path, either straight after high school or with some time lag. Young immigrants with whom I spoke, both in 2003 and 2005, mentioned time and again that their main problem while living in Germany is that of *obsheniye* (a unique Russian term meaning intimate communication). Like their parents (and despite their good command of German), most of them feel alienation from their native German peers and usually limit their contacts with them to instrumental issues. Yet, being a small minority in most German cities (especially outside Berlin), young Russian Jews have no apparent channels for tracking down their co-ethnics whom they could turn into friends, dates, and spouses. The two main networking channels that were mentioned by my young informants are the Russian-German Internet forums and dating sites, and youth clubs emerging in loose affiliation with local synagogues. Having little or no interest in Jewish life and religion as such, many young immigrants attended synagogues and Jewish community centers in order to meet their own kind.

One such club that I visited in Bonn (also frequented by commuters from a neighboring Cologne) has a thriving program of karaoke and dance parties loosely connected with the Jewish holidays, but mainly serving the meeting ground for young Russian immigrants, mostly Jews. Over time, the successful Jewish clubs attract also upwardly mobile youths of Aussiedler origin, diverse students from Russia and Ukraine (who enjoy free education in Germany), and other young Russian speakers who populate German cities. A Bonn club activist told me about several marriages that had their origin in the synagogue dance, and many friendships that spilled over the boundaries of the

Jewish community. Answering my question about their friends, several informants noted that it was much easier for them to establish amicable relations with Germans coming from the East and with other "foreigners" in Germany (e.g., foreign students in German universities), especially those coming from the former Soviet Bloc—Poland, Czech Republic, Hungary, etc.—than with West German peers. In the words of one informant, "we all know what it meant to be Young Pioneer and Komsomol member, we grew up reading the same stories and watching the same movies, and laughing at the same jokes. You cannot start explaining all this to your West German fellow student."

To conclude, young Jewish immigrants in Germany manifest an already familiar social syndrome also found among their counterparts in Israel and America—a combination of upward social mobility and economic success with consistent co-ethnic preference in private communications and social networks. Despite their German proficiency, young Russian Jews find themselves facing a broad cultural gap to their native peers that will probably linger for the lifetime of this 1.5 generation.

Conclusion

In this chapter based on ethnographic research I tried to illuminate some of the identity dilemmas faced by former Soviet Jews who chose Germany as their new home. Coming from the same ethno-cultural background as my interviewees, and being an outsider to the social setting in question, I could elicit open and uncensored accounts of their resettlement experiences. Generally speaking, I have confirmed my initial assumption that many Jewish immigrants feel moral discomfort about residing in the midst of the nation largely responsible for the extermination of European Jewry only several decades ago. For most Soviet Jews the memory of the Great War and the Holocaust is rather fresh, casting a shadow over the lives of two postwar generations. Hence, it is hardly surprising that the predominant expressed attitude towards native Germans is a mix of caution and perceived broad social distance. At the same time, the key identity issue for many immigrants coming from the assimilated ranks of educated Soviet Jewry is: Whether and why remain Jewish at all? It is much easier to assume the neutral identity of a Russian/Ukrainian or former Soviet and pass as any other foreigner in Germany, rather than face multiple possible ramifications of belonging to this "small but special minority." After all, the initial affiliation with the organized Jewish community is temporary and may be seen as a pure formality necessary for obtaining legal status and financial aid from the state. The Gemeinde policy of selecting new members on the basis of ethnic purity is perceived as discriminatory or even racist by many newcomers and, along with power struggles between old and new leadership of the Gemeinde, further repels them from participation in the ethno-religious community they allegedly came to join.

The immigrants whom I interviewed solve these identity dilemmas differently, depending on their age, family history, and the extent of social adjustment in Germany. For the immigrants, who moved to Germany during their peak working years, the chief problem is the loss of professional identity, a harsh choice between lifelong welfare dependence and downgrading to unskilled workforce. Only a handful could re-launch their old careers on German soil, or start a new business from scratch. The comforts of everyday life in the heart of Europe, a thriving consumer market, and cultural life on the "Russian street" help Jewish immigrants cope with insecurity and loss of their former social status. (One middle-aged informant defined his life in Germany as "living in a golden cage"—comfortable and secure, but never free, equal, and at home). The more educated and philosophically inclined immigrants try to elaborate on historic and ideological justifications of their return to Germany as the cradle of Ashkenazi Jewry and part of enlightened Europe, stressing their role as potential supporters of Israel from abroad. The less sophisticated among the immigrants openly admit that they had been attracted by the possibility of a comfortable life at the expense of a wealthy German state, often adding the point of "historic dues" and retribution for past grievances.

Age is also a factor involving personal memories of the war and family loss in the Holocaust (especially for those coming from Western parts of the USSR occupied by the Nazis). Older migrants tend to feel more insecure living among Germans and are intimidated by the possibility of anti-Semitic attacks in the future. One expression of this insecurity is refraining from being alone in open social spaces (i.e., in fact anywhere outside immigrant residential enclaves), and exclusive social networking with other Russian Jews. The majority of older migrants did not even try to contact or befriend native Germans, being convinced in their arrogance towards foreigners and intrinsic anti-

Semitism. At the same time the older generation feels entitled to material support from the German state as its due for old historic grievances. Veterans of the Soviet army living side by side with their former foes often underscored their military deeds and the role in defeating fascism, interpreting institutional aid and the polite silence of the Germans as signs of their appreciation and respect. Few were ready to admit to a black irony, if not absurdity, of their current relations with the German state and people. None of the older informants could call Germany their home, but rather "a comfortable resort to which I had been sent a few years ago and luckily forgotten," in an ironic definition of one man.

Conversely, younger and more successful migrants, who have learned German and found relevant employment, were typically free from moral dilemmas and apprehensions. Although most of them experienced social distance from native Germans and preferred the company of their co-ethnics, their attitudes towards the host society were much more positive and their social inclusion is probably only a matter of time. Younger immigrants often espouse a universalistic philosophy: they see themselves as citizens of unified Europe, a new geopolitical entity without borders and with growing economic opportunities. In their opinion, younger Germans are no different from other West Europeans in their general outlook and tolerance of "others" and are not directly responsible for the Nazi crimes against Jews. If anti-Semitism is still lingering among some Germans, it is not a specific German phenomenon but universal human bigotry found in every country. Younger immigrants were more diverse in their social networks both within the "Russian street" (befriending and dating Jews, Aussiedler, and other Russian speakers) and beyond it, gradually including some Germans and other nationals into their social networks. Most of them could say that they felt at home in German cities at least as much or more than they had felt in Russia or Ukraine.

My research has endorsed the view that Russian/Soviet-Jewish identity is split along the lines of cultural affiliation and may include various shares of Russian and Jewish components. Immigration generally, and settling in Germany especially, highlight this identity split and compel Jewish immigrants to choose the main path. The strength of the pre-migration affinity to Jewishness emerges therefore as another salient predictor of psychosocial adjustment of Russian Jews in Germany. Those who have a strong Jewish identity have either to live in tension and lingering sense of insecurity or to rationalize their choice of Germany by the moral and/or religious mission to reconstruct Jewish life in Germany after the Holocaust. The immigrants with greater interest in Jewish traditions, the Hebrew language, and Israel as the center of modern Jewish life have also to tackle a difficult question of choosing Germany over Israel. My findings seem to indicate that recent immigrants with a more universalistic and cosmopolitan orientation, that is, perceiving Germany mainly as part of Europe, have a better chance for expedient acculturation and psychological well-being than their counterparts with a stronger Jewish identity. Many older immigrants speak of Israel as their symbolic home and take Israeli problems close to heart, but few would consider living there. Being pragmatics, they have found their Promised Land in the heart of comfortable Europe.

Notes

1. Native Germans fail to imagine how Jewish refugees can make ends meet, receiving a monthly survival minimum of some 350 Euros per person and 650 Euros per couple. Yet, given that all the basic expenses (housing, health care, subsidized public transportation) are covered by the state, most immigrants manage to make a decent living with this small allowance, shopping in cheaper stores, not eating out, etc. Many even manage to save some money for travel, both within Europe and to the FSU.

2. Reflecting the overall crisis of the German welfare system and growing ranks of economically inactive population, new regulations have been recently introduced in some Lands, requiring from all working-age welfare recipients (regardless of their education and former work status) to participate in public works such as street cleaning for a minimal hourly wage (one to three Euros). Their earnings are then deduced from their welfare check, so they receive the same allowance but are required "to pay back to society" by their work. This new practice causes much indignation among Russian Jews, used to get their meal ticket for free.

3. Many immigrants invest lots of intellectual energy to understand the complex regulations of the German welfare system to milk it for all it is good for. One example includes a lobby formed by a group of elderly Russian Jews in Berlin, trying to engage the established German Jewish leaders into political action aimed at lifting the existing limitations of the assignment of the status of the "Nazi regime's victim." In Berlin-Brandenburg Land, only those who had immigrated before January 1, 1991 (i.e., a small minority of all the arrivals) can claim this status, with the ensuing financial benefit—a higher pension not contingent on one's presence in the country (vis-à-vis regular welfare benefit waived when a refugee leaves Germany for over two weeks). As many Russian Jews have relatives, property, and nostalgic links to their former homeland, many would like to

travel to the FSU without losing German welfare income. So far, the attempts to redefine the rules to embrace all Jewish immigrants who had suffered during the War, have failed, as that would mean high additional expenses for the Land, suffering lately of great budgetary problems.

7

Lost Relatives or Strangers?
Jews or Former Soviets? In Search
of the Common Denominator

"The German political establishment did not prepare the German public for the kind of immigrants it was going to receive from the former Soviet Union. Kindhearted burghers had romantic illusions about their suffering brothers from the East: Germans were expecting to welcome their lost tribe of Aussiedler, *and the Jews opened their arms to embrace* Ostjuden *fleeing anti-Semitism and craving a Jewish life. Instead, German taxpayers of any faith received a crowd of dispossessed Soviet people who came to Germany with a simple and clear goal—to partake in the riches of the German welfare state. Regardless of their blood and ethnic roots, the Soviet mentality is their chief common heritage. Many of them left the FSU to escape this mentality, but they still carry it in their bones."*—Gasan Guseinov, 2005 (my free translation from Russian)

After depicting specific experiences of former Soviet Jews in the four main countries of their immigration, these concluding notes will attempt reflective integration drawing (as I did throughout this book) on the nexus between macro and micro analytical tools. I will start from a table summarizing at a glance the key macro-level characteristics of the 1990s immigration wave in terms of the host countries' policies and conditions. Apparently, the frameworks of integration manifest both similarities and differences. Common for most receiving societies (and politicians who brokered this immigration wave) was the construction of Soviet Jews as a population in need, fleeing persecution, lacking financial resources, and entitled to support from the welfare system. At the same time, given their high rates of post-secondary education, the policymakers had expected that after a short period of orientation and public support Soviet Jews would become economically self-sufficient (Sicron, 1998; Brym, 2001; Chiswick and Wenz, 2004; Jasper, 2005). In all receiving countries, Russian Jews were given access to citizenship and political rights—in Israel immediately, in the Western countries after a few years of residence—as opposed to some other groups of refugees and labor migrants (e.g., Turks in Germany or guest workers in Israel). It was also expected that the newcomers' integration in the mainstream would mainly occur via their participation in established Jewish communities.

Yet, declared ideological goals do not always go hand in hand with economic realities; occupational adjustment of Soviet immigrants was often thwarted by rigid regulations of the labor market and blocked entry to most professions for carriers of foreign credentials. These obstacles were most prominent in Germany and Canada, where local governments and professional associations de facto barred former Soviet doctors, engineers, educators, and other professionals from regaining their former occupations. In The U.S., the regulation of the labor market is minimal and competition with native professionals was fairer, but poor command of English held back many former Soviets. In Israel, the majority had to adjust their expectations to the reality of small and saturated skilled labor market. In all the host economies, former Soviet professionals often faced the misfit of their experience to the demands of the Western labor market and had to acquire new skills in technology, languages, and self-marketing, starting from such basic skills as composing one's resume. While in Germany many immigrants could stay out of the labor force for years thanks to generous welfare aid, in all the other host countries former professionals had to take any available jobs to make a living. The resulting occupational downgrading and detachment from the local peer milieu discouraged many skilled immigrants from seeking social integration and relegated them to life on the social margins. Reflecting these different structural conditions and broad variance in immigrants' human (and lately also financial) capital, Russian-speaking Jews are found in all economic tiers of the host societies, from chronic welfare recipients and manual laborers to thriving professionals and business owners. Reflecting self-selection of the more independent individuals and carriers of higher

Table 1
Macro-Characteristics of the Post-Soviet
Jewish Immigration in the Main Host Countries

Characteristics	Israel	Germany	USA	Canada
Official framing of Jewish immigration	Ethnic return, Zionist nation building	Religious refugee, paying historic dues to Soviet Jewry	Religious refugee, saving from anti-Semitism	Independent economic migrants & small number of refugees
Access to citizenship	Immediate for the Jews	Pending 6–8 years of residence	Pending 5 year residence and and exam	Pending 3 year residence and exam
Size of the Soviet Jewish group among:	Large (1 million among 5.3 million Jews)	Small in general	Small in general	Small
* general population	* 14 percent	* 0.001	* 0.001	* 0.001
**Jewish population	** 20 percent	** 85 percent of JG, 100 percent in some towns	** 13 percent (700,000 in 5.9 million)	** 10 percent (80,000 among 800,000)
Resettlement package & welfare aid	Modest, short-term but comprehensive, incl. occupational adjustment & health care	Generous and long-term, incl. housing & health care	Refugee rights: short-term for working age, life-long for seniors	None: economic self-reliance, welfare like all Canadians
Access to skilled occupations	Licensure needed for regulated occupations; labor market small but dynamic & flexible	Foreign credentials seldom accepted; labor market regulated & unionized	Licensure required for few occupations; labor market large, liberal & flexible	Barriers to foreign credentials; public sector unionized & regulated
Host expectations toward immigrants	Rapid assimilation in the Jewish mainstream	No specific expectations	Participation in Jewish life, economic self-reliance	Economic self-reliance
Economic success in 10–15 years	Moderate; Occupational downgrading, but middle-class lifestyle	Low by local standards: high unemployment and reliance on welfare	High income & rapid accent to middle-class & prosperity	Moderate: occupational downgrading
Political power	High: large size, voting rights, political parties	Low: small group of non-voters	Moderate, as part of U.S. Jewry	Moderate, as part of Canadian Jewry

human capital (e.g., occupations demanded on most Western labor markets), the U.S. and Canada probably attracted a more industrious and self-reliant sub-stream of the former Soviet immigrants, vis-à-vis Israel and Germany. Their demographic profile[1] was also rather different, with Israel accommodating the highest share of older immigrants (30 percent being in the age bracket fifty-five+, compared to 24 percent in Germany, and 16 percent in the U.S.), as well as those coming from the periphery of the FSU, including Central Asia and the Caucasus, and endowed with poorer human capital necessary for occupational and social adjustment. These gaps in the structure of personal and demographic resources of the immigrants, as well as their attitudes towards self-reliance versus public aid, shaped the resulting diverse patterns of economic mobility.

In the beginning of the Israeli chapter, I have offered some theoretical reflections on the nature of integration and acculturation processes under conditions of mass influx of same-origin immigrants, especially when it is framed as ethnic return or ethnically privileged migration (which is mostly the case with former Soviet Jews). I have also introduced a heuristic model allowing us to follow-up the integration process in more specific terms, drawing on the four major indicators of social incorporation: employment in the mainstream economy, inclusion of the natives in migrants' personal social networks, and incorporation of the mainstream media and cultural products in immigrants' basket of cultural consumption. The fourth factor shaping the pace and scope of integration is the dominant majority attitudes towards the specific immigrant groups. More open and inclusive disposition of the hosts is conducive to mutual tolerance and greater participation of the newcomers in the host social institutions. Successful integration usually emerges in a form of biculturalism, based on bilingualism. Tamar Horowitz (2001) writes about the "hybridism script" of integration in a similar sense. Integrative strategy implies a double cultural competence, flexibility and an effective situational switch between the two cultures (Berry, 1990; Nauck, 2001). Bilingualism and double cultural competence may also be seen as signs of acculturation (this is where the two concepts overlap). Immigrants' ability to pursue integration in the new society hinges on the human/cultural capital they are endowed with (education, professional and linguistic skills), as well as the amount of social support (from both personal and institutional sources) available to them during the initial difficult years of readjustment. On the individual level, age and facility with the languages are of paramount importance: younger migrants are usually prone to faster social learning and greater adaptability, while better language command improves the chances for successful employment, informal networking with the locals, and an easier shift to mainstream cultural products.

My comparative exploration of the experiences of the post-communist Jewish immigrants on the four larger isles of the emerging Russian-Jewish diaspora (or archipelago) endorsed the heuristic value of the described model of social integration. Employment on par with one's skills and qualifications has been shown to be the major gateway for the newcomers to both economic well-being and gradual social insertion in the mainstream. Multiple structural and cultural barriers experienced by the immigrants on professional labor markets (proving foreign credentials, skill incompatibility, blocked access to public sector jobs, etc.) resulted in occupational downgrading of former professionals in all receiving countries. In the wealthy social democracy of Germany this meant chronic dependence on welfare, in all the other countries, the need to seek retraining and new paths to economic survival. For younger and more dynamic immigrants this meant taking a fresh start (often for the better!) but for middle-aged professionals, especially men, the inability to get back to their original line of work meant severe damage to self-esteem and further estrangement from the host society. Across post-Soviet Jewish diaspora, the share of professionals who could regain their former occupations probably lies between 15 percent in Germany and 30 percent in the U.S. and Israel. Occupational adjustment was especially hard for members of humanistic and culturally dependent occupations (highly prestigious in the FSU but often useless in the West) who could not make a living as educators or writers in the new cultural milieu. Sometimes they found an outlet for their talents in various educational and cultural ventures targeting Russian immigrant youth (e.g., after-school Russian language and art classes). On the other end of the scale were computing and IT specialists, whose skills were easily convertible and universally in demand.

Significant numbers of the dropouts from the mainstream labor market found shelter in the ethnic economic sector, giving a strong push to the mushrooming of Russian groceries, garages, travel agencies, book/music/video stores, and other small businesses forming together the thriving "Russian street" of New York, Tel Aviv, Berlin, and Toronto. The share of self-employed among former Soviet immigrants is hard to measure due to different legal definitions in the four countries, but the estimates vary between 8 percent in Israel and 35 percent in some U.S. cities (Light and Isralowitz, 1997). Some members of the free professions (e.g., lawyers, accountants, physicians, and dentists) who managed to obtain local licenses opened their offices catering mainly for the Russian-speaking clientele. Yet the majority of former "big shots" and current "nobodies" had to toil in manual or semi-skilled labor force in industry and services, hardly making ends meet. The older segment of educated Russian Jews had to rely on their pre-migration reputation and achievements as a basis for identity and self-esteem; thus all the former "senior engineers" and "chief constructors" (everyone turned to be "senior" in their old life) were frozen in time and psychologically dwelled on their solid past rather than shaky present and unclear future. A minority of well-adjusted bicultural and bilingual immigrants is found mainly among those who found their place in the mainstream organizations and companies.

The workplace is also the meeting ground between the immigrants and their local peers, giving rise to new social relationships and personal friendships that over time may transcend the boundaries of the ethnic community. Gradual inclusion of the members of the hegemonic majority into immigrants' personal networks is a potent signifier of the ongoing integration. Given their limited contact with the mainstream institutions and low proficiency in the host languages, the expansion of immigrants' social networks has been slow in all the four countries. Personal narratives collected in my fieldwork largely point to the explicit co-ethnic preference in all informal communications manifested by Russian-speakers in all their major hubs of immigrant life. Between 65 percent and 85 percent of adult immigrants state in interviews that most or all of their personal friends, dates and potential spouses are other Russian immigrants. Even in contexts potentially conducive to cross-cultural contacts (workplace, studies, cultural venues, etc.) Russians pick up other Russians as their counterparts in various social transactions. The tendency of many immigrants, especially older ones, to settle in Russian residential enclaves additionally hampers their chances to befriend native neighbors. The ability to bridge the social gap to the majority is stronger among olim in Israel than among Russian Jews living in the West, probably due to immigrant origins of most Israelis and an informal style of interpersonal interactions typical for the natives. Few adult Russian immigrants in other countries could say that they count non-immigrant Americans, Canadians, or Germans among their personal friends, although this tendency is apparently stronger among younger immigrants.

The co-ethnic social preferences of Russian Jews reflect their feelings of cultural superiority over other immigrants and often the natives too, drawing on the proverbial cultural legacy of great Russian literature, philosophy, and the arts. By way of historic irony, Russian Jews— a mistrusted minority themselves—got infected by the virus of Russian chauvinism and imperial arrogance towards other cultures, outlooks, and lifestyles. Many educated Soviet Jews (especially intellectuals) are embittered by the lack of appreciation of their finesse by the host society. Without actually knowing much about the mainstream cultural life (due to the language barrier and social alienation), they often judge the local media and cultural scene as inferior and unworthy of the attempt to learn it better. For many years the cultural consumption of the immigrants is limited to the Russian language press, radio, and television channels, which often create a one-sided or even biased picture of the local and international events. The shift to the mainstream cultural basket occurs faster in North America (where the selection of Russian cultural products is limited) and is slower in Germany and Israel, probably because the language barrier there is perceived as higher. In these two countries, the bulk of reading for news and pleasure among the immigrants still occurs in Russian (the work-related reading has to be in Hebrew or German), with this trend challenged only among younger immigrants who completed all or part of their education in the host country. Younger Russian immigrants consume diverse media sources, with the increasing share of Internet communications in both Russian and host languages.

The last component of my analysis, which sets the tone for the integration process, is the feedback received by the immigrant community from the hegemonic majority. It would be fair to say that even in Israel, where every fifth Jew today speaks Russian, the Hebrew mainstream is largely indifferent to the life of the "Russian street" and not really interested in its alleged cultural riches. Although most Jewish Israelis give a lip service to the contributions of the Great Russian Aliyah to the Israeli economy and society, fewer Israelis express personal interest in befriending Russian immigrants, learning Russian, or visiting Russian cultural events (Remennick, 2003a). The ongoing process of cultural production in Russian (new books, literary almanacs, etc.) goes unnoticed by the mainstream educated public, even where Hebrew translations are offered. Although there is little institutional discrimination of Russian immigrants (who are full fledged citizens from day one), the negative attitudes towards their professional competence (e.g., as doctors or educators) and traces of the Soviet mentality often lead to practices of exclusion and stifled promotion (Remennick, 2004b). In the U.S. and Canada, Russian Jews try to build their primary social networks within the established local Jewry, and are largely perceived by the mainstream as its integral part. In Germany, the position of New Russian Jews vis-à-vis local Jewry, other immigrants, and native German majority is still contested and vague. In all host countries, the Russian component of their dual social identity includes these immigrants in the negative associative chain of images such as "Russian mafia," "Russian ethnic violence," "Russian sex workers," etc. The mainstream media has the major role to play in the social construction of the collective image of Russian immigrants generally and Russian Jews specifically, and unfortunately the negative scoops and profiles featuring Russian names tend to predominate in the media discourse (Lemish, 2000). These general trends do not undermine multiple personal stories of warm welcome and generous aid that the newcomers had received from Israelis, Americans, and Germans, Jewish or not, during their initial harsh years of resettlement.

Given the diversity of Russian immigrant experiences, it is hard to draw a universal bottom line as to the extent of social integration of former Soviets in Israel and in the West. On the macro-level, the first post-Soviet immigrant generation has manifested faster upward mobility than most other minorities, often entering local middle class in a matter of five to ten years. In a cross-country comparison, Russian-Jewish immigrants in the U.S. probably achieved the highest and fastest socio-economic mobility in comparison to both other U.S. minorities and Russian-speakers in other countries (Chiswick and Wenz, 2004). It is estimated that in terms of average annual income, Russian Jews in the U.S. recently surpassed Indian immigrants—another highly educated and dynamic minority—and became number one (www.migrationpolicy.org). As a community, Russian Jews on all three continents display both the signs of socio-cultural continuity verging on self-isolation and successful instrumental insertion into Western economies and lifestyles. A significant fraction of Russian speakers became in fact bilingual and can effectively function in both cultural domains—

old and new. Yet, their encounters with the receiving societies have been tainted with intrinsic conflict over their identity and disposition vis-à-vis established Jewish community and the hegemonic majority.

I opened this chapter with a quotation from Gasan Guseinov—cultural historian, linguist, and sharp observer of Russian life in Germany. His somewhat cynical but savvy diagnosis can serve as a blueprint for the encounter between Russian immigrants of the 1990s and the receiving societies. The mass influx of former Soviet citizens (Jews and others) to Israel and to several Western countries can be described as a crisis of mutual failed expectations. Although the political motivation that underpinned this immigration was different in every host country (usually a mix of ideology and pragmatics), Jewish communities of the U.S., Canada, and Germany were deemed the main beneficiaries of this population increment and shouldered the heavy responsibility for resettlement of the newcomers. In Israel, the Jewish majority is represented by the state, but the underlying expectation was rather similar: to embrace more Jews in need and mold them expediently into regular Israelis. In the preceding decade, the American and Israeli governments and Jewish organizations put their joint efforts into the historic endeavor of "liberating Soviet Jews." In return for their investment and services, the hosting Jewish communities expected to witness appreciation and eagerness of the newcomers to live as "real Jews" after decades disguised as Soviet citizens. They were shocked to discover that the saved Russian Jews did not intend to "get out of the closet"—the closet became part of their identity, the mask stuck firmly to their skin.

What did ex-Soviet Jews expect from the hosting countries and local established Jews? To be accepted on their own terms, for who they are—hard-working, educated, ambitious people whose efforts at social and economic mobility had been curbed by the anti-Semitic state in the Slavic countries where they had never felt at home. They left the FSU in search of self-actualization, higher living standards, and better futures for their children rather than return to the Jewish religion and lifestyle, which their forefathers had left behind in the shtetls of Russia and Ukraine many decades ago. They assert that no one has a right to teach them how to be Jews: they had experienced the full measure of humiliation and grief due to their "ethnic disability" in the FSU, lost family members in the Holocaust and Stalin's purges, and moved to the West simply to be free and pursue their life goals unhampered. At the same time, most of them gladly accepted their new rights as Jews, perceiving the services and aid offered by the hosting Jewish communities as their "natural entitlement," a fair tribute for their past privations offered by the wealthy Jews of New York, Hamburg, or Toronto. As citizens molded by socialist ideology (which many of them adamantly rejected!), deep in their hearts they believed in equality as synonym of justice. They were shocked to discover the wealth of most Western and some Israeli Jews vis-à-vis their own shabby suitcases filled with old clothes and books.

Struggling to find an economic and social foothold in the new country, they did not hurry to return the favors to their new beneficiaries by paying synagogue fees, coming to *minyan* for prayer or volunteering for community causes. For one thing, this was never part of their past experience or identity, for another they had not enough spare time and expendable income to behave like good American, Canadian, or German Jews. However, when the initial shock and anger were over, many Russian Jews appreciated the benefits of belonging to the Jewish community, both in terms of social identity and informal networking. Slowly but surely, they came to adopt many of the less religious and more cultural practices of American and European Jewry, sending their children to Jewish after-schools and camps, celebrating bar mitzvahs and high holidays. In Israel, this drift towards cultural Judaism has been precluded by the single-handed rule of the Orthodox and limited exposure of the newcomers to the more liberal modern versions of Judaism. In any event, the participation of Russian Jews in formal Jewish organizations and religious congregations is still rather low across the post-communist diaspora.

In the early years of their encounter with the receiving societies many former members of the Soviet intelligentsia experienced an acute identity crisis reflecting the uselessness of their old cultural baggage under new conditions. Nurturing a flattering self-image of the cultural and professional elite of their old homelands, they discovered themselves overnight relegated to the status of social outcasts living on the handouts of the generous state. In the words of my German informant, a sixty-year-old unemployed chemistry professor from Kharkov: "Every day I make believe that I am still a university professor, but I know that I am fooling myself. . . . It's all behind me, now I am no better than any illiterate Turkish laborer working in a construction site. . . . In fact I am worse, as he is making his living honestly and I am just a parasite." The loss of social identity was augmented by the linguistic muteness, recasting former articulate and intelligent people to the status of seeming half-wits unable to express themselves properly (Yelenevskaya and Fialkova, 2003). Yet, regardless of these identity crises, most immigrants manifested good survival skills in the new economic environment (the cultural toolbox of Homo Sovieticus came in handy), finding sources of income in the ethnic economy and relying on the informal Russian networks for solving their multiple problems of adjustment. In many ways, the condition of former Soviet immigrants in Western societies resembled the destiny of those who stayed back in the FSU and struggled for a new foothold in the transitional economy with little or no welfare support. Both had to redefine their professional and social identities, adjust their lifestyles, and learn how to swim in the unpredictable surf of market capitalism, either in its more civilized or "jungle" versions. In many cases, women turned out to be better equipped for coping with these challenges, manifesting better social skills, occupational flexibility, and drive for novelty, vis-à-vis their male partners.

The lingering complex of social dependency on the state and expectation of public aid for solution of personal problems formed a salient psychosocial barrier for successful adjustment of former Soviets in Western democracies. It was especially expressed in the countries with a developed welfare system, that is, Israel and Germany, also because Russian Jews felt "invited" there by the governments (in Canada reliance on welfare was contained by the independent economic framing of their immigration). The conviction in their legitimate right to pensions and benefits in countries where they had not worked at all or worked for just a few years (often in the untaxed cash economy) is more often espoused by older Soviet immigrants molded by the "womb to tomb" Soviet welfare system. Often immigrants' expectations reflected their misunderstanding of the workings of the civil society and Western welfare state construed by them along familiar Soviet lines. They often perceived caseworkers of HIAS and NYANA in America and Judisches Gemeinde in Germany not as representatives of voluntary organizations but as governmental officials whose duty was to take good care of their needs. Used to manipulating and bribing Soviet bureaucrats, some of them looked for the "right approach" to their caseworkers to get a larger cut of the communal resources or secure their help in conflicts with federal authorities.[2] When they encountered limited resources or goodwill among their new beneficiaries, Soviet immigrants lamented over the heartless American (Israeli, German, Canadian) bureaucracy and their failed hopes for a better life (Yelenevskaya and Fialkova, 2005). Fewer immigrants, exemplified by the above-cited professor of chemistry, were deeply humiliated by their forced leisure and the need to rely on welfare.

Coming mainly from ethnically and socially homogeneous Soviet cities, many immigrants experienced cultural shock at the face of ethno-racial diversity of all receiving societies. As they often entered the host social structure from its bottom, living in poorer neighborhoods and working in unskilled jobs, Russian Jews mainly crossed paths with people of color and other disadvantaged minorities (Turks in Germany, Arabs and Moroccan Jews in Israel, Blacks and Hispanics in the U.S., Asian immigrants in Canada). This social encounter comprised a stark contrast to their former social milieu of the educated Soviet intelligentsia, and it often gave rise to ethnic prejudice and negative attitudes towards their new co-workers and neighbors, especially when they had to compete with them for scant resources. As many newcomers gradually worked their way up the host social ladder and met their middle-class peers, their attitudes towards the hosting societies generally improved and they grew more willing to adopt elements of the new lifestyle and everyday culture. Yet, many educated former Soviets are prone to believe in their cultural superiority over the hosts (Israeli sabras, German burghers, and American suburban dwellers alike), labeling them as overly materialistic, ignorant, lacking in cultural and spiritual interests, and (the gravest sin!) indifferent to the problems and privations of the recent migrants. Those who proudly wear their cultural superiority on their sleeves are often the least successful and poorly integrated immigrants, who know little about the actual lives of the locals, do not read mainstream press and literature, and build their opinions from ethnic media sources. It seems that Russian cultural supremacy is the last line of psychological defense for those of the immigrants who found themselves socially displaced; in a way it is another downside of the identity crisis and socio-economic marginality (Kishinevsky, 2004; Yelenevskaya, 2005; Guseinov, 2005).

The process of cultural transition experienced by former Soviets in their new homelands is typified by preservation of their core cultural values (Smolitz et al., 2001), with simultaneous drift towards local lifestyles in more external and instrumental domains. The core values of the former Soviet Jewry include the preservation of the Russian language and cultural consumption and attempts to transfer it to their children; the indisputable value of education, hard effort, and social mobility; closely knit families with life-long exchange of intergenerational support; reliance on informal social networks rather than formal institutions, and clear in-group preference in personal relationships. In line with these core values, Russian-Jewish immigrants have established thriving ethnic cultural and educational institutions, such as Russian libraries, amateur drama, literary and music societies, afterschool enrichment activities for the children, multiple printed and electronic media channels in Russian. Although over time these Russian-language institutions incorporate more local elements (e.g., drama groups stage not only Russian classics but also local plays or perform in the host language), their style, management, and membership remain Russian. Some unique forms of cultural production dating back to the Soviet times—amateur song festivals (KSP), humor contests between student teams (KVN), and brain-ring games (*Chto-Gde-Kogda*)—have all found their way into the lives of Russian cultural diaspora in Israel and in the West.

Russian-speaking communities in Israel and in Western countries are internally diverse, including "core" Jews, partial Jews and non-Jewish spouses and children of the Jews (the Jewish "periphery"), as well as many others groups of former Soviets who moved there as students, legal and illegal labor migrants, spouses and sponsored relatives, Diversity Lottery winners, etc. In some host countries (Israel and U.S.), Jews form a majority among former Soviet migrants, while in others they comprise about half (in Canada), or even a minority (vis-à-vis Aussiedler in Germany). On top of ethnic diversity (Jews of European or Asian origin and non-Jews) and different frameworks of integration shaped by the entry route (e.g., job visa holders in the high-tech sector vs. illegal domestic workers; refugees vs. sponsored spouses), former Soviets come from different republics and cities of the FSU and are endowed with different human capital. All these parameters shape complex hierarchies and webs of prestige and social status within the emerging "Russian street" of each host country. These traits, reflecting both the Soviet past and current achievements, influence social relations between the immigrants, the exchange of paid work and unpaid favors, and mutual stereotypes reflected in the immigrant press and folklore (Yelenevskaya and Fialkova, 2005). Here is another paradox of Homo Sovieticus: raised in an ostensibly egalitarian society, former Soviets are always alert to the signs of social status of other social actors and try to build their personal networks from the individuals perceived as equal or superior to themselves. Immigrant condition, with its built-in streak of trial and differentiation of success, further reinforces the sense of competition and social comparison between former Soviets. While in their old Soviet lives the valued symbolic assets of intelligentsia pertained to educational and spiritual realm (size of the home library, academic degrees, access to elite cultural events), in materialistic Western societies immigrants adopt universal symbols of status and success (income, housing location and quality, Ivy League colleges attended by the children). The ethnographic research of the intricate social relations within diverse communities of Russian-speakers is in its cradle, but more work will hopefully be done in this fascinating anthropological field as young researchers emerge from the ranks of Russian immigrants themselves.

Although former Soviet immigrants are prone to social apathy and mistrust of any establishment, their political participation in the host countries usually increases with receiving citizenship and full voting rights. In Israel, their immediate access to citizenship and high demographic weight in the electorate led to rapid ethnic mobilization for lobbying of the mutual interests and the formation of "Russian" parties (Al-Haj, 2004). In the Western countries, where they comprise a small minority, Russian immigrants have a weaker sense of political power and seldom participate in mainstream democratic institutions. Yet, they are usually quite active in both local and national elections, voting for the candidates whose policies they deem beneficial for immigrants like themselves. They often manifest poor understanding of the local political scene, and their choices are strongly influenced by the local Russian media and their immigrant friends. With other variables kept constant, former Soviets typically lean towards conservative, Republican, and right-wing politicians, whom they construe as consistent and reliable, fighting against social evils such as crime, terrorism, ethnic conflict, and declining morals (e.g., gay marriage). Despite their dislike of formal organizations, over time most Russian immigrant communities have built their own voluntary associations catering for their cultural and social needs, providing self-help and legal advice, and, more rarely, expressing a specific political agenda (e.g., Russian Jews of America for Israel recently formed in New York). Yet, the share of Russian-speakers who actively participate in any community organizations remains insignificant, the way it was in the mid-1980s when Fran Markowitz conducted her research in Brooklyn. They still prefer the grapevine of informal social connections as a tool for solving their problems and meeting personal goals, remaining a "community in spite of itself."

Russian ethnic economies are thriving in all the host countries, providing employment and income to both legal immigrants and many other categories of former Soviets seeking better lives abroad. As was already said, opening a small business was an attractive alternative for some educated immigrants who could not (or would not) return to their original occupations. Some others had entrepreneurial experience either from the times of the socialist shadow economy or from post-communist times of "jungle capitalism." Their opportunistic and informal mode of business operation learned in the old country and excellent skills in "beating the system, bending the rules" proved to be useful also in the global capitalist economy (Morawska, 1999). The client body of the immigrant businesses (especially those in food and catering, music, and other services that are less language-dependent) gradually expands to embrace not only Russian-speakers but also local residents, who appreciate Russian cuisine and folk singers. Many Russian-owned businesses rely on transnational social networks (e.g., for the supply of groceries, books, records, and other cultural products) and gradually create small-scale but lasting economic ties between the FSU and its diasporas—in Israel, North America, and Europe.

Reflecting their firm roots in the Russian language and culture, former Soviet immigrants living on four continents (Europe, Asia, America, and Oceania) are gradually weaving a web of a transnational community spanning all the Soviet successor states and their new homelands. As opposed to the Soviet times when émigrés had to burn all the bridges to their past, in the 1990s Russia, Ukraine, and other newly independent states turned their face towards their co-ethnics abroad as a valuable economic and political resource. Significant shares of ex-Soviet immigrants (between 25 percent in Israel and 70 percent in Germany) keep their Russian, Ukrainian, and other former Soviet passports, and some have residential property in their former homelands. Fortified by time- and space-compressing technologies—modern communications, easy travel, and the omnipotent Internet—Russian-speaking immigrants can stay in touch with their friends and relatives in the FSU and other branches of the post-Soviet diaspora, run joint businesses with their compatriots and vote in their national elections. Global Russian press and TV networks (represented by the *RTVi* channel in New York, the *Europe Express* newspaper in Berlin, and *Inostranetz* [Foreigner] magazine in Moscow) further reinforce the interest in the former homelands and the life on the "Russian street" in other countries. Celebrities of the Russian theater, music, and show business regularly tour the main Russian hubs of Israel, Europe, and America, becoming household icons in Haifa and Los Angeles, Munich and Toronto. KVN and *Chto-Gde-Kogda* teams from Kiev, Jerusalem, and San Francisco come to Moscow for their global league contests, broadcast by the Russian satellite TV networks in at least twenty countries. Thus, the human links in the Russian-speaking global community are both physical (enacted in visits and activities transcending national borders) and virtual (multiple Internet contacts via Russian websites, featuring dating, file sharing, topical forums, intellectual games, and more). So far, most transnational ties among former Soviets living in different countries have emerged from below, that is, as individual initiative rather than institutional effort, and it embraced mainly social and cultural rather than economic domains. One can envision further expansion of economic and institutional forms of Russian transnationalism with the growing prosperity and invest-ment capacity of the former Soviets abroad, pending greater political stability and predictable financial environment in the FSU.[3]

Reader can legitimately ask: how long would the global "Russian street" outside Russia last in its current forms? No one can pretend to know the answer, but it apparently has to do with the social and cultural dispositions of the young immigrants—the 1.5 and second generation. Will children of Russian-speaking families enact their ethnicity in a practical or purely symbolic way, like descendants of Armenian refugees in the U.S. (Bakalian, 1992), who gradually drifted from *being* to *feeling* Armenian? Will they still speak Russian among themselves and with their own children another fifteen or twenty years down the road? Current literature on immigrant ethnicity suggests that processes of integration and assimilation of subsequent migrant gen-erations are hard to predict (Faist, 2000; Portes and Rumbaut, 2001). Few contemporary scholars endorse the linear model of assimilation that was popular in the 1970s and 1980s, especially in light of apparent revival of ethnicity and fortification of ethnic diasporas in all pluralist modern societies. The available research on the incorporation of young Russian-Jewish immigrants in Israel, U.S., and Germany points to a combination of good instrumental integration in the host country's institutions with a definite preference for co-ethnics in informal social networking and continued interest in Russian cultural products. Many immigrant children manifest social mimicry at the outset seeking acceptance by their local peers, only to discover later their unique cultural baggage as an asset. It is not uncommon for the young immigrants who grew up in large American cities or in Israeli kibbutzim to suddenly rediscover Russian literature and cinema, or travel to the cities in the FSU their parents came from. Some will eventually opt for a transnational lifestyle, splitting their time and interests between Moscow, New York, and Jerusalem. Influenced by the core values espoused by their parents and co-ethnic milieu, many young Russian Jews of today feel alienated by their local peers. Yet, among children born to Russian immigrants abroad the gravity center of interests and values clearly shifts towards the mainstream peer culture, despite conscientious efforts of the parents to preserve their Russianness (e.g., by sending them to Russian kindergartens, hiring Russian teachers, etc.). It goes without saying that the extent of cultural continuity among young Russian immigrants depends on their parents' background and attitudes towards host societies, as well as their own educational and occupational mobility and experiences with local peers. The bottom line is that the thriving cultural and economic life on the "Russian street" will surely persist during the lifespan of the current adult generation of former Soviets, and will perhaps linger for several decades among their children. I would not dare to make a longer forecast, but fifty years seem quite enough for a follow-up study of one of the most diverse, energetic, and upwardly mobile ethnic diasporas of today's world.

Notes

1. The demographic profile and vital balance of former Soviet Jews has been largely improving due to resettlement to the countries with higher living standards and better health care, but to various extents. In Israel, the rise in fertility rates and reduction in premature deaths among Russian olim is already apparent, promising to improve the age composition in the next generation, while in Germany, Jewish fertility rates remain very low. No direct demographic data are available

for Russian-Jewish immigrants in North America, but some indirect sources point to a slow increase in birth rates and mortality reduction also there.

2. The setting of the Jewish community services in New York is hilariously depicted in Gary Shteyngart's novel *The Russian Debutante's Handbook,* where an elderly Russian immigrant tries to bribe his young caseworker to secure his help in gaining U.S. citizenship he had been denied for his bad behavior (assaulting a fellow Arab immigrant) at the ceremony.

3. Some buds of transnational cooperation in science and technology have appeared in the form of multilateral research projects initiated by the Israeli Ministry of Science in the areas of traditional strength of Russian/Soviet scientists (such as physics and aerodynamics), with the goal of attracting Russian-speaking specialists residing in different diaspora countries.

Glossary

Acculturation is a process of cultural adaptation by immigrants and minorities to the dominant cultural norms of their new societies. As opposed to more inclusive terms *assimilation* and *integration*, acculturation refers mainly to learning the language and cultural ways of the host society (including dress, hairstyles, and other external changes), as well as increased cultural consumption of the local cultural products (TV shows, the press, literature, etc.). Acculturation mainly occurs among first generation immigrants who were born and socialized in the old country; its pace depends on age, gender, social class, and other personal traits.

Aliyah (immigration to Israel) and *olim* (new immigrants) are Hebrew terms, or rather, ideological labels, ensuing from the Zionist tenet of homecoming. Aliyah means ascent or pilgrimage, derived from the ascent to Jerusalem as a holy site located in the hills of Judea. Olim literally means the rising ones, or the pilgrims. These terms are still in common use in contemporary Hebrew, despite multiple challenges to the Zionist master narrative and growing realization that aliyah is no different from any other immigration experience, entailing losses, adjustments, and cultural gap with the hegemonic majority.

Ashkenazi Jews are the Jews whose ancestors come from Central and Eastern Europe, historically spreading from Ashkenaz – the ancient Yiddish name of Germany. Most Ashkenazi Jews spoke both Yiddish and the language of their country of residence. The majority of the world Jewish population (including the FSU, North and South America, Europe and Oceania) are of Ashkenazi descent. Ashkenazi Jews coming mainly from Poland, Russia, Germany and Austro-Hungary formed both the leadership and the masses of the Zionist movement and founded the State of Israel. Until this day they largely retain their privileged status as the country's political and economic elite, although in younger generations this is changing due to mixed marriage and upward mobility of non-European (*Mizrahi*) Jews.

Assimilation is a social process of dissolution of a minority (ethnic, linguistic, religious, etc.) in the surrounding majority, via severing their old identity and lifestyle and adopting those of the hegemonic or majority population. Until recently, theories of linear assimilation process from one migrant generation to the next were predominant in both American and Israeli immigration research; yet in Israel "absorption" (*klita*) was expected to occur already in the first adult generation of return migrants (olim). Actual immigrant experiences in most countries have challenged linear models of assimilation, and the alternative terms, such as *integration* and *acculturation*, have emerged in the discourse to describe the social insertion of immigrants.

Aussiedler is a German term for ethnic Germans who have lived for many generations in the Russian Empire and the USSR. Over 2.5 million of ethnic Germans returned to their historic homeland—unified Germany—after 1989. Like their counterparts in Israel, Greece and some other countries receiving ethnic return migrants, they are granted German citizenship and full political rights soon upon migration. Some German scholars have compared the integration experiences of aussiedler and a much smaller group of former Soviet Jewish immigrants, finding both similarities and differences.

Blat is a Soviet version of informal networking and exchange of goods and favors hard to procure under the "shortage economy," an omnipresent form of barter used as a survival tool by most Soviet citizens. To get something (e.g., quality winter boots, French perfume or tickets to a fashionable theatre play) *po blatu* means to procure it via informal social ties, usually on the basis of reciprocity.

Core Jews, as well as Jewish *periphery*, or *enlarged Jewish population,* are demographic and ethnologic terms. The former refers to those who have two Jewish parents and self-identify in censuses and surveys as Jews; the latter – to persons with one Jewish parent or grandparent, as well as non-Jewish spouses of Jews. Reflecting processes of assimilation, the ratio between the Jewish core and periphery in the FSU has been growing from one generation to the next, being now close to 1:2.

Diaspora literally means dispersion, referring usually to ethnic groups living outside their historic homelands. The archetypal Diaspora has been that of stateless Jewish people before the foundation of the State in 1948; afterwards the term denoted Jewish communities outside Israel (although some critics deem this dichotomy irrelevant, re-defining modern Jewish world as multi-centric—see, for example, Shneer and Aviv's 2005 book "New Jews"). For the former Soviet émigrés of any ethnicity, Russia, Ukraine, and other parts of the FSU had been, until recently, their historic homelands. This was the home they left after the fall of communism, while retaining multiple symbolic and practical ties to it, and this allows me to speak of the *post-communist diaspora.*

Ethnically-privileged (or return) migration is a type of late twentieth-century migrations ideologically framed as in-gathering of diasporas, or home-coming by co-ethnics (*ex sanguinis*) historically detached from their homelands by wars, demise of multinational empires, change of borders, political regimes and economic opportunities. The examples or ethnic return migration (also called repatriation) include the return of ethnic Germans to Germany from parts of Eastern Europe and the USSR; the return of Pontiac Greeks from Southern Russia to Greece, and of Japanese from Brazil, Chile and other Latin American countries to Japan. Most countries receiving back their diasporas typically grant the returnees citizenship soon upon entry.

Ethnography is an approach to data collection based on unobtrusive methods of study of various social groups observed in their natural environs (the home, workplace, and other social settings). Originally used in ethnology and anthropologic research among non-European ethnic groups, this methodology became popular in *qualitative social research* generally. Besides observations (participant and non-participant), ethnographic research includes in-depth interviews with key informants and sometimes also discussion (focus) groups. Ethical issues in this kind of research revolve around researcher-informants relationship, for example, the extent to which s/he is willing to uncover the research questions and goals, ways of ensuring unbiased attitude towards the participants, etc.

Giyur is the procedure of conversion to Judaism (*ger* is a covert). As opposed to other monotheistic religions, Judaism does not proselytize and deliberately makes conversion very difficult and demanding. The candidates must study the oral and written Hebrew tradition, be well versed in the main religious texts and comply with the strict regulations of the everyday life (keeping kosher, dressing modestly, performing Sabbath rituals, etc.). Most converts to Judaism in Israel are non-Jewish women married to Jews, as their *giyur* is the only way for their children to join the Jewish mainstream. Only full Orthodox conversion is recognized by rabbinical courts and the Ministry of the Interior as basis for changing registration in the ID cards, while the more lenient Reform and Conservative versions of *giyur* are not taken into account. During the 1990s, only about 3 percent of non-Jewish immigrants from the FSU in Israel became Jews through *giyur*.

Goy (m) / goya (f) is a non-Jew, Gentile man or woman (Yiddish).

Halacha is ancient Hebrew Common Law code used until this day by the rabbis and religious courts in Israel. Halacha posits a strict definition of a Jew as a person who was born of a Jewish mother or else underwent the full Orthodox conversion (*giyur*); it also regulates the main life-cycle rites of marriage, divorce, burial, and coming-of-age (circumcision and bar/bat-mitzvah), all of which are controlled and managed by Israeli religious authorities.

HIAS, Hebrew Immigrant Aid Society, is one of the oldest American Jewish organizations, actively involved in resettlement of Jewish immigrants in North America since the nineteenth century. HIAS was instrumental in the resettlement and initial socio-economic adjustment of over 400,000 former Soviet Jews who immigrated since the early 1970s. After providing initial aid in housing, school placement for children and other practical matters, HIAS usually refers new immigrants to other Jewish social services, such as JVS (Jewish Vocational Services), Jewish Child and Family Services, the English language classes, etc.

Homo Sovieticus is a term (usually ironic or pejorative) used to describe the social type molded by State Socialism over its seventy+ years of ideological indoctrination and meager living standards. Usually implies such features as social dependency, lack of initiative, and compliance with social control, along with manipulation of the state bureaucracy at all levels ("working the system, bending the rules") as a survival tool. The novelist Alexander Zinoviev coined this term in his sharp 1976 satire *Ziyayushie Vysoty* (*The Yawning Heights*) denouncing collaborationism of Russian intelligentsia with the Soviet regime.

Hyphenated identity, also known as multiple or salami-style identity – are all part of the discourse on immigration and identity change. Sociologists typically see identity as malleable and context-bound, but in immigrant circumstances this plasticity has to increase in the process of social and cultural adjustment. While keeping their identity core from their prior life (including their native language, occupation, social class affiliation, etc.), adult immigrants usually add new identity layers resulting from their new experiences. External expressions of identity (appearance, dress, home decoration, some forms of leisure) are more prone to rapid change than more intrinsic and private ones (family lifestyles, choice of friends and dates/spouses, religious practices). Immigrants often prefer hyphenated identity labels (e.g., Russian Israeli, Turkish German, or Chinese American) that offer them more flexibility in self-definition and lifestyle.

Integration is a more realistic way (vis-à-vis *assimilation*) to describe the process of social insertion of immigrants and minorities in the host country's mainstream. Integration usually implies successful instrumental adaptation to the host country's labor market, with the ensuing economic mobility, and successful navigation of its social institutions (schools, financial, legal, social welfare, and health care systems). At the same time, integration does not assume the severance of the old identity, but rather adding to it new layers and facets facilitating adjustment and success in the new society. Well-integrated immigrants of the first and 1.5 generations are usually bilingual, bicultural and able of effective situational switch between their old and new cultures.

Intelligentsia is a Russian term referring broadly to the educated class of citizens, as well as to people endowed with social consciousness and broad cultural interests. In the Soviet vernacular, there was a further distinction between scientific and technical intelligentsia, on one hand, and creative intelligentsia (writers, artists, etc.), on the other. Intelligentsia not directly involved in "material production" was often juxtaposed with the "working class."

Intifada, the Palestinian uprising against Israeli occupation of the West Bank and Gaza. The first Intifada took place in the late 1980s-early 1990s and caused, among other factors, the 1993 Oslo accords; the second one stared in September 2000 and ended around the time of Arafat's death in November 2004. If the first Intifada was fought mainly with stones and homemade explosives, by the second one Palestinians have accumulated enough automatic weapons and rockets to cause greater damage and multiple causalities on both sides.

Judisches Gemeinde, German for the Jewish Community, an officially recognized religious congregation (mainly of Orthodox denomination) receiving funding and support from the German state. *JG* was the main social force that lobbied for and organized the immigration of the 1990s wave of Russian Jewish immigrants in the German lands. Yet, given the Halachic principle in establishing its membership (i.e., accepting only Jews born of Jewish mothers), just about half of some 220,000 allegedly Jewish newcomers from the FSU could join the *JG*.

Klita, Hebrew for absorption, that is, the dissolution of the added immigrant minority in the hegemonic Israeli majority. This term reflects the aspiration for rapid social and cultural assimilation of the newcomers in line with the "melting pot" principle, including their expedient switch into Hebrew as a primary language. The assimilationist ideology and policy have been applied to all the waves of immigration to Israel from both Western and Middle Eastern countries as part of the nation building strategy.

Mizrahi Jews originate in the countries of the Middle East, including North Africa, Yemen, Iran, and Iraq. They lived in these countries for thousands of years as a result of Babylonian exile, speaking different dialects of the Arabic and Farsi as their native languages. The massive wave of Mizrahi Jews arrived in Israel in the early 1950s, mainly from Morocco and Yemen, over the years forming the underclass in the Ashkenazi-dominated Israeli society. Social mobility of Mizrahi Jews was limited by the low human capital of the adult generation, residency in peripheral Israeli towns with poor educational opportunities, and common prejudice of the Ashkenazi mainstream (see *Orientalism*). Although by now the economic and social status of the second-generation Mizrahi Jews has greatly improved, they are still underrepresented among key professions and in many social institutions.

NAYANA, New York Association for New Americans, an arm of the New York Jewish charities assisting recent immigrants (mainly of Jewish descent) to get their initial foothold in Metropolitan New York by providing social services, English classes, etc.

Orientalism is a concept coined by the Palestinian-American social philosopher Edward Said in his book *Orientalism* (1978), which gave rise to the research stream known as post-colonial studies. Orientalism is a frame of reference or a discourse, in which the peoples and cultures of the East (mainly those drawing on Islam) are viewed as inherently different from and inferior to those of the West, based on the Judeo-Christian tradition. Orientalist discourse is a powerful tool of "othering" of the Arabs and other Moslems, as well as of "Arab Jews" or Mizrahim, whose cultural roots lie in the East. Russian immigrants in Israel often partake in the orientalist interpretations of culture and lifestyle in Israel generally (as a Levantine country) and of behavior and demeanor of dark-skinned Mizrahi Jews.

Point System is the procedure of selecting potential immigrants on the basis of their human capital and adaptive potential in the host country (as opposed to ethnic affinity, family reunification, political asylum or other principles). Variations of this approach to immigrant policy are applied in Canada, Australia, New Zealand, the UK, and some other countries. The most common criteria used to screen the applicants are age, education, occupation and professional experience, host language proficiency, an interest of potential employer (or a job offer), and availability of help in resettlement from the family and friends already living in the country. All these are aimed at diminishing social dependency of the prospective immigrants and maximize the benefit to the host country's economy.

Qualitative research methods (personal interviews, observations, discussion groups) are increasingly popular in social sciences as they allow tapping on the subjects that are difficult to quantify and measure by traditional statistical methods. Theoretical approach used by many qualitative researchers is *grounded theory* developed by Barney Glaser and Anselm Strauss, the main tenet of which is that theoretical explanations should rise from the "ground," that is, draw on constantly compared empirical findings. Qualitative inquiry does not seek to establish social/behavioral patterns in large representative samples, but rather aims at in-depth understanding of people's subjective interpretations of their social and personal reality. As rich and lengthy personal interviews can only be given by motivated (i.e., self-selected) informants, qualitative findings do not claim to be broadly generalizable. Rather, they help sociologists glean insight into unique personal experiences (e.g., childbirth, breast cancer or immigration),as well as the mechanisms of personal decision-making, beliefs, biases, and generally to answer the question of *why* people do what they do.

Quantitative research methods in sociology try to imitate "objective" research methods used by the "hard sciences" by means of quantification of research tools and statistical analysis of the findings. Often the existing or new social theory is tested by means of empirical quantitative study, being either refuted or endorsed. Surveys in large, representative population samples, with structured questionnaires (i.e., with closed answers formulated by researcher), usually administered in an impersonal way (i.e., by telephone or post) to save the costs of face-to-face interview, form the backbone of current quantitative social research. Survey research usually aims at identifying facts and patterns of human behavior, while seldom attempting at in-depth explanations. As response rates are dropping in most "over-surveyed populations," the value and generalizability of mass surveys become more questionable.

Refusniks (also spelt as *refuseniks*) is an anglicized version of a Russian word *otkazniki*, from otkaz – refusal – meaning thousands of former Soviet Jews who had been denied exit visa to Israel by the Soviet regime between the early 1970s and mid–1980s. Most refusniks lost their jobs and many were under KGB surveillance. Refusniks formed an active part of the Soviet dissident movement; most of them left for Israel or the USA in the late 1980s and early 1990s.

Regulated occupations are those deemed socially-important and/or potentially damaging to the well-being of citizens in case of malpractice, with the ensuing testing of professional competence and/or retraining for foreign-educated practitioners. This testing is in the form of state or bar exams, accreditation by local professional associations, etc. Most occupations in human services (medicine, nursing, law, social work, counseling, school teaching), as well as some kinds of engineering (e.g., civil and construction) are subjected to regulations in most developed countries. Hence, immigrants who had been trained and experiences in these occupations abroad, have to undergo licensure procedures upon migration in order to get back to practice in the host country.

Russian Jews is an inclusive category for the purposes of this volume, referring to all former Soviet Jews united by their Russian linguistic and cultural background. The majority of Soviet Jews lived in Russia, Ukraine, and Belorussia, with about 25 percent spread across the Baltic states, the Caucasus and Central Asia. About 90 percent of former Soviet Jewry is of Ashkenazi ethnic origin and 95 percent were urban residents.

Sabra, an Israeli-born Jew.

Sephardic Jews (*Spharadim* in Hebrew) are Jews historically originating from Spain (*Spharad* in Hebrew) and Portugal, who resettled mainly in Southern Europe and the Balkans after their expulsion from Spain in the fifteenth century. This term used to denote non-Ashkenazi Jews in general, but its original meaning refers mainly to the Jews of Greece, Turkey, Bulgaria, Southern Italy, and other Mediterranean countries. Ladino was the native language of Sephardic Jews. In a popular dichotomy between Ashkenazi (Western) and Mizrahi (Eastern) Jews, Sephardic Jews (who actually form a separate category) are often associated with Mizrahi Jewry.

Shtetl, a small Jewish town, usually in the former Pale of Settlement, that is, remote areas where Jews were allowed to settle in the Russian empire (Western parts of Russia, Ukraine, Belorussia, Poland, Lithania, etc.).

Sochnut (or The Jewish Agency for Israel) – an international Jewish organization, whose chief goal is the preparation and implementation of Aliyah of Jews to Israel, as well as the preservation of the Jewish life in the Diaspora. The examples of the current Sochnut programs are Birthright Israel in the Anglophone countries (offering fee or subsidized trips to Israel for the Jewish youth) and programs NAALE and SELA for high school students in the Soviet successor states wishing to continue their education in Israel.

SSI, supplemental social security, a monthly benefit low-income immigrants (including the elderly) are entitled to under American welfare laws. Individuals, who qualify for the SSI, usually also receive federal health care program for the poor, Medicaid.

Thaw is a metaphoric name denoting a short-lived period of political liberalization of the Soviet regime soon after Stalin's death in 1953. The impetus to the Thaw has been given by Nikita Khrushchev's famous speech at the Twentieth Communist Party Congress in 1956, denouncing the "excesses" and outright "crimes" of the Stalinist past. The Thaw was associated with mild political and economic reforms and relaxation of political censorship in literature, press, and the arts, with the ensuing outburst of creative potential (some of the best Soviet films and novels, as well as scientific discoveries, have appeared during these years). The decade of the Thaw gradually wilted after Leonid Brezhnev became the general secretary in 1964; his conservative and corrupt rule led to stagnation in all spheres of life in the USSR over the 1970s and early 1980s.

Ulpan is a mandatory Hebrew language class that every *Ole* (newcomer) is expected to attend during the initial months of his/her life in Israel. The Ulpans are funded by the state and their students get a subsistence stipend, so that they can devote most of their time to the study of Hebrew and some religious and cultural traditions. In practice, many students of the 1990s had to supplement this small income by part-time work, depleting their time and energy and impeding their advancement in Hebrew. The "Hebrew-in-Hebrew" teaching method used in most Israeli Ulpans proved to be of dubious efficiency for adult Russian-speakers who had never been exposed to this language in their Soviet lives.

Yerida (Hebrew for descent) means leaving Israel for good, or for a long time. Out-migrants are called *ha-yordim*. By existing estimates, between 500,000 to 700,000 of Israeli citizens permanently live abroad, most commonly in the U.S., Canada, and Western Europe.

Bibliography

Adams Friend, Bruce (2005). *Tiny Revolutions in Russia: Twentieth Century Soviet and Russian History in Anecdotes.* Taylor and Francis.

Adva Center (2002). *Single Motherhood in Israel: Facts and Comparisons.* Tel-Aviv: Adva Center Reports (Hebrew).

Agozino, Biko, ed. (2000). *Theoretical and Methodological Issues in Migration Research. Interdisciplinary, Intergenerational and International Perspectives.* Aldershot: Ashgate.

Alba, Richard D. (1990). *Ethnic Identity: The Transformation of White America.* New Haven, CT: Yale University Press (1990)

Alba, Richard and Nee, Victor (1997). Rethinking Assimilation Theory for a New Era of Immigration. *International Migration Review,* 31(4), pp. 826–874.

Al-Haj, Majid (2002). Ethnic Mobilization in an Ethno-National State: the Case of Immigrants from the Former Soviet Union in Israel. *Ethnic and Racial Studies,* 25(2), 238–257.

Al-Haj, Majid (2004). *Immigration and Ethnic Formation in a Deeply Divided Society: The Case of the 1990s Immigrants from the FSU in Israel.* Leiden: Brill.

Althausen, Leonid (1993). Journey of Separation: Elderly Russian Immigrants and Their Adult Children in the Health Care Setting. *Social Work in Health Care,* 19(1): 61–75.

Altshuler, Mordecai (1987). *Soviet Jewry Since the Second World War: Population and Social Structure.* Westport, CT: Greenwood Press.

Altshuler, Mordechai (1998). *Soviet Jewry on the Eve of the Holocaust: A Social and Demographic Profile.* Jerusalem: Center for Research on East European Jewry, The Hebrew University of Jerusalem, and *Yad Va-Shem* Museum of the Holocaust. Chapters 2–4.

Anisef, Paul, Baichman-Anisef Ellen, and Siemiatycki, Meyer. (2002). *Multiple Identities and Marginal Ties: The Experience of Russian Jewish Immigrant Youth in Toronto.* Center of Excellence for Research on Immigration and Settlement (CERIS), Working Paper No.19. Toronto: CERIS Publications.

Anthias, Floya (2001). New Hybridities, Old Concepts: The Limits of 'Culture.' *Ethnic and Racial Studies,* 24(4), pp.619–641.

Ashwin, Sara (2002). "A Woman is Everything": The Reproduction of Soviet Ideals of Womanhood in Post-Communist Russia. In: A. Smith, A. Rainnie, and A. Swain (Eds.) *Work, Employment and Transition: Restructuring Livelihoods in Post-Communist Eastern Europe.* London: Routledge.

Ashwin, Sara and Lytkina, Tatiana. (2004). Men in Crisis in Russia: The Role of Domestic Marginalization. *Gender and Society*, 18(2): 189–206.

Aroian, K.J., Khatutsky G., Tran, T.V. and Balsam A.L. (2001). Health and Social Service Utilization among Elderly Immigrants from the Former Soviet Union. *Journal of Nursing Scholarship*, 33 (3): 265–271.

Aroian, K.J., Norris, A.E., and Chiang, L. (2003). Gender Differences in Psychosocial Distress among Immigrants from the Former Soviet Union. *Sex Roles*, 48(1/2): 39–51.

Axelrod, Toby (2005). More Russian Jews Expected as Germany Amends Immigration Law. The Jewish Agency for Israel Website: www.jafi.org.il, posted on June 28, 2005.

Azarya, Victor and Kimmerling, Baruch (1998). New Immigrants as a Special Group in the Israeli Armed Forces. In: J.T. Shuval and E. Leshem (eds). *Immigration to Israel: Sociological Perspectives*. Studies of Israeli Society Series, Vol.VIII. New Brunswick: Transaction, pp. 229–252.

Bakalian, Anny (1992). *Armenian-Americans: From Being to Feeling Armenian*. New Brunswick: Transaction.

Bardach, Rebecca (2005). Israel: A Country of Immigration. In: *World Migration 2005: Costs and Benefits of International Migration*. Geneva: International Organization for Migration.

Basok, Tanya (1991). Soviet Immigration to Canada: The End of the Refugee Program? In T. Basor and R. Brym (eds) Soviet Jewish Emigration and Resettlement in the 1990s, Toronto: York Lanes Press, pp. 141–158.

Basok, Tanya (1997). Occupational Experience of Soviet Immigrant Physicians in Canada. In J.T. Shuval and J. Bernstein (eds), *Immigrant Physicians: Former Soviet Doctors in Israel, Canada and the United States*. Westport, CT: Praeger, pp. 93–115.

Basok, Tanya and Brym, Robert J. (2000). *The Jewish Community from the former USSR in Toronto*. A Report for the Department of Canadian Heritage, Multiculturalism Canada (unpublished paper).

Barankin, T., Konstantareas, N., and De Bosset, F. (1989). Adaptation of Recent Soviet Jewish Immigrants and Their Children in Toronto. *Canadian Journal of Psychiatry*, 34 (6), 78–85.

Bell, Duncan S.A. (2003). Mythscapes: Memory, Mythology, and National Identity. *British Journal of Sociology*, 54: 63–81.

Ben-David, Amit and Lavee, Yael (1994). Migration and Marital Distress: The case of Soviet Immigrants. *Journal of Divorce and Remarriage* 21(3/4): 133–146.

Ben-Rafael, Eliezer, Olshtain, Elite, and Geijst, Idith. (1998). Identity and Language: The Social Insertion of Soviet Jews in Israel. In: J.T. Shuval and E. Leshem (eds). *Immigration to Israel: Sociological Perspectives*. Studies of Israeli Society, Vol.VIII. New Brunswick: Transaction, 333–356.

Bensimon, Doris (2003). Jews in Today's Germany. *The Jewish Journal of Sociology*, 45 (1–2): 20–33.

Berkowitz, M., Tananbaum, S.L. and Bloom, S.W. (eds) (2003). *Forging Modern Jewish Identities: Public Faces and Private Struggles*. London and Portland, OR: Valentine Mitchell Press.

Bernstein, Julia (2004). *Coping with "Capitalism:" How Jewish Immigrants from the Former Soviet Union in Israel and Germany Experience and Interpret their New Societies.* Paper presented at the Conference *"Russian Jews in Germany in the 20ᵗʰ and 21 Centuries,"* Sussex University, Brighton, UK, December 2004.

Berry, John W. (1990). Psychology of Acculturation: Understanding Individuals Moving between Cultures. In Brislin R.W. (ed) *Applied Cross-Cultural Psychology.* London: Sage, pp.232–253.

Berry, John W. (2001). A Psychology of Immigration. *Journal of Social Issue,* 57(3), pp. 615–631.

Bezmozgis, David (2004). *Natasha and Other Stories.* Farrar, Straus, and Giroux.

Bloemraad, Irene (2004). Who Claims Dual Citizenship? The Limits of Postnationalism, the Possibilities of Transnationalism, and the Persistence of Traditional Citizenship. *International Migration Review* 38(2): 389–426.

Bodemann, Michael, Ed. (1996*). Jews, Germany, Memory: Reconstruction of Jewish life in Germany.* Ann Arbor: University of Michigan.

Boym, Svetlana (2001). *The Future of Nostalgia.* New York: Basic Books.

Branover, Herman, Sir Isaiah Berlin, and Zeev Wagner (1998). *The Encyclopedia of Russian Jewry. Biographies.* Northvale, NJ & Jerusalem: Jason Aronson Inc.

Brubaker, Rogers (1998). Migrations of Ethnic Un-Mixing in the "New Europe". *International Migration Review,* 32(4): 1047–1065.

Brym, Robert J.(with the assistance of Rosalina Ryvkina) (1994). *The Jews of Moscow, Kiev and Minsk: Identity, Antisemitism, Emigration* NY: New York University Press.

Brym, Robert J. (2001). Jewish Immigrants from the Former Soviet Union in Canada, 1996. *East European Jewish Affairs,* 31(2): 36–43.

Brym, Robert J. (2003). Russian Antisemitism: 1996–2000. In: Z. Gitelman, M. Goldman, and M. Glanz (eds). *Jewish Life After the USSR.* Bloomington: Indiana University Press, pp. 99–116.

Capo Zmegac, Jasna (2005). Ethnically Privileged Migrants in their New Homelands. *Journal of Refugee Studies,* 18(2): 199–215.

Caspi, Dan, Adoni, Hanna, Cohen, Akiba A, and Elias, Nelly (2002). The Red and the White and the Blue: Russian Media in Israel. *Gazette* 64 (6): 551 —570.

Castells, Miguel (1997). *The Power of Identity.* Oxford: Blackwell.

CBS –Central Bureau of Statistics of Israel. *Statistical Yearbooks of 2000, 2002, 2004.* Jerusalem, CBS Publishing.

Cherviakov, Valeriy, Gitelman, Zvi, and Shapiro, Vladimir (2003). *E Pluribus Unum?* Post-Soviet Jewish Identities and Their Implications for Communal Reconstruction. In: Chiswick, Barry R. (1997). Soviet Jews in the United States: Language and Labor Market Adjustments Revisited. In: N. Lewin-Epstein et al. (eds). *Russian Jews on Three Continents: Migration and Resettlement.* London: Frank Cass, pp.233–260.

Chiswick, Barry R. (2000). Soviet Jews in the United States: Language and Labor Market Adjustments Revisited. In: E. Olshtain and G. Horenczyk (eds). *Language, Identity and Immigration.* Jerusalem: Magnus Press, 275–300.

Chiswick, Barry R. and Wenz, Michael (2004). *The Linguistic and Economic Adjustment of Soviet Jewish Immigrants in the United States, 2000: A Preliminary*

Report. Paper delivered at the International Conference on the Economic Aspects of International Migration. Bar-Ilan University, June 2004.

Chlenov, Mikhail (1997). Jewish Community and Identity in the Former Soviet Union. In: *Jews of the Former Soviet Union: Yesterday, Today, and Tomorrow.* Conference Proceedings. New York: The American Jewish Committee, pp.11–16.

Cohen, Rina (2001). The New Immigrants: A Contemporary Profile. In R. Klein and F. Diamant (eds), *From Immigration to Integration: The Canadian Jewish Experience. A Millennium Edition.* Toronto: Institute for International Affairs and B'nai-Brit Canada, pp.213–227.

Cohen, Yinon and Haberfeld, Yitchak (1998). Second-Generation Jewish Immigrants in Israel: Have the Ethnic Gaps in Schooling and Earnings Declined? *Ethnic and Racial Studies,* 21(3): 507–528.

Cohen, Yinon and Kogan, Irena (2005). Jewish Immigrants from the Former Soviet Union to Germany and Israel in the 1990s. In: J.A.S. Grenville and R. Gross (eds.). Leo Baeck Institute Year Book, 2005. London: Leo Baeck Institute Publications.

Cooper, Alanna (2003). Feasting, Memorializing, Praying, and Remaining Jewish in the Soviet Union: The Case of the Bukharan Jews. In: Z. Gitelman, M. Goldman, and M. Glanz (eds). *Jewish Life After the USSR.* Bloomington: Indiana University Press, pp. 141–151.

Crabtree, Brian F. and Miller, William L. (1992). A Template Approach to Text Analysis: Developing and Using Codebooks. In B.F. Crabtree and W.L. Miller (Eds). *Doing Qualitative Research.* Newbury Park, CA: Sage, pp.93–109.

Darieva, Tsypylma (2000). Managing Identity: Some Insights into Post-Soviet Russian Language Media in Berlin. Center for Independent Social Research, St. Petersburg. Online: www.indepsocres.spb.ru/sbornik8/8e_Darieva.htm.

Della Pergola, Sergio (2004). Demographic Trends in Israel and Palestine: Prospects and Policy Implications. In: D. Singer and L. Grossman (eds.) *American Jewish Year Book,* 2003. NY: American Jewish Committee, pp.3–70.

Dershowitz, Allan M. (1997). *The Vanishing Jew: In Search of Jewish Identity for the Next Century* New York: Simon & Schuster.

Deutsch Kornblatt, Judith (2003). Jewish Converts to Orthodoxy in Russia in Recent Decades. Gitelman, Zvi et l.(eds). *Jewish Life After the USSR.* Bloomington: Indiana University Press, pp. 209–223.

Dietz, Barbara (2000). German and Jewish Migration from the Former Soviet Union to Germany: Background, Trends and Implications. *Journal of Ethnic and Migration Studies,* 26: 635–52.

Dietz, Barbara, Lebok, Uwe, and Polian, Pavel (2002). The Jewish Emigration from the Former Soviet Union to Germany. *International Migration,* 40: 30–47.

Dion, K.K. and Dion, K.L. (2001). Gender and Cultural Adaptation in Immigrant Families. *Journal of Social Issues* 57(3): 511–521.

Donitsa-Schmidt, Smadar. (1999) *Language Maintenance or Shift: Language Preferences among Former Soviet Immigrants in Israel.* Unpublished Ph.D. Thesis. Tel Aviv University, School of Education.

Dominitz, Yehuda (1997). Israel's Immigration Policy and the Dropout Phenomenon. In: *Russian Jews on Three Continents. Migration and Resettlement.* Ed by N.

Lewin-Epstein, Y. Ro'i and P. Ritterband. London, UK & Portland, OR: Frank Cass, pp. 113–127.

Doomernik, Jeroen (1997). Adaptation Strategies among Soviet Jewish Immigrants in Berlin. *New Community*, 23: 59–79.

Druzhnikov, Yuri (1991). *Angels on the Head of a Pin*. Translated from Russian by Thomas Moore. London: Peter Owen/UNESCO, 566 pp.

Eisikovits, Rivka A. (2000). Gender Differences in Cross-Cultural Adaptation Styles of Immigrant Youths from the Former USSR in Israel. *Youth and Society*, 31(3): 310–331.

Eisikovits, Rivka A. (2006). Intercultural Learning among Russian Immigrant Recruits in the Israeli Army. *Armed Forces and Society*, 32(2): 292–306.

Elias, Nelly (2003). *From the Former Soviet Union to Israel and Germany: The Role of Mass Media in the Social and Cultural Integration of Immigrants*. Unpublished Doctoral Dissertation. The Department of Communications, Tel-Aviv University.

Elias, Nelly (2005). Living in Germany, Longing for Israel: The Old Jewish Immigrants from the FSU in Germany. *East European Jewish Affairs*, 35(2): 167–187.

Epstein, Alek and Kheimets, Nina (2000a). Immigrant Intelligentsia and its Second Generation: Cultural Segregation as a Road to Social Integration? *Journal of International Migration and Integration (JIMI/RIMI)*, 1: 461–476.

Epstein, Alek and Kheimets, Nina (2000b). Cultural Clash and Educational Diversity: Immigrant Teachers' Efforts to Rescue the Education of Immigrant Children in Israel. *International Studies in Sociology of Education*, 10(2): 191–210.

Faist, Tomas (2000). *The Volume and Dynamics of International Migration and Transnational Social Spaces*. Oxford: Oxford University Press.

Fearon, Jack and Laitin, David (2000). Review Essay: Violence and the Social Construction of Ethnic Identities. *International Organization*, 54: 845–77.

Feldman, Eliezer (2003). *Russkii Izrail': Mezhdu Dvuh Polusov*. ("Russian" Israel: Between the Two Poles). Moscow: Market DS (in Russian).

Feliciano, Carol (2001). The Benefits of Biculturalism: Exposure to Immigrant Culture and Dropping out of School Among Asian and Latino Youths. *Social Science Quarterly*, 82(4): 865–879.

Fialkova, Larisa and Yelenevskaya, Maria (2004a). Motifs of Antisemitism in FSU Immigrants' Personal Narratives. *Jews and Slavs*, 13: 137–154.

Fialkova, Larisa and Yelenevskaya, Maria (2004b). How to Find the West in the Middle East: Perceptions of the East and West among Russian Jews in Israel. In: A. Paladi-Kovach (ed.). *Times-Places-Passages: Ethnological Approaches in the New Millennium*. Budapest: Hungarian Academy of Sciences.

Fialkova, Larisa (2005). Emigrants from the FSU and the Russian-Language Internet. *Toronto Slavic Quarterly—Academic Electronic Journal in Slavic Studies*, University of Toronto, No 12 (www.utoronto.ca/tsq/12).

Finckenauer, James O. and Waring, Elin (2001). Challenging the Russian Mafia Mystique. *National Institute of Justice Journal*, April 2001. See online version at: http://ncjrs.org./pdffiles1/.

Fishman, Joshua A. (1991). *Reversing Language Shift: Theoretical and Empirical Foundations of Assistance to Threatened Languages*. Clevedon ,UK: Multilingual Matters.

Fishman, Joshua A. (2000). Who Speaks What Language, to Whom, and When? In: J.A. Fishman (ed.). *The Bilingual Reader*. New York: Free Press (first published in 1965).

Friedberg, Robert (2000). "You Can't Take it with You?" Immigrant Assimilation and the Portability of Human Capital. *Journal of Labor Economics*, 18(2): 221–251.

Friedgut, Theodore H. (1989). Passing Eclipse: The Exodus Movement of the 1980s. In: R.O. Freedman (ed). *Soviet Jewry in the 1980s. The Politics of Anti-Semitism and Emigration and the Dynamics of Resettlement*. Durham: Duke University Press, pp.3–25.

Friedgut, Theodore H. (2003). Nationalities Policy, the Soviet Regime, the Jews, and Emigration. In: Gitelman, Zvi et al.(eds). *Jewish Life After the USSR*. Bloomington: Indiana University Press, Pp. 27–48.

Fussel, Paul (2000). *The Great War and Modern Memory*. 2nd Edition. New York: Oxford University Press.

Galasinska, Agnes and Galasinski, Demetri (2003). Discursive Strategies for Coping with Sensitive Topics of the Other. *Journal of Ethnic and Migration Studies*, 29: 849–63.

Geertz, Clifford (1973). Thick Description: Towards an Interpretive Theory of Culture. In C. Geertz, (ed.) *The Interpretation of Culture*. New York: Basic Books.

Gershenson, Olga (2005). *Gesher: Russian Theatre in Israel. A Study of Cultural Colonization*. New York: Peter Lang.

Gershenson, Olga (2006). Russian Jews on Screen. Unpublished article.

Geva-May, Iris (2000). On Impacts of Comparative Policy Analysis. Immigration to Israel: What Other Countries Can Learn. *International Migration*, 38(1): 3–45.

Gitelman, Zvi (1997). "From a Northern Country:" Russian and Soviet Jewish Immigration to America and Israel in Historical Perspective. In: N. Lewin-Epstein et al. (eds). *Russian Jews on Three Continents: Migration and Resettlement*. London: Frank Cass, pp.21–44.

Gitelman, Zvi (1999). Soviet Jews: Creating a Cause and a Movement. In: M. Friedman and A.D.Chernin (eds). *A Second Exodus. The American Movement to Free Soviet Jews*. Hanover & London: Brandeis University Press, pp. 84–93.

Gitelman, Zvi (2003). Thinking About Being Jewish in Russia and Ukraine. In: Z. Gitelman, M. Goldman, and M. Glanz (eds). *Jewish Life After the USSR*. Bloomington: Indiana University Press, pp. 49–60.

Gladilina, Nataliya and Brovkine, Vadim (2005). Sprache und Identitat Judischer Immigranten in Deutschland. In: Schoeps, J.H., Grozinger, K.E., Jasper, W., and Mattenklott, G. (Eds). *Russische Juden und Transnationale Diaspora*. Menora: Publication of Moses Mendelssohn Center for European Jewish Studies, Potsdam University. Berlin: Philo Verlag, pp.151–182.

Glick Schiller, Nina, Basch, Linda, and Szanton Blanc, Carol (1995). From Immigrant to Transmigrant: Theorizing Transnational Migration. *Anthropological Quarterly* 68(1): 48–63.

Glikman, Yaacov (1996). Russian Jews in Canada: Threat to Identity or Promise of Renewal? In H. Adelman and J. Simpson (eds), *Multiculturalism, Jews and Identities in Canada*. Jerusalem: Magnes (The Hebrew University Press), pp. 192–218.

Gold, Steven J. (1997). Community Formation Among Former Soviet Jews in the US. In: N. Lewin-Epstein et al. (eds). *Russian Jews on Three Continents: Migration and Resettlement*. London: Frank Cass, pp.261–283.

Gold, Steven J. (1999). From "The Jazz Singer" to "What a Country!" A Comparison of Jewish Migration to the US: 1800–1930 and 1965–1998. *Journal of American Ethnic History* 18(3): 114–141.

Gold, Steven J. (2003). Israeli and Russian Jews: Gendered Perspectives on Settlement and Return Migration. In: P. Hondagneu-Sotelo (ed.) *Gender and US Immigration: Contemporary Trends*. Berkeley: University of California Press, pp.127–150.

Goldman, Marshall I. (2003). Russian Jews in Business. In: Z. Gitelman, et al.(eds). *Jewish Life After the USSR*. Bloomington: Indiana University Press, pp.76–98.

Goldscheider, Calvin (1996). *Israel's Changing Society. Population, Ethnicity, and Development.* Boulder, CO: Westview Press.

Grillo, Ralph D. (1998). *Pluralism and the Politics of Difference: State, Culture and Ethnicity in Comparative Perspective.* Oxford: Clarendon.

Gross Revital, Brammli-Greenberg Shulamit, and Remennick Larissa (2001). Self-Rated Health Status and Health Care Utilization Among Immigrant and Non-Immigrant Israeli Jewish Women. *Women and Health*, 34(3): 53–70.

Guarnizo, Louis E. and Smith, M.P. (eds.) (1998). *Transnationalism from Below*. New Brunswick, NJ: Transaction Publishers.

Guseinov, Gasan (1997). Observations on the Speech Patterns in the Newly Formed Russian Enclaves in Germany. In: *Fortbildungstagung fur Russischlehrer an bayerischen Gymnasien*. Regensburg: Staatsministeruium fur Unterricht, Kultur, und Kunst (in Russian).

Guseinov, Gasan (2005). Russian Language in German Politics (*Russkii Yasyk v Nemetskoi Politike*). *Toronto Slavic Quarterly, No 12*. On-line version: http://www.utoronto.ca/tsq/12/gusejnov12.shtml.

Hoffman, Betty N. (2001). *Jewish Hearts. A Study of Dynamic Ethnicity in the United States and the Soviet Union*. Albany: State University of New York Press.

Heitman, Sidney. Jewish, German, and Armenian Emigration from the USSR: Parallels and Differences. In: R.O. Freedman (ed). *Soviet Jewry in the 1980s: The Politics of Anti-Semitism and Emigration and the Dynamics of Resettlement*. Durham & London: Duke University Press, 1989, pp. 115–140.

Hondagneu-Sotelo, Pierrette (ed.) (2003). *Gender and U.S. Migration: Contemporary Trends*. Berkeley: University of California Press.

Horenczyk, Gabriel (2000). Conflicted Identities: Acculturation Attitudes and Immigrants' Construction of their Social Worlds. In: E. Olshtain and G. Horenczyk, (eds). *Language, Identity and Immigration*. Jerusalem: Hebrew University Press (Magnes), pp.12–30.

Horowits, Tamar. Integration Without Acculturation: The Absorption of Soviet Immigrants. *Soviet Jewish Affairs*, 1982, 12(3):19–33.

Horowitz, Tamar, and Leshem, Eliezer (1998). The Immigrants from the FSU in the Israeli Cultural Sphere. In: M. Sicron and E. Leshem (Eds.) *Profile of an Immigrant Wave: The Absorption Process of Immigrants from the Former Soviet Union, 1990–1995*. Jerusalem: The Hebrew University (Magnes), pp. 291–333.

Horowitz, Tamar (Ed.) (1999). *Children of Perestroika in Israel.* Lanham, MD: University Press of America.

Horowitz, Tamar (2001). The integration of immigrants from the former Soviet Union: Four scripts of integration. In: S. Avineri and W. Weidenfeld (eds). *Politics and Identities in Transformation: Europe and Israel.* Berlin: Europa Union Verlag.

IMIA—Israeli Ministry of Immigrant Absorption. *Statistical Reports and Special Releases*, Jerusalem: IMIA, 1998, 2000.

Ilatov, Zena and Shamai, Shmuel (1999) "Segmented absorption": Israeli Students' View of Soviet immigrant Students. In: Horowitz, T. (Ed.) *Children of the Perestroika in Israel.* Lanham, MD.: University Press of America, pp. 205–217.

Iredale, Robin R. (1997). *Skills Transfer. International Migration and Accreditation Issues. A comparative study of Australia, Britain, Canada, New Zealand and the United States.* S. Australia: University of Wollongong Press.

Israeli, Dafna and Bejaui-Fogel, Sylvia (eds.) *Sex, Gender, and Politics (Min, Migdar ve Politika).* Tel-Aviv: Tel Aviv University Press (Hebrew).

Isralowitz, Richard, and Friedlander, Jonathan (Eds.) (1999). *Transitions: Russians, Ethiopians, and Bedouins in Israel's Negev Desert.* Ashgate Publications.

Jansen, Carol and Lam, Linda (2003). Immigrants in the Greater Toronto Area: A Socio-Demographic Overview. In P. Anisef and M. Lanphier (eds). *The World in a City.* Toronto: University of Toronto Press, pp. 103–127.

Jasinskaja-Lahti, Inga and Liebkind, Karmela (1999). Exploration of Ethnic Identity among Russian-Speaking Adolescents in Finland. *Journal of Cross-Cultural Psychology,* 30(4): 527–539.

Jasper, Willi and Vogt, Bernhard (2000). Integration and Self-Assertion, In: O. Romberg and S. Urban-Fahr (eds.) *Jews in Germany after 1945. Citizens or "Fellow Citizens"?* Frankfurt: Tribune, pp.217–227.

Jasper, Willi (2005). Deutschland, Europa und die Russisch-Judische Diaspora. Anmerkungen zur Identitatsproblematik in der Forschungsdiskussion. In: Schoeps, J.H., Grozinger, K.E., Jasper, W., and Mattenklott, G. (Eds). *Russische Juden und Transnationale Diaspora.* Menora: Publication of Moses Mendelssohn Center for European Jewish Studies, Potsdam University. Berlin: Philo Verlag, pp. 133–150.

Jones, Allan (ed.) (1991). *Professions and the State: Expertise and Autonomy in the Soviet Union and Eastern Europe.* Philadelphia: Temple University Press.

Joppke, Christian and Rosenhek, Zeev (2002). Contesting Ethnic Immigration: Germany and Israel Compared. *Archives of European Sociology,* XLIII: 301–335.

Joppke, Christian (2005). Resilience Versus Demise in the Diaspora Constellation: Israel and Germany. In: *Selecting by Origin: Ethnic Migration in the Liberal State.* Cambridge: Harvard University Press, pp.157–216.

Jurgens, Jeffrey (2001). Shifting Spaces: Complex Identities in Turkish-German Migration. In: Ludger Pries (ed.) *New Transnational Spaces. International Migration and Transnational Companies in the Early 21 Century.* London and New York: Routledge.

Kaminer, Vladimir. *Russian Disco* (2000); *Journey to Trulala* (2002); *Mama, I am Worried,* (2004). All published by Berlin: Manhattan Verlag (in German).

Kandinov, Veliyam (1996). *Russian Immigration: Bukharan Jews in America*. Translated by Todd Bludeau). New York: Forum Publishers.

Kapphan, Andreas (2000). Russian Entrepreneurs in Berlin: The Role of Ethnicity and Opportunity Structures. Center for Independent Sociological Research, St. Petersburg, Online: www.indepsocres.spb.ru/sbornik8/8e_kapph.htm.

Kasinitz, Philip, Zeltzer-Zubida, Aviva, and Simakhodskaya, Zoya (2001). *The Next Generation: Russian Jewish Young Adults in Contemporary New York*. Russell Sage Foundation Publication. See also: www.russelsage.org/publications/workingpapers

Kasinitz, Philip, Mollenkopf, John, and Waters, Mary (2003). Becoming Americans, Becoming New Yorkers: Immigrant Incorporation in a Majority Minority City. In: J. G. Reitz, (ed) (2003). *Host Societies and the Reception of Immigrants*. La Jolla, CA: Center for Comparative Immigration Studies.

Kay, Rebecca (1997). Images of an Ideal Woman: Perceptions of Russian Womanhood Through the Media, Education and Women's Own Eyes. In M. Buckley (Ed) *Post-Soviet Women: From the Baltic to Central Asia*. Cambridge, UK: Cambridge University Press, pp. 77–98.

Khanin, Zeev (2000). Political Behavior and Voting Patterns among Russian immigrants. In: A. Epstein and A. Fedorchenko (eds). *Mass Migration and its Impact on the Israeli Society*. Jerusalem-Moscow: Hebrew University (In Russian), 198–227.

Kheimets, Nina and Epstein, Alek (2001). Confronting the Languages of Statehood: Theoretical and Historical Frameworks for the Analysis of the Multilingual Identity of the Russian Jewish Intelligentsia in Israel', *Language Problems and Language Planning* 25(2): 151–62.

Kimmerling, Baruch (2001). *The Invention and Decline of Israeliness. State, Society, and the Military*. Berkeley: University of California Press.

King, Jeremy and Naveh, Gedalia (1999). *The Absorption into Employment of Immigrant Engineers*. Jerusalem: JDC-Brookdale Institute for Gerontology and Adult Human Development. (Hebrew).

Kishinevsky, Vera (2004). *Russian Immigrants in the United States: Adapting to American Culture*. NY: LFB Scholarly Publishing.

Kliger, Samuel (2001). The Religion of New York Jews from the Former Soviet Union. In: T. Carnes and A. Karpathakis (eds). *New York Glory: Religions in the City*. NY: New York University Press, pp. 148–161.

Kliger, Samuel (2004). *Presidential Election 2004: Russian Voters*. NY: The American Jewish Committee Report.

Kon, Igor S. (1995). *The Sexual Revolution in Russia: From the Age of Tsars to Today*. New York: Free Press.

Kopeliovich, Shulamit (1999) *Intergenerational Transmission of Russian Literacy in Immigrant Families with Multicultural Orientation*. Unpublished MA Thesis. Bar-Ilan University, Israel.

Krakhmalnikova, Zoya (ed) (1994). *The Great Russian Idea and the Jews*. Collection of Articles. (*Russkaya Ideya I Evrei*). Moscow: Nauka (in Russian).

Kraemer, Roberta, Zisenwine, Dian, Keren, Michal L., and Schers, Dina (1995). A study of Jewish Adolescent Russian Immigrants to Israel: Language and Identity. *International Journal of the Sociology of Language* 116: 153–159.

Krausz Ernest and Tulea Gita (eds) *Jewish Survival: The Identity Problem at the Close of the 20th Century.* New Brunswick, NJ and London: Transaction.

Krutikov, Mikhail (2003). Constructing Jewish Identity in Contemporary Russian Fiction. In: Gitelman, Zvi et al.(eds). *Jewish Life After the USSR.* Bloomington: Indiana University, pp.252–274.

Lazin, Fred A. (2005). *The Struggle of Soviet Jewry in American Politics: Israel Versus American Jewish Establishment.* NY: Lexington Books.

Ledeneva, Alena (1998). *Russia's Economy of Favors: Blat, Networking, and Informal Exchange.* Cambridge and NY: Cambridge University Press.

Lemish, Dafna (2000). The Whore and the Other: Israeli Images of Female Immigrants from the Former USSR. *Gender and Society*, 14: 333–349.

Lerner, Julia (1999). *By Way of Knowledge: Russian Migrants at the University.* Shaine Working Papers, No 5. Jerusalem: The Hebrew University (Hebrew).

Lerner, Miri and Hendeles, Yitzhak (1996). New Entrepreneurs and Entrepreneurial Aspirations among Immigrants from the Former USSR in Israel. *Journal of Business Research*, 36: 136–151.

Lerner, Miri and Menahem, Gila (2003). Decredentialization and Recredentialization: The Role of Governmental Support in Enhancing Occupational Opportunities of Immigrants: The Case of Russian Immigrants in Israel in the 1990s. *Work and Occupations*, 30 (1): 3–29.

Leshem, Eliezer and Lissak, Moshe (1998). The Israeli Public's Attitudes toward the New Immigrants of the 1990s. In: E. Leshem and J.T.Shuval (Eds.), *Immigration to Israel: Sociological Perspectives* (pp. 307–330). New Brunswick: Transaction.

Leshem, Eliezer and Lissak, Moshe (1999). Development and Consolidation of Russian Community in Israel. In S. Weiss (Ed.), *Roots and Routs: Ethnicity and Migration in Global Perspective* (pp.136–171). Jerusalem: Hebrew University (Magnes).

Levy, Daniel and Sznaider, Norman (2002), Memory Unbound: The Holocaust and the Formation of Cosmopolitan Memory. *European Journal of Social Theory,* 5: 87–106.

Levy, Daniel and Weiss, Yifat (eds) (2002). *Challenging Ethnic Citizenship: German and Israeli Perspectives on Immigration.* New York and Oxford: Berghahn Books.

Levinson, Alexei G. (1997). Attitudes of Russians towards Jews and their Emigration, 1989–1994. In: N. Lewin-Epstein et al. (eds). *Russian Jews on Three Continents. Migration and Resettlement.* London, UK & Portland, OR: Frank Cass, pp.222–231.

Lewin-Epstein, Noah, Ro'i, Yaakov, and Ritterband, Paul. *Russian Jews on Three Continents. Migration and Resettlement.* London, UK & Portland, OR: Frank Cass, 1997, 557 pp.

Liakhovitsky, Dimitri (2004). Survey of Russian Immigrants Living in the U.S. (Age 20–40) Conducted in May-June 2004. Website: www.elinagorelik.net/emigrantsurvey.

Liakhovitsky, Dimitri (2005). *Community Conversations with Young Russian Speak-*

ing Jewish Professionals. Report on Findings. NY: United Jewish Appeal Federation of New York.

Liebler, C.A. and Sandefur, G.D. (2002). Gender Differences in the Exchange of Social Support with Friends, Neighbors, and Coworkers at Midlife. *Social Science Research* 31(3): 364–391.

Light, Ivan and Gold, Steven J. (2000). *Ethnic Economies.* San Diego: Academic Press.

Light, Ivan and Isralowitz, Richard E. (1997). *Immigrant Entrepreneurs and Immigrant Absorption in the United States and Israel.* Ashgate: Avebury Books.

Lissak, Moshe and Leshem, Eliezer (1995). The Russian Intelligentsia in Israel: Between Ghettoization and Integration. *Israel Affairs* 2(2): 20–36.

Lisitsa, Sabina and Peres, Yohanan (2000). New Immigrants and Old Timers: Identity and Interrelations—Research Findings. In : A. Epstein and A. Fedorchenko (eds) Mass Migration and its Impact on the Israeli Society. Moscow—Jerusalem: Hebrew University (in Russian), 244–278.

Litwin, Howard (1995). *Uprooted in Old Age: Soviet Jews and their Social Networks in Israel.* Westport, CT: Greenwood.

Lomsky-Feder, Edna and Rapoport, Tamar (2001). Homecoming, Immigration, and the National Ethos: Russian-Jewish Home-comes Reading Zionism. *Anthropological Quarterly,* 74(1): 1–14.

Lomsky-Feder, Edna, Rapoport Tamar, and Lerner, Julia (2005). Orientalism and the Challenge of Migration: "Russian" Students Read *Mizrahiyut. Theory and Criticism,* 26: 119–147 (Hebrew).

Lowenstein, Ariela (2002). Solidarity and Conflicts in Co-residence of Three-Generational Immigrant Families from the Former Soviet Union. *Journal of Aging Studies* 16(3): 221–241.

Markowitz, Fran (1993). *A Community in Spite of Itself: Soviet Jewish Émigrés in New York.* Washington, DC: The Smithsonian Institute Press.

Martin, Terry (1998). The Origins of Soviet Ethnic Cleansing. *The Journal of Modern History,* 70(4): 846–861.

Menachem, Gila and Geijst, Idith (2000). Language and Occupation among Soviet immigrants to Israel in the 1990s. In E. Olshtain and G. Horencyk (eds). *Language, Identity and Immigration.* Jerusalem: Hebrew University Press (Magnus), 301–324.

Merridale, Chris (1999). War, Death and Remembrance in Soviet Russia, In: E. Sivan and J. Winter (eds.) *War and Remembrance in the Twentieth Century.* Cambridge: Cambridge University Press (1999).

Min, P.-G. and Kim, R. (2000). Formation of Ethnic and Racial Identities: Narratives by Young Asian-American Professionals. *Ethnic and Racial Studies* 23(4): 735–760.

Mirsky, Julia and Kaushinsky, Freda (1989). Migration and Growth: Separation and Individuation Processes in Immigrant Students in Israel. *Adolescence* 23: 725–740.

Mirsky, Julia (1998). Psychological Aspects of Immigration and Absorption of Immigrants from the Soviet Union. In: M. Sicron and E. Leshem (Eds.) *Profile of an*

Immigrant Wave: The Absorption Process of Immigrants from the Former Soviet Union, 1990–1995. Jerusalem: The Hebrew University (Magnes), pp.334–367.

Mondak, Jeffery J. and Gearing, Adam F. (2003). Why Post-Communist Citizens Do Not Join Voluntary Organizations? In: G. Badescu and E.M. Uslaner (eds). *Social Capital and The Transition to Democracy.* London: Routledge.

Morawska, Ewa (1999). The Malleable *Homo Sovieticus*: Transnational Entrepreneurs in Postcommunist East Europe. *Communist and Postcommunist Studies,* 32: 359–378.

Morawska, Ewa (2004). Exploring Diversity in Immigrant Assimilation and Transnationalism: Poles and Russian Jews in Philadelphia. *International Migration Review* 38(4): 1372–1412.

Munz, Rainer and Ohliger, Rainer (eds.). *Diasporas and Ethnic Migrants. Germany, Israel, and Post-Soviet Successor States in Comparative Perspective.* London, UK and Portland, OR: Frank Cass, 2003.

Naiditch, Larissa (2004). Russian Immigrants of the Last Wave in Israel: Patterns and Characteristics of Language Use.Wiener Slawistischer Almanach (Vienna University Publication), B53.

Nakhimovski, Alice (2003). Mikhail Zhvanetskii: The Last Russian-Jewish Joker. In: M. Berkowitz, S.L. Tananbaum, and S.W. Bloom (eds). *Forging Modern Jewish Identities.* London and Portland, OR: Valentine Mitchell Press.

Naon, David, King Judith, and Habib, Jack (1993). Resettling Elderly Soviet Immigrants in Israel: Family Ties and the Housing Dilemma. *Journal of Psychology and Judaism* 17(4): 299–313.

National Jewish Population Survey (2001). See the website: http://www. jewishvirtuallibrary.org/jsource/US-Israel/ujcpop.html

Nauck, Bernhard (2001). Social Capital, Intergenerational Transmission and Intercultural Contact in Immigrant Families. *Journal of Comparative Family Studies* (Special Issue: *Immigrant and Ethnic Minority Families*), 32: 465–88.

Naveh, Gedalia, Noam, Gila and Benita, Esther (1995). *The Employment and Economic Situation of Immigrants from the Former Soviet Union: Selected Findings from a National Employment Survey.* Jerusalem: JDC-Brookdale Institute (Hebrew).

Nosenko, Elena E. (2004). Byt' ili chuvstvovat'? Osnovnye aspekty formirovaniya evreiskoi samo-identifikatsii u potomkov smeshannykh brakov v sovremennoi Rossii. (To Be or to Feel Jewish? The Expressions of Jewish Identity among Offspring of Mixed Marriage in Contemporary Russia). Moscow: Institute of Oriental Sciences, Russian Academy of Sciences (in Russian).

Olshtain, Elite and Kotik, Bella (2000). The Development of Bilingualism in an Immigrant Community. In E. Olshtain and G. Horenczyk (eds.) *Language, Identity and Immigration.* Jerusalem: The Hebrew University (Magnes), 201—217.

Orleck, Annelise (1999). *The Soviet Jewish Americans.* "The New Americans" Series, Westport, CT: Greenwood Press.

Palatnik, Yevgenyi and DeAngelis, Pat (2001). Voices of New York: Survey of the Use of the Russian Language in the Brighton Beach Area of Brooklyn. New York University website: http://www.nyu.edu/classes/blake.map2001/russia.html

Peck, Jeffrey M. (2005). *Being Jewish in the New Germany*. New Brunswick, NJ: Rutgers University Press.

Pesmen, Dale (2000). *Russia and Soul: An Exploration*. Ithaca: Cornell University Press.

Pessar, Patricia R. and Mahler, Sarah J. (2003). Transnational Migration: Bringing Gender In. *International Migration Review* 37(3): 812–846.

Pincus, Benjamin (1988). *The Jews of the Soviet Union. The History of a National Minority*. New York: Cambridge University Press.

Portes, Alejandro and Rumbaut, Ruben G. (2001). *Legacies: The Story of the Immigrant Second Generation*. Berkeley: University of California Press. Chapters 3 and 10.

Portes, Alejandro, and DeWind, Josh, eds (2004). Conceptual and Methodological Developments in the Study of International Migration. Special Issue of *International Migration Review,* 38(3).

Primor, Avi (2003). *The Resurrection of the Jewish Community in Germany, from an Israeli Perspective*. Retrieved in June 2005 from the Goethe-Institute website: www.goethe.de/kug/ges/rel/thm/en66123.htm.

PROMPT—*Policy Roundtable: Mobilizing Professions and Trades* (2004). In the Public Interest: Immigrant Assess to Regulated Professions in Today's Ontario. July 2004 (URL: www.promptinfo.ca).

Raijman, Rebecca and Semyonov, Moshe (1998). Best of Times, Worst of Times, and Occupational Mobility: The Case of Soviet Immigrants in Israel. *International Migration* 36(3): 291–312.

Rapoport, Tamar, Lomsky-Feder, Edna, and Heider, Angelika (2002). Recollection and Relocation in Immigration: Russian Jewish Immigrants "Normalize" their Anti-semitic Experiences. *Symbolic Interaction* 25(2): 175–198.

Rapoport, Tamar, and Lomsky-Feder, Edna (2002). Intelligentsia as an Ethnic Habitus: The Inculcation and Restructuring of Intelligentsia among Russian Jews. *British Journal of Sociology of Education*, 23(2): 233–248.

Rebhun, Uzi, and Waxman, Chaim (eds.) (2004). *Jews in Israel: Contemporary Social and Cultural Patterns*. Waltham, MA: Brandeis University Press.

Reitz, Jeffrey (2001). Immigrant Success in the "Knowledge Economy": Institutional Change and the Immigrant Experience in Canada, 1970–1995. *Journal of Social Issues* 57(3): 579–613.

Remennick Larissa, Amir Delila, Elimelech Yuval, and Novikov, Ilya. (1995). Family Planning Practices and Attitudes Among Former Soviet New Immigrant Women in Israel. *Social Science and Medicine,* 41(4): 569–577.

Remennick Larissa and Shtarkshall, Ronny (1997). Technology Versus Responsibility: Immigrant Physicians from the Former USSR Reflect on Israeli Health Care. *Journal of Health and Social Behavior*, 38 (September): 191–202.

Remennick, Larissa (1998). Identity Quest among Russian Jews of the 1990s: Before and After Emigration. In: E. Krausz and G. Tulea (eds) *Jewish Survival: The Identity Problem at the Close of the 20th Century*. New Brunswick, NJ: Transaction, pp.241–258.

Remennick, Larissa and Ottenstein, Naomi (1998). Reaction of Soviet Immigrants to

Primary Health Care in Israel. *International Journal of Health Services* 28(3): 555–574.

Remennick Larissa (1999a) 'Women with a Russian Accent' in Israel. On the Gender Aspects of Immigration. *The European Journal of Women's Studies* 1999, 6(4): 441–461.

Remennick Larissa (1999b). Women of the 'Sandwich' Generation and Multiple Roles: The Case of Russian Immigrants of the 1990s in Israel. *Sex Roles,* 40(5/6): 347–378.

Remennick Larissa (1999c). Preventive Behavior among Recent Immigrants: Russian—Speaking Women and Cancer Screening in Israel. *Social Science and Medicine,* 48(11): 1669–1684.

Remennick, Larissa (2001). "My Life is One Big Nursing Home." Russian Immigrant Women in Israel Speak about Double Caregiver Stress. *Women's Studies International Forum* 24(6): 685–700.

Remennick Larissa and Segal Rosie (2001). Socio-Cultural Context and Women's Experiences of Abortion: Israeli Women and Russian Immigrants Compared. *Culture, Health and Sexuality,* 3(1): 49–66.

Remennick Larissa (2002a). Transnational Community in the Making: Russian Jewish Immigrants of the 1990s in Israel. *Journal of Ethnic and Migration Studies,* 28(3): 515–530.

Remennick, Larissa (2002b) Survival of the Fittest: Russian Immigrant Teachers Speak about their Professional Adjustment in Israel. *International Migration* 2002; 40(1): 99–121.

Remennick, Larissa (2002c). Immigrants from Chernobyl-Affected Areas in Israel: The Link between Health and Social Adjustment. *Social Science and Medicine* 2002; 54(2): 309–317.

Remennick, Larissa and Shakhar, Gila (2003). "You Never Stop Being a Doctor:" The Stories of Russian Immigrant Physicians Who Converted to Physiotherapy. *Health: An Interdisciplinary Journal for the Study of Health, Illness and Medicine,* 2003, 7(1): 87–108.

Remennick, Larissa (2003a). What Does Integration Mean? Social Insertion of Russian Jewish Immigrants in Israel. *Journal of International Migration and Integration,* 4(1): 23–48.

Remennick, Larissa (2003b). Career Continuity among Immigrant Professionals: Russian Engineers in Israel. *Journal of Ethnic and Migration Studies* 2003, 29(4): 701–721.

Remennick, Larissa (2003c). Retired and Making a Fresh Start: Older Russian Immigrants Speak about their Adjustment in Israel. International Migration, *41(5): 153–173.*

Remennick, Larissa (2003d). Language Acquisition as the Main Vehicle of Social Integration: The Case of Russian Jewish Immigrants in Israel. International Journal of the Sociology of Language, *# 164: 83–105.*

Remennick, Larissa (2003e). The 1.5-Generation of Russian Jewish Immigrants in Israel: Between Integration and Socio-Cultural Retention. *Diaspora: A Journal of Transnational Studies* 2003, 12(1), 39–66.

Remennick, Larissa (2004a). *From Russian to Hebrew via HebRush: Inter-Generational Patterns of Language Use among Former Soviet Immigrants in Israel.* Journal of Multilingual and Multicultural Development, *24 (5): 431–453.*

Remennick, Larissa (2004b). Work Relations between Immigrants and Old-Timers in an Israeli Organization: Social Interactions and Inter-Group Attitudes. *International Journal of Comparative Sociology*, 45(1–2); 43–69.

Remennick, L. (2004c). Language Acquisition, Ethnicity and Social Integration among Former Soviet Immigrants of the 1990s in Israel. *Ethnic and Racial Studies,* 27(3): 431–454.

Remennick, Larissa (2005a). Cross-Cultural Dating Patterns on an Israeli Campus: Why are Russian Immigrant Women More Popular than Men? *Journal of Social and Personal Relationships*, 24 (2): 435–454.

Remennick, Larissa (2005b). Immigration, Gender, and Psychosocial Adjustment: A Study Among 150 Immigrant Couples in Israel. *Sex Roles*, 53(11–12): 847–864.

Ritsner, Michael and Ponizovsky, Arie (2003). Age Differences in Stress Process of Recent Immigrants. *Comprehensive Psychiatry*, 44(2): 135–141.

Ron, Pnina (2001). The Process of Acculturation in Israel among Elderly Immigrants from the Former Soviet Union. *Illness, Crisis and Loss*, 9(4): 357–368.

Roosen, Jacob (1989). *Creating Ethnicity.* Newbury Park, CA: Sage.

Rubina, Dina (1999). *Here Comes the Messiah*! Translated from Russian by Daniel M. Jaffe. NY: Zephyr Press.

Rubina, Dina (2004). *The Syndicate*. Moscow: EXMO (in Russian).

Rumbaut, Ruben G. (1996). The Crucible Within: Ethnic Identity, Self-Esteem, and Segmented Assimilation Among Children of Immigrants. In: A. Portes (ed). *The New Second Generation.* New York: Russell Sage Foundation, pp. 119–170.

Rumbaut, Ruben G. (1997). Assimilation and its Discontents: Between Rhetoric and Reality. *International Migration Review*, 31(4), pp.923–960.

Ryvkina, Rosalina (2005). *Kak Zhivut Yevrei v Rossii?: Sociologicheskii Analiz Peremen.* [How Do Jews Live in Russia?: Sociological Analysis of Changes]. Moscow: Dom Yevreiskoi Knigi (Jewish Book Publishers).

Saffran, William (1999). Comparing Diasporas: A Review Essay. *Diaspora: A Journal of Transnational Studies*, 8(3): 255–291.

Sarna, Jonathan (2004). *American Judaism: A History.* New Haven: Yale University Press.

Schoeps, Julius H., Jasper, Will and Vogt, Bernhard (1999). *Ein Neues Judentum in Deutschland: Fremd—und Eigenbilder der Russisch-Judischen Einwanderer.* Potsdam: Verlag fur Berlin-Brandenburg.

Schoeps, Julius H. (2003). Russian Jewish Immigration to Germany and its Impact of the Jewish Communities. Presentation at the Conference: *Soviet and Post-Soviet Jewry.* Jerusalem: The Hebrew University of Jerusalem, Institute for Contemporary Jewry, December 30, 2003.

Shamai, Shmuel and Ilatov, Zena. (2001). Assimilation and Ethnic boundaries: Israeli Attitudes towards Soviet Immigrants. *Adolescence,* 36 (144): 681–695.

Shapiro, Inna (2005). *Reverse Immigration to Russia Falls by 20%.* Retrieved on 03.01.2005 from www.haaretz.com.

Sharot, Stephen (1998). Judaism and Jewish Ethnicity: Changing Interrelationships and Differentiations in the Diaspora and in Israel. In: E. Krausz and G. Tulea (eds) *Jewish Survival: The Identity Problem at the Close of the 20th Century.* New Brunswick, NJ: Transaction, pp. 87–105.

Shasha, Dennis and Shron, Marina (2002). *Red Blues: Voices from the Last Wave of Russian Immigrants.* New York: Holmes and Meier Publishers.

Shifman, Limor and Katz, Elihu (2005). "Just Call Me Adonai": A Case Study of Ethnic Humor and Immigrant Assimilation. *American Sociological Review*, 70(5): 843–859.

Shkolnikov, Vladimir M., Andreev, Evgenii M., Anson, John, and Mesle, Fransua (2004). The Peculiar Pattern of Mortality of Jews in Moscow, 1993–1995. *Population Studies,* 58(3): 311–329.

Shneer, David and Aviv, Caryn (2005). *New Jews: The End of the Jewish Diaspora.* New York: New York University Press, Chapter 4.

Shteyngart, Gary (2002). *The Russian Debutante's Handbook.* New York: Riverhead Books.

Shumsky, Dimitri (2002). Ethnicity and Citizenship in the Perception of Russian Israelis. In: D. Levy and Y. Weiss (eds). *Challenging Ethnic Citizenship: German and Israeli Perspectives on Immigration.* NY & Oxford: Berghahn Books, pp 154–180.

Shuval, Judith T. (1995). Elitism and Professional Control in a Saturated Market: Immigrant Physicians in Israel. *Sociology of Health and Illness*, 17(4), 550–65.

Shuval, Judith T. (1998). Migration to Israel: The Mythology of "Uniqueness." *International Migration,* 36(1), pp. 1–23.

Shuval, Judith T. and Bernstein, Judith (eds) (1997). *Immigrant Physicians: Former Soviet Doctors in Israel, Canada, and the United States.* Westport, CT: Praeger.

Sicron, Moshe (1998). Social Capital of Recent Russian Immigrants and the Process of their Occupational Integration. In: Sicron, M. and Leshem, E. (eds) *The Social Profile of the Immigrant Wave. The Integration Process of the Immigrants from the Former Soviet Union in Israel, 1990–1995.* Jerusalem: Magnes, pp. 127–179.

Siegel, Dina (1998). *The Great Immigration. Russian Jews in Israel.* New York: Berghahn.

Silberstein, Laurence J. (2000). *Mapping Jewish Identities.* New York: NY University Press.

Simanovsky, Stanislav, Strepetova, Margarita P., and Naido, Yuri G. (1996). *Brain Drain from Russia: Problems, Prospects, and Ways of Regulation.* New York: Nova Science Publishers.

Simon James, Rita (1997). *In the Golden Land. A Century of Russian and Soviet Jewish Immigration in America.* Westport, CT: Praeger.

Simon James, Rita (Ed). (2001). *Immigrant Women.* New Brunswick, NJ: Transaction.

Singer, David and Grossman, Lawrence (2004). Jewish Population of the United States, 2002. In: Singer, D. and Grossman, L. (eds.) *American Jewish Year Book, 2003.* New York: The American Jewish Committee.

Slezkine, Yuri (1994). The USSR as a Communal Apartment, or How a Socialist State Promoted Ethnic Particularism. *Slavic Review*, 53(2): 414–452.

Slezkine, Yuri (2004). *The Jewish Century.* Princeton, NJ: Princeton University Press.

Slutzki, Cynthia. (1979). Migration and Family Conflict. *Family Process* 18: 379–390.

Smolicz Jerzy J., Secombe, Margaret J., and Hudson, Dorothy H. (2001). Family Collectivism and Minority Languages as Core Values of Culture among Ethnic Groups in Australia. *Journal of Multilingual and Multicultural Development* 22(2), 152–172.

Spolsky, B. and Shohamy, I. (1999) *The Languages of Israel: Policy, Ideology and Practice.* Multilingual Matters Series. London: Clevedon.

Steinbach, Anna (2001). Intergenerational Transmission and Integration of Repatriate Families from the Former Soviet Union to Germany. *Journal of Comparative Family Studies* (Special Issue: Immigrant and Ethnic Minority Families), 32(4): 505–516.

Stern, Susan (2001). *Jews in Germany.* Retrieved on June 14, 2005 from the website: "http://www.dickinson.edu/glossen/heft16/stern.html" http://www.dickinson.edu/glossen/heft16/stern.html.

Stevens, Gerald (1992). The Social and Demographic Context of Language Use in the United States. *American Sociological Review,* 57: 171–185.

Stier, Haya. and Levanon, Vered (2003). Finding an Adequate Job: Employment and Income of Recent Immigrants to Israel. *International Migration,* 41(2): 81–105.

Stolovich, Leonid (2001). *The Jews Are Joking. Jewish Anecdotes and Witticisms, as well as Aphorisms about Jews.* St. Petersburg, 1999, 2001. (in Russian).

Tolts, Mark (1997). The Interrelationship between Emigration and the Socio-Demographic Profile of Russian Jewry. In: Lewin-Epstein, N., Ro'i, Y., and Ritterband, P. *Russian Jews on Three Continents. Migration and Resettlement.* London, UK & Portland, OR: Frank Cass, 1997, pp. 147–176.

Tolts, Mark (2003). Demography of the Jews in the Former Soviet Union: Yesterday and Today. In: Gitelman, Zvi (ed). *Jewish Life After the USSR.* Bloomington: Indiana University Press, pp. 173–208.

Tolts, Mark (2004). The Post-Soviet Jewish Population in Russia and the World, *Jews in Russia and Eastern Europe* 1(52): 37–63.

Tolts, Mark (2005). Demographische Trends unter den Juden der Ehemaligen Sowjetunion (Demographic Trends among the Jews of the Former Soviet Union). In: Schoeps, J.H., Grozinger, K.E., Jasper, W., and Mattenklott, G. (Eds). *Russische Juden und Transnationale Diaspora.* Menora: Publication of Moses Mendelssohn Center for European Jewish Studies, Potsdam University. Berlin: Philo Verlag, pp. 15–44.

Tong, Y.-Y., Hong, Y.-Y., Lee, S.L., and Chui, C.-Y. (1999). Language Use As a Carrier of Social Identity. International Journal of Intercultural Relations, *23: 281–96.*

Toren, Nina (2003). Tradition and Transition: Family Change in Israel. *Gender Issues,* 21(2): 60–76.

Tress, Madeleine (1997). Foreigners or Jews? The Soviet Jewish Refugee Populations in Germany and in the United States. *East European Jewish Affairs,* 27(2), pp. 21–38.

Van Etten, Ida (1893). Russian Jews as Desirable Immigrants. *Forum* 15 (1893): 172–182.

Van Hear, Nicholas (1998). *New Diasporas: The Mass Exodus, Dispersal and Re-grouping of Migrant Communities.* London: University College of London Press.

Vertovec, Steven (2004). Migrant Transnationalism and Modes of Transformation (1). *International Migration Review,* 38(3): 970–998.

Vinokurov, Andrey, Birman, Dina, and Trickett, Edison (2000). Psychological and Acculturation Correlates of Work Status among Soviet Jewish Refugees in the United States. *International Migration Review* 34(2): 538–559.

Weissbrod, Lilly (2002). *Israeli Identity: In Search of the Successor to the Pioneer, Tsabar and Settler.* London and Portland, OR: Frank Cass. Chapter 5. Blurry Boundaries.

Werbner, P. & Modood, T., Eds. (1997). *Debating Cultural Hybridity.* London: Pluto.

Wierzbicka, Anna (1996). *Understanding Cultures Through Their Key Words.* Oxford: Oxford University Press.

Yelenevskaya, Maria and Fialkova, Larisa (2003). From Muteness to Eloquence: Immigrants' Narratives about Language. *Language Awareness,* 12(1): 3–48.

Yelenevskaya, Maria and Fialkova, Larisa (2004). My Poor Cousin, My Feared Enemy: The Image of an Arab in Personal Narratives of Former Soviets in Israel. *Folklore,* 115(2): 77–98.

Yelenevskaya, Maria (2005). A Cultural Diaspora in the Making: Former Soviets in Israel and in Germany. *Jews and Slavs,* No 15.

Yelenevskaya, Maria and Fialkova, Larisa (2005). Russian Street in the Jewish State: The Study of the 1990s Immigrants' Folklore (*Russkaya Ulitsa v Evreiskoi Strane. Issledovanie folklora emigrantov 1990 godov v Israile*). Moscow: The Institute of Ethnology and Anthropology, Russian Academy of Sciences (in Russian).

Yu Zhou (2000). The Fall of "The Other Half of the Sky"? Chinese Immigrant Women in the New York Area. *Women's Studies International Forum,* 23(4): 445–459.

Zaika, Jana (2006). *Battalion Aliya*—The Military Facet of Social Activism among Russian Immigrants. Paper Presented at the Annual Meeting of Israeli Sociological Society, Bar-Ilan University, February 2006 (Hebrew).

Zaslavsky, Victor and Brym, Robert, J. Soviet Jewish Emigration and Soviet Nationality Policy. London: Macmillan, 1983.

Zeltser, Arkadii (2004). Jews in the Upper Ranks of the NKVD, 1934–1941. *Jews in Russia and Eastern Europe* (Publication of the Hebrew University of Jerusalem), 1(52): 64–91.

Zeltzer-Zubida, Aviva (2000). *Beyond Brighton Beach. Russian Jews in the American Mosaic. Common Quest* (NY) 4(3): 42–49.

Zilberg, Narspy (2000). The Russian Jewish Intelligentsia in Israel: The Search for Models of Integration. In: A. Epstein and A. Fedorchenko (eds). *Mass Migration and its Impact on the Israeli Society.* Jerusalem-Moscow: Hebrew University, 198–227 (in Russian).

Zilberg, Narspy and Leshem, Elazar (1996). Russian-Language Press and Immigrant Community in Israel. *Revue Europeenne des Migrations Internationales (REMI)* 12(3): 173–189.